The Science and
Psychology of Music

The Science and Psychology of Music

From Beethoven at the Office
to Beyoncé at the Gym

William Forde Thompson and
Kirk N. Olsen, Editors

BLOOMSBURY ACADEMIC

NEW YORK · LONDON · OXFORD · NEW DELHI · SYDNEY

BLOOMSBURY ACADEMIC
Bloomsbury Publishing Inc
1385 Broadway, New York, NY 10018, USA
50 Bedford Square, London, WC1B 3DP, UK
29 Earlsfort Terrace, Dublin 2, Ireland

BLOOMSBURY, BLOOMSBURY ACADEMIC and the Diana logo
are trademarks of Bloomsbury Publishing Plc

First published in the United States of America by ABC-CLIO 2021
Paperback edition published by Bloomsbury Academic 2025

Library of Congress Cataloging-in-Publication Data
Names: Thompson, William Forde, editor. | Olsen, Kirk N., editor.
Title: The science and psychology of music : from Beethoven at the office
to Beyoncé at the gym / William Forde Thompson and Kirk N. Olsen, editors.
Description: Santa Barbara : Greenwood, an imprint of ABC-CLIO, 2021.
| Includes bibliographical references and index.
Identifiers: LCCN 2020010260 (print) | LCCN 2020010261 (ebook) |
ISBN 9781440857713 (hardcover) | ISBN 9781440857720 (ebook)
Subjects: LCSH: Music—Psychological aspects. | Music—Social aspects.
Classification: LCC ML3830 .S29 2021 (print) | LCC ML3830 (ebook) |
DDC 781—dc23
LC record available at https://lccn.loc.gov/2020010260
LC ebook record available at https://lccn.loc.gov/2020010261

ISBN: HB: 978-1-4408-5771-3
         PB: 979-8-2162-0161-8
         ePDF: 978-1-4408-5772-0
         eBook: 979-8-2161-4219-5

To find out more about our authors and books visit www.bloomsbury.com
and sign up for our newsletters.

This book is dedicated to all the musicians around the world whose craft and creativity have enhanced human experience, enriching our emotional lives, identities, friendships, and well-being. We also dedicate this book to the hundreds of scholars, ranging from fine arts to neurosciences, who have brought deep insight and understanding to the science and psychology of music.

Contents

Preface   xi

Acknowledgments   xv

Part 1: Understanding Music

What Is Music?   3
    1. Defining Music   3
    2. Sound Waves: The Music inside Sound   7
    3. Pitch, Timbre, and Rhythm   14
    4. Scales, Intervals, and Tuning Systems   21

Music across Cultures   31
    5. Defining Culture   31
    6. Cross-Cultural Research in Music Psychology   36
    7. Nature versus Nurture   41
    8. Musical Universals   47

Musical Expertise   53
    9. What Is Musical Expertise?   53
    10. Musical Genius   58
    11. Genetics and Musical Expertise   64
    12. Competitions: Judging Expertise   69

Musical Prodigies and Savants   75
    13. Becoming a Musical Prodigy: Hard Work or Born That Way?   75
    14. Prodigies in Performance   80
    15. Prodigies in Musical Creativity   84
    16. Musical Savants   89

Music and the Brain   95
    17. Contemporary Approaches to the Neuroscience of Music   95
    18. Music and the Brain across the Life Span   100
    19. Tone Deafness   105
    20. Music and Language   111

Part 2: Psychological and Social Implications of Music

Music and Identity   119
    21. Defining Ourselves through Music   119
    22. Music and Cultural Identity   124
    23. Gender Bias in Music History   129
    24. Music and Social Class   135

Music and Personality   140
    25. Personality and Listeners   140
    26. Personality and Musicians   145
    27. Who Likes Sad Music and Why?   150
    28. Violence and Music   154

Music and Ritual   161
    29. Maternal Songs as Bonding Rituals   161
    30. Music and Ecstatic States   167
    31. Music and Rites of Passage   172
    32. Music and Death   177

Music and Belief   183
    33. Religion and Music   183
    34. Music and Lyrics   188
    35. Music and Advertising   192
    36. Music and Healing Rituals   197

Music and Social Bonding   205
    37. Lullabies   205
    38. Love and Music   210
    39. Intercultural Relations through Music   214
    40. Music as Social Grooming   220

Part 3: Impact and Applications of Music

Music and Emotion   227
    41. Why Is Music Emotional? Theories of Music and Emotion   227
    42. Contemporary Research on Music and Emotion   233
    43. Music as Emotion Management   238
    44. Music and Emotion across Cultures   243

Music and Memory   249
    45. What Is Memory for Music?   249
    46. Music and Studying   253
    47. Earworms   258
    48. Music-Evoked Autobiographical Memories (MEAMs)   263

Music and Movement   269
    49. Movement and Music Performance   269
    50. The Case of Ensemble Performance   274
    51. Music and Dance   278
    52. Why Do People Exercise to Music?   284

Music and Health   290

    53. Defining Music, Health, and Well-Being   290
    54. Five Healthy Ingredients of Music   295
    55. Music Therapy   300
    56. Music and Healthy Aging   305

Music Education   311

    57. Music in Schools   311
    58. Music Learning across the Life Span   316
    59. Music in the Community   321
    60. Media and Technology in Music Education   325

About the Editors and Contributors   331

Index   341

Preface

Music is everywhere. Every society worldwide engages in musical activities, and our engagement begins in infancy with lullabies and continues in various forms throughout our lives. Music is a constant—like the air we breathe or the blood that flows through our veins. For this reason, we often take music for granted and rarely stop to think about why it plays such a crucially important role in our lives. Why should a sequence of human-made sounds, produced in inventive ways and in a range of contexts, be a source of worldwide activity, fascination, and appreciation?

In 2018, it was estimated that Beyoncé and Jay-Z, as a couple, were worth roughly $1.25 billion. From one standpoint, they accumulated this enormous wealth because they are talented at imagining and stringing together sounds in ways that people appreciate. Bono, with the band U2, has sung to huge stadiums of fans all around the world. At one concert in Pasadena, California, close to one hundred thousand people packed into the Rose Bowl to hear them play. An outsider to their music might be forgiven for wondering what the fuss was all about. Bono can sing a memorable tune, but why the worldwide adulation? In the 1960s, protest songs by musicians such as Joan Baez, Judy Collins, Pete Seeger, Phil Ochs, and Bob Dylan helped to build and then fuel a global peace movement in response to the Vietnam War, including the famous anti-war student movement that began at the University of California, Berkeley.

In 2020, the global pandemic profoundly impacted the careers of musicians, with classical and popular music concerts cancelled across the globe, and venues that would normally support local musicians shut down. Musical communities were also disrupted as people went into isolation. Yet as people adjusted to the new reality, music began to re-emerge from the balconies in Italy, to online collaborations and performances such as virtual choirs and orchestras. Music was a natural human response to the isolation and anxiety that people were experiencing, and it was a source of healing and hope.

The profound power of music to affect people from all walks of life is one of the great mysteries of science. It is being vigorously investigated by musicologists, psychologists, neuroscientists, physicists, and a range of other scholars. The aim of this book is to provide an introduction to some of the main scientific investigations, theories, and discoveries about music and how it affects our emotions, thoughts, identities, and social lives. All the chapters have been authored by world-leading experts on the science and psychology of music. They bring first-hand experience and knowledge of their chosen topics to provide exciting and accessible accounts of each topic area.

Just as music is found in many different contexts and is used for different reasons, there are many intriguing questions that can be asked about music. What is special about the sounds that are used as the building blocks of music—the notes, chords, drumbeats, and vocalizations? Is music different in every culture or are there certain commonalities in the various musical sounds and activities that occur across cultures? What does it take to become an expert musician? Why are some people gifted at music, whereas others, no matter how hard they try, are tone deaf? What happens in our brains when we listen to music, and what are its effects on memory, emotion, and health?

Rather than answering all possible questions about the science and psychology of music in one long explanation spanning hundreds of pages, we have instead organized the book into three parts: (1) Understanding Music, (2) Psychological and Social Implications of Music, and (3) Impact and Applications of Music. Each part addresses a distinct and coherent set of issues related to the science and psychology of music and can stand on its own as an independent resource for teachers, students, and interested readers. Each part also addresses five core topic areas, giving rise to fifteen topics across the entire book.

Part 1, Understanding Music, describes the various ways that scientists think about music: (1) how they attempt to define music (What Is Music?); (2) how they understand and compare musical practices around the world (Music across Cultures); (3) how they investigate the nature of musicianship (Musical Expertise); (4) how they understand child prodigies (Musical Prodigies and Savants); and (5) how they investigate music through the lens of the human brain (Music and the Brain). Because every topic addresses a complex question, it is further divided into distinct questions that are addressed across four chapters written by different scientists and theorists.

Part 2, Psychological and Social Implications of Music, deals with five different topic areas: (1) how music helps us to construct or reinforce a sense of our identity (Music and Identity); (2) how musical preferences and skills are affected by personality (Music and Personality); (3) why music is used to accompany and celebrate rituals such as births, marriages, and birthdays (Music and Ritual); (4) the influence of music on religious and other beliefs (Music and Belief); and (5) how music can bring people together, strengthening our friendships and reinforcing the trust that we form with people around us (Music and Social Bonding). Such issues speak to the powerful ways that music shapes and helps constitute our identities and human societies. As in part 1, each topic area in part 2 is addressed across four chapters.

Part 3, Impact and Applications of Music, considers the impact and applications of music, that is, how music affects us in ways that change how we think and feel, with consequences for health and education. The chapters in this section deal with the following topics: (1) the effects of music on emotional states (Music and Emotion); (2) the strong connection between music and memory (Music and Memory);

(3) the intimate association between music and movement (Music and Movement); (4) the application of music for health (Music and Health); and (5) the application of music for education (Music Education).

We believe the organization of this book will help readers tease apart and digest the many distinct and fascinating questions and issues surrounding the science and psychology of music and that this comprehensive collection of chapters will inspire the next generation of researchers in the field. Music is an extraordinary aspect of human life, and its power to affect us can only be understood by considering its psychological implications. For without our psychological input and appreciation, music would not exist. Philosopher George Berkeley (b. 1685), after whom the University of California, Berkeley, was named, once wrote, "All the choir of heaven . . . which compose the frame of the world—have not any subsistence without a mind" (Berkeley 1710/2002). The same can be said for music: it exists only because we conceive it in our minds and then engage in musical activities, to be forever affected by our own creations. The sixty chapters contained in this book explain how and why music affects us so deeply.

Reference and Further Reading
Berkeley, G. (2002). *A Treatise Concerning the Principles of Human Knowledge* (D. Wilkins, Ed. & Trans.). (Original work published 1710). https://www.maths.tcd.ie/~dwilkins/Berkeley/HumanKnowledge/1734/HumKno.pdf.

Acknowledgments

This project has brought together sixty-six leading researchers from around the world in the psychology and science of music. They have skillfully distilled and communicated the most important and complex issues in the field into what we believe are highly engaging, readable chapters that will inspire the next generation of researchers. As editors, we are grateful for their dedication and enthusiasm for the project and feel privileged to have led a project with such esteemed contributors.

We would also like to thank all the scholars who reviewed drafts of chapters, providing valuable feedback that helped authors to further refine their contributions. Maxine Taylor from ABC-CLIO also provided excellent advice and guidance throughout the project. Finally, we are deeply appreciative of the continued support of the members of the Music, Sound and Performance Research Group at Macquarie University and to our families for their unconditional support and understanding.

PART I

Understanding Music

What Is Music?

1. Defining Music

William Forde Thompson and Kirk N. Olsen

Has it ever occurred to you how strange it is that humans seem to enjoy concocting sounds by hitting objects with sticks, blowing air across a small opening in hollowed-out cylinders, buzzing lips into a mouthpiece, and scraping stretched steel strings with the stretched fibers of horse hair? If humans were being investigated by an alien species from another planet, what would they make of this peculiar activity? If they wanted to understand this behavior, the first step they would need to take is to define it.

DICTIONARY DEFINITIONS OF MUSIC

What is music? According to a 1947 version of the *Random House College Dictionary*, *music* can be defined as "an artistic use of sound to express thoughts and feelings through the elements of melody, harmony, and rhythm." One problem with this definition, however, is that it makes a lot of assumptions. First, it assumes that we make music to express our thoughts and feelings, which defines music as an act of communication. Not everyone would agree that communication can explain everything about our experience and enjoyment of music. In some cases, we enjoy listening to music for the same reason that we enjoy listening to the sounds of waves on a beach or a summer rainstorm. That is, we sometimes enjoy the sounds in music for their own sake, even if nothing specific is being communicated to us. Second, it identifies quite specific ingredients of music: melody, harmony, and rhythm. Is that all there is to music? And does *all* music contain these three ingredients? Unfortunately, the answer to both questions is probably no.

Consider, for example, the traditional music of indigenous Australians (also called Aboriginal Australians). One of the instruments commonly used in this music is the didgeridoo—a type of instrument classed as an *aerophone* (other aerophones include the harmonica and the trumpet). Skilled players of the didgeridoo use a technique called *circular breathing* to create a continuous sound that they can control, often using vocal and breathing techniques that change the overall sound quality of the instrument, or *timbre*. The didgeridoo does not produce melodies in the conventional sense of the word, and when it is accompanied by other instruments, such as clapsticks or vocals, the combination does not sound like the kind of harmonies that we hear in popular Western music. Thus, this form of music does not fit well with the dictionary definition of music and its emphasis on melody, harmony, and rhythm.

The 1955 edition of the *Oxford Universal Dictionary* offers an improved definition of music. It describes *music* as "the art of combining sounds with the aim of achieving beauty of form and the expression of thought and feeling." This definition was an improvement because it allowed for any possible sounds to be used, not just melody, harmony, and rhythm. In that way, the definition can be applied to many musical practices around the world. However, the definition is not perfect because it can be applied to activities that are not music, such as spoken poetry, and there are forms of music that the definition does not seem to capture, such as dance music and music therapy.

Around the world, music is used for a range of other purposes, not just to achieve beauty of form and the expression of thought and feeling. Music is used to establish or strengthen social bonds, to induce physical movement (usually in the form of dancing), to highlight important cultural rituals, and to foster healing. Take the traditional music of the Bushmen people of Southern Africa, also known as the !Kung people. (The ! sound is made by clicking your tongue against the back of the roof of your mouth while mouthing the vowel *O*. Try pronouncing *!Kung*). One kind of music practiced by the Bushmen people helps a spiritual leader make a transition into a trancelike stake (*!kia*). The music often involves men and women chanting, singing, and clapping rhythmically until the music intensifies enough for the spiritual leader or healer to enter a realm in between the human world and the spirit world. Well-being and health are bestowed on all those who attend the musical ritual. In other words, the music does not function for aesthetic beauty or to express thoughts or feelings but to assist a spiritual leader in bringing about freedom from illness.

IS MUSIC RESTRICTED TO SOUND?

Some dictionaries such as the American Heritage Dictionary have opted for a simple definition of *music*, for example, "the art of arranging sounds in time." Although such a definition is not very specific, can we agree that it is accurate? Probably not. First, it describes activities that are not music, such as speech, Morse code, laughter, and the applause of an audience. To get around this problem, the American Heritage Dictionary clarifies that music is an arrangement of sounds so as to create a music composition, but this clarification is circular, like saying "music is the art of making music." Moreover, many forms of music do not fit this definition. In many cultures, music is not restricted to sound but always involves movement and social interactions. Indeed, sound is not even necessary to enjoy music. This may seem like a surprising claim, but music is enjoyed by millions of people who are profoundly deaf.

Barbie Parker, a Texas native, earns her living by signing and interpreting music concerts, thereby enhancing the experience of profoundly deaf and hard of hearing audience members. Barbie not only signs the lyrics; she also moves expressively to the music, often playing air guitar and air drums. Many music listeners are deaf, and many great musicians are also deaf. Beethoven went profoundly deaf later in life, but that did not stop him from composing his masterpiece, the Ninth Symphony.

The ability of deaf individuals to enjoy and produce music is also evident in the all-deaf contemporary rock and roll band Beethoven's Nightmare, which has a busy touring schedule. For these musicians, music comes from within and exists irrespective of hearing. How can we make sense of this idea when most of us experience music as fundamentally about sounds? The answer lies in having an open mind and in contemplating the many forms of musical behaviors around the world.

Although most of us enjoy "listening" to music, it is important to recognize that music is not restricted to sound; it often involves movement that we can appreciate in our bodies and with our eyes. This artful creation of sound, sight, and movement carries not a single kind of meaning but many different meanings and functions depending on the context. Along these lines, music cognition researcher Ian Cross (2001) proposed that music can be understood as the creation of sounds and movements that have the potential to play different roles in our lives depending on the context. He was careful not to pinpoint what role music might play because he argued that we are free to think about music in any way that makes sense to us. This freedom to think about music in any way lies at the crux of his definition. For Cross, experiences of music are not *fixed* across contexts but are *floating*. Cross calls this property "floating intentionality," where the term *intentional* should be understood in the philosophical sense, that is, *mental phenomena* such as thoughts, plans, and memories. In effect, this description holds that the way we think about music, including its meaning and function, depends on the context in which that music is created and experienced.

An attractive feature of the definition offered by Cross is that it captures music across many cultures and contexts. However, in trying to be inclusive, it accidentally includes activities that we would not normally describe as music. Gossiping with friends involves making sounds, and the way we think about gossiping may depend on context. Should we consider gossiping a form of music? Most people would argue no. Other activities that are consistent with this definition include sighing loudly, groaning, drumming your fingers, blowing a whistle, clapping your hands at the end of a lecture, and cracking your knuckles. Are these musical activities? A broad definition of *music* ensures we are not too restrictive, given the diversity of music around the world. But by casting such a wide net, we may end up capturing activities that extend beyond music.

WHAT ARE THE INGREDIENTS OF A GOOD DEFINITION?

Some people believe that a good definition of a concept should possess the qualities of *necessity* and *sufficiency*. Put differently, we want a definition that identifies *all* (necessity) instances of a concept and *only* (sufficiency) instances of that concept. If a definition has the property of necessity, the qualities included in the definition exist in all instances of the concept. For example, all fish have gills, so gills are a necessary condition of being a fish. If an animal does not have gills, it is not a fish. Conversely, if the definition of a concept has the property of sufficiency, the features identified only refer to the concept being defined and no other concept. For example, a sufficient definition of a triangle is a closed figure consisting of three straight lines connected to form exactly three angles. The definition is sufficient because only triangles possess these features. The definition of music outlined by Cross does not fulfill the condition of sufficiency because it accounts for not only musical activities but also many other human activities as well.

UNIVERSALS AND FAMILY RESEMBLANCES IN MUSIC

One strategy of defining music is to characterize features that seem to be *universally* present in all instances of musical behavior. If a particular attribute, function, or experience is always present in the behaviors that we classify as music, it could be listed as part of our definition of music. The concept of universals in music is discussed in the four entries in chapter 2; for now, we will consider some of the features that seem to be associated with all musical systems.

Features of music that have been identified as potentially universal have included the properties of music and human responses to music. One possible universal characteristic is the tendency to group certain elements together and to separate those groups from one another. For example, when we listen to a sequence of notes in music, some notes seem to go together to form larger units, such as phrases and melodies. We perceive these phrases and melodies to be distinct entities, sometimes because they are physically separated from each other by a slight pause or are shaped in a way that makes them sound coherent and distinct. Another characteristic that may be universal is the tendency of listeners to entrain to the temporal dimension of music. By this, we mean the experience of paying close attention to the rhythm of the music. The term *entrainment* can refer to the way our attention can be locked into the rhythm, and it can also refer to the tendency to synchronize our body movements to the beat of the music, as in dancing or performing music with others.

Another approach is to list all of the features that are observed in instances of music across cultures and acknowledge that only a subset of these features may be evident in any one form of music. This approach suggests that various instances of music are related to one another not by defining features but by a "family resemblance." Just as members of the same family tend to share various features with one another, but no one feature in particular, various forms of music may not have any one common feature, even though they all resemble each other in various ways. Take six attributes that are common, but not universal, to many musical systems: (1) musical behaviors around the world often involve song; (2) the sounds are often restricted to a particular set of pitches, called the *scale*; (3) instruments are typically used to produce sound; (4) participants are often encouraged to synchronize with each other in time; (5) the sounds are often associated with social interaction; and (6) the sounds and accompanying activity are often experienced in an emotional way.

First, *song* refers to any complex, nonverbal, learned vocalization, and we see instances of song in most musical systems around the world. Second, songs tend to be built around a small set of notes called the *scale*. Third, music tends to involve the production of sounds by purpose-built instruments, such as flutes and drums. Fourth, music often encourages us to synchronize our bodies to the rhythm of the music (also called *entrainment*). Fifth, music is typically a social activity. This may be true even when we are listening to music on our own because we tend to experience music as a social surrogate, such that the music becomes a kind of "friend" that we relate to on an emotional level. Finally, music tends to have an emotional effect on us, energizing or calming us, giving us pleasure, and helping us to make sense of our inner emotional experiences, both happy and sad. None of these features is present in all musical systems around the world, but all musical systems likely have a subset of these attributes.

CONCLUSION

Renowned ethnomusicologist John Blacking famously called music a "gloss word," writing that "although every known human society has what trained musicologists would describe as 'music,' there are some that have no word for music or whose concept of music has a significance quite different from that generally associated with the word music" (Blacking 1995, pp. 224–225). Given the various definitions and understandings of music across cultures, and the absence of an overall concept of music in certain cultures, one might wonder how an ethnomusicologist would decide whether a particular activity is an instance of "music." Given the complexities of defining this human behavior, it is tempting to avoid using the gloss word *music* and to focus instead on describing specific human activities, such as singing together to create beautiful harmonies, chanting as part of a religious experience, or creating sounds and movement for the purposes of healing. There are many concepts we use that we would not be able to define if asked: What is *time*? What is *happiness*? Music is perhaps one of those concepts that is difficult, if not impossible, to define.

We do not need to define music before we can recognize it, describe it, and appreciate it. Some ethnomusicologists have adopted this approach, providing richly detailed understandings of particular behaviors across various cultural contexts—a strategy that is sometimes called *thick description*. And it is hard to deny that all these forms of musical behavior play powerful roles in our lives and may have a deep psychological connection and common evolutionary origins. For this reason, understanding this collection of human behaviors, in all their colorful and complex manifestations, will remain a key focus of investigation within the psychology and science of music.

References and Further Reading

Bispham, J. C. (2009). Music's "design features": Musical motivation, musical pulse, and musical pitch. *Musicae Scientiae, 13*, 41–61.

Blacking, J. (1973). *How Musical Is Man?* Seattle: University of Washington Press.

Blacking, J. (1995). *Music, Culture, and Experience: Selected Papers of John Blacking.* Chicago, IL: University of Chicago Press.

Cross, I. (2001). Music, cognition, culture, and evolution. *Annals of the New York Academy of Sciences, 930*, 28–42.

Davies, S. (2012). On defining music. *Monist, 95*, 535–555.

2. Sound Waves: The Music inside Sound

Alex Chilvers

The composer Edgard Varèse (1883–1965) used a very simple phrase to define music: organized sound. Working with any means of sound production available—from conventional musical instruments, to hand-cranked fire sirens, to electronic tape—his creations were limited only by his imagination. Varèse, and other pioneers of the early twentieth century, inspired future generations of musicians to think of music in terms of *sound* rather than the abstract entities we call *notes*. Modern technology has since led to the development of tools that allow us to closely analyze the properties of sound. Thus, today's musicians—that is, people interested in organizing sound for creative purposes—are able to understand their medium in greater detail than ever before.

THE ORIGINS OF SOUNDS

Before we examine the music inside sound, let us first recall a climactic scene from *The Sound of Music*. After the Captain's stirring rendition of "Edelweiss," the von Trapp family singers bid their audience a long-winded goodbye and sneakily flee their Nazi escort to take refuge among the sympathetic nuns of the local abbey. As the military search party closes in on them, the family hides in the cemetery. Although they are safely hidden from view, Maria and the children huddle together and try their best to remain perfectly still.

This raises a simple question: why is it so imperative that one must avoid making even the slightest movement when trying to avoid detection? The answer is also simple: because movement causes sound. Although different kinds of movement produce different sounds, all sounds are the result of movement. Furthermore, every audible movement—from the warble of Maria's vocal cords, to the twang of the Captain's guitar strings, to the rustle of Friedrich's lederhosen—reaches our ears through the air disturbances we call *sound waves*.

When an object moves, it creates changes in air pressure that travel outward as sound waves (imagine the ripples created when a pebble is dropped into a pond). When these waves reach an ear, having traveled at the constant speed of sound, they are transmitted to the brain and ultimately perceived as sound. Every such sound wave has a unique profile that is shaped by the properties of that original moving object.

FROM FREQUENCY TO PITCH

Most musical instruments produce sounds of definite pitch. We speak of *pitch* in terms of height (by singing the "do re mi . . ." scale, made famous in the above-mentioned movie, you are singing an ascending scale of pitches). Pitched sounds are created when vibrations occur in a consistent repetitive pattern. A plucked string, for example, will vibrate at a constant frequency—not slowing down until it is muted by touch or allowed to naturally decay to silence. This consistency is called *periodicity*, and it allows a stable pitch to form. Some musical instruments, particularly in the percussion family, produce waves that are not periodic and therefore have no definite pitch. A snare drum, a hi-hat, and a tambourine all produce unpitched sounds.

The simplest example of a pitched sound is a pure tone. Pure tones are represented by the smooth and consistent shapes of sine waves (as in figure 2.1) and are

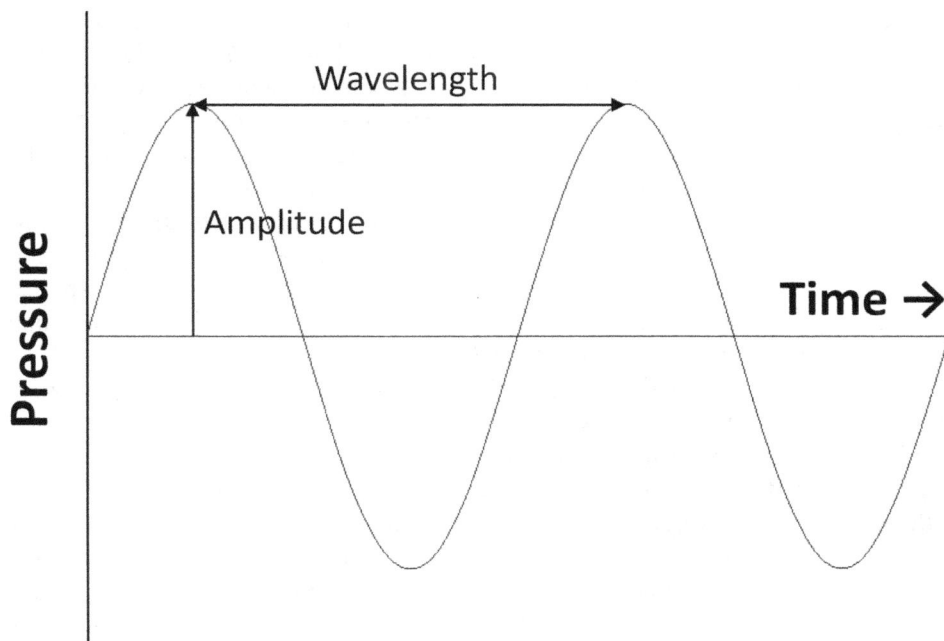

Figure 2.1 Vibrating Pattern of a Sine Wave.

generally only produced electronically or in controlled environments. The frequency of such a wave determines the pitch of the tone produced. Frequency is measured in hertz (Hz) and tells us the number of complete vibrations per second. Higher frequencies are perceived as higher pitches.

Humans are generally capable of perceiving tones of between 20 Hz and 20,000 Hz (20 kHz), although we find it harder to perceive higher pitches as we get older. Anything outside that range will go unheard (if the tone is pure) or will sound like unpitched noise. Yet, different kinds of animals hear different frequency ranges. Dogs, for example, can hear up to around 45 kHz. This is why dog trainers often use whistles that are pitched above 20 kHz, enabling them to train their pooches without annoying the neighbors.

Shorter wavelengths require less time for a single vibration, thus completing a greater frequency of vibrations per second. Higher pitches therefore also correspond to shorter wavelengths. Furthermore, shorter wavelengths are generally created by physical materials of shorter lengths. This is why small musical instruments have higher pitches than their large counterparts. A piccolo, for example, sounds higher than a flute, and a viola sounds higher than a cello. This relationship between length and pitch also explains the shape of a harp. The strings closest to the harpist are very short and produce the highest pitches, while the farthest strings are the longest and lowest. Many musical instruments allow the performer to manually alter the length of a vibrating object to control pitch. For example, cello players use their fingers to determine what portion of a string is allowed to vibrate. This is referred to as *stopping* the string (when a string is played without being stopped, it is referred to as *open*).

When a string vibrates, it moves up and down across its entire length at a frequency that produces the pitch we hear. This is called the *fundamental frequency*. For example, if you pluck the lowest string on a conventionally tuned guitar, the pitch you hear is the low E-natural, which corresponds to that open string's fundamental frequency (82.4 Hz). If you use your finger to stop the same string at the first fret and pluck again, the vibrating portion of the string is shortened, the fundamental frequency is raised, and the pitch increases to an F-natural. If you continue up to the twelfth fret, you halve the vibrating portion of the string. Halving the length of a string causes its vibrating frequency to double, which corresponds to a pitch increase of one octave. Thus, you will produce the E-natural that is one octave higher (with a frequency of 164.8Hz).

Although the relationship between size and pitch (smaller = higher) is fairly intuitive due to our interactions with musical instruments, the relationship between speed and pitch (faster = higher) is a little harder to visualize. Consider a plane propeller. As it starts to turn, you hear each cycle as a discrete noise—a "whoosh" as the blade whips through the air. These unpitched noises soon take on a rhythmic nature, creating an ever-quickening pulse as the propeller speed increases. Eventually, the individual noises are no longer discernible; however, a single continuous pitch has now formed. As the speed continues to increase, those now indistinguishable pulses move closer and closer together. This both shortens the length and increases the frequency of the resulting wave, and you begin to hear an upward-gliding tone. This example also demonstrates that pitch exists on the same continuum as rhythm (albeit with much higher speeds involved).

FROM AMPLITUDE TO LOUDNESS

Just as the frequency of a sound wave influences our experience of pitch, the amplitude of a sound wave relates to our experience of loudness. As can be seen in figure 2.1, amplitude can be visualized as the *height* of a sound wave's cycle and is often referred to as the *intensity of sound*, which is measured in decibels (dB). In real-world scenarios, breathing reaches about 10 dB, a quiet conversation reaches about 50–60 dB, and a rock concert often reaches 110 dB. In basic terms, the higher the decibel, the louder the sound will be perceived. However, this is not always the case. For example, take a pure tone with a very low frequency of 20 Hz and compare it with a pure tone of 1000 Hz. Both are in the range of human hearing; however, for these tones to be perceived (i.e., to reach the threshold of hearing), the 20 Hz tone needs to be presented to the ear at approximately 80 dB, whereas the 1000 Hz tone only needs to be presented at approximately 5 dB. This is an example of how the frequency of a sound wave interacts with its amplitude to influence how loud a sound is perceived.

MANY TONES MAKE TIMBRE WORK

Timbre refers to the quality of a sound, and discussions of timbre tend to rely on adjectives such as *shrill*, *mellow*, *bright*, and *nasal*. Timbre allows us to tell the difference between notes played on a flute, a trumpet, and a violin—even when their pitch, dynamic, and duration are all equal. Alongside pitch and rhythm, timbre is fundamental to the sounds of music. However, timbre is really just the result of many pitches sounding simultaneously.

Musical instruments are made of complex physical materials that vibrate in complex patterns. Therefore, they produce tones that are much more complex than the pure tones discussed above. When you play a note on a guitar string, the pitch you hear most prominently corresponds to the fundamental frequency of vibration. However, you also hear a whole spectrum of frequencies that make up the timbre of that particular guitar.

The additional frequencies that create timbre are variously called *overtones*, *partials*, or *harmonics*. These are simply multiples of the fundamental frequency (so, if the fundamental is 100 Hz, the overtones are 200 Hz, 300 Hz, 400 Hz, and so on). Overtones occur because a vibrating portion of string (or other material) naturally divides itself into an infinite number of smaller segments that vibrate simultaneously (see figure 2.2).

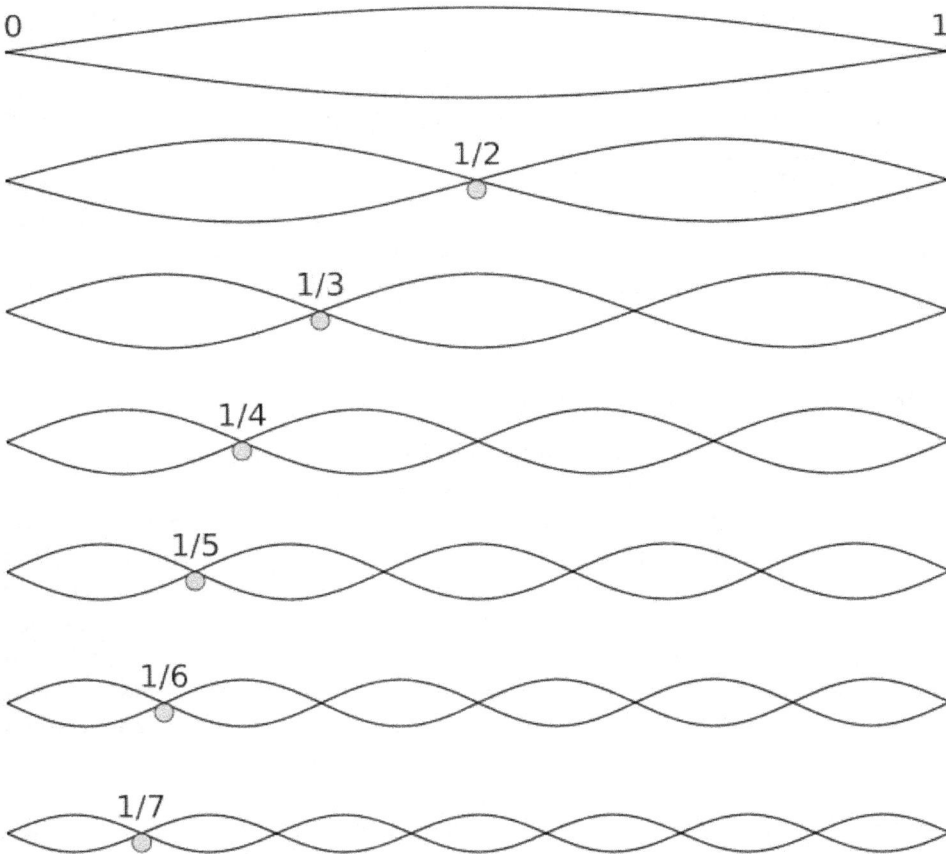

Figure 2.2   Vibration Patterns of a String, from the Fundamental (1) to the Seventh Harmonic (1/7).

Consider again the open low E string on a guitar. It vibrates at a fundamental frequency of 82.4 Hz to produce that E-natural pitch. Where the string divides into two, with a stationary node at the midpoint, the fundamental frequency is doubled. This second harmonic therefore vibrates at 164.8 Hz and produces a higher E-natural pitch. The third harmonic, created by segments of one-third the string length, sees the fundamental tripled to 247.2 Hz, which is very close to the pitch we know as B-natural. The fourth harmonic is just the second harmonic doubled (329.6 Hz) and thus produces another E-natural pitch (now two octaves above the fundamental). Although there is no theoretical limit to the number of overtones that are produced, these harmonics eventually produce frequencies that are beyond the range of human hearing.

Harmonics are always produced at multiples of a note's fundamental frequency, regardless of the instrument playing that note. The difference in timbre, and what allows us to distinguish between a flute, a trumpet, and a violin, is the relative loudness of each overtone. You can thus think of timbres as recipes: all instrumental timbres contain the same ingredients, but each has different quantities of those ingredients.

Another factor that contributes to an instrument's timbre is *sympathetic resonance*, which is caused by the fact that vibrations of sound waves are infectious (so to speak). If an object is prone to vibrating at a particular frequency, and a wave matching that frequency comes into contact with it, the object itself will begin vibrating. You can observe this phenomenon by again plucking the low E-natural on a guitar. Because the highest guitar string is tuned to the E-natural two octaves higher (329.6 Hz), the fourth harmonic of the note you play will cause that higher string to vibrate sympathetically, thus contributing to the overall spectrum of sound. Indeed, a sound wave will trigger the sympathetic resonance of any material with which it has overlapping overtones. You can imagine this kind of chain reaction taking place inside the body of a piano whenever a low note is played.

INTERVALS ON THE SPECTRUM

The relationships between individual pitches in a harmonic series can be discussed in terms of the intervals used in Western music. We have already seen that octaves are created each time a frequency is doubled. The second harmonic is an octave above the first harmonic (the fundamental), the fourth harmonic is two octaves, the eighth harmonic is three octaves, the sixteenth harmonic is four octaves, and so on. Perfect octaves are the only intervals in the harmonic series that have been maintained by the equal temperament tuning system with which we are most familiar. While this will be discussed in more detail elsewhere, suffice to say that the division of an octave into twelve equal semitones has resulted in interval relationships that differ slightly from those produced by natural overtones.

Figure 2.3 shows the pitches of the first seven harmonics produced by the open lowest guitar string. Between the second and fourth harmonics, we find the first nonoctave overtone. As mentioned above, this overtone is very close to a B-natural (in fact, the difference between this overtone and a tuned B-natural is

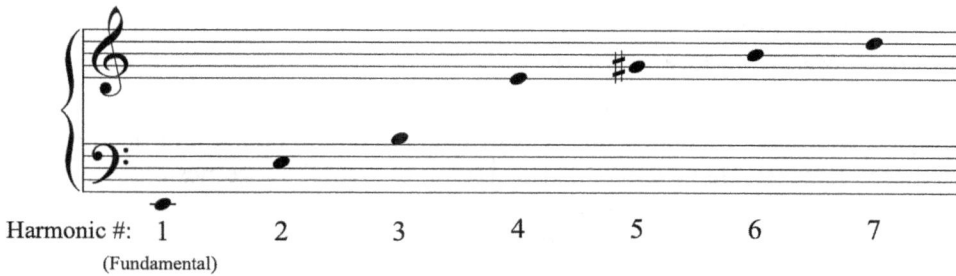

Figure 2.3 First Seven (Approximate) Pitches of the Harmonic Series Beginning on E2.

imperceptible). The next nonoctave overtone is the fifth harmonic. This is followed by the sixth harmonic (which is double the frequency of the third harmonic and therefore another B-natural).

If we continue up through the series, the intervals produced get progressively narrower and weaker, contributing less to the sound that we hear. It is therefore important to note that those intervals that we consider to be consonant (i.e., more pleasant and stable) occur naturally and most prominently in the harmonic series. This suggests that our appreciation of consonance stems from this natural system of overtones. Given that our imperfect tuning system only manages to approximate these intervals, however, the concepts of *consonance* and *dissonance* (the opposite of consonance) are primarily learned through exposure to music that conforms to the rules of our particular Western harmonic system.

CONCLUSION

Sound begins with movement. The many properties that define the quality of a particular sound originate with that initial movement. It is helpful to keep this in mind if you are trying to avoid making sound: simply stop moving! Yet, this information is far more important to those of us who are interested in making and understanding music. By examining the fine details of sound production, we see that the experience of *pitch* is defined by the timing of repetitive events, namely, fluctuations in air pressure or a sound's frequency. On the other hand, *loudness* is defined by the amplitude of those fluctuations in air pressure. Furthermore, the many complex timbres that allow us to distinguish one instrument type from another are simply combinations of pitches, blended according to an instrument's unique recipe of fundamental frequencies, harmonics, and amplitudes.

References and Further Reading

Campbell, M., & Greated, C. (1994). *The Musician's Guide to Acoustics*. Oxford, UK: Oxford University Press.

Gough, C. (2014). Musical acoustics. In T. Rossing (Ed.), *Springer Handbook of Acoustics* (pp. 567–701). New York, NY: Springer Handbooks. Springer.

Moore, B. C. J. (2012). *An Introduction to the Psychology of Hearing* (6th ed.). Cambridge, UK: Emerald Publishing.

Photinos, P. (2017). *Musical Sound, Instruments, and Equipment*. San Rafael, CA: Morgan & Claypool Publishers.

3. Pitch, Timbre, and Rhythm

Andrew J. Milne and Kirk N. Olsen

Pitch, timbre, and rhythm are fundamental building blocks of music and, in almost all cultures, music is created through the deliberate manipulation of one or more of these elements. Importantly, pitch, timbre, and rhythm are not objective features of the acoustic signal but subjective experiences within the listener's mind. In this chapter, we will show how the psychological experiences of pitch, timbre, and rhythm are linked to physical characteristics of sound. As we shall see, these links are surprisingly complex.

PITCH

Of the three elements, pitch has the most straightforward relationship with a physical attribute of sound. Pitch is a sensation that can be ordered from low to high. For example, keys on a piano are ordered from low pitches on the left of the keyboard over to high pitches on the right. We experience pitch whenever there is a sound that is *periodic*, that is, when sound occurs as a series of waves through the air. Pitch is related to the frequency of these periodic waves; as the frequency increases (more waves per second), the perceived pitch of the sound becomes higher.

Pitch is the most important building block for melodies to be created. A *melody* can be defined as a sequence of pitches ordered in time so that the set of pitches seem to cohere with one another. The result is often a memorable and sometimes meaningful phrase. Pitches are also the foundation for *harmony*, which is the musical art of simultaneously sounding more than one pitch at a time. Harmonious combinations of several different pitches are called *chords*. In Western music, the arrangement of pitches into major and minor scales and chords (see chapter 4) can have happy and sad emotional connotations, respectively.

Although the sensation of pitch is strongly related to the frequency of sound waves, the relationship requires some detailed explanation. First, most sounds comprise numerous simultaneous frequencies rather than a single frequency. When we play a key on the piano, we hear a single pitch, but the sound consists of many different frequencies. The lowest frequency corresponds to the pitch that we hear, whereas the higher frequencies, and how they all fade over time, give the note its unique piano sound. To understand this concept better, imagine watching a wave in the ocean and then noticing that there are smaller waves moving along the top of the wave, like ripples, and on those ripples are even smaller waves moving along the ripples. Normally, the pitch that you hear corresponds to the biggest wave, but the other waves also influence what you experience.

Figure 3.1 shows the frequency spectra of three different sounds: a train clackity-clacking over tracks, a cymbal, and a bowed violin. Frequency spectra are graphs that show the intensity of each frequency component of a sound. The higher the gray bars for each frequency, the greater the intensity of that frequency in the sound.

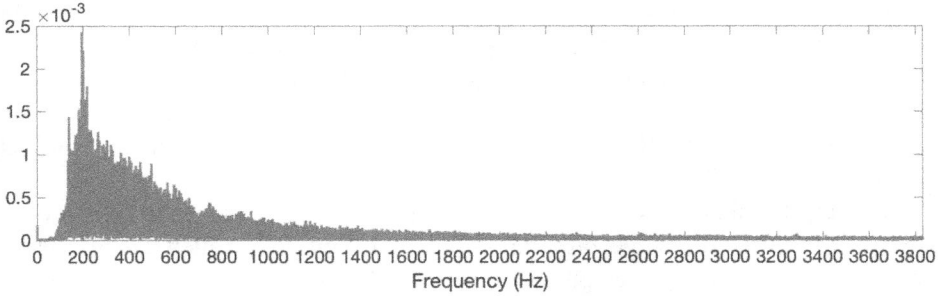

Figure 3.1a Spectrum of Train Sound. Most Listeners Would Say That This Sound Has No Discernibe Pitch and That It Is, Instead, "Noisy."

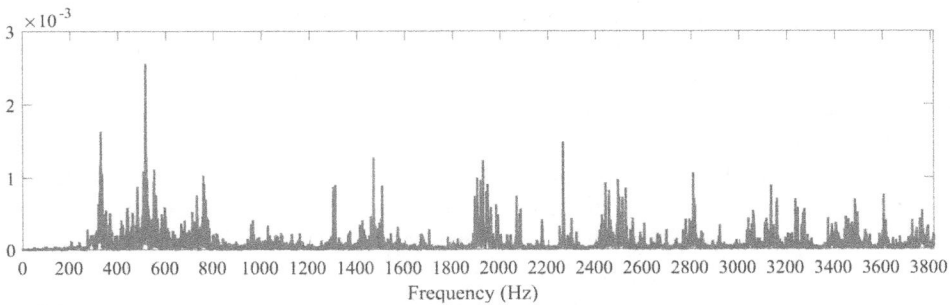

Figure 3.1b Spectrum of a Ride Cymbal. Most Listeners Would Say This Sound Is Mostly "Noisy," but There Are Hints of Multiple Possible Pitches.

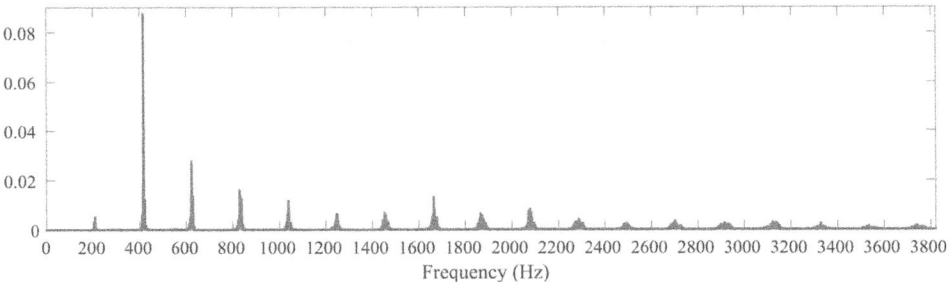

Figure 3.1c Spectrum of Violin Playing the Note A-Flat Below Middle-C. Most Listeners Would Say This Sound Has a Single Clear and Unambiguous Pitch.

The first thing to notice is that all these sounds have multiple frequency components. Indeed, it is a natural property of physical objects to vibrate simultaneously at different rates when struck, plucked, or stroked in some way. Any sound with more than one simultaneous frequency component is called a *complex tone*. These complex tones give rise to different experiences of pitch. The train sound has a "noisy" sound, and there is no clear pitch. This is because it is densely packed with multiple frequencies, mainly in the lower-frequency range, as can be seen on the left side of figure 3.1a. If you hear the sound of a train, you will probably find it difficult to sing in tune with it because it has no obvious pitch.

The cymbal sound in figure 3.1b is a partially or *ambiguously pitched* sound. Most people would agree that some cymbals sound higher than others, but it is still hard to sing along with a cymbal because it also does not have a very clear pitch. With very careful listening, a number of different pitches can be heard, and each of these different pitches corresponds to a peak in the spectrum (e.g., at 320 Hz, 510 Hz, and 1470 Hz).

However, the pitch we experience from the violin sound in figure 3.1c is quite different from the others. Despite the presence of multiple frequencies, we hear a *single* clear and unambiguous pitch. This results from the specific arrangement of frequencies in this spectrum: every single frequency component (each blue peak in figure 3.1c) occurs at (or close to) a frequency that is a multiple of a single *fundamental* frequency. In the violin spectrum, the fundamental frequency is the first peak at 207.65 Hz (A-flat below middle-C). The second peak is at $2 \times 207.65 = 415.3$ Hz and is called a *harmonic* or *overtone*, the third harmonic is at $3 \times 207.65 = 622.95$ Hz, the fourth harmonic is at $4 \times 207.65 = 830.6$ Hz, and so on. Sounds such as these—where all frequency components are multiples of a fundamental frequency—are known as *harmonic complex tones*.

Harmonic complex tones are unique in that they are the only set of simultaneous frequency components that ensures that only a single pitch is heard. Furthermore, that particular pitch always corresponds to the pitch produced by the fundamental (lowest) frequency. If the frequency of any single component in a harmonic complex tone is sufficiently altered, that altered frequency component will suddenly pop out as a clearly audible additional pitch. Due to the clarity and singularity of their pitches, instruments that produce harmonic complex tones are privileged in styles of music that make use of melodies or harmony (e.g., Western tonal music); these include stringed instruments (plucked or bowed), wind instruments, brass instruments, and even the human voice.

TIMBRE

Imagine listening to a saxophone playing a single pitch. Now imagine listening to a flute playing the same pitch and at the same loudness. In your mind's ear, do the two instruments sound the same? Most people would say that despite their having the same pitch and loudness, they sound quite different and are fairly easy to tell apart. This demonstrates that there must be more to auditory perception than just pitch and loudness. This additional perceptual feature is known as *timbre*.

However, this singular word gives a misleadingly simple impression of what is actually a complicated perceptual phenomenon. It is complicated because timbre encompasses numerous different perceptual attributes that are neither pitch nor loudness. Indeed, there is no consensus as to precisely what these perceptual attributes are or even how many there are. A small selection of adjectives commonly used to describe aspects of timbre include bright/dark, rough/smooth, heavy/light, nasal, reedy, and hollow. The first three make reference to other sensory modalities (vision, touch, proprioception), whereas the final three make reference to common physical characteristics of sound-producing devices. It seems that humans have not developed a distinct vocabulary to describe timbre, and so they often draw upon similarities with qualities from other senses.

One way to address this confusion of adjectives is to identify the dimensions of sound that best explain the similarities and differences between timbres. What dimensions of sound, for example, can best explain why a violin sounds more similar to a cello than it does to a harmonica? One procedure that has been used for this purpose is called *multidimensional scaling*. In an experimental setting, participants are played numerous different pairs of sounds, and they rate how similar the two sounds are in each pair. Let us imagine four sounds—saxophone, flute, recorder, and piano—with the following hypothetical, yet plausible, dissimilarity ratings that are made by comparing two instruments on a ten-point scale. The greater the number, the more dissimilar they are perceived to be:

- *saxophone vs. flute* = 6
- *saxophone vs. recorder* = 5
- *saxophone vs. piano* = 8
- *flute vs. recorder* = 3
- *flute vs. piano* = 9
- *recorder vs. piano* = 10

From these hypothetical dissimilarity ratings, we can see that the flute and recorder sound the most similar with a relatively low score of 3, whereas the recorder and piano are the most dissimilar with a maximum score of 10. The idea of multidimensional scaling is to use the dissimilarity ratings as an index of "distance" between the two sounds. By plotting the distance of dissimilarity ratings between two sounds on a three-dimensional graph—such as in figure 3.2—we can compare multiple sounds on multiple dimensions and begin to see that some sounds are perceived to be quite similar on some dimensions, whereas some are quite different due to their relative distance in the three-dimensional space.

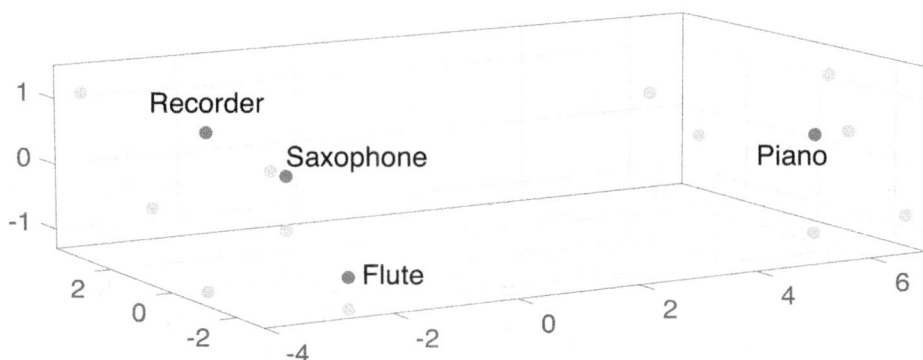

Figure 3.2 The Three-Dimensional Representation of the Distances between the Saxophone, Flute, Recorder, and Piano Timbres.

From such a graph, we can then begin to interpret and name each dimension to best summarize what perceptual or acoustic attribute characterizes them. For three-dimensional timbre spaces, there is usually convergence on two of the dimensions. The first dimension is often called *rise time*, which refers to the attack of a sound. In other words, the characteristics of the very beginning of a sound. For example, compare the fast percussive attack of a piano or plucked violin with the slow attack of a flute or bowed violin. The second dimension is called *spectral centroid*. If a sound has many, or loud, high-frequency components, it has a high spectral centroid, if it has few, or quiet, high-frequency components, it has a low spectral centroid. Spectral centroid is commonly associated with the timbral descriptor of "brightness." For example, compare a bowed violin with a flute when both are playing the same musical pitch; the violin produces more higher frequencies than the flute and so sounds more "shrill" or "bright," even though the main pitch does not change.

There is less consensus on a third dimension of similarity, but two qualities of sound may be important. The first quality is *spectral flux*, or how much a spectrum of a sound *changes* over time. For example, an organ sound does not change very much over time, whereas a gong sound changes a lot over time. A second quality is *spectral flatness*, which corresponds to the noisiness of a sound. For example, a cymbal has high spectral flatness, whereas a single note played on an oboe has low spectral flatness.

RHYTHM

The timing of musical sounds when pitches are played or when drums are struck is not random; it is organized or patterned in some way. *Rhythm* refers to the patterns of sounds over time. Rhythmic patterns may be simple and obvious to the listener, but sometimes they can be quite complex. However, in all cases, they respect certain constraints related to time. They also make use of the human brain's propensity to recognize certain patterns and for neural activity to *synchronize* (or entrain) to sounds that are equally spaced in time (equally spaced sounds are called *isochronous*).

Perceptual Time Scales

When isochronous musical sounds—for example, evenly spaced drum hits—are played with only a small gap between them (less than one-tenth of a second), they will be perceived as one continuous sound. The sounds are too close together to be heard separately. When they are played with long gaps between them (more than about 1.5 seconds), they tend to sound disconnected. It is actually quite difficult for musicians to accurately perform rhythms at these long gap durations without subdividing them. For example, to play a rhythm accurately when the gaps are two seconds apart, a typical strategy used by a musician is to subdivide the 2 seconds into four 0.5 second intervals and mentally count these out as 1, 2, 3, 4, 1, 2, 3, 4, 1, 2, 3, 4 but only strike the drum on the 1. Indeed, when adults are asked to tap a regular beat but not told how fast, they typically tap every 0.5–0.6 seconds. These tap rates correspond to a musical tempo of 100–120 beats per minute (bpm), and tempi such as these are very common in music.

Isochronous Beats and Entrainment

People are highly sensitive to isochronous patterns—beats that are regularly spaced in time. When we hear a steady drumbeat, it sounds intentional and orga-nized, and even small deviations from a regular drumbeat can be easily heard. How is music able to capitalize on this natural sensitivity for isochrony while also making rhythms interesting? There are at least three musical techniques, one or more of which are common in a variety of musical cultures and styles. They are called *metric hierarchies*, *asymmetric rhythms*, and *polyrhythms*.

Metric Hierarchies, Asymmetries, and Polyrhythms

Metric hierarchies refer to rhythms with numerous levels, where each faster level equally subdivides each slower level. This is the most common metrical framework in Western music. For example, consider a common but simple rock drum rhythm, notated graphically in table 3.1.

Here, the hi-hat cymbal plays a fast and isochronous rhythm. The snare drum also plays an isochronous rhythm. Note how the hi-hat subdivides or splits each snare beat into eight faster beats. The kick drum, however, is not playing an iso-chronous rhythm; there is an additional strike just before the count of three, which means that its three beats are of different lengths. But, crucially, every kick drum beat occurs at the same time as a hi-hat beat.

Rhythmic *asymmetries* such as these, where instruments play a *non-isochronous* subset of a faster isochronous pulse, are common. Sometimes, the isochronous pulse may not even be sounded, leaving the listener to fill in the gaps. An example of a non-isochronous rhythm commonly used in Latin American music is called the *clave* rhythm, as seen in the top rhythm outlined in table 3.2. Another example commonly used in West African music is called the *Yoruba timeline*; it is outlined in the bottom panel of table 3.2.

Table 3.1   A familiar rock drum rhythm. The drums playing each rhythmic level are shown on the left. The row labeled Count is how a musician might mentally count out the rhythm while practicing it

Count	1	e	&	a	2	e	&	a	3	e	&	a	4	e	&	a
Hi-hat cymbal	x	x	x	x	x	x	x	x	x	x	x	x	x	x	x	x
Snare drum					x								x			
Kick drum	x								x	x						

Table 3.2   In the *clave* rhythm at the top, the percussion instrument is played with an irregular (non-isochronous) pattern that repeats every sixteen pulses; the *Yoruba timeline* at the bottom is also irregular but repeats every twelve pulses. The Count row is how a musician might mentally count out the rhythm while practicing it

Count	1	&	2	&	3	&	4	&	1	&	2	&	3	&	4	&
Clave	x				x			x				x		x		

Count	1	&	2	&	3	&	1	&	2	&	3	&
Bell	x			x		x	x		x			x

Rhythms where sounds frequently occur on weak beats are called *syncopated* rhythms. Syncopated rhythms are often used to create rhythmic *groove*—the ability of music to elicit foot tapping, body swaying, head banging, or dancing. It is not fully understood why syncopated rhythms create a strong feeling of groove, but one possibility is that when we hear notes played on weak beats, we have to work a bit harder to imagine the strong beat; this compels us to want to move to the music, whether by clapping, tapping or dancing.

Polyrhythms are another method for creating complex and groovy rhythms. In polyrhythms, simple rhythms with different speeds (the speeds often have ratios of 2:3 or 3:4) are combined to form interesting rhythmic combinations. Polyrhythms such as these are common in some South American, African, and Caribbean traditions. For example, Ricki Martin's *Livin' La Vida Loca* employs polyrhythms that give the music a strong groove.

CONCLUSION

Pitch, timbre, and rhythm are the core building blocks of music. Individually, they can have strong effects on the mind and body—for example, a sad melody, the rich and fascinating timbres of a didgeridoo performance, or the driving rhythmic groove of a Latin American carnival band. Musicians use these building blocks to create songs that can then be played again and again by different performers in their own style. The song's core musical elements should remain fairly close to those of the original so that listeners will be able to recognize it from performance to performance, but musicians often make small adjustments to the pitch, timbre, and timing in subtle and individual ways, giving each performance its own unique flavor.

References and Further Reading
London, J. (2004). *Hearing in Time: Psychological Aspects of Musical Meter.* Oxford, UK: Oxford University Press.
Martineau, J. (2008). *The Elements of Music: Melody, Rhythm, and Harmony.* Somerset, UK: Wooden Books.
McAdams, S. (2013). Musical timbre perception. In D. Deutsch (Ed.), *The Psychology of Music* (3rd ed., pp. 35–68). London, UK: Academic Press.
Peterson, N. (2008). *An Introduction to the Concepts of Music.* Sydney, NSW, Australia: Cengage Learning Australia.

4. Scales, Intervals, and Tuning Systems

William A. Sethares

Why are there so many different kinds of music? Why do people in different cultures use different musical instruments? Why are those instruments tuned in so many different ways? This chapter tackles these questions by looking at the many ways musical instruments from around the world are tuned. Most are tuned based on musical scales, which are themselves composed of intervals. The word *scale* has a specific meaning: a musical scale is the set of all the pitches in a song or a musical performance. Although different musical cultures prefer to use different scales in their songs, almost all cultures choose to use scales that contain a modest number of tones.

WHY USE SCALES AT ALL?

Your voice, the pluck of a guitar string, the blowing of a trumpet, the vocalizations of a whale, and the song of a bird—these sounds all have a clear pitch. Sometimes these pitches vary continuously over time. For example, a smooth gliding or sliding up and down characterizes the calls of a whale or the voice of an eastern meadowlark. Sometimes, the pitches are separated into discrete steps, such as the notes produced by the keys of a piano or when fretting and plucking a guitar. Figure 4.1 contrasts these two situations: the pitch of the songbird on the left sweeps smoothly up and down, and the notes of the piano on the right jump from pitch to pitch as different keys are pressed.

As suggested by the wavy line in figure 4.1, people can perceive many thousands of different pitches. Why would music makers so often choose to use just a small number? One possible answer is that a song needs to be memorable; by using only a small subset of the existing pitches, a melody may be easier to remember. Another answer is that songs made from scales are easier to perform than songs made up of continuous pitches; restricting the full range of pitches to a small set of discrete scale notes makes it easier to sing or to play a piece of music.

Musical scales are usually ordered (either ascending or descending), and so the scale of the piece represented on the right side of figure 4.1 is shown by the four round gray circles, which correspond to specific notes on the piano keyboard. In principle, musical scales can consist of any set of pitches, but, in practice, the same sets of pitches reoccur over and over; common scales are given names such

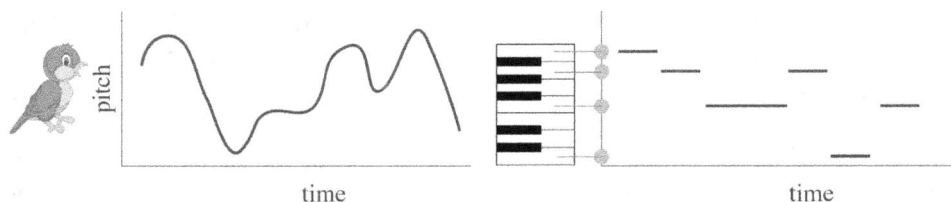

Figure 4.1 Pitch Can Vary Continuously, Like the Warbling of a Songbird, or May Assume a Small Number of Values, Like the Notes of a Musical Instrument.

as *major* and *minor* (Western Europe), *slendro* and *pelog* (Indonesia), *Uşşak* and *Hicaz* (Turkey), and *Segāh* and *Māhur* (Iran). These are not just different names for the same scales; they also contain different intervals in different patterns. In some traditions, scales are associated with various emotional states or feelings; in others, scales may be associated with the seasons, with holidays, with the time of day, or with particular geographic regions.

NAMING NOTES

In many musical cultures, the tones in a scale are given names. One early naming system is based on a Gregorian chant called *Ut Queant Laxis* that honors John the Baptist:

> *Ut* queant laxis *re*sonare fibris
> *Mi*ra gestorum *fa*muli tuorum,
> *Sol*ve polluti *la*bii reatum, Sancte Iohannes.

With the substitution of *do* for *ut* and the addition of *ti*, this is the familiar *do–re–mi–fa–sol–la–ti–do* of Western music. Another common naming system is numerical: the eight notes of the *do–re–mi* scale can be identified with the first eight integers. In the Indonesian system, a melodic line in the slendro scale may be notated numerically:

$$3\,6\,5\,\underline{1}\,2\,3\,5\,6\,1\,2\,3\,5\,6\,1\,2\,3\,5\,6\,1\,2\,3\,\ddot{5}$$

Notations such as these are relative, in the sense that the 1, or the *do*, can represent any pitch (called the *root* or the *tonic*), and all others are relative to this root. Such pitch differences are called *intervals*, and these intervals also typically have names.

INTERVALS

The simplest interval is the octave from low *do* to high *do*, which occurs naturally when a man and a woman (or a woman and a child) sing together. On vibrating strings, octaves occur when one string is twice as long as another. The modern way of stating this fact (known to the ancient Greeks) is that the octave represents the sounding of two pitches with fundamental frequencies that are separated by a factor of two. The octave, this factor of two to one, is often notated with the fraction 2/1.

The octave is special perceptually. In general, as the frequency difference (and the interval) between two tones grows, the pitch difference increases, as shown on the left-hand side of figure 4.2. As the separation between the two tones nears the octave, however, the two tones appear to become "the same" again (this is called *octave equivalence*). Octave equivalence is reflected in the repeating pattern of the piano keyboard and the repeating pattern of the naming of the notes: for instance, the same *do–re–mi* pattern recurs in every octave. Perceptually, intervals can be thought of as stacked, where all the *do*s or all the Cs are placed above

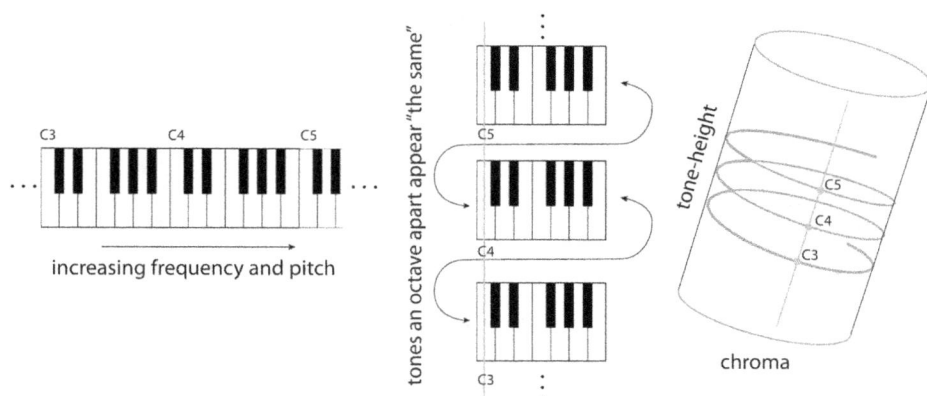

Figure 4.2 The Perception of Pitch Intervals Has Two Aspects: The Chroma Relates Tones Within an Octave, and the Tone Height Specifies Which Octave the Interval Belongs to. Most Musical Scales Repeat at the Octave.

each other. Thus, there are two notions of distance in the perception of pitch: the distance caused by nearness or farness in frequency and the distance within the octave. This may be pictured as in the right-hand portion of figure 4.2, which shows the frequency difference displayed along a spiral that is wrapped around a cylinder. For any interval (the octaves of C are shown), the tone height specifies the loop of the spiral, and the chroma locates the position around the cylinder.

The next simplest interval is the musical fifth, which occurs when two vibrating strings are in the ratio 3/2 (for instance, thirty inches to twenty inches). Similarly, other ratios n/m, where both n and m are small integers, are called *pure* or *just*; several are shown in figure 4.3. Intervals can be combined by multiplying the ratios as fractions. For example, combining a fifth (3/2) and a major third (6/5) gives the interval

$$3/2 * 6/5 = 18/10 = 9/5$$

which is called the just minor seventh in figure 4.3. If the product becomes larger than the octave, it is reduced back to its chroma value by multiplying by 1/2. For example, a stack of two fifths gives $3/2 * 3/2 = 9/4$. To see that this is an octave plus a major second, multiply 9/4 by 1/2 to arrive at 9/8. Figure 4.3 shows that 9/8 is indeed a major second.

Ratios and fractions are often cumbersome, and the size of a complicated fraction is not always obvious. For instance, is 19/12 larger or smaller than 17/11? An alternative is to adopt a measurement system called *cents* (abbreviated ¢) that translates products of fractions into sums of cents. In the cents system, the octave is defined to be 1200 cents, and so each adjacent key of the piano is 100 cents apart. A formula[1] that involves logarithms relates the size of an interval expressed

---

1 An interval expressed as a ratio f_2/f_1 can be translated into cents with the formula $1200 * Log_2(f_2/f_1)$. If this calculation seems intimidating, there are websites that contain interactive ratio-to-cent (and cent-to-ratio) converters.

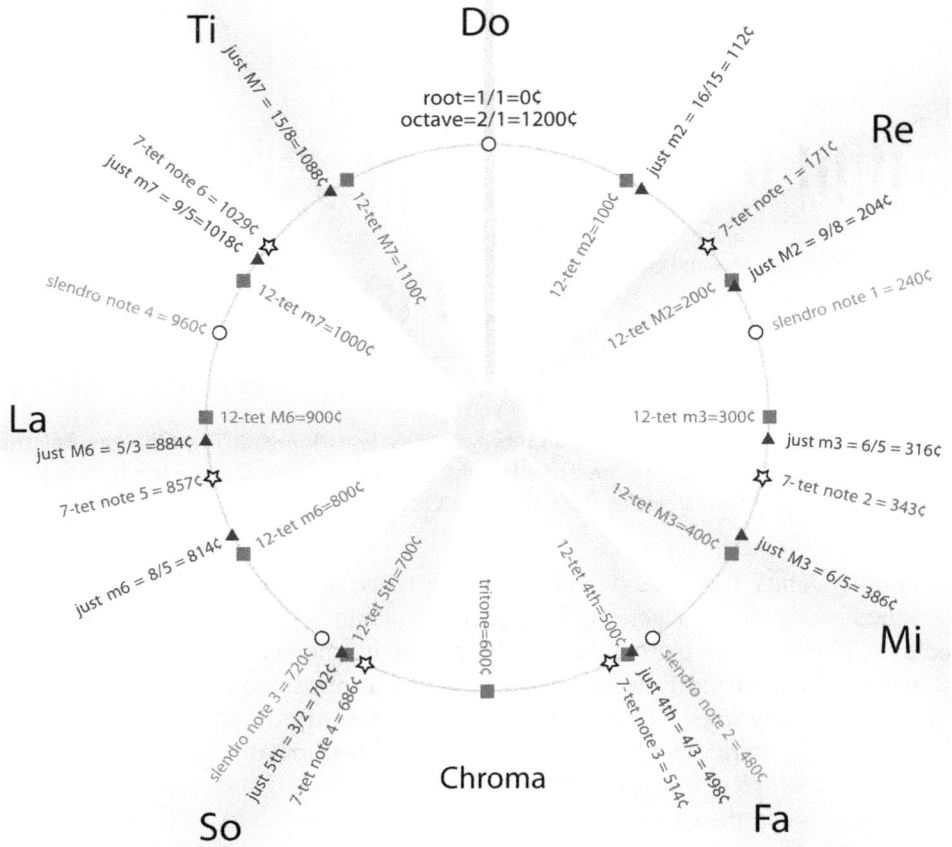

Figure 4.3 Shows one octave divided in many ways. The equally spaced squares mark the twelve steps of the Western equal-tempered chromatic scale. A collection of just intervals (those defined by small-integer ratios) are shown by the small triangles. Both of these have many intervals that lie within the regions marked *do–re–mi*, indicating that a variety of nearby intervals can play these melodic and harmonic roles. The seven equal steps of the traditional Thai scale are shown with stars, and the five steps of the Indonesian slendro are indicated by the circles. Several abbreviations are used: ¢ for cents; m2 and M2 for minor and major second, respectively; m3 and M3 for minor and major third, respectively; and so on.

as a ratio to the size of the interval expressed in cents. Converting shows that 19/12 is 796 cents, and 17/11 is 754 cents. Clearly, 796 is larger than 754. Cents make it easy to compare the sizes of intervals and their location on the circular pitch chroma of figure 4.3.

NAMING SCALES

In the Western tradition, musical scales are drawn from notes of the 12-tone equal-tempered scale (often written 12-tet, called the *chromatic scale*, and shown in figure 4.3 by the equally spaced square markers). In 12-tet, each octave is segmented into twelve equal sounding divisions, like the hour markers on the face of a clock. Depending on the exact ordering of the intervals, subsets of 12-tet may be major or minor, and a variety of modes differ based on the starting point. From a historic perspective, such scales and modes based on subsets of 12-tet are fairly recent. Ancient Greeks such as Aristoxenus constructed scales based on tetrachords and just intervals (like those indicated by small triangles in figure 4.3), and Pythagoras is often cited as designing a scale by stacking just fourths and just fifths. Tetrachords (where a pure fourth is divided into three subintervals) also appear in traditional Turkish *makam* music and can be used to create scales with many more than twelve pitches as well as diatonic scales with unusual intervals. Scales that use intervals based on small-integer ratios, that is, fractions with small integers in the numerator and denominator (Doty 1993), are called *just intonation scales.* Harry Partch created a scale with forty-three unequal tones per octave, designed a family of musical instruments (some of which are shown in figure 4.4), and composed a repertoire of music to perform on his instruments. Many other historical scales, such as meantone tunings and well temperaments, are essentially different ways of approximating just intervals while attempting to retain the ability to modulate to distant keys.

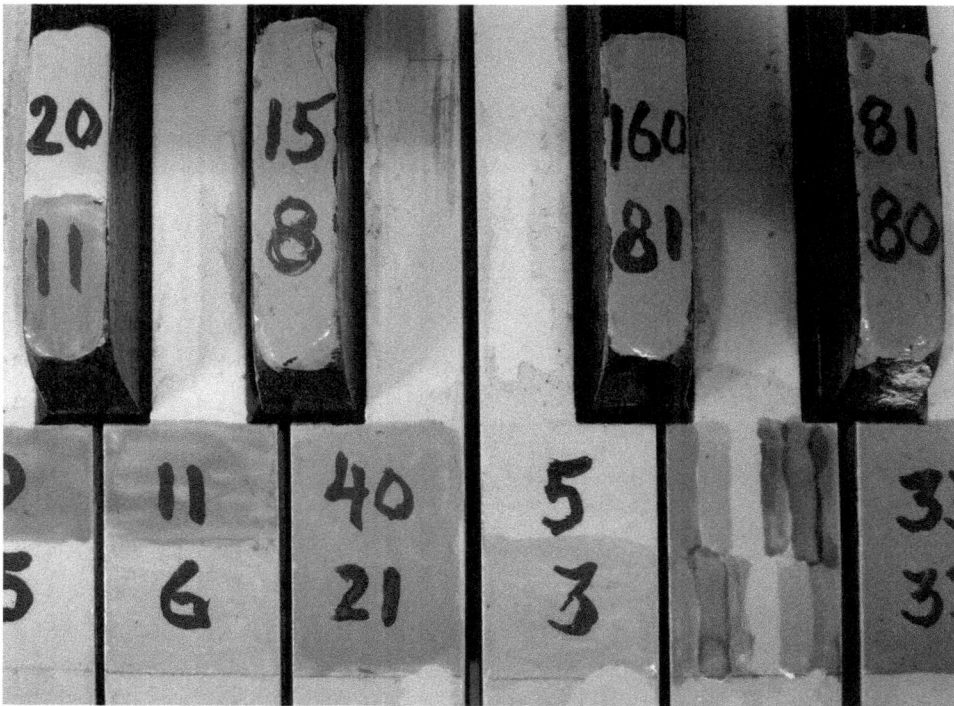

Figure 4.4a Harry Partch designed Many Instruments to Play in His 43-Tone Just Scale. This is the Chromelodeon (Keyboard Detail Shown). (Danlee Mitchell, Courtesy of the Harry Partch Estate)

Figure 4.4b Harry Partch designed Many Instruments to Play in His 43-Tone Just Scale. This is the Cloud-Chamber Bowls. (Danlee Mitchell, Courtesy of the Harry Partch Estate)

Figure 4.4c Harry Partch designed Many Instruments to Play in His 43-Tone Just Scale. This is the Quadrangularis Reversum. (Danlee Mitchell, Courtesy of the Harry Partch Estate)

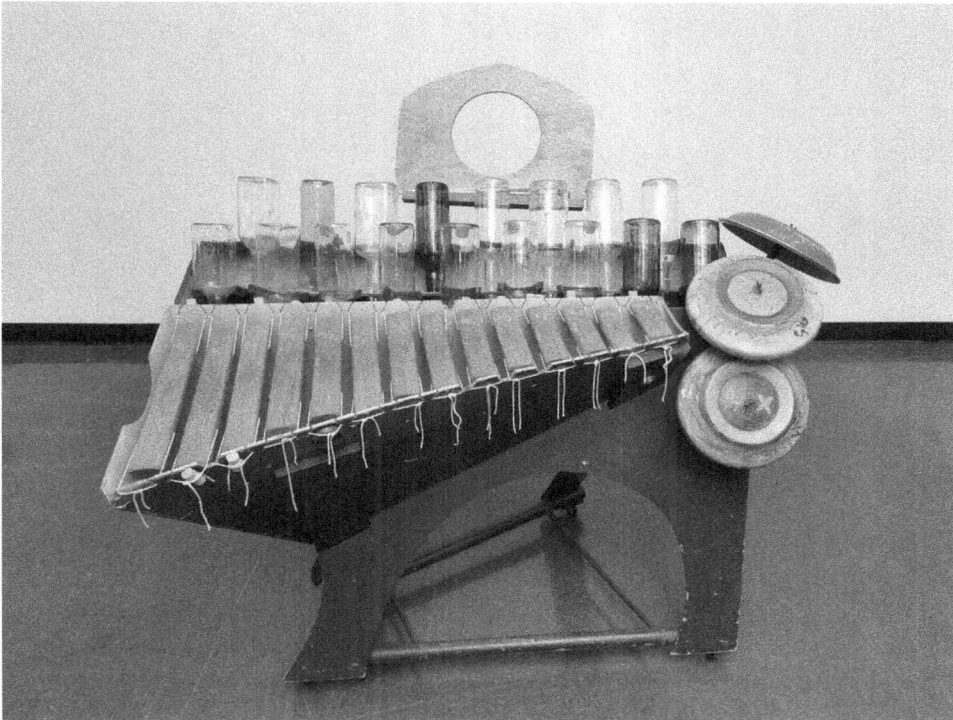

Figure 4.4d Harry Partch designed Many Instruments to Play in His 43-Tone Just Scale. This is the Zymo-Xyl. (Danlee Mitchell, Courtesy of the Harry Partch Estate)

Of course, other cultures use intervals and scales that are quite different. For example, the traditional music of Thailand uses a scale that is approximately seven-tone equal temperament, which is shown in figure 4.3 by the stars, where the interval between adjacent tones is 172 cents. Certain Arabic music is played in scales with twenty-two unequally spaced tones per octave, though the exact intervals are a matter of some discussion. Indonesian gamelan orchestras are tuned to either the five-note slendro (shown in figure 4.3 by the small circles) or the seven-tone pelog scales. Neither of these scales has intervals that correspond to 12-tet, and neither lies completely within the *do–re–mi*. Moreover, each gamelan is tuned idiosyncratically, with "octaves" that are stretched or compressed by up to 25 cents from the standard 1200-cent octave.

TUNING INSTRUMENTS

Scales and their associated intervals are ways of dividing pitch into useful chunks, and the musical instruments of a culture are commonly set to a *tuning* that makes it easy to play in the scales of that culture. The classical piano keyboard is tuned to the steps of the 12-tet chromatic scale. The white keys are tuned to the major scale (the 12-tet *do–re–mi* of figure 4.3). The frets of a guitar mimic the 12-tet tuning of the piano keyboard, but the frets of other stringed instruments,

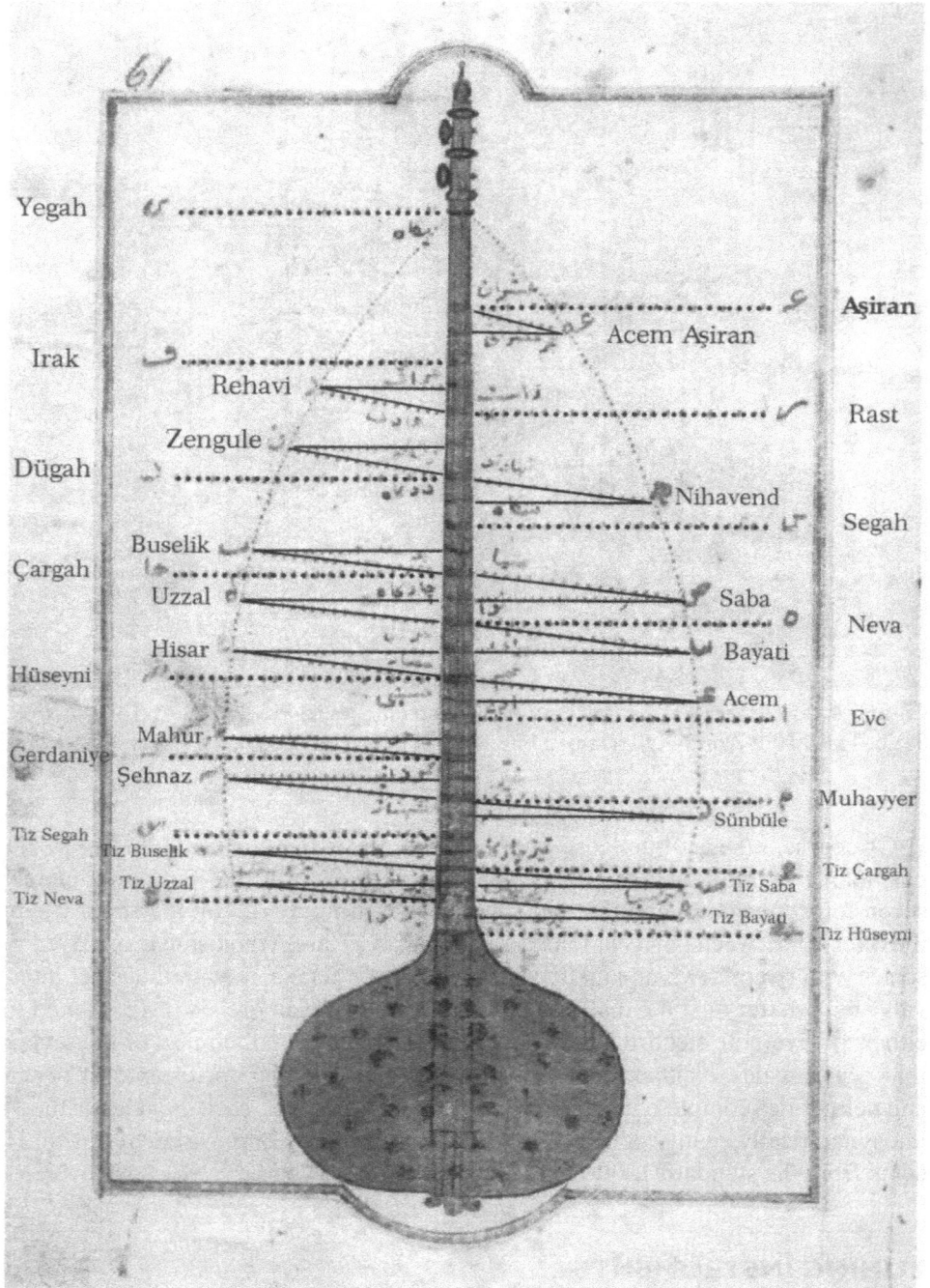

Figure 4.5 Not All Stringed Instruments Are Fretted Alike. Kantemir's Early Eighteenth-Century Tuning Instructions Explicitly Describe the Tuning (and hence the Intervals of the Scale) of the Tanbur. (Kantemir's Tanbur from Kitabu Ilmi'l-Musiki ala vechi'l-Hurufat, p. 131.)

Figure 4.6 Gamelans Contain a Variety of Metallophones, Drums, and Gongs and May Be Tuned to Either the 5-Note Slendro Scale of Figure 4.3 or to a Seven-Note Pelog Scale. (Asian Civilizations Museum, Empress Place. Photo by Sengkeng.)

such as the Turkish tanbur of figure 4.5, are tuned to the tones of a Turkish *makam* (scale).

Yet, other musical cultures use instruments that sound quite different from the familiar stringed and air-column instruments common in the West. The inharmonic instruments of the Indonesian gamelan (see figure 4.6) are built from an orchestra of metallophones (instruments made of metal), drums, gongs, and other instruments tuned to traditional scales. The orchestra often accompanies singing, dancing, or shadow puppet shows, and the music can be stately and contemplative or loud and energetic.

CONCLUSION

Why are there so many different intervals, scales, and tunings in use throughout the world? One answer is that each musical tradition has followed a unique path that reflects its cultural and historical setting; common music binds a people together and is part of the fabric of a society. Another answer rests on the tone quality of the musical instruments. Overtones of string and wind instruments are harmonic: they lie in a harmonic series. Since harmonic overtones overlap each other when notes are played in simple integer ratios, just intonation explains musical intervals and scales in relation to the harmonic series. But some musical traditions (such as the gamelan) use instruments with inharmonic overtones that overlap each other when tones are played in different intervals (such as those of the slendro and pelog scales (Sethares 1998)). This suggests that the tone quality of the instruments is tied to the scales of the musical tradition and may have been adopted, at least partially, in response to each other.

References and Further Reading

Deutsch, D. (Ed.). (1982). *The Psychology of Music*. San Diego, CA: Academic Press.

Doty, D. B. (1993). *Just Intonation Primer*. San Francisco, CA: Just Intonation Network.

Harrison, M. (1999). *Contemporary Music Theory*. Winona, MN: Hal Leonard Publishing, Co.

Partch, H. (1974). *Genesis of a Music*. New York, NY: Da Capo Press.

Sethares, W. A. (1998). *Tuning, Timbre, Spectrum, Scale*. Springer-Verlag. https://sethares.engr.wisc.edu/consemi.html

Surjodiningrat, W., Sudarjana, P. J., & Susanto, A. (1993). *Tone Measurements of Outstanding Javanese Gamelan in Yogyakarta and Surakarta*. Yogyakarta: Gadjah Mada University Press.

5. Defining Culture

Tia DeNora

We come to culture early in the course of life. From the moment an infant and a parent begin the rhythmic, improvised vocalizations known as baby talk, culture is there, and it is being informally taught as a shared patterned activity.

CULTURE AS OBJECT AND AS ACTIVITY

Culture enters our lives as an explicit *thing*—as works of art and music, magazine images, rules and norms about how to behave where and when, and material objects. But culture is also implicit, working as a kind of silent partner in much of what we do, feel, think, and say. When we ride a bicycle, for example, or greet someone on the street, we are unlikely to ponder, "How should this be done?" Rather, we "just do it"—relying on deeply ingrained habits, routines, and, perhaps, muscle memories (how to balance on the cycle, how to smile when you are greeting someone). The fact that we are rarely aware of culture's implicit presence is brought home to us every time something seems to go wrong, socially speaking (e.g., times when we feel confusion or embarrassment and ask ourselves, "Was it something I said?" or "Is s/he crazy?"). At those times, some of the unwritten or tacit features of culture that govern human action become visible because they are seen against the backdrop of what should have happened but did not. (Imagine you fall off the bicycle. You then say to yourself, "Aha! This is what I forgot to do to keep my balance.) Breaches in cultural order highlight what we otherwise take for granted in action. Most of the time, though, we operate on a kind of cultural autopilot, and when we speak about having "cultural competence," we are referring to just how complex cultural operating systems can be. Culture's seemingly automatic features actually save us a lot of effort as we move through the various scenes and situations that make up any given day.

Explicit and implicit culture are of course interrelated. Explicit culture often informs, or "gets into," implicit culture; for example, if we begin to imitate the talk or walk of a film star and do it so often that we forget we are doing it, an explicit feature of culture has become implicit, at least until someone tells us that we walk or talk like (film star X or Y). Then we might say, "Ah, yes, I was very impressed by him/her when I was younger."

One of the founding fathers of sociology, Emile Durkheim (1858–1917), once said that culture "lifts" us into a realm that is above individual experience and in ways that actually come to shape individual experience. We can often trace culture as it gets into and informs situations and scenes. Indeed, we can think of our lives as consisting of interlinked cultural events.

CULTURAL EVENTS

A cultural event may be something *special*, such as a celebration (holidays, birthdays), or it may involve strongly bounded procedures, as in a game (scoring a goal in ice hockey or playing in tune or in rhythm within an orchestral string section). It may involve a very formal set of rules about what is to be done, by whom, and how, for example, certain rituals (graduations, initiations) or ceremonies (requiem masses, civil partnerships). Conversely, a cultural event may also be mundane or *everyday*. It can be a situation (school lesson, concert, family meal). It may even involve a private or personal activity for only one person (thinking about a problem, writing a poem, listening to music using earbuds).

Culture is not tightly bounded to geographical area, despite all the talk about national cuisines and customs or regional variations in culture. Geography may inform culture, but culture also transcends physical space—and never more so than today with the proliferation of digital media and travel. So today's idea of "national" or "regional" culture is increasingly complicated by other cultural currents. These currents crosscut physical topography and lead to the blurring of earlier contexts (traditions, "authentic" practices), which, as they are transported, get redefined and recombined in ways that change them—often with social consequences.

For these reasons, it is perhaps less interesting to ask, "What is the culture of [X country or Y region or even Z group]?" than it is to ask, "What does culture do, and how is it employed in ways that structure action?" These questions also draw together different academic perspectives that are concerned with what culture does. It combines anthropology's and sociology's concern with cultural norms, rules, and social behaviors with social psychology's focus on individual experience to examine how culture can be seen to organize, or "get into," and give definition to even our seemingly most personal, subjective experiences.

For example, think about how quickly your mood can change when listening to a piece of music. Here, music, which is something that exists independent of you (it is in the world, not in your mind or your bloodstream), can get, as people sometimes say, "under your skin" in ways that can powerfully affect how you feel and the kinds of memories and associations you have while listening. Indeed, it may even have some bearing on what you then choose to do after the music stops. No wonder music is so vital to our sense of identity and our attachments to other people (and groups of people).

Think about the music playlists you may have made for personal listening. Would you be willing to share these with just anyone? If your answer is no, you recognize that other people often judge us according to our cultural (in this case musical) values and tastes. Now think about how you might, without even thinking about it, judge people according to the music they say they like or dislike. Now imagine that you hang out more with people who share your tastes and musical practices; you are now part of what cultural sociologists speak of as a *cultural scene* (a hip-hop scene, a jazz scene), a *taste public* (consumers of X or Y music), or a *musical subculture* (though this last term may cause problems because it tends to imply that some cultures are general and shared by everyone and others are subsets, which tends to rank cultures in ways that might disrespect some of them).

In each of these examples, whether *special* or *everyday*, people are doing things in real times and spaces in ways that make use of media (words, objects, symbols) and that, to some extent, can be recognized by others as *common* or *shared* activities, that is, activities that stand outside any one individual but, rather, between two or more individuals. To speak about things that stand outside an individual is to speak about things that exist in a public (or quasi-public) domain. Culture is, in short, publicly available ways of doing, thinking, and acting that have been developed by people in space and time and that have the capacity to draw people together. Culture is the medium through which human sociability is produced—we would, simply put, not be sociable without the work that culture does.

WHAT DOES CULTURE DO?

Durkheim said that culture fulfills important functions for human society: it is culture that motivates us, that captures our imagination, and that makes mutual orientation possible. Emblems and embodied representations, as Durkheim describes, give rise to shared feelings and shared social forms. As a simple example of how representations give rise to collective feelings, consider the names we give to sports teams. While it may be easy to imagine a sports team called the Bulls, or the Eagles (indeed, there are teams with these names), it is less easy to imagine a team called the Cows or the Turkeys. If this example strikes a humorous chord, it is because naming matters. The name, as a symbolic totem, stands on behalf of the team's characteristics; it embodies and exemplifies what kind of players there are on this or that team. People who study *semiotics*, the meaning and social force of symbols, examine how our different symbolic codes are interrelated. For example, it might not have escaped your notice that while the Bulls is masculine, the Cows is feminine; so this might be read to undercut the conventional association of basketball with masculinity (although nowadays these associations are increasingly challenged as previously marginalized groups seek to participate in what were unfairly segregated forms of activity).

The cultural meanings and symbols attached to sports teams thus stand as forms of explicit culture. They become implicit (and facilitate forms of action) when they are internalized by the team's players and supporters. For example, if you are a player, feeling empowered during a game often involves a kind of imaginative participation; the imagination is fired up by symbols and symbolic associations ("We are the Bulls—we are strong and tough like bulls!"). To speak of internalization is to point to how culture gets into acts and motivations.

So, without culture, we would not be able to coordinate, communicate, or create shared meaning, and we would not have forms with which, and within which, to imagine, to dream, or to feel. For this reason, Durkheim believed that one of the greatest forms of misery was to be without guiding cultural structures, which, he said, created a feeling of being cast adrift from human sociability. The result of this feeling is often distressing, it is isolating, and, ultimately, it can be dangerous to mental health and health in general.

For example, imagine for a moment that you somehow landed on a distant planet, one where there are human beings. But you cannot understand the language, and even gestures seem to mean entirely different things. What people eat and how they dress are totally different, and you do not know how to act. Moreover, you do not even know how to ask about how to act. The feeling is frightening, and the lack of cultural connection means you are isolated. When this happens at a collective level—at times, whole groups of people lose their focus and motivation—culture becomes, in Durkheim's sense, deregulated and *anomic*—it has failed to provide direction and structure in ways that lead to a crisis in literally knowing what to do, feel, and think. In other words, culture is the thing that binds us together, and, along with connecting us, culture makes us feel secure. It is perhaps not surprising then that, for these reasons, cultural participation can promote well-being. Indeed, at times, culture can be so powerful that it can actually prevent us from noticing physical pain (e.g., when placebos are effective).

CULTURAL POWER, SEGMENTATION, AND CONFLICT: THE CASE OF MUSIC

The case of music as it becomes culturally implicit is good to examine because we can often follow music as it gets into and lends particular kinds of capacity to our embodied actions. It is because of music's ability to organize the body that we often choose to exercise to music; we become entrained, or move in sync, along with its pulse or rhythms. But music can also support and maintain our motivation at times of stress or difficulty, and for these reasons, music can be seen to structure action, thought, and mood in ways that promote well-being. When people face harsh conditions or circumstances, such as during times of political oppression or forced migration or in relation to ill health or sadness, it is not surprising, then, that many researchers have described how music can help to keep hope and action alive (Ansdell & DeNora 2016; Hagen 2019).

But culture can have negative as well as positive effects. Culture is, paradoxically, both the thing that draws us together and the thing that can drive us apart, as many arguments begin because of cultural clashes. Often, the more powerful a person's or group's commitment to culture, the more likely they will be intolerant of practices or values that are different from their own. As one cultural sociologist has put it (Reed 2007), there is a danger in having "too much reality," that is, in believing that cultural categories and values are sacred, given, or preordained and thus must be defended, even with violence. The cultural anthropologist Mary Douglas has described in her famous book, *Purity and Danger*, how culture orders things into binary categories—things that are clean, for example, or that make sense to us, and things that are dirty or polluting and make no sense. When we encounter the latter, she says, we feel the need to tidy it up, or remove it, to preserve the symbolic order. Of course, what counts as clean or dirty is context dependent—that is, it is cultural. And for this reason, the impulse to order is simultaneously a potential threat to anyone who might cleave to the things that others seek to "fix" (the forms of "disorder").

On a daily basis, we experience a multitude of shared events. In all of these, we participate with varying degrees of feeling, devotion, passion, and commitment. These varying degrees highlight our relative attachment to culture or, rather, to cultural features that define a particular type of shared event. Sometimes we are detached and cool, sometimes we are hostile, and sometimes we are totally taken over by a cause, event, or situation in ways that move us deeply. To the extent that it is possible to speak of group identification with cultural forms or formats, we can speak about the relative strength of culture—the varying degrees of social solidarity—across a group, tribe, region, nation, virtual community, or, indeed, globally.

Music history offers many examples of cultural conflicts and attempts to create or restore cultural "order." Some of these have been linked to socioeconomic status and the attempts of elites to confer status on "high culture" forms of music while degrading popular forms. The sociologist Pierre Bourdieu's famous study of the social structure of cultural tastes and preferences suggests that "nothing more clearly affirms one's class, nothing more infallibly classifies, than taste in music" (1984, p. 19), because, during the nineteenth century, the musical tastes in Europe and the United States became stratified, that is, linked to class and status backgrounds of taste publics. So-called serious music (classical, symphonic music) came to serve as a powerful symbol of status among elites and those who wished to be like elite members of society.

The history of popular music has also been subject to conflicts, and, in particular, it has frequently been associated with moral panics, that is, with collective attempts to suppress the music because it is deemed to promote immoral, violent, or deviant forms of activity that threaten the fiber of society as a whole (the *whole* being itself a problematic term because how it is defined is often subject to conflict). Jazz, heavy metal, club music, hip-hop, and, most recently, drill (in Chicago and London) have all been accused of encouraging illicit or risky behaviors in ways that show how conflicts over music are often aligned to class, racial discrimination, and stereotyping.

CONCLUSION

The study of culture highlights what it means to be a human social animal. Culture is produced by and produces social action and draws people together while simultaneously sketching the fault lines that lead to conflict and dissent. A focus on how explicit forms of culture can "get into" how we act, feel, and think— in concert—is a focus on how, metaphorically speaking, the medium within which we operate (and have to operate) if we are to remain social beings. As Durkheim put it more than one hundred years ago, "Society cannot make its influence felt unless it is in action, and it is not in action unless the individuals who compose it are assembled together and act in common" (1912/2001, pp. 417–418). It is culture that, for better or worse, draws us onto the plane where action in common occurs.

References and Further Reading
Ansdell, G. and T. DeNora. (2016). *Musical Pathways in Recovery: Community Music Therapy and Mental Wellbeing*. London: Routledge.
Bourdieu, P. (1984). *Distinction: A Social Critique of the Judgement of Taste* (R. Nice, Translator). Cambridge: Polity.
DeNora, T. (2014). *Making Sense of Reality: Culture and Perception in Everyday Life*. London, UK: Sage.
Douglas, M. (1966). *Purity and Danger*. London: Routledge, Keagan and Paul.
Durkheim, E. (2001). The *Elementary Forms of Religious Life*. Oxford, UK: Oxford University Press. (Original work published 1912).
Garfinkel, H. (1967). *Studies in Ethnomethodology*. New York, NY: Free Press.
Goffman, E. (1959). *The Presentation of Self in Everyday Life*. New York, NY: Doubleday.
Hagen, T. (2019). *Living in the Merry Ghetto*. Oxford: Oxford University Press.
Reed, I. (2007). Why Salem made sense: Culture, gender and the Puritan persecution of witchcraft. *Cultural Sociology, 1*(2), 209–234.

6. Cross-Cultural Research in Music Psychology

William Forde Thompson and Kirk N. Olsen

People differ in the types of music they like, how they make music, how they relate to it, and how they are affected by it. Around the world and across history, there are vast differences in the forms that music can take, what music sounds like, and the activities that involve music. Hindustani music of Northern India sounds nothing like Western electronic dance music, and these styles of music sound different from the klezmer music of the Ashkenazi Jews of Eastern Europe. Similarly, classical piano music such as that of Mozart and Beethoven sounds nothing like American rap music. What about the psychological basis of these divergent forms of music? Is it possible that, despite the many differences in what these forms of music sound like, they have similar psychological effects on people? For example, maybe all music affects people emotionally, stimulates creativity, or brings people together. Cross-cultural research on the psychology of music seeks to understand the similarities and differences between forms of music around the world and listeners' experience of such music.

Cross-cultural research is not the norm in the psychology and science of music. Between 1983 and 2010, over half of all research on the psychology of music focused on Western classical music such as Mozart and Beethoven, and many genres of music around the world have never been considered in any psychological investigation to date. But the situation is changing. In the past several decades, researchers have begun to consider other genres of music, and not just genres from around the globe but also overlooked music from within our own society, such as death metal, jazz, and rap. As cross-cultural research expands to consider various traditions of music worldwide, we will gain a better understanding of the science and psychology of music. But time is running out. With increasing globalization, there are few musical traditions that have not been heavily influenced by the music of Western countries such as the United States and the United Kingdom, which is heard around the world on radio, on the Internet, and through various other music-delivery systems.

UNDERSTANDING MUSIC ACROSS CULTURES

Specific forms of music in Western countries, such as popular songs on the radio, rock concerts, piano recitals, and music for films, are not found in all cultures. Defining music in one society is difficult enough, but defining music across all the world's cultures poses a significant challenge. Many languages, such as the Mafa language spoken in northern Cameroon, do not even have a word for *music*, although they have words for specific behaviors and rituals that tend to involve music. Thus, a single understanding of music does not exist cross-culturally. However, it is still possible to scientifically investigate and compare a range of music-like phenomena from different cultures by looking at the sounds that make up the music, the behaviors of people performing and listening to the music, and what happens in the mind when people engage in musical activities.

A comparison of sounds might consider the set of notes that are used in the music, called the *scale*; the kinds of melodies and rhythms that occur; and the types of instruments and vocalizations that are involved. A comparison of behaviors might examine whether the music is accompanied by social rituals (e.g., marriages, religious celebrations) or by physical responses such as dancing or singing along. A comparison of what goes on in the mind would require psychological investigations that uncover what people perceive and remember about their music and how it affects them psychologically. Does music change the way people feel and how they interact with others? Does it influence what they believe? And how do these experiences differ across cultures? These are all important questions in cross-cultural research in music psychology.

CHALLENGES OF CROSS-CULTURAL RESEARCH

Is it possible to make neutral or objective observations about unfamiliar music from another culture? Up until the middle of the twentieth century, most genres of music associated with non-Western societies were described as "primitive" by scholars who were only familiar with Western music. When they listened to this unfamiliar music, it sounded "wrong" to them. The perceptions of Western scholars reflected a lack of experience and understanding of this music, and they typically concluded that the music was unsophisticated, badly conceived, or undeveloped. They genuinely believed they were making neutral scientific observations, but hindsight tells us that their perceptions reflected a Western bias. In other words, their lifelong experience listening to Western music had changed the way they perceived and evaluated music from non-Western societies. In the same way, someone who has only ever experienced classical piano music might perceive extreme metal music as unmusical noise, but many extreme metal songs have a complex musical structure and are performed by elite-level musicians. Fans of this music have learned to hear the various qualities of the music and thoroughly enjoy it, whereas nonfans have not.

For these reasons, cross-cultural research is difficult. Researchers need to identify a musical culture and familiarize themselves with the music until they understand its many features and complexities. They must also learn about the experiences, values, and behaviors of the people who listen to that music while also ensuring their own biases do not impact their results. Only then can they begin to investigate what goes on in the mind when people from a specific culture or segment of the population engage in a musical experience, whether those people are associated with a particular geographical region, such as Tibet or Northern India, or a defined subset of society, such as the death metal or rap community.

UNDERSTANDING FIELDWORK

Many cross-cultural investigations involve fieldwork, where researchers immerse themselves in the culture of interest for a period of time, making observations, learning about the people and their music, and sometimes running controlled experiments. Tom Fritz, a researcher working at the Max Planck Institute in Leipzig, Germany, was interested in studying the Mafa people who live in the extreme north of Cameroon, a country in Central Africa next to Nigeria. Knowing that in Western society we can all tell if a piece of music seems "happy" or "sad," his aim was to determine whether the Mafa people in this region could also perceive emotional connotations in Western music. The Mafa do not have a word for *music*, but music-like activities play an important role in many of their rituals and harvesting activities. To find Mafa people with little or no experience with Western music, he traveled to remote villages in the Mandara Mountains, where the people often pursued a conservative way of life. Within these settlements, he found Mafa people who had never participated in any event at which Western music might be playing in the background, such as a Christian service or a market with access to electricity.

To gain the trust and cooperation of these people, Fritz first made visits to several chiefs of villages in traditional settlements, who invited him to share in food and millet beer. Adjusting to a new environment can be challenging, and Fritz experienced many health challenges during his visit, including salmonella poisoning, malaria, typhoid, and bronchitis. At one point, he participated in a traditional flute-playing ritual, an activity that can lead to trance states among participants. He also befriended individuals who spoke Mafa and French, and they were happy to work as translators for his research. The research involved playing short piano sequences and asking participants to select a face that best expressed the emotion that was conveyed by the music. Three faces were shown with an emotional expression that conveyed either happiness, sadness, or fear. He found that the Mafa could often recognize happiness, sadness, and fear in the Western music excerpts, and certainly above the level expected if they had just guessed the answer. The ability for Mafa people to tell whether Western music is happy or sad suggested to Fritz and his colleagues that there may be a natural or universal ability for all humans to recognize emotions in music.

EXPLAINING CROSS-CULTURAL SIMILARITIES AND DIFFERENCES

Why would certain musical behaviors and experiences be similar across cultures? One reason is that the human brain works in fairly similar ways across all populations globally, affecting how we perceive, experience, and perform music. As an example, all people around the world have limits in how much they can remember, and short-term memory tends to be limited to around seven to nine items, so about the number of digits in a typical phone number. These memory limitations may influence the length of melodies that people create and enjoy around the world. Melodies cannot be too long and complicated or they would be too difficult to recall. For this reason, most melodies found in music around the world tend to be a length that is relatively easy for people to remember, and they are also constructed to allow perceptual grouping of notes together, which further reduces the burden on memory. For the same reason, the scales of music all around the world tend to be built on a limited number of notes. Most Western music is built on major and minor scales that consist of seven notes (do, re, mi, fa, sol, la, ti).

Physical constraints may also play a role in music. Humans sing melodies, but they also need to breathe. Breathing is a physical constraint, so the duration of a melody must permit ease of breathing while a person is singing. As another example, some musical notes blend well together (the basis of harmony), and others do not. Physical acoustics can partially account for this difference. All notes are made up of many sound frequencies, and notes that have many frequencies in common usually blend well together, such as notes that are separated by an octave. These common frequencies help to "fuse" the notes together, creating blended sounds, or *harmony*. By sharing some of the same acoustic frequencies, notes can camouflage other notes that have overlapping features. When this happens, we tend to hear a single fused musical event, or chord, rather than distinct notes, like a stick insect that blends perfectly into a habitat that has the very same visual features.

These psychological and physical constraints may explain why there are similarities in musical systems around the world, but commonalities can also arise from the powerful influence of media. Western music is widely propagated in media around the world, and there are few cultures that have not been inundated with Western media. This means that, through the influence of media, Western music can affect the music that is produced around the world. For this reason, researchers who observe cross-cultural similarities in music often attempt to evaluate the potential role of cultural influences such as media as well as psychological and physical constraints. The impact of media can be powerful, and we can learn a lot from studying societies that have had no or little exposure to Western media. But only a few such societies still exist, and soon there will be none.

Cross-cultural researchers also need to account for the many differences in musical systems around the world by analyzing the psychosocial functions of that music. Understanding the psychosocial functions of music involves answering some questions: Is the music of a particular population used for entertainment, to heal the sick, or to accompany a cultural ritual such as marriage? Do participants socialize more easily while listening to music? Do they go into a trance state? Once differences in musical sounds, behaviors, and psychosocial functions are identified, researchers can then attempt to explain these differences.

THE PSYCHOLOGICAL BASIS OF CROSS-CULTURAL SIMILARITIES AND DIFFERENCES

One of the most important psychological influences on music is the way we form expectations while listening to music. After many years of listening to the music of our culture, people form expectations for which notes or chords will come next in a piece of music. These expectations not only occur for familiar songs that people have heard many times before but also for songs that they have never heard. These expectations reflect what we know about music. When comparing two different musical cultures, such as Western popular music and North Indian music (e.g., ragas), researchers have determined that listeners from both cultures form expectations while they are listening to music, but these expectations are based on the music with which they are familiar. For this reason, when an American teenager listens to unfamiliar music from North India, he or she will not be very good at anticipating the sequence of notes in a melody and so may perceive many of them as "bad notes." This effect demonstrates another cultural bias in how we perceive music.

However, other research has shown that some of the expectations we form while listening to music are actually similar across cultures. For example, all people generally expect the notes that follow one another in a melody to be close in pitch. As a result, melodies that contain too many jumps in pitch tend to sound surprising. Importantly, melodies with unexpected changes are not necessarily bad; they are just more surprising and less conventional than melodies that conform with our expectations. In fact, most people like a balance between predictable and unpredictable changes in a melody. Imagine one of your favorite melodies. Are the notes that follow one another close in pitch? Are there large jumps in pitch during the melody that make the melody interesting? These effects reflect the importance of expectations on our perception and appreciation of music.

As an illustration of the importance of expectancy, researcher David Huron played a traditional Balinese melody to a group of American and Balinese musicians. As the melody was played, he assessed how certain they were about upcoming events by asking them to make "bets" on which note might come next. Overall, uncertainty was much higher for the American musicians than the Balinese musicians, and this difference was most obvious at the beginning of the melody.

Along with expectancy, research has considered whether people from different cultures are sensitive to other properties of music, such as tempo and loudness. Does fast and loud music affect people in similar ways around the world? Research on lullabies suggests that when mothers are soothing their babies, they use similar strategies across cultures. If you wanted to sooth a baby, it would not make sense to sing a fast and loud lullaby, so most lullabies around the world tend to be slow and soft to create a sense of calmness. More generally, music can express emotions in similar ways all around the world. One study revealed that Japanese listeners could judge the emotional connotations of unfamiliar Western and North Indian music, and they did so by focusing on aspects of the music such as the tempo and the complexity of the music. In other words, despite enormous differences in musical sounds and behaviors around the world, we are still all human, and people from all walks of life often respond to music in similar ways.

CONCLUSION

There is enormous diversity in musical systems around the world. Each musical culture exhibits differences in musical sounds, behaviors, and psychosocial functions of musical activity. When we contemplate the music of Tunisia, the Sami *yoiks* of northern Finland, extreme metal communities in the United States, and Italian opera, it is difficult to imagine finding commonalities. However, people from all populations are constrained by the physics of sound and by the psychological mechanisms that allow us to appreciate music. We all experience emotions, we all form expectations about what will happen next, and we all have memories that are limited. Such factors provide the foundation for cross-cultural studies in the psychology and science of music.

References and Further Reading

Fritz, T., Jentschke, S., Gosselin, N., Sammler, D., Peretz, I., Turner, R., . . . Koelsch, S. (2009). Universal recognition of three basic emotions in music. *Current Biology, 19*, 573–576.

Nettl, B., Danielson, V., Stone, R. M., Porter, J., Fisher, A. J. Marcus, S. L., . . . Witzleben, J. L. (Eds.). (2001). *The Garland Encyclopedia of World Music* (Vols. 1–10). London, UK: Routledge.

Thompson, W. F., & Balkwill, L.-L. (2010). Cross-cultural similarities and differences. In P. Juslin & J. Sloboda (Eds.), *Handbook of Music and Emotion: Theory, Research, Applications* (pp. 755–788). Oxford, UK: Oxford University Press.

Thompson, W. F., Sun, Y., & Fritz, T. (2019). Music across cultures. In P. J. Renfrew & D. J. Levitin (Eds.), *Foundations of Music Psychology: Theory and Research* (pp. 503–541). Boston, MA: MIT Press.

7. Nature versus Nurture

Elizabeth Hellmuth Margulis

A central aim of the science of psychology is to understand the root causes of human behavior. Broadly speaking, answers to these kinds of questions fall into two categories: nature and nurture. These debates often play out in relation to behaviors of wide relevance to society; scientists argue, for example, about the degree to which overeating stems from a genetic predisposition versus environmental factors. But scientists also weigh the influence of culture and experience on musical behaviors, such as the ability to sing in tune.

It may be the case that people who can flawlessly sing back tunes on pitch were simply born with genes that encode the appropriate mechanisms. According to this view, nature plays an important role in singing ability. But it may also be the case that nurture plays an important role. According to this view, the environment in which people are raised and the experiences that they have can promote singing in tune. For example, they may grow up in a household where music is always playing, with raucous full-family sing-alongs and karaoke nights from earliest childhood. The influence of nurture can refer either to explicit learning, such as voice lessons or choir participation, or to enculturation, the more passive absorption of customs and norms, as in the case of a child raised in a family of people who love to sing.

But most argue that complex behaviors such as singing arise out of a combination of factors related both to nature and to nurture. Disentangling the influence of these various factors calls for careful research design. For example, if researchers want to determine whether a certain environmental factor leads to the capacity to sing in tune, they have to make sure that members of the two groups do not also differ systematically in terms of genetic makeup. Otherwise, they might conclude that the environmental factor shaped the singing ability when the underlying genetic differences really contributed as well.

SIMILARITIES AND DIFFERENCES IN MUSICAL BEHAVIORS ACROSS CULTURES

The nature/nurture debate plays out in the study of other musical behaviors too. On the one hand, all known human cultures make music, although it is important to note that these behaviors aren't always conceptualized as music—some languages have a superordinate word that blends music, dance, and ritual and others have words for song and for instrumental music, but no word for what might be shared between them. When a behavior is prevalent in this way, it tends to raise the prospect that it emerges as a result of human biology—from being encoded in genes, for example. Universality is not enough to conclude that nature outweighs nurture, however, as unknown commonalities among environmental factors might suffice to account for the emergence of musical behaviors in cultures around the world. So although universality does not *prove* the predominance of nature, it is at least consistent with the hypothesis that biology plays a role.

On the other hand, although all known human cultures make music, they do so in fantastically diverse ways. They use different vocabularies of notes, different rhythms, and different instruments. They make music in different settings for different purposes, and they speak differently about what music is and what role it plays in their society. The diversity of musical behaviors found throughout the world argues for the influence of nurture.

The shared tendencies (similarities) and diversity (differences) of musical behaviors seem to set up two contradictory accounts: either that musical behaviors are primarily determined by biology or that they are primarily determined by culture. But another view conceptualizes biology and culture as co-constitutive. How do researchers decide between these theories?

ARE WE BORN WITH MUSICAL ABILITY?

One strategy is to investigate whether musical capacities are innate—whether people are born with them or whether certain experiences must occur for them to develop. To pursue this strategy, researchers often try to study infant musicality, reasoning that tiny babies are the closest to blank musical slates that they will find. Studying infants, who cannot directly answer questions, requires special techniques. Infant studies tend to use the preferential looking paradigm, an experimental technique that uses the amount of time babies spend looking at a stimulus to infer things about their cognitive processing of it, or electroencephalography (EEG), a way of measuring electrical activity in the brain, to try to understand how infant brains work.

Studies using such methodologies have found that infants as young as a few months can tell that melodies are the same even when they are transposed to start on a different pitch. Babies also prefer consonant sounds (notes that adults think sound good together) to dissonant ones (notes that adults think do not). These studies seem to make a clear case for nature, but keep in mind that as fetuses develop within the womb, they are exposed to all the typical sounds of the mother's musical environment. Thus, even very young infants have had months for nurture to shape their abilities and preferences.

Another strategy for pulling apart the impact of nature and nurture on music is to conduct cross-cultural research by presenting the same stimuli and recording responses from people who have been exposed to vastly different musical and cultural environments. By examining the similarities and differences between their responses, researchers can learn what musical behaviors remain invariant across diverse environments (reflecting the influence of nature) and what behaviors change depending on exposure and experience (the influence of nurture). However, research like this is expensive and complicated to carry out.

A third strategy is to look for genetic markers of musical abilities. Methodologies include studying whether a trait runs in families, studying how a trait develops in twins, and using various approaches from molecular genetics.

Scientists have taken advantage of all these methodologies to explore the nature/nurture debate in music. The rest of this chapter explores the contours of this debate as it relates to three distinct areas:

1. Musical aptitude—who becomes particularly skilled at music and how?
2. Musical preferences—what kinds of music do people tend to like and why?
3. Musical structure—what characteristics does music tend to have and why?

MUSICAL APTITUDE

Musical ability seems to be unevenly distributed in the population. Most people are able to make sense of music and enjoy it—they can tap along to the beat or tear up at an especially moving passage—but not everyone possesses these capacities to the same extent. Some people are especially keen musical responders; they amass vast record collections and spend all their free time listening. Others do not especially seek out musical experiences. Similarly, some people can detect even the slightest wrong note or mistuning, while others lack as robust a sense of pitch.

These differences appear larger when considering not just the ability to listen and understand music but the ability to perform and make it. Some people sing beautifully; others struggle to eke out the right notes in "Happy Birthday." Some people become violin or marimba virtuosos, while others cannot seem to get their two hands to work together, no matter how hard they try. What causes these differences? Is it something about the different life experiences people have, or do unequal capacities start at birth?

Consider the case of absolute pitch—the ability to identify the precise identity of a note without any context. People with absolute pitch can hear a note presented in isolation and quickly and correctly respond with its name. Some estimates claim that only about one in every ten thousand people has this ability. Certain populations are more likely to possess absolute pitch than others. It is more prevalent among speakers of tonal languages, such as Mandarin Chinese, in which pitch contour forms a part of the defining characteristics of a word: *ma* spoken with a level high tone means *mother*, but *ma* spoken so that it first dips and then rises in pitch means *horse*. It is also more common among people of East Asian descent, people with Williams syndrome and autism, or people who have been blind from birth.

The higher incidence of absolute pitch in East Asian populations suggests that it may be genetic; indeed, some studies have provided evidence of specific sets of genes in families with absolute pitch. But others argue that the East Asian advantage is attributable to environmental factors, such as the higher prevalence of tonal languages in the region. Similarly, the high rate of absolute pitch among people with specific developmental disorders may result from underlying genetic differences or from different life experiences. People with autism, for example, tend to devote more attention to details than to relational thinking. This increased focus on absolute pitch characteristics from a young age could explain the frequent emergence of the ability within this population. It can be difficult to disentangle the contributions of nature and nurture.

SINGING

Singing ability also varies widely within the population, although not as widely as you might think; many more people classify themselves as bad singers than would be registered as such on tests measuring their intonation. Actual poor singing, as reflected by a failure to reproduce correct pitches, actually afflicts only around 10–20 percent of the population. Studies have demonstrated that poor singing can result from multiple root causes: some people have a condition called *amusia*, a perceptual deficit that prevents them from registering pitch differences between notes that are relatively close to one another. However, most poor singers have normal perceptual skills but lack the motor control to correctly produce them with their vocal chords. Although good singing sometimes runs in families—such as the Jackson 5 or the von Trapps—this may merely suggest that parents who like to sing engage their children with it early and effectively, not that they share a gene for it.

But perhaps nowhere is the nature/nurture debate more heated than in the conversation surrounding musical ability on instruments. Studies that sought to account for differences in the proficiency of violinists training at a prestigious conservatory found that what most people perceive as "talent" is largely reducible to the number of hours spent in quality practice with the instrument, with the students who practiced more being perceived as more innately talented. Yet, subsequent research on over a thousand pairs of identical twins showed that musical ability was shared within a pair and not dependent on the amount of practice time.

These divergent results likely stem from the different measures the studies used to assess musical aptitude (ratings of violin performance talent on the one hand versus success on pitch and rhythm detection tasks on the other), reflecting how daunting it can be to look for biological roots of a complex human behavior. Success on a musical instrument depends on a host of factors, ranging from basic perceptual skills to motor control and executive function—having the grit to keep practicing day in and day out even when more immediately rewarding activities beckon. Identifying the source of this behavior depends on pulling apart these component abilities, which is not always an easy task.

MUSICAL PREFERENCES

Musical preferences seem like a more straightforward case for nurture. One person's favorite song is another person's instrument of torture. There seem to be few identifiable characteristics that make music liked the world over. Rather, one artist can be hot in a particular place but gain absolutely no traction in another. Some people love alt country and others live for electronica.

These differences exist not just at the level of genre preference (whether a person likes hip-hop or folk music) but also at the level of preferences for specific musical features, even features that seem not to invite disagreement. Consider the case of *consonance*, the smooth quality of sound that occurs when two or more notes or vocalists blend well together, and *dissonance*, the harsh quality of sound that occurs when notes seem to clash. For hundreds of years, Western scholars have attributed consonance to biology, hypothesizing that certain sounds take advantage of the structure of the ear in ways that lead to them sounding sweet. Yet, recent work with the Tsimané, an indigenous tribe in Bolivia with little exposure to Western music, showed that they like consonant and dissonant sounds equally. Culture, not biology, seems to shape notions of what sounds "good." The way scholars have sometimes historically appealed to nature to assert the inevitability or superiority of certain types of music (namely, Western classical music) marks a troubling phase in the history of music and psychology.

Certain patterns do seem identifiable in the way culture intersects with biology to give rise to musical preferences. For example, an inverted U-shaped response tends to characterize preference across repeated exposures to a musical piece or style. People tend to like a piece more as they hear it more frequently, until a saturation point is reached, beyond which repeated hearings tend to diminish enjoyment. Just as nature might endow all babies with the capacity to learn language, leaving the specifics of exactly which language up to the surrounding culture, nature might endow people with a capacity to become enculturated to musical styles—to make sense of them through immersion—but exactly which styles people learn depends on exposure.

CONCLUSION

People often wonder whether nature plays a role in determining the materials and structure of diverse forms of music from around the world. Does biology influence the forms songs take, the rhythms they use, and the way the pitches are patterned? The most common way to investigate this question is to survey music from world cultures and tally the commonalities, assuming that features that appear universally are the ones that reveal innate tendencies.

All known human cultures register octave equivalence—the sense that every C or A, no matter how high or low, features some essential C- or A-ness that remains invariant. Moreover, most cultures divide that octave into an unequal set of scale steps (often seven or fewer) that form the basic material for generating music. They recognize transpositions—restating a pattern starting on a different pitch—as different instances of the "same" thing. They tend to rely on repetition, both in the sense that patterns repeat within a piece and in the sense that people tend to perform and reperform the "same" discrete pieces.

Many of these commonalities may reflect the limits and affordances of human memory rather than anything specific about musical communication. This reflects the general lack of consensus about whether music is a product of natural selection or simply takes advantages of a number of other cognitive capacities that evolved for other purposes. This debate is best encapsulated by evolutionary psychologist Steven Pinker's (1997) infamous assertion that music is "auditory cheesecake"—a concoction that takes brilliant advantage of underlying predilections but was not itself selected for. At the other end of the spectrum are researchers who argue that the capacity for music evolved prior to the capacity for speech. Future decades will likely bring more insight from animal studies, longitudinal studies carried out over many years, and cross-cultural studies carried out in many places. Until large-scale studies of this type can be carried out, the nature/nurture debate will likely continue to rage.

References and Further Reading

Honing, H. (2018). *The Origins of Musicality*. Cambridge, MA: MIT Press.

McDermott, J. H., Schultz, A. F., Undurraga, E. A., & Godoy, R. A. (2016). Indifference to dissonance in native Amazonians reveals cultural variation in music perception. *Nature, 525*, 7611.

Mosing, M. A., Madison, G., Pedersen, N. L., Kuja-Halkola, R., & Ullén, F. (2014). Practice does not make perfect: No causal effect of music practice on music ability. *Psychological Science, 25*, 1795–1803.

Pinker, S. (1997). *How the Mind Works*. New York: W. W. Norton.

8. Musical Universals

Stephen Davies and Matteo Ravasio

Every known human society has music. Even more significantly, almost every individual has some sort of involvement with music as a performer, composer, or listener. Even in modern-day Western societies, in which listening to music is more common than performing, most people listen more or less attentively to music every day through the TV, an iPod, or on the Internet.

The fact that every society has something that we could call music does not mean that all societies have a word equivalent in meaning to the English *music*. For instance, the Blackfoot language uses the term *saapup* to refer to singing, dancing, and ceremony. The ancient Greek concept of *mousikē* was similarly broader than ours, indicating a union of singing, dance, and spoken words. Despite these verbal ambiguities, all human societies engage in musical behavior, and the result is readily recognized as music, even by people who are unfamiliar with the musical tradition in question. You may not be able to appreciate central Javanese gamelan at the first hearing, but you will recognize that it is music (see photo 8.1).

Although the search for universal traits in music has long been neglected, recent contributions have shown that many, if not all, known musical traditions share important common features. These traits are not limited to the way music sounds and is organized; they also regard the social uses of music.

In this chapter, we will see that all known musical traditions share some important features. Certain organizational principles are common to the music of

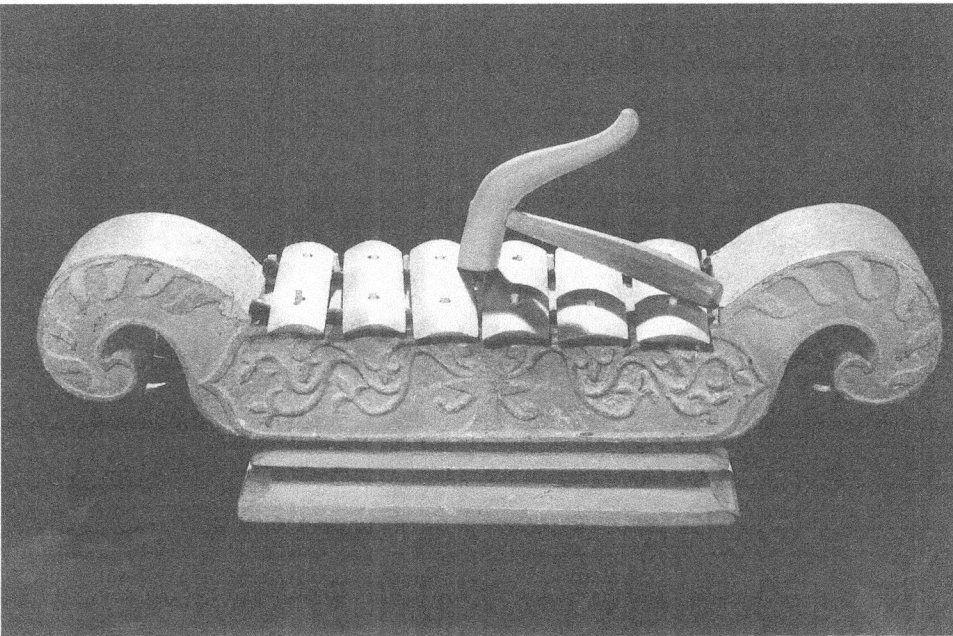

Photo 8.1   Javanese Saron Panerus. (The Crosby Collection of Musical Instruments, 1889. Metropolitan Museum of Art, New York.)

different cultures. But beyond this, the social use of music and its connections with emotion are shared by all music traditions.

THE SEARCH FOR MUSICAL UNIVERSALS

Given the universal presence of some kind of music in all cultures, one might wonder whether there are elements common to the music of every society. In other words, are there elements that are found in all musical traditions, other than that we are inclined to describe them as music?

Musicologists have long been skeptical. Ethnomusicological research, which deals with the study and comparison of different musical cultures, has mainly been interested in stressing the differences between musical traditions rather than their shared features. Bruno Nettl, a musicologist who helped overturn this skeptical view, recalls how he was taught that every proposed universal should be contrasted with an exception that shows that the alleged universal is not actually a universal.

However, thanks to the efforts of Nettl and many others, the search for musical universals has gained significance in the past three decades. This is also partly due to the development of our understanding of musical abilities as a product of our evolution as a species. If we can isolate traits that are common to all musical traditions that we are aware of, these features may be linked to a fundamental evolved nature that all human beings share.

AN OVERVIEW OF MUSICAL UNIVERSALS

The following sections will consider some candidates for universality based on the available evidence. It is important to keep in mind that these attributions of universality are always made on the grounds of partial evidence, as we presently do not know every musical culture that has existed on the planet, as at least some have been lost. Because of this, researchers sometimes speak of "statistical universals" to stress that these traits are almost invariably found in every musical tradition with which we are acquainted. We are aware of lost traditions, without knowing how they sounded.

Pitches and Scales

An important universal in music processing is octave equivalence: notes that are an octave apart are perceived as the same note but at a higher or lower place in musical space. Accordingly, we would call a melody the "same" melody when played at different octaves. This equivalence is recognized by every musical culture. This is unsurprising, as the perception of octave equivalence arises very early in infants and also occurs in some other species.

All musical cultures organize the auditory space into discrete pitches. These pitches are in turn arranged as elements in scales. By far, the most common scales employ five or seven tones. In almost every instance, the intervals that constitute these scales are uneven. In the Western C major scale, for instance, the interval between the notes B and C is smaller than the one between A and B. There are exceptions to this, as some scales from Thailand and Indonesia have more or less equal intervals. However, it remains true even for these traditions that they have at least one scale made of uneven intervals.

Why are scales almost invariably composed of uneven intervals? There are various reasons why this may be the case, but one in particular is worth mentioning because it is another candidate universal: tonal hierarchy. Uneven intervals favor characteristic relationships between the tones that make up a scale, and these relationships in turn give us a sense of the tones' function in the scale. This means that some tones have a more prominent role in particular scales, and this role is often linked to the scale's interval structure. To go back to the example of the C major scale, consider how the first note of the scale is experienced as the stable tonal center partly because of the semitone interval that separates it from the leading tone, B. All known musical scales structure the tones that compose them according to some hierarchy.

In addition to the octave, most of the world's scales feature the perfect fourth or the perfect fifth above the first note of the scale (in the C major scale, the notes F and G). Why are these three intervals so widespread? It could be because they are easier for our brain to process. Imagine a vibrating string producing a certain note, as on a guitar. Now imagine cutting the string in half. The note produced by the vibrating half will be an octave above the original note. This means that the frequency ratio of the octave is 2:1: the frequency of the octave is twice the frequency of the original note. The frequency ratio of the perfect fifth is 3:2, and that of the perfect fourth is 4:3. Other intervals are characterized by more complex frequency ratios. It is possible that the universal preference for the octave and the perfect fourth and fifth may be related to their simple frequency ratio, which allows our brain to process these intervals more effectively.

Grouping and Regularity

Psychologists have known for a long time that human beings tend to perceive things in characteristic configurations. For instance, if faced with six vertical lines paired two by two, we are inclined to group the three pairs as single entities, as if they were columns. A similar grouping occurs in music, except that the organization is of course not spatial but, rather, temporal. Grouping by tempo and rhythm are two central features of music.

Most music has a steady tempo and features repetitive rhythmic patterns. Even though many cultures have unmeasured music (such as Western pieces indicated as being in free rhythm), these cultures also have measured musical styles. There is also a universal propensity to simple duration ratios, especially 1:2. This means that when two consecutive notes have different durations, it will often be the case that one is twice as long as the other. It has been suggested that this feature may depend on a tendency to perceive time intervals as either twice as long or twice as short as a reference interval. More generally speaking, all human beings seek patterns, repetitions, and closure and consistently agree on how to break up the stream of sound in terms of these.

Entrainment and Social Uses of Music

Regularity in tempo and repeating rhythmic patterns facilitate entrainment, that is, coordinated movement to music, such as tapping your foot to a jazz piece or headbanging at a heavy metal concert. Human beings, unlike other animals, automatically do this from a very early age.

Our ability to entrain to music is likely one of the reasons why music is so widely used in social activities, especially when these involve regular movements—think of work songs or marches. In these cases, music facilitates coordination between us because of our propensity to synchronize our movement to it. But music is also important in a number of communal activities that do not necessarily involve regular movement. For instance, every known culture uses music to supplement the power of rituals.

Other Nonstructural Universals

No musical tradition lacks vocal music, and almost every known society has musical instruments. Wind instruments and drums are the most common.

Another feature shared by all known music traditions is the presence of a repertoire. People do not just play music; they play particular pieces, songs, tunes, and the like. In other words, every musical tradition has identifiable musical pieces that may be performed on different occasions. This is true despite the fact that different musical traditions keep track of their works in very different ways, some transmitting the repertoire orally and others writing it down or even recording it.

A striking example of a musical universal is the lullaby. Lullabies are universally widespread, and they also share some common features. For instance, in terms of structure, they typically include more descending intervals than other melodies, have a slow tempo, and are rather repetitive. Another obvious common feature of lullabies is their function. In every culture, lullabies serve the purpose of soothing children and encouraging them to sleep.

When people sing lullabies to their babies and infants, they perform the lullaby in a distinctive manner that is different from the way they would sing it to, say, an adult who wanted to learn it. If listeners are asked to identify which version of a lullaby was sung to a child, they normally judge correctly.

The universality of lullabies is certainly related to the importance of human beings' relation to their children. In this regard, another music-like human behavior is worth mentioning because of its universality. This is infant-directed speech, sometimes referred to as "motherese", that is, the exaggerated, sing-song way in which parents talk to their very young children. Although one would not, strictly speaking, describe motherese as music, it is important because it is an example of music-like behavior that is universally widespread.

Both lullabies and motherese are related to the parent's attempts to regulate the child's mood. For instance, the aim of a lullaby is to sooth the baby through its gentle and delicate character. It is common for us to speak of music in these emotional terms, such as when we say that a melody is "happy" or "sad". Similar attributions of emotions to musical pieces are found in other cultures, such as with respect to Indian ragas. This raises an important question: to what extent do people from different cultures agree when it comes to identifying the emotions attributed to a certain piece? The empirical research on these topics is still growing, but psychologists tend to be moderately optimistic: it looks as if people can correctly detect some emotions in a piece of music, even if they are completely unfamiliar with its style.

The widespread tendency to perceive music as happy, sad, and the like is matched by music's universal power to arouse emotions in listeners. Every music listener is familiar with the experience of reacting emotionally to music. Although music listening in Western society is often a private activity, music's capacity to arouse emotions is particularly important when music is used in social contexts. In these cases, where music arouses the same emotion in different listeners, it helps create an emotional bond among the members of the group.

CONCLUSION

All known cultures have music, and most human beings engage in music, either directly or indirectly. Despite this, musicologists have long doubted the possibility of isolating musical universals, that is, features common to all musical cultures. However, recent research has overturned that trend, showing that some traits are found in virtually all known musical traditions.

Structural musical universals include the subdivision of musical space into discrete units (pitches) and their organization in scales. Scales are always structured hierarchically and are almost invariably constituted by uneven intervals. A regular tempo and regular rhythmic patterns are also widespread features. There are also universals in the social roles played by music. For instance, different groups all use music to bond emotionally and to coordinate rhythmic activities. A more specific example is the lullaby, the only known universally widespread musical genre. Despite local variations, lullabies across cultures are similar both in their calming function and in some of their characteristic musical features, such as the slow tempo and frequent descending intervals.

Research on these topics is ongoing, and it can be expected that the joint efforts of ethnomusicologists and psychologists will produce a more accurate picture in the next few decades. It is also important to stress that none of these traits can be conclusively deemed musical universals because future discoveries may cast doubt on their universality. Despite this note of caution, it is fair to conclude that all forms of music that are known to us share some fundamental features and that these common features are likely to be grounded via evolution in our shared human nature as well as in common patterns of social life.

References and Further Reading

Brown, S., & Jordania, J. (2013). Universals in the world's musics. *Psychology of Music, 41*(2), 229–248.

Higgins, K. M. (2006). The cognitive and appreciative import of musical universals. *Revue Internationale de Philosophie, 4*(238), 487–503.

Justus, T., & Hutsler, J. J. (2005). Fundamental issues in the evolutionary psychology of music: Assessing innateness and domain specificity. *Music Perception: An Interdisciplinary Journal, 23*(1), 1–27.

McDermott, J., & Hauser, M. (2005). The origins of music: Innateness, uniqueness, and evolution. *Music Perception: An Interdisciplinary Journal, 23*(1), 29–59.

Nettl, B. (2001). An ethnomusicologist contemplates universals in musical sound and musical culture. In N. L. Wallin, B. Merker, & S. Brown (Eds.), *The Origins of Music* (pp. 463–472). Cambridge, MA: MIT Press.

Stevens, C., & Byron, T. (2009). Universals in music processing. In S. Hallam, I. Cross, & M. Thaut (Eds.), *Oxford Handbook of Music Psychology* (pp. 14–23). Oxford, UK: Oxford University Press.

Thompson, W. F., & Balkwill, L. (2010). Cross-cultural similarities and differences. In P. N. Juslin & J. A. Sloboda (Eds.), *Oxford Handbook of Music and Emotion: Theory, Research, Applications* (pp. 453–489). Oxford, UK: Oxford University Press.

Musical Expertise

9. What Is Musical Expertise?

Eric Taylor, Christina M. Vanden Bosch der Nederlanden, and Jessica A. Grahn

We know a good musician when we hear one. Whether you are thinking of legendary musicians such as Mozart, Liszt, and Rachmaninoff or modern-day legends such as Thelonious Monk, David Bowie, and Beyoncé, there is a pretty good chance you have a clear idea of what a musician is. Musicians are highly trained individuals who have both natural talent and years of diligent practice on their instrument of choice, be it voice, computer, or ukulele. If we look back at the musicians described above, many of them had extensive formal music training from an early age. Beyoncé attended an arts school from age eleven and took dance lessons from an even earlier age. Liszt took piano lessons from age seven and moved to Vienna to be taught by masters of piano performance. Mozart's father began teaching him piano at age three, and Mozart also played and learned at court in Vienna.

It is tempting to begin to define musical expertise in terms of how much formal musical training a person has amassed in their lifetime and how early that musical training began. But what about those who have never had formal music training? Thelonious Monk and David Bowie were both self-taught musicians who started with natural talent, interest, and the opportunity to learn the piano and other instruments on their own. We could count their informal music sessions as formal music training, but does that work for everyone who has ever dabbled around with an instrument? It can be difficult to equate a year of informal musical practice from one person to another. To make matters more complicated, the type of practice may differ significantly between musical genres. If your goal is to play violin for a concerto competition, then formal music lessons are likely the best route. If your goal is to fiddle as part of a bluegrass band, then group jam sessions may be the best way to hone your musical skills.

Musical expertise cannot be summed up by simply counting the sheer number of years or hours an individual has been practicing. Different types of practice may develop different musical skills, such as reading music versus playing by ear. What does it mean to have musical expertise? How much musical knowledge do nonmusicians have? We will now describe some of the existing studies on expertise and how researchers have defined *musicianship*, and we will then explain how musical training is related to the way we think (cognitive processing) and the way we perceive (perceptual processing) the world.

MUSICAL KNOWLEDGE IN THE GENERAL POPULATION

When we think of *musical expertise*, we often imagine musical geniuses, forgetting that, from an early age, we have all learned much about the many important features of music. You only need to search YouTube or scroll through your social media feed to see countless examples of babies and toddlers enjoying music, dancing and singing along even if they are not perfectly in time or in tune. To enjoy and make music, you need knowledge about how notes fit together because that enables you to predict what happens next in the music. Music is engaging because it plays with the rich set of musical knowledge and expectations we build through experience. Your experience is why you can tell whether a song has a wrong note and also why it can be difficult to follow along with music outside your musical culture, such as Chinese opera, Indonesian gamelan music, or African polyrhythms. As babies listen and move to music that is sung by their caregivers or that is playing in the background, they eventually become enculturated listeners; that is, they learn the structures of the music they hear most often. Adults continue to engage with music by dancing, creating playlists, and sharing music among friends, even if they do not become paid musicians.

The most common way to measure enculturation is by comparing how we listen to music from our own culture compared to music from other cultures. Western adults are better at detecting pitch changes in Western (e.g., major or minor) scales than Javanese pelog scales, which use different spacing between pitches than Western musical scales. In contrast, at six months, infants are not better at detecting pitch changes in Western scales than they are at Javanese scales, which suggests that they have not yet been enculturated to Western scales. However, by twelve months of age, infants are already worse with Javanese scales than Western scales, just like adults.

Western adults are also better at detecting *rhythmic* changes in regular Western musical excerpts compared to Balkan musical excerpts, which have a different underlying rhythmic structure; Western six-month-old infants detect these changes equally well. In short, the way infants hear music appears more culture-free than the way adults hear music, but by twelve months, and certainly by five years of age, listeners' experience has shaped the way they perceive music. So even nonmusicians perceive the rules of their culture's music, such as harmonic and melodic relationships or rhythmic patterns, demonstrating a rich set of musical abilities that are learned implicitly through exposure.

There have been many ways to define, or operationalize, *musical expertise* over time. Test batteries used to primarily assess the abilities of musicians with formal training rather than individuals without formal training. This can lead to misclassifications: musicians making a living in their craft can be labeled as nonmusicians despite clear musical ability, individuals with extensive training but who remain wholly unmusical are labeled as musicians ("sleeping musicians"), and individuals with excellent musical perceptual abilities but without a musical outlet are labeled as nonmusicians (musical sleepers). Two new assessments, the Profile of Music Perception Skills (PROMS; Law & Zentner 2012) and Goldsmiths Musical Sophistication Index (Gold-MSI; Müllensiefen, Gingras, Musil, & Stewart 2014), address this problem by examining a range of perceptual abilities with simple musical stimuli to measure rhythm or pitch ability and rich musical excerpts to examine skills in a natural musical context. These tests provide better measures of overall musical ability than self-reports. Further, the number of subtests makes these measures well suited to examine how certain types of musical training lead to improvements in some domains but not others. For example, musical training in percussion may improve a musician's rhythm or tempo but not their fine pitch discrimination.

FORMAL MUSICAL TRAINING

We regularly encounter situations that highlight the importance of starting young: learning a second language, playing a musical instrument, or becoming an elite athlete. For instance, immigrants who moved to the United States before age six tend to have no discernable foreign accent. This is because the developing brain is in a stage of greater plasticity—pruning away extra synaptic connections and tuning existing connections based on the input from the environment. During this period of increased plasticity, or a sensitive period, input from the environment has a more pronounced effect than later in life. Therefore, there may also a sensitive period for gaining musical expertise.

Several studies have highlighted that starting music lessons before age seven is associated with higher rates of perfect pitch, better auditory and motor synchronization, and brain changes. Although early musical training may lead to increased perceptual and motor skills, late learning musicians (after age seven) still show better performance than nonmusicians, suggesting that musical training at any age, even if it takes more practice to achieve proficiency, can bring about real and lasting changes in the brain. Given all the differences between late and early learning musicians, how do we explicitly define what it takes to be an expert musician?

One possible criterion for the expert label is to measure the amount of practice. One of the world's leading experts in the psychology of expertise, K. Anders Ericsson, argues that expertise emerges after ten years—and ten thousand hours—of deliberate, structured practice. It may seem arbitrary to put a number on the amount of time it takes to reach expertise, but there is evidence that the difference between a ten thousand–hour musician and a novice is significant.

Ericsson, Krampe, and Tesch-Römer (1993) compared the lifetime practice habits of novice violinists in a music education program against young violinists who were identified as having the potential for careers as concert soloists. Over the first twenty-one years of life, the soloists had amassed ten thousand hours, whereas the novices had not yet reached five thousand. Similarly, there is little variability in the lifetime hours of practice required to achieve a standardized high level of proficiency (nationally graded performance exams). This suggests that there is merit to defining expertise partly as a function of the early onset of frequent, deliberate practice. Interestingly, recent studies suggest that how much and how well a person practices may be inherited; therefore, genes may help determine who is willing to put in the hard work to become an expert (Thomson, Mosing, & Ullen 2017).

DEFINING EXPERTISE BY ABILITY

The violinists in Ericsson's study were judged to be expert performers, which means the researchers had an idea of what an expert should be able to do. Intuitively, this seems like a plausible way of defining expertise: ask what a person can do, not how much they have practiced. If someone achieves the same skill after seven thousand hours, is he or she still not an expert just because he or she has not reached ten thousand hours? Instead, we can define *expertise* by measuring ability.

Some expertise is perceptual, meaning musicians can hear music differently than a novice. Their ears are the same, of course, but they perform better on various tests of perception. Unsurprisingly, musicians are better at detecting pitch changes and focusing on one sentence over another. Some benefits appear to draw on musicians' expert knowledge of musical structure. Musicians do not remember a piece note by note. They group the notes into structures, or "chunks," such as chords, according to the cultural rules of musical composition, which makes the music easier for them to remember. This is also why, when an expert *incorrectly* remembers a piece of music, the mistake is still likely to be consistent with the piece's structure. Interestingly, chess players remember complicated chess patterns similarly, having better memory for plausible arrangements than random arrangements. Thus, musicians have great memory for pieces that follow the rules of music and poor memory for pieces that do not.

In addition to perceptual expertise, expert musicians are also special because they can perform music—and some fascinating abilities arise from their ability to do so. For example, when an expert musician hears music, their motor system— the part of the brain that controls the body's movement—is more active than in novices. This implies that motor processing may be part of the experience for an expert performer: the part of the brain responsible for movement is activated while listening to another performer's actions. Indeed, musicians have greater connectivity between auditory and motor areas when listening to rhythms. This may make it more difficult for musicians to ignore motor information present in music. When asked to perform a simple action, such as imitating the fingering for a certain chord, expert musicians are slower if they are simultaneously listening to music made by a different action, such as hearing a chord that uses a different finger pattern. This slowing implies that experts cannot ignore the motoric information implied by the music they hear. Novices do not show the same slowing. For expert musicians, music perception and production seem to be intertwined. When expert violinists silently tap out the fingering to a popular concerto, their auditory cortex is active, even though no sound is present. Novices do not show this activity. Moreover, pantomiming actions that are similar to musical actions can cause musicians to actually hear a sound differently, biasing perception to be more in accordance with the pantomimed movement. This intricate connection between hearing and action, in which hearing musical sounds brings to mind movements and movements bring to mind musical sounds, is a hallmark of musical expertise.

In addition to having superior abilities in perception and production, musical experts appear to have other cognitive enhancements outside the musical domain.

For example, musical experts are better at inhibiting distracting information, and switching between tasks. These abilities are abstract and unrelated to music, and although they likely help with musical performance, these benefits may also assist with everyday challenges outside the music hall. Along with these high-level cognitive advantages, musical expertise, especially in performance, can involve skills in emotional expression. One example of expert expression is the ability to perform music with emotional variations in style. If we wanted the music played exactly as written, we could let a computer do it. Instead, we prefer to hear music played by performers who introduce human intonation, accentuation, and expression. Expert performers are remarkably consistent when reproducing their expressive performances, and it is often the most celebrated performers who differ most from the written music.

When studying expertise, there are few true experiments. In a true experiment, scientists randomly assign participants to different experimental conditions. But no one has ever randomly assigned people to become experts and nonexperts because such a lifelong experiment would be difficult to conduct. Consequently, we cannot know whether experts have better pitch perception because of musical training or whether individuals who pursue music have better musical perceptual abilities from the start. For instance, a child's *openness-to-experience* personality trait is the best predictor of the number of years that child takes music lessons, even after controlling for parents' personality, socioeconomic status, and the child's IQ. Thus, expert abilities may be driven by personality, rather than training, and these traits may in turn be largely influenced by genetic factors.

One way to determine whether training actually changes abilities is to take two groups of nonmusicians and randomly assign one to music training, then test for cognitive ability differences against the untrained group. For example, researchers Bangert and Altenmuller randomly assigned two groups of musically naïve subjects to learn a simple piece on a normal piano or a scrambled piano where the pitches were out of order. After a short time, participants who trained on the normal piano showed more activity between auditory and motor brain areas, suggesting that practice does strengthen the sound and movement connections that were described earlier for experts. This is evidence for the role of experience in developing traits associated with expertise. However, these kinds of studies are rare, and the participants did not become experts; therefore, the jury is still out on the contributions of nature versus nurture to musical expertise.

CONCLUSION

Musical expertise is hard to define. Researchers want to define *expertise* in quantitative terms—to operationalize it—to be able to measure, control, and analyze it in experiments. Expertise is challenging because, as we have seen, it is difficult to quantify. Researchers have designed standardized tools such as the Gold-MSI and PROMS to quantify musical ability in the lab. However, fully characterizing musical expertise likely depends on a complex interplay between a number of different factors, including musical skills, deliberate practice, personality, genetic predispositions, and environmental factors. So, we can define expertise by the years or hours of practice, by measuring performance, or even by describing differences in personality, genetic expression, and access to musical interactions. Overall, expertise may be best understood as a combination of factors, including time practiced, standardized measures of ability, changes in the brain, and cognitive markers of advanced musical skill.

References and Further Reading

Ericsson, K. A., Krampe, R. T., & Tesch-Römer, C. (1993). The role of deliberate practice in the acquisition of expert performance. *Psychological Review, 100*(3), 363.

Law, L. N. C., & Zentner, M. (2012). Assessing musical abilities objectively: Construction and validation of the profile of music perception skills. *PLoS One, 7*(12), e52508. https://doi.org/10.1371/journal.pone.0052508

Mullensiefen, D., Gingras, B., Musil, L., & Stewart, L. (2014). The musicality of non-musicians: An index for assessing musical sophistication in the general population. *PLoS One, 9*(6), e101091. https://doi.org/10.1371/journal.pone.0089642

Thompson, W. F., Mosing, M. A., & Ullen, F. (2017). Musical expertise: Genetics, experience, and training. In R. Ashley & R. Timmers (Eds.), *The Routledge Companion to Music Cognition* (pp. 415–426). New York, NY: Taylor & Francis.

Trainor, L. J., & Hannon, E. E. (2012). Musical development. In D. Deutsch (Ed.), *The Psychology of Music* (3rd ed., pp. 423–497). San Diego, CA: Academic Press.

10. Musical Genius

Dean Keith Simonton

Among the vast numbers of people who have achieved high levels of expertise in music, who can be called a "musical genius"? Certainly, every well-established genre of music has examples of great musicians who might qualify for that appellation. Western music lovers might point to examples such as Ludwig van Beethoven in classical (see Photo 10.1), Billie Holiday in jazz, Stephen Sondheim in musical theater, Richard Wagner in opera, John Williams in film, Jimi Hendrix in rock, Paul McCartney in pop, Bob Marley in reggae, Tupac Shakur in rap, Wendy Carlos in electronic, and Hildegard of Bingen in religious music—just to offer a very partial list. But what does it actually mean to call someone a musical genius? Music is a broad category that can encompass a vast variety of forms. Yet, it is equally true that genius has multiple meanings. So, before we can discuss musical geniuses, it is first necessary to define the term *genius*.

GENIUS DEFINITIONS

The word *genius* dates back to ancient Roman mythology, when it meant something akin to the English expression "guardian angel." Like most Latin words, it has acquired multiple meanings over the centuries. In contemporary times, the term often carries three connotations: high intelligence, exceptional talent or

Photo 10.1 Ludwig van Beethoven, an Iconic Genius in the Classical Music Repertoire. (Library of Congress)

giftedness, and extraordinary eminence. The first two connotations of genius refer to the potential and actual abilities possessed by an individual; the third requirement is necessary for the label to be applied across large segments of society and over time. Thus, not all people with exceptional musical talent can be considered geniuses. Indeed, even the most impressive musical prodigies and savants typically do not go on to achieve extraordinary eminence.

General Intelligence: High IQ

In popular culture, genius is sometimes associated with having a high IQ. One dictionary says that a genius is someone with an IQ of 140 or higher. Such a score would place this person in the top 1 percent of the population in tested intelligence. Even so, some might argue that this score is either too high or too low. To join Mensa, a society for high-IQ people, a person only needs to score in the top 2 percent, or roughly around IQ 130. On the other side, to belong to the Mega Society, the individual must represent one out of a million—a score so high that a special IQ test is required. The test is so difficult that most people cannot even understand the questions!

However, this definition of genius suffers from two major problems. First, musical geniuses seldom take IQ tests and rarely report their scores if they happen to do so. Second, and even worse, standard IQ tests do not contain any questions concerning *musical* ability. Hence, even if musicians were to score high enough on such a test to count as bona fide geniuses, that performance would tell us nothing about whether they should count as *musical* geniuses. To be sure, IQ scores have been estimated for several classical composers. Wolfgang Amadeus Mozart's IQ was supposedly between 150 and 155, Ludwig van Beethoven's between 135 and 140, and Johann Sebastian Bach's between 125 and 140 (depending on the specific estimates). However, none of these composers actually took an IQ test, so these estimates are highly speculative. Instead, their scores were based on biographical information about their precocious intellectual development, and that development was predicated only on their musical accomplishments, not on any other capacities.

At this point one might ask this question: why not create an IQ test that measures *musical* intelligence? Wouldn't that solve the problem? Maybe, but standardized tests of musical talent usually concentrate on basic perceptual and cognitive skills that have little bearing on what geniuses achieve. For instance, although perfect (or absolute) pitch is readily measured (the ability to name individual notes such as F-sharp just by hearing the pitch), musical geniuses do not necessarily have that skill. The French classical composer Camille Saint-Saëns showed this ability before he was three years old, but many composers have no more than relative pitch (the ability to judge the *difference* between two notes). Musical geniuses clearly must have advanced levels of expertise; otherwise, we would not know that they are geniuses. But it is surprisingly hard to define exactly what those skills are.

Talent or Giftedness

The words *talent* and *giftedness* are often used interchangeably, albeit *talent* would seem more appropriate for music and *giftedness* for academic schoolwork. Another way to distinguish these terms is to consider *gifts* as one's inborn potential (what is *given* by your genes) and *talent* as the outcome of a process of developing these skills. In either case, a person has a talent or gift for a specific domain, such as sports, chess, music, or school. This talent or gift manifests itself as exceptional precocity within the particular domain; that is, exceptional achievement far earlier in life than normally expected. This usage fits nicely with the IQ estimates mentioned earlier for Beethoven, Mozart, and Bach. It also has the advantage that it can be applied to musicians in any genre.

To illustrate, the Colombian songwriter Shakira has an IQ estimated around 140, a figure that can easily be justified by her precocious development in music and music-related domains. She began writing poetry at four years old—a definite prelude to song writing—and started her music writing just four years later. By the time she entered her teens, her musical talents sufficed to earn her a recording contract with Sony. Although she could not claim a genuine success until almost a decade later, her musical precocity cannot be denied. Hence, if precocity alone equates to genius, then Shakira counts as one, and so would all musical prodigies.

That said, a definition of genius that requires precocious ability has its own drawbacks. One problem is that precocious musicians, called *prodigies*, rarely grow up to become famous or even exceptional musicians as adults. This surprising fact is evident from the many musical prodigies who become mediocre adult musicians, if they continue in music at all. The same is true of many musical *savants*: people with exceptional musical ability who are otherwise intellectually disabled.

A famous example of a savant in classical music is the Australian concert pianist David Helfgott, whose life became the subject of the 1996 *Shine*, which won actor Geoffrey Rush an Academy Award. Helfgott started learning piano at five, and in his preteen years, he began winning local performance competitions. At nineteen, he earned a scholarship at London's Royal College of Music, where he continued his progress and won awards, including recognition for his rendition of the notoriously difficult "Rach 3" (Rachmaninoff's Third Piano Concerto). But in a few years, he began showing signs of a psychotic disorder, and from that point onward, his musical development slowly declined. Although he made some effort to revive his virtuoso career, riding on the wake of the film's popularity, that endeavor was not really successful. His performances and recordings were panned by the critics, making it clear that whatever pianistic talent he had originally possessed had dissipated. His recording of the "Rach 3" is said to be ill-advised, manifestly designed to appeal to audiences who liked the film.

But even if Helfgott had continued to perform impeccably, should he be called a *musical genius*? He did not compose anything creative himself, not even writing his own cadenzas. In contrast, Shakira composed the songs that she sings. Some individuals acquire the capacity to listen to a musical piece and play it back with the perfection of a tape recorder. Yet, if they exhibit no ability to compose or improvise, those achievements are unlikely to earn them the label of *genius*. Even the capacity to compose at a young age may not be sufficient to call someone a genius. Hikari Ōe is the autistic son of the Japanese author and Nobel laureate Kenzaburō Ōe. Hikari learned to speak through music, and his compositions can be ordered online and heard on YouTube. Yet, he is not considered a musical prodigy: He never became a virtuosic performer, and his first recordings did not appear until he was in his thirties. His abilities are impressive, but, ultimately, he did not make a widespread and enduring contribution to music.

Achieved Eminence: Extraordinary Impact

If an individual's work is overlooked or unappreciated, they are unlikely to be considered a genius by many people. Furthermore, if an individual has the potential to create great works of art but never actually produces anything, can we really call that person a "genius"? With these points in mind, a third definition of musical genius requires that an individual make a widespread and enduring contribution to a recognized musical genre. Most often, this contribution takes the form of original compositions, such as popular hits that are frequently covered, arranged, quoted, or expropriated by other musicians, such as film composers. Furthermore, the music should have a sustained influence for a considerable amount of time so that the hit becomes a recognized classic or standard that may even transcend genre. Johann Pachelbel's Canon in D, though beginning in the classical repertoire, has become familiar—perhaps even overly familiar—in cinema, pop, jazz, and new age.

More rarely, an instrumentalist or vocalist will exhibit a technique or style that ends up being so effective that it becomes widely imitated and eventually becomes an integral part of the genre, if not a new genre altogether. Since the advent of recordings, many top-notch musicians have devoted their youths to listening and attempting to replicate the innovations of past masters. Whatever the medium, these performance traditions can sometimes extend multiple generations. In classical piano, for example, many virtuosos could trace their teachers back through Franz Liszt, to Carl Czerny, and thus to Beethoven. The latter's contributions to later piano playing can thus count toward his musical genius.

Of course, musicians are not the only ones who can have an extraordinary and sustained influence. Scientific genius can also be gauged by influence over fellow scientists. Albert Einstein was a genius, even though only a small percentage of the human population would have any idea what his equations meant. The famous $E = mc^2$ is nothing more than a mysterious multisyllable chant for most people, but it still has scientific importance. Yet, in the case of music, it is the audience who decides whether music is good or bad, even if they have little or no understanding of the genre. After a work's performance, if an audience fails to applaud or responds with booing, the work will have failed to make a musical contribution in that context. Admittedly, avant-garde movements in any genre, from classical to jazz and beyond, can sometimes take a while to catch on. American jazz saxophonist John Coltrane's expressive innovations did not immediately earn universal acceptance, but his genius is certainly recognized today as an essential influence on the subgenre of free jazz.

Discussion of genius, musical or otherwise, often evokes the touchstone of surviving the test of time. Contemporaries as well as distant members of posterity are the final judge. Musical geniuses have to satisfy this criterion by producing works that remain popular with both professionals and audiences long after they pass away. In one way or another, the work enters a standard repertoire known to anyone who appreciates that genre. Performances and recordings of the pieces in this stable canon will continue indefinitely, and the corresponding music scores will become archived, as seen in *The Great American Songbook*. Of course, ups and downs in fashions will always take place. Yet, the value placed on the works of genius will often preserve enough recurrent interest to permit revivals at later times. The German composer Hildegard of Bingen died in 1179, over eight centuries ago. Despite the long period of history separating her time and ours—a period that included several catastrophic wars—her compositions somehow survived to be frequently performed and recorded today. How many times during that lengthy interval did some obscure monk or nun decide to laboriously make a manuscript copy for the enjoyment and edification of future generations? After all, music printing did not begin until almost three centuries after her death!

CREATIVE PRODUCTIVITY

Achieved eminence as a genius is not a simple yes-or-no attribute. Rather, genius varies on a continuum. This gradation is especially manifest in the case of composers. Although performers may display more or less proficiency at their chosen instrument, how does one quantify the differential impact on later performers? By comparison, the magnitude of creative genius in music is basically a function of productivity—the total number of major works that the composer creates in their favorite genre. The more pervasive and lasting contributions they make to the canon, the greater the amount of genius. This statement leads to a preliminary distinction between one-hit wonders and lifelong creators.

Regarding the former, in every music genre, a huge number of composers established their claim to fame on a single successful work. In popular music, these might include "99 Luftballons" by Nena, "Come on Eileen" by Dexys Midnight Runners, "Ice Ice Baby" by Vanilla Ice, "Mickey" by Toni Basil, "My Sharona" by the Knack, "Tainted Love" by Soft Cell, "Tubthumping" by Chumbawamba, "Video Killed the Radio Star" by the Buggles, and "Who Let the Dogs Out?" by Baha Men. Besides Pachelbel's Canon in D, classical music examples could cite the minuet from the String Quintet in E by Luigi Boccherini, the toccata from Symphony for Organ no. 5 by Charles-Marie Widor, the *Adagio for Strings* by Samuel Barber, the "Meditation" from the opera *Thais* by Jules Massenet, the "The Flower Duet" from the opera *Lakmé* by Léo Delibes, the "Dance of the Hours" from the opera *La Gioconda* by Amilcare Ponchielli (famously used in Walt Disney's animated *Fantasia*) as well as the entire opera *Cavalleria rusticana* by Pietro Mascagni (which plays a major role in the film *The Godfather, Part III*).

It deserves emphasis that not all one-hit wonders did it the easy way by composing a single success and then resting on their laurels. Pachelbel composed more than five hundred works in his lifetime, of which only one secured a prominent place on the classical charts. Others are more fortunate. Anton Karas, a minor Viennese zither player, was working for tips at a local restaurant when director Graham Greene, who was filming *The Third Man* on location, walked in, heard his playing, and decided that this music had exactly the right sound for the film's theme. The result was one of the most popular cinematic compositions ever created! Given his otherwise very low output of minor works, Karas might be considered a very marginal musical genius.

The supreme music geniuses, in stark contrast to the one-hit wonders, are not only extremely prolific, but they also produce multiple hits. The first hit typically appears sometime in their late twenties and the last hit somewhere in their fifties, with their best hit emerging in the late thirties to early forties. To be more precise, the exact location of these hits depends on the composer's total output. The more the composer produces, the earlier the first hit and the later the last hit—provided the creator lives long enough to get everything out of their system before dying!

Consider the great Johann Sebastian Bach, who composed more than a thousand works during his sixty-five years. His first notable compositions appeared in his early twenties, and he was still working on his unfinished magnum opus, *The Art of the Fugue*, on his death bed. The greatest musical geniuses devote thirty to forty years of their lives to composition, creating undoubted masterworks along the way. A necessary consequence is that their posthumous reputations are more stable over long periods of time. Their eminence does not depend on a single work. For instance, some scholars have questioned whether Bach actually composed the great organ Toccata and Fugue in D minor. Does it really matter? Removing that one work from his list of masterpieces would put only the tiniest dent in his total musical achievement.

CONCLUSION

Like the general definition of a genius, a *musical genius* can be defined in three ways: high general intelligence, exceptional talent or giftedness, and extraordinary eminence. Of these definitions, the third seems the most important because it alone acknowledges the need for any genius to make creative contributions to a genre's repertoire. Given this third definition, it becomes necessary to distinguish degrees of genius, ranging from the one-hit wonders to the super geniuses who essentially define the best in the repertoire. The latter are tremendously productive, creating their first hit at a very young age and offering their last hit close to their final year of life. By that definition, creative genius can appear in every musical genre.

References and Further Reading

Simonton, D. K. (2009a). Creative genius in classical music: Biographical influences on composition and eminence. *Psychologist, 22*, 1076–1079.

Simonton, D. K. (2009). *Genius 101*. New York, NY: Springer.

Simonton, D. K. (2018). *The Genius Checklist: Nine Paradoxical Tips on How You Can Become a Creative Genius*. Cambridge, MA: MIT Press.

11. Genetics and Musical Expertise

Miriam A. Mosing and Fredrik Ullén

Do musical skills have a biological and genetic base? There are at least four reasons to suspect that they might. First, music is a universal feature of human culture and can be traced back more than forty-thousand years based on an old bone flute found in Slovenia. If people all around the world engage in musical activities, it stands to reason that musicality may be a human trait that is part of our biology and not something that is specific to particular societies. Even without any formal music training, humans have the ability to not only perceive and appreciate music but also to produce music. For example, across all cultures, humans can generate a relatively steady beat or coordinate their movements with an external beat with impressive precision. Children all around the world clap and dance along with music, although there is variation in their skills. Some of the cognitive skills underlying musicality seem to be universal and tend to develop spontaneously and early during child development, such as pitch processing, metrical encoding of rhythm, and beat induction. Even newborns are naturally interested in music, and they can tell when a note from a familiar music piece is omitted.

Second, musical skills seem to aggregate in families: if one family member is highly musical, it is likely other family members will also be highly musical. One of the most famous musical families was the Bach family, which had more than fifty highly accomplished and well-known musicians, including several notable composers. Such families also exist today, such as the Marley family (the most famous member being Bob Marley) and the Jackson family (which included Michael Jackson). In the nineteenth century, the scientist Sir Francis Galton observed that exceptional abilities often clustered in families, and he interpreted this observation as evidence for hereditary influences on musical skill. Of course, it is difficult to draw strong conclusions about the relative importance of genetic influences from such cases because family members not only share genes but also a common environment.

When considering several family members with exceptional musical talent, an assessment of the amount of familial aggregation can help to determine whether a trait clusters in a family more than would be expected by chance. Two music-related traits that have been studied within this framework are (1) *congenital amusia*, a specific impairment in processing of music, also referred to as *tone deafness*, and (2) *absolute pitch* (AP), the ability to identify pitches without relying on external reference notes. Congenital amusia has been shown to aggregate in families, with family members of individuals with amusia at greater risk of having the impairment than unrelated individuals. The same finding has been reported for AP, with siblings of individuals with AP being more likely to also develop AP, even when controlling for music training. However, familial aggregation studies do not allow for the distinction between genetic and nongenetic (cultural or family environment) influences on music-related traits: both genetic factors and family environment could contribute to the aggregation.

Third, musicians vary widely in the number of hours of music practice they have accumulated during their lifetime, even when they are matched for their musical skills. This variability means that practice alone does not determine how skilled a person becomes, so genetic factors may also be important. Even the benefits of each practiced hour will vary between individuals. In a classroom, the same lesson can result in large individual differences in learning between pupils, with some benefiting enormously from a single hour of training while others receive little benefit. Some individuals need fewer practice hours to reach a certain skill level compared to others, which suggests that some people are more talented from the outset or have a faster learning pace.

Two recent analyses considered the combined results of several past studies on the relationship between music practice and music skill level. They showed that music practice could only account for about one-third of the differences in the quality of music performances. This means that factors other than practice account for close to two-thirds of the differences in the quality of these performances. Such observations strongly suggest that genetic influences and talent play a considerable role in musicality and probably interact with environmental factors and music practice.

Fourth, individuals diagnosed with certain genetic syndromes show altered musical skills. The most relevant syndromes are caused by an abnormality on chromosome 7. Williams-Beuren syndrome (WBS) is caused by a heterozygous gene deletion and can result in serious cognitive deficits, but the affected individuals tend to have surprisingly good music skills. They also show high musical interest as well as strong emotional responses to music. The second syndrome is caused by a rare mutation that results in severe speech and language problems along with reduced musical skills. In both cases, musicality is altered, and gene mutations are clearly the cause, suggesting that our genes (on chromosome 7) are likely important for normal musical development.

The four observations presented above suggest that genetics plays an important role in musical expertise. But can we establish the precise degree to which genetics are important? This research challenge will be discussed in the next section.

MEASURING GENETIC INFLUENCES ON MUSICALITY

The most popular method to quantify genetic influences underlying individual differences in human traits is the classical twin design. This method provides an overall estimate of how much of the observed variation in a trait can be attributed to genetic variation, but it does not allow us to identify the specific genes that are involved. To explore the particular genes influencing a trait, a number of other methods are used. These methods will be discussed later.

The Classical Twin Design

The classical twin design makes use of the fact that identical or monozygotic (MZ) twins share 100 percent of their genes (i.e., they are genetically identical), whereas fraternal or dizygotic (DZ) twins share on average only 50 percent of their genetic makeup (just like ordinary siblings). As twins usually grow up simultaneously in the same family, they share their home environment, the prenatal environment (i.e., their mother's womb), and many other family-related factors, such as teachers, schools, and friends, with each other. Such *shared environmental factors* make the two twins of a pair more similar to each other. Of course, each twin in a pair can have unique experiences, and these distinctive environmental experiences can make the two twins of a pair different from one another (*nonshared environmental influences*). Such differences may include different teachers, separate friends, and experiences only one twin went through (e.g., trauma), including random experiences. Based on these known facts, predictions can be made about the average resemblance of MZ and DZ twin pairs, depending on the strength of the three types of influences on a trait (genetic influences, shared environmental influences, and nonshared environmental influences). If individual differences between people were entirely due to genes, we would expect MZ twins to be exactly the same in every way whereas DZ twins would share 50 percent of their characteristics on average. Of course, we know that genes cannot explain everything because twins are never identical in every way.

To estimate the degree to which genes are responsible for behaviors and skills such as musical ability, we first need a way to measure similarities between people. In research, similarity is usually measured using a statistic called *correlation*, where 100 percent similarity results in a correlation value of 1.0, a correlation of zero corresponds to no association, and negative values correspond to opposing tendencies (where high values on one variable are associated with low values on the other). Using a musical example, if singing ability were purely genetic, identical pairs would always perfectly resemble each other on those skills (correlation value of 1.0) because they share the same genetic makeup, whereas DZ twins would only correlate 0.5 on average. Similarly, if singing ability were entirely due to shared environment, both MZ and DZ pairs should perfectly resemble each other on those skills (correlation of 1.0) because "shared environment" by definition means all the experiences that both twins of a pair have in common. Finally, if all variance were due to nonshared environmental influences, the musical skills of twin pairs should be quite different, whether they are MZ or DZ twins. Based on these peculiarities of twin pairs and the advancement of complex statistical methods, we can quantify the percentage of genetic, shared, and nonshared environmental influences underlying individual differences in a given trait and explain the relationships between two or more traits.

Gene Finding Methods

Our genetic makeup is coded in DNA, which contains four to five million single-nucleotide polymorphisms (SNPs), or genetic variants. Several methods can be used to identify specific genetic variants associated with differences in human traits, such as eye color, height, or musical ability. Recent advances in technology allow us to look at the DNA sequence of any individual—a process called *genotyping*. Genotyping helps us determine differences in the genetic makeup between individuals and to identify genes that may be relevant to particular traits. A popular and commonly used method to identify genes relevant for human complex traits is the *genome-wide association study* (GWAS).

The GWAS tests for relationships between SNPs across the entire genome and variation in a trait in the population. As there are so many SNPs, one problem with this approach is that a huge number of tests need to be conducted, and this leads to some complications in drawing conclusions. Furthermore, most genetic variants can only explain a small fraction of differences between people in a given trait. For this reason, hundreds of thousands of people are typically needed to reliably identify a genetic variant that is genuinely associated with a given trait, such as musical ability. If researchers have a specific hypothesis of a genomic region of interest, they can consider fewer SNPs in their study. This strategy is called *candidate gene study*, and it has the advantage in that fewer tests are required. There are other gene-finding methods not discussed here, and the field of genetics is rapidly advancing.

GENETIC CONTRIBUTIONS: FINDINGS OF TWIN STUDIES

In the last few years, a lot of research based on twin studies has suggested that individual differences in music expertise and related traits are to a considerable degree genetically influenced. To date, a number of independent twin studies have estimated the heritability (the proportion of total variance explained by genetic influences) of various musical skills. These skills include musical achievement (outside school), musical aptitude, exceptional musical talent, and achievement in the music world, as well as more objective measures of musicality, including AP, relative pitch, rhythm and beat processing, and melody discrimination tasks. These studies observed quite different heritability estimates, with some estimates quite low and others up to 86 percent, attributing most differences observed in the traits to genetic differences. However, almost all studies indicate considerable genetic influences on music-related traits, with the majority of heritability estimates ranging around 30–50 percent.

One of the most exciting and surprising findings in this field of research came from two twin studies that explored the heritability of *music practice*. Both studies found surprisingly high heritability estimates, suggesting that individual differences in propensity to practice, play, and engage in music are strongly influenced by genetic factors. Why is this surprising? We usually assume that practice is a behavior that anyone can achieve if we just put our minds to it, and with enough practice, anyone can become highly skilled. That differences in our *willingness* to practice (e.g., music playing) are partly due to genetic influences is a game changer. The importance of genetic influences on practice has led (among other research findings) to a shift in understanding or model, whereby both genetic and environmental factors and their interplay are thought to be responsible for musical expertise. This new model is called the *multifactorial gene-environment interaction model* (MGIM), and it will be further discussed toward the end of this chapter.

THE GENES OF (POTENTIAL) INTEREST

DNA molecules are packaged into threadlike structures called *chromosomes*, and genetic researchers can determine whether differences in specific SNPs or genes on a certain chromosome are associated with particular human traits, such as singing ability. Several studies have reported associations between loci (SNPs) on chromosome 8q and AP and music perception as well as between chromosome 4 and musical aptitude, accuracy of pitch perception, and pitch accuracy during singing and composing. The gene AVPR1A on chromosome 12 is associated with music perception and music listening, whereas the gene SLC6A4 on chromosome 17 is associated with choir participation. Both genes are also associated with music memory and social behavior.

Although these results are encouraging, it should be mentioned that other studies tried and failed to replicate these associations. In other words, there is considerable uncertainty about exactly which genes are associated with musical expertise, so many more studies with larger sample sizes are needed. Given the complexity of musicality and its many facets, it is likely that there will be many genetic variants that are relevant for music-related traits, and it will be challenging to identify all of them, even using excellent measures and large samples.

CONCLUSION

Although very little is known about the genes that underlie music-related traits, individual differences in most, if not all, traits involved in human music playing are at least partly due to underlying genetic influences. And this even includes music practice. Both genes and the environment play essential roles in musical expertise, as predicted by the multifactorial gene-environment interaction model. This model recognizes that practice alone cannot explain expertise, and it acknowledges the importance of the interplay between genes and environment. To become a top-level musician, various factors and skills are involved, and many critically depend on neural circuits in the brain and spinal cord that are optimized to allow performance at a high level (e.g., timing ability, excellent hearing, fast and accurate motor skills—skills likely under relatively strong genetic influence).

Other skills are largely influenced by an individual's environment, such as the opportunity to hold an instrument or engage in music. Beyond such abilities, there must be a willingness, drive, and joy to practice and spend long hours on the same task. The combination of a genetic predisposition toward musicality with a conducive environment is the best predictor of high musical expertise. Anyone with either talent or opportunity (but not both) will have a hard time in getting to the top. However, most of us do not aim to reach the highest levels of expertise but are happy to enjoy music as a recreational activity.

References and Further Reading

Mosing, M. A., Madison, G., Pedersen, N. L., Kuja-Halkola, R., & Ullén, F. (2014). Practice does not make perfect: No causal effect of musical practice on musical ability. *Psychological Science, 25*(9), 1795–1803.

Tan, Y. T., McPherson, G. E., Peretz, I., Berkovic, S. F., & Wilson, S. J. (2014). The genetic basis of music ability. *Frontiers in Psychology, 5*, 658.

Ullen, F., Hambrick, D. Z., & Mosing, M. A. (205). Rethinking expertise: A multifactorial gene-environment interaction model of expert performance. *Psychological Bulletin, 142*(4), 427–446.

12. Competitions: Judging Expertise

Chris Dromey and William Forde Thompson

Competitions play a significant role in the music industry. Whether a televised reality contest, an international classical music competition, or a Battle of the Bands in a local bar, competitions enable musicians of various ages and experiences to judge, promote, and, in principle, better themselves. Even so, as the number and type of competitions have grown tremendously in the past half century, questions about their purpose and legitimacy have surfaced. Some critics also argue that immensely popular television shows such as *The X Factor* and *The Voice* present a distorted impression of the nature and function of professional music competitions, whose formats, goals, and participants are more diverse than we see on popular television shows.

PAST AND PRESENT MUSIC COMPETITIONS

From a modern perspective, competitive music making can be traced to late eighteenth-century Britain, with its array of brass band contests, choral and instrumental competitions, and revival of the *Eisteddfodau* (a Welsh festival of competitive music and poetry dating to the eighth century). By the 1800s, a competition *movement* had emerged. Contests became formal and popular, with audiences attracted to them as much by musical rivalries as by the higher-quality performances that competitions promoted. One prestigious competition that still runs today, notable for its long history, is the British Open Brass Band Championship (f. 1853). The Stratford Festival (f. 1882) is another prominent competition. It was originally founded by John Spencer Curwen with the goal of establishing a strong connection between competition and education. The event is now managed by teachers and choirmasters and consists of multiple classes and sections of competition. It embraces both amateur and professional music making. Such competitions laid the foundation for a thriving competition scene in the twentieth and twenty-first centuries.

In parallel to these annual events, there are many one-off competitions in which solo musicians are pitted against each other for entertainment, patronage, or simply to debate the merits of those involved. One historical example is the famous rivalry between the pianist-composers Franz Liszt and Sigismond Thalberg, which was showcased in a benefit concert held in 1837 in Paris. Such musical duels have a modern equivalent in the showy, sudden-death finals of televised contests such as *The Voice*. These mass media contests are immensely popular and a source of huge revenues for the television industry. Although they typically focus on popular music, they have also (controversially) started to include classical music.

CLASSICAL MUSIC

Classical music competitions became popular in the twentieth century and were gradually designed to meet a set of criteria. For example, there are frequently age restrictions for entrants, and performances are heard and adjudicated by a panel of adjudicators (often called a *jury*). The music that is performed is often set from a repertoire (occasionally with a commissioned test piece of music), and the competition finals are often public events. To assist adjudicators in making reliable judgments, a number of formalized methods have been developed. One such method is called the Music Performance Assessment (MPA) tool, but there are many others. Most of these methods identify some core qualities that adjudicators are advised to consider, such as technique, phrasing, balance, articulation, timing, and dynamic range. By breaking down a performance into specific qualities, adjudicators are encouraged to listen in an analytical way.

Music competitions with the most prestigious reputations attract the best musicians. In their attempt to attract the best musicians, classical music competitions must themselves compete against one another, in the same way that popular competitions such as *The Voice* compete for high ratings and prime-time programming slots. One prestigious competition, Belgium's annual Queen Elisabeth Competition, was established in 1937 in memory of violinist Eugène Ysaÿe, and it has continued to this day. Many people consider this competition among the most challenging and prestigious of all classical music competitions. Currently, the competition rotates annually between performances by violinists, pianists, cellists, and singers, but it previously also included composition. The stakes are high, as winning such a competition can help to launch a musician's career. Soviet musicians did particularly well early on, with violinist David Oistrakh winning the competition when it was first held and pianist Emil Gilels winning its second presentation. Both musicians were star performers of classical music.

Many competitions rely on external sources of support and are therefore vulnerable to periods of economic downturn. Some competitions found that they had insufficient financial means to continue during the global financial crisis, when funding for the arts was generally reduced. Nonetheless, the most established competitions found ways to continue and, in some cases, to thrive. The M-Prize chamber arts competition (Michigan, f. 2016), for example, offers traditional and open categories to accommodate and encourage improvisation, music technology, and cross-genre creativity. The Leeds (triennial since 1961), Tchaikovsky (Moscow, quadrennial since 1958), Busoni (Bolzano, biennial since 1949), and Chopin (Warsaw, quinquennial since 1927) competitions attract the world's very best young pianists. Violinists vie for the Paganini (Genoa, since 1954, now biennial), Indianapolis (quadrennial since 1982), Joseph Joachim (Hannover, triennial since 1991), and Michael Hill (Auckland, biennial since 2001) titles. Prestigious string quartet competitions are held in Banff (triennial since 1983) and Bordeaux (originally Evian, triennial since 1981). Conductors compete at the Solti competition (Frankfurt, biennial since 2002). Other single-discipline events include the BBC Cardiff Singer of the World (biennial since 1983), the USA International Harp Competition (Bloomington, Indiana, triennial since 1989), and the Kobe International Flute Competition (quadrennial since 1985). Solo instrumentalists of all kinds, if aged eighteen or under, are eligible to enter the BBC Young Musician of the Year (London, biennial since 1978).

POPULAR MUSIC

The runaway success of reality television has transformed the meaning of competition in popular music. The globally imitated series *Popstars* (first broadcast in New Zealand in 1998) was the first to televise auditions for a pop group. Its prominent successors in the United Kingdom include *Pop Idol*, and in the United States, they include *American Idol*, *The X Factor*, and *The Voice*. *America's Got Talent* is part of the "Got Talent" franchise created by Simon Cowell and is now mirrored by similar shows in most countries around the world. A distinguishing feature of this competition is that it attracts competitors from across the performing arts and beyond, including singers, dance troupes, magicians, comedians, and other forms of entertainment—a throwback to the first-ever televised talent contests, for example, *Opportunity Knocks* (1949–1990).

At the time New Zealand's *Popstars* began, some sections of the media thought that its groundbreaking style would reveal the age-old "manufacturing" of musical stars. In fact, such competitions proved to be more docudrama than documentary, as they charted the emotional and musical ups and downs of their contestants' progress. Winning the contest became an end in itself and far more important than whether the finalists actually went on to become successful musicians in the industry. Some people have raised concerns that reality television competitions make their profits from exploiting, and even humiliating, their entrants. They point to the fact that many winners of such competitions have not enjoyed lasting success. However, defenders of such competitions argue that most entrants have benefited enormously from the exposure, including winners such as Carrie Underwood and Kelly Clarkson; runners-up such as Adam Lambert; and even entrants who were voted out long before the finals, such as Jennifer Hudson, who finished seventh in season three of *American Idol*. Beyond the benefits to contestants, such competitions also have an undeniable benefit to the music industry, and the excitement they generate encourages many young viewers to take up music lessons, especially in voice and guitar.

The competition scene for popular music is having a global impact. Member countries of the European Broadcasting Union founded the annual Eurovision Song Contest in 1956. Originally contested by seven countries, in 2018, musicians representing forty-three countries took part, of which twenty-six qualified as finalists. Notable past winners include Sandie Shaw (United Kingdom, 1967), ABBA (Sweden, 1974), Céline Dion (Switzerland, 1988), and Dana International (Israel, 1998). Once judged by national juries, then voted for by the public, and nowadays decided by a mixture of the two, the contest gives each country equal weighting, no matter its size.

As several European nations devolved in the late twentieth century, Eurovision "voting blocs" became more pronounced. That is, people tend to vote for the competitor who represents their country, and this motivation dominates voting patterns, causing groups of people to vote in the same way. Citizens of countries tied to other countries by geography or politics often reward such countries' entrants without much consideration of the actual merits of their performances—a strategy that has frustrated commentators and sometimes given rise to surprise winners. Whether such events constitute valid competitions is debatable. Are the winners of events such as the Eurovision Contest the best contestants in terms of their creative contributions and technical expertise, or are they just the most popular personalities or representing the most popular nationalities? The fairness of such competitions is questionable, to say the least, and many established artists shun them for this very reason.

JUDGING EXPERTISE

Concerns about the validity of popular music competitions led to broader questions about the nature of adjudication and what it means to judge a performance. What are the best criteria for judging the quality of a music performance? Should we judge a performance based on whether we enjoy the music, or should other factors be considered? What if the performance is highly enjoyable but merely repeats what other musicians have already done with the same song? If a musician sings a song by Coldplay and mirrors the original performance in every detail, we may enjoy the performance, but what creative contribution has the musician really made? Conversely, if a performer tries to do something different with a song, should this attempt at innovation be rewarded? What if a musician performs the adjudicator's favorite song of all time but the performance itself is not very good? Can adjudicators set aside their personal preferences to judge the performance on its own merits? Somehow, an adjudicator must form a judgment on the *relationship* between music and its expressive interpretation in performance without being swayed (i.e., biased) by personal preferences.

Other considerations will also influence and moderate an adjudicator's judgment of a performance, from the difficulty and stylistic conventions of the music itself, to technical matters particular to the instrument(s) or voice. Opinions on the desirability of certain expressive choices also vary, such as the expressive use of vibrato by a violinist or vocalist, the dynamic (loudness) range, and the chosen tempo (pace) of a performance. Such decisions will almost always affect the outcome of a competition, and so they are important pedagogical considerations for teachers who may be encouraging students to enter competitions.

Studies have shown that the evaluations of adjudicators are not very consistent or reliable. In one study, experienced adjudicators were given a large number of performances of the same piece of music and were asked to rate the quality of each performance. What the adjudicators did not realize is that every performance was presented twice, so the adjudicators ended up providing two separate evaluations of each performance. Surprisingly, there was a very weak relationship between the two sets of ratings of the same performances, indicating that their judgments were unreliable.

Research has also uncovered serious bias effects to which adjudicators can be susceptible. One study showed that classical musicians who appeared on the final day of a competition stood a significantly better chance of being ranked higher. Such a bias can be explained as a *recency effect*, whereby performances that are fresh in an adjudicator's mind will stand out and are more likely to be assigned a higher ranking. It is also possible that fatigue plays a role, whereby repeatedly hearing performances may cause adjudication criteria to be relaxed as the competitions progress. Many competitions, including the Queen Elisabeth, have since introduced precompetition screening, serving to reduce the number of competitors appearing before juries in the public rounds of competition and thereby lessening the danger of fatigue.

The psychology of expectation, of who is *expected* to perform well, is another confirmed bias. For example, when adjudicators are given a set of performances arbitrarily labeled "professional musicians" and another set of performances labeled "amateur musicians," they will assign higher ratings to the former set of performances, even when the labels are random and inaccurate. Such effects also point to the fact that certain groups of people can be disadvantaged, for example, because of gender, race, or sexuality. They also demonstrate that aspects of performance beyond the sounded music, including bodily gestures and facial expressions, can affect performance evaluations. In recognition of these biases, some orchestras hold "blind" auditions, with candidates performing behind a screen. *The Voice* also made this tactic its raison d'être when it was first launched in the Netherlands in 2010. The trade-off is clear: bias is countered, but on the other hand, musicians cannot exploit the type of visual "extramusical" information that, for better or worse, has been a historic sway on audiences. Most people prefer live performances to recorded music because they enjoy seeing the performers as well as hearing them. As Robert Schumann famously remarked on Liszt, "If [he] played behind a screen, a great deal of poetry would be lost."

Some competitions have taken other steps to address the problem of bias. The World Federation of International Music Competitions insists that no more than half of the jury members should hail from the host country of a competition. Further policies implemented by competitions include no-discussion rules to forbid jury members from conferring and abstentions when jury members have a student in the competition. Commentators have called for competition organizers to combat the risk of nepotism, for example, by publishing adjudicators' scores postcompetition or even after each round.

CONCLUSION

Music competitions are big business, whether they are prestigious classical music competitions or televised competitions for musical "idols." Aside from the financial incentives to host a competition, one might reasonably ask whether competitions actually benefit musicians. Common sense suggests that they may be a source of motivation for musicians, but does the process of competing create better musicians? Studies cast doubt on this possibility. Extensive research indicates that creativity in children thrives in cooperative environments, but it tends to diminish in competitive situations. Nonetheless, audience members seemingly cannot get enough of high-stakes competitions, so it is unlikely that such events will disappear anytime soon.

References and Further Reading

Bouckaert, T. (2001). *Elisabeth's Dream, A Musical Offering: Fifty Years of the Queen Elisabeth Competition* (P. King & S. Montgomery, Trans.). Brussels: Complexe.

Goertzen, C. (2008). *Southern Fiddlers and Fiddle Contests.* Jackson: University Press of Mississippi.

McCormick, L. (2015). *Performing Civility: International Competitions in Classical Music.* Cambridge, UK: Cambridge University Press.

Raykoff, I., & Deam Tobin, R. (Eds.). (2007). *A Song for Europe: Popular Music and Politics in the Eurovision Song Contest.* Aldershot, UK: Ashgate.

Musical Prodigies and Savants

13. Becoming a Musical Prodigy: Hard Work or Born That Way?

Jane W. Davidson

A prodigy is usually thought of as someone who has the capacity to develop extremely quickly and to display very rapid learning. Thus, prodigies are precocious, developing their abilities during childhood, most often before ten years of age. Typically displaying abilities equivalent to an elite adult expert, prodigies often inspire feelings of wonder in others. How *was* it possible, for example, for Alma Deutcher to compose an opera at age seven or for Emily Bear to give a piano recital at the White House for the president of the United States at age six, when these achievements are intellectually and physically challenging for adult professional musicians?

One of the first concepts that comes to mind when thinking of a prodigy is natural "gifts." Although the terms *gifted* and *talent* are often used casually to refer to exceptional skill, they are subtly different. Major theoretical work to distinguish the terms has been undertaken by Françoys Gagné, who considers *gifts* as those skills that are *given* to us and that do not require development, whereas *talent* is the final outcome of an exceptional capacity to *develop* skills and knowledge over time. Thus, if a person sings beautifully the first time he or she tries and has never had a singing lesson, we would call that person *gifted*. But if another person takes music lessons, progresses rapidly through the various levels, and ultimately becomes an exceptional musician, we might call them *talented*.

Prodigies are often gifted, and their given abilities place them at the very top of their cohort *before* training. Which abilities do gifted musicians possess? Human abilities have been shown to fall into a range of domains, including those associated with intellectual, creative, social, perceptual, muscular, and motor control skills. It is possible to be gifted in just one specific domain, but *musical* skill often engages all these human abilities.

Talent reflects an individual's *capacity for developing* knowledge and skills systematically. Talent displays the pinnacle of knowledge and skill acquisition attainable by the individual. Whereas a gift simply exists regardless of circumstances, talent can only be achieved through a developmental process that relies on catalysts. These catalysts include those from within the individual (intrapersonal) and those from the world in which he or she lives (the environment).

Music prodigies have a unique combination of gifts and talents, and they often grow up in an environment that supports their interest in music. But make no mistake: being a prodigy requires a lot of hard work, even when born with exceptional gifts.

GIFTS AND TALENT DEVELOPMENT

Our development is partly controlled by our genes, or *genetic heredity*. In other words, some individuals are more genetically primed to concentrate harder, identify salient perceptual information more readily, process this information more efficiently, and control their bodies more easily than others. Measurable factors can be identified that provide a theoretical account of the prodigy's gifts and also help us explain differences between them and us. For example, it is possible to calculate response times for mental processes such as perception, memory, judgment and reasoning. Similarly, it is possible to track how body joints move and trace the speed of muscle responses, thus enabling us to show genetic advantage in these dimensions.

Personality is also rooted in genetic heredity. Psychological surveys have been developed to assess personality, and many people believe that our core personalities can be described as a combination of five major factors: openness to experience (similar to open-mindedness), extraversion, conscientiousness, agreeableness versus antagonism, and neuroticism versus emotional stability. Musicians vary in their personalities, but as a group, they tend to display increased openness to experience, introversion, agreeableness, and some neuroticism. These personality types vary according to the instrument played, suggesting that people with certain personalities tend to be attracted to particular musical instruments.

For individuals to develop as a musical prodigy, they need to have a lot of self-awareness. This individual also needs to be highly motivated and have exceptional willpower. Prodigies are quick to self-identify as musicians and often having a strong talent goal, for example, playing a particular piece of music. The capacity to dedicate themselves to the task of music learning is a core attribute of prodigies. Strong willpower sustains daily engagements with music, such as practice, especially when facing boredom or some failures to improve immediately.

People have looked at the biographies of musical prodigies compared with other music learners of similar ages, and the prodigies did show significant initial spontaneous engagements with music that occurred much sooner than the music engagements observed in their peers. The prodigies' intense and self-generated fascination with music revealed that the music had a profound impact on their thought processes that resulted in *absorption* in the music. These children were also reported as producing music very early through singing or free spontaneous explorations with musical instruments in the home.

Harnessing and nurturing gifts is where talent development begins. In many cases, the very young and attentive musical children are often assisted by caregivers who provide supporting structures to scaffold the child's learning. For example, the caregiver may expose the child to many different kinds of musical listening or allow the child freedom to experiment with musical sounds and instruments. Trial and error and creative play entwine to enable the fulfillment of informal learning. Other social contacts and even a role model in the form of a hero to emulate are also reported as key motivators for prodigies.

Renowned classical music prodigies, including Wolfgang Amadeus Mozart (1756–1791), Erich Korngold (1897–1957), and Bejun Mehta (b. 1968), all had fathers who were very involved in their learning. Mehta spoke of the many inspiring hours he spent sitting with his father at the keyboard playfully learning about the instruments, sounds, and possibilities of music more broadly. Jazz prodigy Louis Armstrong (1901–1971) did not meet this criterion; he was born into extreme poverty, and his mother used to leave him to follow other children out on the streets. But even with a very disrupted childhood that involved moving in and out of state and foster care, Armstrong had peers and role models who were highly encouraging and supportive of his efforts in his early years, which are also factors common to those who go on to high levels of achievement.

This supported engagement with music during which the "rules" can be assimilated without any formal teaching has been referred to as the *sampling* stage and is where musical identity formation begins. In addition to informal creative opportunity, prodigies also engage in many hours of what might be called *formal practice*. This includes scales, technical exercises, and repertoire. A range of studies of music practice has been undertaken, and one major study of prodigies and other young music learners revealed that those who went on to professional musician status had invested a minimum of ten thousand hours of accumulated practice across their years of childhood study. This is usually where talent is identified, and it has been referred to as the period of *specialization*. For prodigies, music is absolutely the prioritized area of life.

For this intense focus on music to occur, prodigies are also the center of attention in their homes, and their parents are often found to make the most incredible personal sacrifices, including moving the home and changing their own work habits to support and invest in their child's musical pursuit. Beyond the parents, teachers also invest significantly in these children. Most distinctive here is that the prodigy works with teachers and others in highly collaborative relationships, thereby increasing the rate at which expertise is realized. A classic example of the fast-progressing and well-supported prodigy is Erich Korngold, who was not only playing the piano exceptionally well at a very young age, but working under the mentorship of the world-renowned composers Gustav Mahler and Alexander von Zemlinsky, he also composed a ballet, *The Snowman*, at only eleven years of age.

Self-generated learning is a crucial part of every prodigy's background and so too is a context where competencies can be developed. This could be in the formal context of school, but other contexts can also provide opportunities for systematic training. Erich Korngold spent his childhood in the exceptional cultural milieu of early twentieth-century Vienna. Many centuries earlier, the Abbess-composer Hildegard of Bingen (1098–1179) was immersed in the extensive musical practices of the convent from an early age. Having received no formal music training, she had learned to compose her music by osmosis. More recently, the world-renowned jazz trumpeter Louis Armstrong offers another intriguing case. He grew up in the jazz capital of the world, New Orleans. Engaging with music all day, every day, Armstrong joined informal ensembles with other children, and from just three years old, he could be found singing on street corners and begging for money. Born into poverty, the incentive to improve his musical skills was high. Further, Armstrong was able to spend time with adult professionals who informally let him try their instruments and little by little offered expert guidance.

There has been a trend across the twentieth and twenty-first centuries in Europe and North America to create talent programs for the gifted. Although the models of these school programs vary, there are some music specialist schools. They legally have to cover all the subjects of the compulsory school curriculum, but music is at the center of the child's learning experience. Before official classes start, practice time is allocated, for which practice supervisors are present to help students problem-solve. School life is suffused with music: lunchtime concerts, after-school performances, and multiple music ensembles with which to engage. Music learning comprises a major part of the child's life. The many different opportunities for music learning include aural training, harmony and counterpoint, analysis, practice one-to-one tuition, small ensembles, large ensembles, and coaching.

But, of course, even within these curricular offerings designed to foster gifts, a range of achievements eventuate, with not all students continuing to develop their musical gifts in an even manner across their education. Such outcomes highlight that the concept of a prodigy is not something absolute: a prodigy's rate of development may slow down, diminishing their status in the musical arena, or the prodigy may cease their musical pursuits as adulthood approaches. But why?

POTENTIAL, CHANCE, AND PERSONAL CHANGE

The fulfillment of an individual's potential is not only subject to the alignment of gifts and talents but also to the ways in which certain psychological and emotional states and environmental factors happen to align. This has been referred to as the *chance factor* because the child is dependent on the random alignments in their environment coupled with a roll of the dice in how their heredity aligns. It is essential to understand that genetic endowment, environmental factors, and chance opportunities intermingle in complex and sometimes unpredictable ways, for it may be that identical environmental circumstances offer a good blend of challenges and opportunities for one individual but prove to be too demanding or not sufficiently demanding for another.

In addition to psychological and environmental factors, maturational processes related to hormonal changes affect all humans, and the child demonstrating prodigious musical gifts and talents is no exception. Adolescence is a particularly challenging period when many physical changes align with the person's growing awareness of their values and ideals.

One very striking example of these kinds of change is found in the career of the singer Bejun Mehta. As a young child, Mehta showed remarkable gifts and talents as a boy soprano, receiving worldwide critical acclaim. His voice broke quite late, so remaining a soprano for most of his teenage period was undoubtedly a great advantage, as he was able to perform complex arias that demanded great physical and intellectual focus (like works by Handel and Britten). But when his voice broke, his musical identity was challenged because he could not sing as before. He also found external pressure from his father to succeed in music too intense. Initially, he focused on cello and then conducting, but he decided to focus his attention on studying German literature at Yale University. It was only in his late twenties that the passion and focus for singing reemerged. After several experiences as a baritone, Mehta began to train as a countertenor, which means he sang in falsetto, perhaps aspiring to reproduce aspects of his childhood soprano sound. Although Mehta did eventually return to music, his detour into a different area of study revealed that the habits of conscientious learning developed from an early age can also help prodigies acquire other skills quite rapidly, such as the German language for Mehta.

The difficulties of transitioning through adolescence are found in many writings on prodigies. The famous actress and singer Judy Garland (1922–1969) is one notable example who moved from child prodigy to adult star, but not without incredible personal challenges. Judy became renowned for being unreliable, unstable, and psychologically ill, and drug and alcohol abuse ultimately resulted in her taking a drug overdose and dying at only forty-seven years of age. It has been suggested that the pressures placed on her in childhood were exploitative. Although she performed with incredible virtuosity across her life, obedience to the studio system in Hollywood and the extreme pressure of striving for high achievement seemed to be too much to handle.

Many of the key adult figures in music history were prodigies. Classical musician prodigies include Wolfgang Amadeus Mozart, Joseph Haydn, Frederic Chopin, Franz Liszt, Niccolò Paganini, Felix Mendelssohn, and Erich Korngold. In popular genres, examples include Aretha Franklin, Stevie Wonder, Michael Jackson, and Björk. Some of these individuals were known to be socially difficult and challenging individuals. Korngold, for example, was unhappy in adulthood, regretful of the ways his childhood had been shaped through parental dominance. Perhaps epitomizing the spirit of the prodigy who will go on to a happy and fulfilling adult career, the famous classical cellist Jacqueline du Pré once said, "We cannot become what we need to be by remaining what we are," suggesting that flexibility is necessary to transition between the world of the focused prodigy and the adult with multiple challenges and responsibilities.

Modern education can have a favorable impact on prodigies and improve their chances of a smooth transition from childhood to adult music careers. A longitudinal study of prodigies revealed that those students who went on to the highest levels of adult professional musical achievement did so by possessing strong psychological strategies related to self-identity as a musician and also methods of coping with the lifestyle of extreme pressure and singular focus.

CONCLUSION

Prodigies display common characteristics that are indicative of genetic advantage and coupled with talent development that supports the rapid progression of musical skills. This route requires incredibly hard work and dedication from the prodigy and often significant sacrifice by parents. While achievements of musical prodigies are amazing and often persist into adulthood, the dedicated lifestyle can lead to stress factors that make the route of the prodigy far from easy.

References and Further Reading

Gagné. F. (2004). Transforming gifts into talents: The DMGT as a developmental theory. *High Ability Studies, 15*, 119–147.

Howe, M. (1999). *Genius Explained.* Cambridge, UK: Cambridge University Press.

Kaufmann, S. B. (Ed.). (2013). *The Complexity of Greatness: Beyond Talent or Practice.* Oxford, UK: Oxford University Press.

McPherson, G. E. (Ed.). (2016). *Musical Prodigies: Interpretations from Psychology, Education, Musicology and Ethnomusicology.* Oxford, UK: Oxford University Press.

McPherson, G. E., Davidson, J. W., & Faulkner, R. (2012). *Music in Our Lives: Rethinking Musical Ability, Development and Identity.* Oxford, UK: Oxford University Press.

14. Prodigies in Performance

Gary E. McPherson

By far, the most common examples of musical prodigies are those children who perform music. Prodigies of music composition, for example, are less common. Prodigies of performance display extraordinary abilities before puberty and are able to amaze and dazzle adults who find it hard to explain exactly how these children are able to perform with such professional agility on their instruments.

DISTINGUISHING CHARACTERISTICS

Scientists are keen to understand the range of personal and environmental influences that explain musical prodigies' precociousness and shape their musical lives. But what exactly is a *prodigy*? Perhaps the most important distinguishing feature that defines prodigies is the rapid pace with which they are able to learn and memorize works and reproduce this repertoire across multiple performances. One example is Sarah Chang, who could perform much of the Mendelssohn Violin Concerto at the age of six, a feat that normally takes around twelve years of learning by an average violinist to acquire the technical and musical skills necessary to perform such a difficult piece.

The literature on musical prodigies identifies these talented individuals as being able to perform at an adult level before the age of ten within a recognized field of behavior. However, this definition is problematic for a number of reasons. The onset of puberty, which is around ages eleven or twelve for boys and ages ten or eleven for girls, provides a better cutoff, given that this is when a child's body starts to mature into an adult. Referring to a "professional level of performance" is also awkward given how difficult it is to define exactly what this means or implies. Although most examples of music performance prodigies perform classical repertoire on piano or violin, many would argue that this way of thinking about musical prodigies is too limiting and should instead be opened up to include all forms of music making, even rapping and electric guitar. Thus, any explanation of musical prodigies that confines examples to a culturally demanding field of endeavor, such as classical music, should be seriously questioned given the many examples across all forms of music where precocious young musicians can be found to have excelled in their field.

Some people acknowledge that musical prodigies perform with technical perfection, but they argue that because they are so young they lack the maturity to play with real expression. Listening to the early performances of Sarah Chang and other musical prodigies seriously causes one to question the validity of this assumption, and there are many reports of master teachers who were in awe of the expressive skills of young performers who they accepted into their studios.

How rare are musical prodigies in the general population? There are literally thousands of so-called musical prodigy videos on YouTube, but a close examination of these individuals reveals that it is very difficult to evaluate their abilities from a single YouTube video, even though they may have amassed hundreds of thousands or even millions of views. This aspect of becoming noticed is important, for without public recognition, the musical prodigy will not be known outside of their family and, thus, be unable to gain the public recognition needed to embark on a successful commercial career.

NATURAL ABILITIES

One of the natural abilities that appears to give a child a musical advantage is perfect (absolute) pitch—that is, the ability to name any note just by hearing it. Perfect pitch is formed through a complex interaction between genetic endowment and environmental stimulation. Most renowned musical prodigies display this ability, even though the ability is quite rare in the general population.

Musical prodigies also seem to have the ability to mimic what they see and hear and to pick up the specific musicality of an interpretation of a work they hear others perform (e.g., their teacher) as well as the motor ability to reproduce this performance quickly and effectively on their instrument.

The most important capacity of a musical prodigy, however, is the ability to memorize quickly and accurately, and this ability distinguishes a prodigy from all other learners. Wolfgang Amadeus Mozart's father reported that his son was able to learn repertoire in less than an hour and could play these pieces faultlessly and with great delicacy. More recently, the pianist Lang Lang's teacher reported that when Lang Lang was very young, he could memorize four big pieces of music every week.

As one of the first and most celebrated musical prodigies of his day, Mozart's abilities as a performer and composer are still unrivaled. As noted above, he possessed absolute pitch and a remarkable memory for music that culminated in one of the most astonishing feats by any musical prodigy; at the age of fourteen, he attended performances of Gregorio Allegri's *Miserere* at the Sistine Chapel in Rome. This work was forbidden to be performed outside the chapel, so copies of the music were not available at that time. However, the young Mozart is reported to have been able to transcribe this fifteen-minute work from just a couple hearings.

A core ability of musical prodigies is their sensitivity to the physical and emotional properties of sound such that they are able, from a very young age, to make sense of tonality, key, harmony, and rhythm and even the expressive properties of music. This ability both reflects and reinforces their great love for music. There are many reports of how musical prodigies fall in love with music from a very early age and how their love of music provides the basis for developing a very focused attitude about music that drives their passionate involvement with music and strong determination to succeed and often to be the best, even when faced with difficulties or negative influences that would otherwise undermine their development.

For example, despite the emotional and physical abuse that Lang Lang and Michael Jackson experienced from their fathers, both musicians went on to have successful international careers and to gain recognition as the best in their fields. Part of the reason for being able to put up with such abuse appears to have been their love of music and their drive to become the best in their particular field. From a very early age, Michael Jackson wanted to be the king of pop, and Lang Lang was driven to be a star performer. This love for music, combined with a strong determination to be the best, is thought to have triggered an intense desire to learn music and to reproduce on an instrument what these young performers heard on recordings and through live performances.

Possessing a natural flare for music is insufficient for the development of the types of musical performance talent that will be recognized and accepted by others. Although far less evident nowadays, adult attitudes toward young performers have changed markedly across the centuries. Wolfgang Amadeus Mozart's sister Nannerl, by all accounts, showed early promise as a composer and performer; yet, once she reached a marriageable age, her father forbid her to perform in public. We will therefore never know the full extent of her musical abilities. The same is true for many other young girls, such as Fanny Mendelssohn, whose brother Felix is one of the most renowned musical prodigies of all time. Despite her precocious abilities, like Nannerl, she was forbidden to publish her compositions or perform in public lest she compromise the feminine virtues of obedience and love. It was not until Clara Schumann (1810–1896) that female prodigies started to become more widely known and publicly celebrated.

ENVIRONMENTAL INFLUENCES

There is no doubt that Wolfgang Amadeus Mozart was profoundly gifted; yet, even with these natural abilities, he worked extremely hard, probably accumulating as much music practice before he was ten years old as many musically trained eighteen-to-twenty-year-olds today who are auditioning to enter music institutions. This observation aligns with the proposal that it takes ten thousand hours of practice to become an expert in any field, whether that is painting, music, or tennis. Many young prodigies who are exposed to high levels of training of the type offered at major specialized music schools in North America, Europe, and China, however, will have exceeded this figure by their midteens. Some will have even completed up to fifteen thousand hours of practice by the time they reach age twenty.

However, it is not merely the total number of hours of practice but the quality of that practice that counts. K. Anders Ericsson and his colleagues coined the term *deliberate practice* to explain a form of practice they believe is essential to the acquisition of expert skill. Within this conception, deliberate practice is defined as a special kind of practice that is focused, determined, and hard work but not necessarily always fun. Some music psychologists have found evidence in the lives of some prodigies that they embarked on a form of "deliberate play" for a year or more before receiving lessons on the instrument they finally chose to learn and ultimately excel in playing. For example, a prodigy with whom the author has worked spent many hours playing a toy piano as she mimicked the music from her father's hi-fi system. This occurred well before she commenced formal piano lessons. It was felt that this form of deliberate, unstructured play provided the solid foundation from which she developed a love for performing music once she commenced formal piano lessons.

Another form of environmental stimulation occurs when a young learner is exposed to varied opportunities to perform and learn. As an example, Mozart traveled extensively throughout his childhood and was exposed to all the various trends in music within Europe at that time. These experiences provided a springboard for him to subsequently create works that were generations ahead of his time. In addition, having one of the most accomplished teachers of music as his father as well as receiving intense training from the age of three meant that the young Mozart was able to develop musically extremely rapidly. His intense motivation to learn, perform, and compose music added to his father's desire to earn an income from showing off his young son's abilities, which resulted in the young prodigy traveling to over eighty towns and villages before the age of ten. In fact, Mozart spend around a third of his life (3,720 days) traveling, which was unheard of at the time. As well, the acclaim of performing for royalty throughout Europe meant that the young boy obviously felt special, which also would have fed his desire to become the best musician in Europe.

Possessing a range of gifts provides an important foundation from which a young performer can become musically talented. Hard work and determination are also important for the development of ability, especially for performing music. Yet, the various stereotypes of musical prodigies show many misconceptions concerning how these natural abilities flower into musical talent across time. The perception that the young performers were forced into practicing for many hours is not always the case. Many parents of these prodigious individuals report that they find it hard to keep up with their son's or daughter's efforts and feel like they are serving a facilitating role by providing the resources and attention for them to devote many hours to their practice.

Another stereotype is that young prodigies will never realize their abilities unless they transition to learning from a master teacher. While this may have some truth, it is generally the case that the young prodigies displayed remarkable performance abilities even before entering the master teacher's studio. One of the main advantages of studying with a master teacher is that it can open doors if the teacher is well connected within the profession. Prodigies who attend the Curtis Institute of Music in Philadelphia, where many of the world's greatest prodigies have studied, receive tuition, private lessons, living expenses, and access to resources that are unheard of in any other institution. As an example, Lang Lang went from poverty in China to a full scholarship at Curtis, where he enjoyed living in an apartment that had a seven-foot Steinway Model B piano in the living room.

CONCLUSION

The above description highlights some of the more important conceptions used to explain prodigious development and the types of natural abilities and environmental forces that shape a prodigy's development. An important footnote to this information is that such rapid, precocious development is often fragile, and there are many examples of young prodigies burning out before they reach adulthood or deciding that they wish to pursue other activities. We must therefore be cognizant of the young prodigies' emotional needs and allow them opportunities to be part of the decision-making process so that they can grow up to be autonomous adults who look back on their younger musical years with pride, no matter whether they chose to pursue a musical career or decided to devote their attention to another area.

References and Further Reading

Gagné, F., & McPherson, G. E. (2016). Analyzing musical prodigiousness using Gagné's integrative model of talent development. In G. E. McPherson (Ed.), *Music Prodigies: Interpretations from Psychology, Education, Musicology and Ethnomusicology* (pp. 3–114). Oxford, UK: Oxford University Press.

McPherson, G. E. (Ed.). (2016). *Musical Prodigies: Interpretations from Psychology, Music Education, Musicology and Ethnomusicology*. Oxford, UK: Oxford University Press.

McPherson, G. E., & Williamon, A. (2016). Building gifts into musical talents. In G. E. McPherson (Ed.), *The Child as Musician: A Handbook of Musical Development* (2nd ed., pp. 340–360). Oxford, UK: Oxford University Press.

15. Prodigies in Musical Creativity

Naresh Vempala

A *prodigy* refers to someone who is typically ten years of age or under who produces creative output in a specific domain at a level that is equal to or greater than that of highly trained adult performers or practitioners within that domain. However, the definition of *prodigy* is still open to discussion. Several prodigies have graced the field of music in different genres, and many still continue to do so today. There has been a strong and continued interest among researchers in understanding the cognitive and psychological processes that differentiate musical prodigies from others.

Musical prodigies differ in many ways, but they share important characteristics that enable them to perform at a level well beyond their age. First, they have an innate ability to understand and assimilate information at an extraordinarily rapid pace, particularly from their genre of interest. This ability to acquire knowledge helps them to immensely shorten the amount of practice time typically required to build skills toward achieving a basic level of expertise. Their speed of learning is often attributed to exceptional working memory, which is sometimes domain-specific. *Working memory* refers to the retention of previous information and manipulation of new information in relation to what is already stored. A higher level of musical working memory allows prodigies to learn by trial and error, experiment with new ideas, understand the boundaries of a musical genre, and expand their musical knowledge more quickly than what is normally possible. It particularly lends itself well to the process of creative thinking.

Second, musical prodigies are driven by a strong passion for their specific genre of interest early in their lives. This passion, perhaps innate, is triggered or nurtured by a combination of cultural and environmental factors (e.g., early recognition of musical behavior in the child by parents, the child living in a musical environment with family members who are musicians). This combination of innate ability, passion, and favorable conditions for honing that passion, such as parental guidance and encouragement, allows musical prodigies to single-mindedly focus on learning the techniques, idioms, and repertoire pertaining to a music genre, potentially shaving off several years of practice, which is the norm for adult experts.

CREATIVITY AND ITS ASSESSMENT

To understand musical prodigies of composition and improvisation, we first need to know what creativity entails. Creativity is usually ascertained based on a person's ability to produce something novel or original. The product can range from an idea to an invention, and in the case of musical prodigies, it is usually a composition in the form of a score or an audio recording. People who consume this product determine its creative value. There are two broad types of consumers: (1) musicians, expert music critics, and listeners of that music genre with domain-specific knowledge, who act as gatekeepers and judge the creative value of the product by comparing it with other compositions in that domain, and (2) general listeners without specialized expertise who nonetheless popularize the product based on their preferences, which are influenced by their personal opinion and the opinions of other listeners.

To be considered creative, the composition has to represent a degree of uniqueness or originality. An important aspect of originality is novelty—something that determines the newness of a composition in comparison to other compositions within that genre. This novelty associated with a creative product is assumed to arise out of unique combinations of elements from existing knowledge sources in the producer's mind. For instance, the musician might use lesser-known elements of a genre with more common elements in uncommon ways to create something new. The musician's improvisational ability contributes to a large degree in adding to the novelty. But a more primary requirement, perhaps complementing improvisation, is the existence of broad, well-represented knowledge domains that act as schemas in the musician's mind. These schemas are flexible mental frameworks of knowledge, separated into different categories that can be reshaped by the musician based on their compositional goals.

All musical prodigies acquire significant musical knowledge and skill at a young age, but not all prodigies are highly creative. Indeed, most musical prodigies are primarily known for their abilities as performers. Creative musical prodigies begin composing from a very young age. Their early compositions usually display maturity beyond the child's age. Despite these early signs of maturity, most such prodigies do not reach their peak creative potential until roughly fifteen to seventeen years of age. It is therefore common to see this propensity to compose continue from childhood into adulthood in many prodigies. A person's musical creativity can be assessed only after they have produced a body of work. This makes the task of identifying musical prodigies in their childhood challenging.

Many creative musical prodigies have been documented from the 1800s up until today. Let us consider three different creative musical prodigies: Joey Alexander, a jazz pianist; Zakir Hussain, an Indian classical music and jazz fusion drummer; and Quinn Sullivan, a blues and pop rock guitarist.

Joey Alexander

Joey Alexander grew up in Bali, Indonesia, in a musical family. His father, Denny Sila, was an amateur musician. Joey developed an affinity for jazz from the age of six, and he began listening to several jazz albums from his father's collection. This collection included albums from artists such as Louis Armstrong, Thelonious Monk, and John Coltrane. Starting with Monk's songs, Joey learned to play several songs by ear on the piano. Noticing this ability, his father initially taught him a few lessons. Then his parents helped nurture his talent further. They encouraged him to play in jam sessions and in festivals with famous Indonesian jazz musicians. As a musical genre, jazz demands a high degree of improvisation from a performer. As such, these early jam sessions strongly helped Joey in developing his creative and compositional abilities. Joey's parents also moved closer to Jakarta, where jazz was played more actively.

From that point on, Joey's musical knowledge and career grew at a rapid pace, and he began gaining recognition from audiences worldwide. When he was eight, he was invited by UNESCO to play solo piano for the jazz pianist Herbie Hancock. A year later, at nine, Joey played at an all-ages competition in Ukraine that consisted of two hundred competitors from seventeen countries called the Monster-Jam Fest, and he won the grand prize. By age ten, he was regularly performing at jazz festivals in Jakarta and Copenhagen. A year later, after one of his performances on YouTube caught the attention of Wynton Marsalis, the artistic director of Jazz at Lincoln Center, Joey was invited to New York City to play at the Center's Rose Hall. Based on highly positive audience feedback from his performance, he was invited to play at the Jazz Foundation of America at the Apollo and the Arthur Ashe Learning Center at Gotham Hall. These experiences led his parents to relocate from Indonesia to the United States, where Joey received additional invitations to perform at major jazz festivals. Following these performances, Joey has continued to grow and mature as a musician, composer, and as a bandleader, performing at venues throughout the United States and worldwide. He has released two albums, both highlighting his creativity. His first, in 2015, at age twelve, is titled *My Favorite Things*; it received two Grammy Award nominations. His second, in 2016, is titled *Countdown*.

Zakir Hussain

Tabla player Zakir Hussain is well known in jazz, fusion, and world music circles. Although Zakir only gained worldwide fame in his adulthood, he was widely known in India as a musical prodigy. He was born in a musical family in Bombay (now Mumbai), India. His father, Alla Rakha, was a highly accomplished tabla player, who played as the drummer for the North Indian classical (i.e., Hindustani music) and world musician Ravi Shankar, among other notable classical musicians in India. North Indian classical music is essentially an improvisational form of music within a strict melodic framework, similar to jazz, where improvisation is allowed within a harmonic framework.

The tabla serves as one of the primary drum accompaniments in North Indian classical music. It is taught in one of several technical traditions, referred to as *gharanas*. It requires years of regimented practice, similar to jazz, for a practitioner to acquire the necessary level of technical expertise, where the musician has imbibed the repertoire and idioms to a point where he or she is well equipped for improvising with other musicians.

Zakir's father constantly whispered and sang tabla-based rhythmic phrases, referred to as *bol*, in Zakir's ear when he was two years old. He continued this practice until Zakir was seven years old. In later years, Zakir considered this strange form of rhythmic initiation, through his father, at such an early age as being highly influential in making rhythmic phrases seem almost second nature to him. Zakir also considered the environment he grew up in to have contributed significantly to the development of his musical intuition and creativity. This environment consisted of recorded and live music constantly being played by musicians visiting his father and practicing for concerts and through students learning from his father.

When he was seven, Zakir began a rigorous practice schedule under his father's tutelage. He also started playing in concerts at school. By the age of ten, he had already reached a level of technical proficiency that enabled him to accompany his father on tabla at several concerts with prominent Indian classical musicians. Finally, by the age of twelve, Zakir was performing as the main drummer for important classical music artists at major music concerts in India. Throughout this time, he continued to develop his creative musical skills.

Since his teenage years until today, Zakir has performed extensively in India and throughout the world while also composing and producing music in the form of solo and collaborative efforts with several jazz fusion and world music artists and bands. He has also composed and played music for various movie soundtracks. A few of his noteworthy bands and collaborators include John McLaughlin, Shakti, Mickey Hart, and Tabla Beat Science.

Quinn Sullivan

Born in New Bedford, Massachusetts, Quinn Sullivan started playing guitar at the age of three. Encouraged by his father, who was also a musician, Quinn developed a passion for blues guitar after watching a recording of the 2004 Crossroads Guitar Festival. Blues guitarist Buddy Guy's performance particularly caught Quinn's attention. A year later, at age six, Quinn appeared on *The Ellen DeGeneres Show* in the United States and played a version of the Beatles' song "Twist and Shout."

Two years later, when he was eight years old, Quinn joined his idol, Buddy Guy, on stage at the Zeiterion theater in New Bedford, Massachusetts, after meeting him backstage. That same year, he was invited by Buddy Guy to play on his album *Skin Deep*, which was nominated for a Grammy Award. Following his meeting with Buddy Guy, Quinn played at several blues venues, including prominent ones in New York City, Boston, and Chicago. One of these venues involved a performance with B. B. King. Since then, Quinn has played with his own band at major music festivals in the United States and on TV shows. He has also accompanied several famous blues and rock musicians. His exceptional creativity is evident on his three albums: his debut album, *Cyclone*, in 2011, when he was eleven years old; followed by *Getting There* in 2013; and *Midnight Highway* in 2017.

Although blues music served as a musical base, Quinn's musical endeavors reflect a mature and expanding musical repertoire spanning pop and rock music while not being limited to blues alone.

CONCLUSION

The three musical prodigies described came from very different sociocultural backgrounds. They also differed in their instrument of choice. Yet, there are strong commonalities between them. All three musicians discovered their passion for music, for a particular genre, and for a particular instrument at an early age. There may be some debate about how much of this discovery was based on their natural inclination and how much was through an external influence, such as a parent or family member, but they enjoyed this passion enough to focus single-mindedly on perfecting it. They were able to work on their passion in favorable conditions enabled through parental guidance and encouragement.

They worked hard at acquiring knowledge of musical creativity and were able to reach a level of creative expertise that was equal to or better than that of adult musicians working in the same area of music. All three prodigies were provided with opportunities to collaborate with other musicians, and they actively utilized these collaboration opportunities to hone their creative abilities. These opportunities allowed them to experiment with their ideas in functional settings and to understand limitations as well as possibilities for expansion of their creative vocabulary with their instruments and genres.

References and Further Reading
Koestler, A. (1964). *The Act of Creation*. New York, NY: Penguin Books.
McPherson, G. E. (Ed.). (2016). *Musical Prodigies: Interpretation from Psychology, Education, Musicology, and Ethnomusicology*. Oxford, UK: Oxford University Press.
Ruthsatz, J., & Detterman, D. K. (2003). An extraordinary memory: The case study of a musical prodigy. *Intelligence, 31*, 509–518. http://doi:10.1016/S0160-2896(03)000 50-3

16. Musical Savants

Adam Ockelford

Savants are people who have extraordinary abilities despite their learning difficulties. They are almost always on the autism spectrum. Savants' talents include art, sculpture, mathematics, calendrical calculation (knowing which day of the week a particular date falls on), and music. Most savants have one special ability, but some have two or three types.

The label *savant* was introduced by J. Langdon Down in late nineteenth-century England. He used it in conjunction with the term *idiot*, which at the time did not have the negative connections that it has today. It was just a medical term used to describe someone with a low level of intellectual functioning. He took the word *savant* from the French, where it means a "wise or clever person." Hence, an *idiot savant* was a fool who was nonetheless talented.

A century later, the American psychiatrist Darold Treffert coined the term *savant syndrome*, which is more acceptable to modern ears. He distinguished between *talented savants*, whose skills are remarkable in the context of their disability, and the much rarer *prodigious savants*, whose brilliance is spectacular by any standards. It is not known how many savants there are in the world, although it has been estimated that around 10 percent of people on the autism spectrum have some type of special skill. Truly prodigious savants, whose prevalence we can only guess from their public exposure, probably number less than one hundred: that is, around one in seventy million. In line with the autism population more generally, savants tend to be male.

MUSICAL SAVANTS

Music is the most common savant skill—estimated to be the special focus of around two-thirds of those with savant syndrome. Musical savants usually play the piano (although other instruments are possible) and are self-taught, at least in the early stages, learning to play by ear: that is, just by listening and copying what they hear. Savants are able to do this because they have what musicians call *perfect pitch*, or *absolute pitch* (AP), as psychologists refer to it. This means that they can remember what all the notes on an instrument sound like. To someone with AP, every tone does not just sound somewhat high or low but has a distinct character of being C, B-flat, F-sharp, or whatever. To play a piece of music that they have heard, savants merely have to recall the sequence of notes, whose names they know, and find them on their instrument, which, with practice, they are able to do well and very quickly.

AP helps savants to memorize music, which they find much easier to do than most of us. They can often recall hundreds or even thousands of pieces effortlessly. However, they are not just "human iPods"; musical savants can often improvise on the music they hear (like jazz musicians do), and some can compose completely new pieces.

Having AP is *necessary* to becoming a savant, but it is not on its own *sufficient*. No matter how good your musical ear is, there is no shortcut to the countless hours of practice that are required to become technically proficient on an instrument. It has been estimated that becoming a professional musician takes around ten thousand hours of practice, and savants are no different. The remarkable thing is that they will typically play their instrument of choice for many hours each day; indeed, they may become obsessed with it. It is this deep-seated, unshakable interest that drives the development of savant skills.

EXAMPLES OF SAVANTS

Although the term *savant* is an appropriate one to use to describe people who have exceptional abilities in the context of learning difficulties, in reality, the people concerned are just as diverse as the rest of us. To get a sense of the breadth of the musical savant population, five thumbnail sketches of them as children are presented below. Like the majority of musical savants, they are blind.

Savant A

Savant A (S-A) is a twelve-year-old boy with an eye condition called Leber congenital amaurosis (LCA), a rare genetic condition that can cause visual impairment and, in S-A's case, blindness. He has moderate learning difficulties, with a verbal IQ of 75, and he displays many of the characteristics of autism, including impairments in social interaction and communication and a restricted area of interest, being almost wholly preoccupied with music—an obsession that began as a baby.

S-A has universal AP (meaning that he recognizes the pitches of everyday sounds as well as those of musical instruments and the human voice). Tests have shown that he can hear the notes that make up large musical chords with ease. So when an orchestra plays, for example, he knows what each of the instruments is playing.

S-A plays the piano, recorder, clarinet, saxophone, and drum kit. He was initially self-taught on the keyboard at the age of three, but tuition is increasingly helping him with the technical requirements of the other instruments. The levels of his saxophone and kit playing are of a sufficient standard for him to have learned and performed a version of Dave Brubeck's *Take Five* by ear after listening a few times to an original recording that included extended solos for the drum kit and saxophone. S-A then recorded the piece himself, playing both the kit and saxophone parts by overdubbing—a significant achievement given the rhythmic complexities that are involved. The performance is musically persuasive, even though it never moves beyond the "feel" of the original.

S-A's memory is exceptional. For example, he was able to learn the first of Debussy's *Arabesques* for piano by listening to the music being played a page at a time. However, S-A finds it difficult to reproduce what he hears in his head on the keyboard, where his efforts tend to be rather uncoordinated. Hence, having memorized the *Arabesque* in a short space of time, he then spent weeks practicing it from memory and was never able to achieve (for him) a satisfactory standard of performance. In addition to his performance skills, S-A enjoys improvising and composing in a range of popular and classical styles. He has a rudimentary knowledge of music theory and terminology, although he cannot read music (which could potentially be available to him in Braille).

Savant B

Savant B (S-B) is a ten-year-old girl. She was born preterm in a hospital in South Korea but now lives in the United Kingdom. S-B has retinopathy of prematurity (RoP)—a form of severe visual impairment that affects some premature babies. Her verbal IQ is estimated at 65, and she has a diagnosis of autism spectrum disorder. Her capacity to understand and use language—both English and Korean—is limited. S-B has universal AP and, like S-A, can hear the notes that are played in large chords precisely and quickly.

S-B plays one instrument, the piano, which she started to teach herself when given access to an instrument at age four, having been obsessively interested in listening to music. She now has weekly lessons with a teacher experienced in working with visually impaired children. She learns entirely by ear and has memorized a number of pieces from the Western classical tradition. She plays with a limited range of expression, which appears to emulate that of her teacher. S-B also enjoys playing popular music with fellow Korean expatriates in a band, where she supplies the harmonies on a keyboard. These she picks up with apparent ease by listening to the other musicians play the songs through once or twice.

Savant C

Savant C (S-C) is a nine-year-old girl. She has septo-optic dysplasia (SOD), a rare genetic condition that causes developmental anomalies in the midline of the brain. As a result, S-C is totally blind, and she has been under psychiatric care since the age of seven to help alleviate some of the effects of her autism. She has a verbal IQ of 75 and is classified as having moderate learning difficulties.

Although she has mastered the mechanics of reading and writing Braille, S-C's comprehension of language is patchy. She has low muscle tone, and this affects her capacity to play instruments. Nonetheless, tests undertaken as a young adult show that she can reproduce four-note chords with ease on the piano by using her universal AP ability.

S-C's primary avenue of musical performance is her voice. Having shown an early fascination with music, S-C sang when she was very young with an unusual purity of sound, a characteristic that has recently been encouraged through voice lessons. Her repertoire, in the soprano register, largely comprises light and popular music and songs from shows, which she learns by listening to commercially available recordings. She has an uncanny ability to emulate the expressivity of professional performers by imitating their use of vibrato, crescendos and diminuendos, and rubato. She has sung in a number of high-profile charity events in London, and she enjoys the public appreciation of her talents.

Savant D

Savant D (S-D) is an eleven-year-old boy. He was born prematurely at twenty-five weeks. S-D is blind and has severe learning difficulties, with a verbal IQ of 58, and a diagnosis of autism. His grasp of language is limited, and his conversations tend to circle around a limited number of topics pertaining to everyday matters, using speech that is often highly repetitive. S-D has universal AP, and tests show that he can hear and reproduce nine-note chords with 93 percent accuracy on the piano.

S-D taught himself to play a small keyboard when he was two, having been captivated by his nanny's singing, and by the time he was four, he was getting to grips with pieces of some melodic and harmonic complexity on the piano, such as *Smoke Gets in Your Eyes*, Beethoven's *Für Elise*, and Chopin's *Raindrop Prelude*. His technique was idiosyncratic, involving the flats of his hands, karate chops, and even the occasional use of the elbow to enable him to hit notes that would otherwise have been beyond the span of his small hands. S-D's musical ability was noticed at this time by a specialist teacher, who introduced a program of daily musical tuition, involving, among other things, technical exercises in every key, which S-D came to relish.

S-D's favorite genres are light music of the twentieth century, jazz, and pop, although he also has an extensive repertoire of classical pieces, which he performs with gusto, unhampered by concerns of being true to the composer's intentions. He learns all pieces by ear, fluently, and can play them in every key. S-D generally learns new material by listening to it repeatedly over a period of a week or more. During this time, renditions of pieces gradually come into focus: S-D's version eventually becomes almost entirely faithful to the original before serving as a

Photo 16.1 Derek Paravicini. (Photo used by permission of Nic Paravicini)

framework for subsequent improvisation. Here, he can display creativity and even wit as different styles are merged. S-D has not composed original pieces, however. His knowledge of music theory is limited to the names of notes and those of simple chords, and he is unable to read Braille music.

The level of S-D's special abilities can be gauged by the fact that he has appeared with jazz bands and orchestras in international venues such as the Barbican Centre, London (see photo 16.1), and has been featured in the media all over the world.

Savant E

Savant E (S-E) is a five-year-old boy with LCA. He had access to a piano from the age of twelve months, and by twenty-four months, he had taught himself to play simple tunes with simple left-hand parts—always in the appropriate key. S-E is blind and has autism spectrum disorder and severe learning difficulties. He has little meaningful expressive language. Tests show that he can hear six-note chords with ease.

S-E plays the piano on his terms and is reluctant to share his music making with others. He has a natural dexterity and fluency at the keyboard, although he is not yet at the stage of wanting to engage with any form of technical exercises. S-E tends to play fragments of music that he has heard rather than complete pieces from beginning to end. A favorite is the *Rondo alla Turca* by Mozart. He can transpose freely, and he improvises on familiar tunes by adding extra melody notes or changing the harmonies.

TEACHING SAVANTS

It can be very challenging to teach savants because they are invariably autodidactic to begin with: that is, they teach themselves. Moreover, they learn music in a holistic way: rather than breaking a new piece into manageable chunks, which is what most musicians do, they tend to prefer learning things all at once. Gradually, through repeated hearings of a piece and attempts at playing it, details are corrected until a complete rendition takes shape. So, for a savant, learning a new piece is more like a picture gradually coming into focus than a jigsaw being built up from lots of separate tiny components. It is difficult for a teacher to intervene in this process of intuitive learning, although it can be done with patience. Sometimes the relationship between a savant and a teacher can be very special, and it can help with wider issues of developing social skills and empathy, which people on the autism spectrum can find problematic.

CONCLUSION

Savants make up an exceptional group of musicians, whose advanced skills develop in the context of autism and learning difficulties—and, very often, blindness or visual impairment as well. These three difficulties in combination cause the brain to wire itself up differently when a child is very young and can lead to children developing an obsessive early interest in sound and music. In around 40 percent of cases, this leads to the acquisition of AP. Given access to a musical instrument (typically the keyboard), AP is a *necessary* condition, although it is not in itself *sufficient* to drive the self-directed learning that is characteristic of savants. In terms of the way they hear things, savants seem to develop similar listening strategies to nonautistic prodigies. However, the challenges caused by autism spectrum disorder and learning difficulties mean that they are likely to develop an intuitive understanding of music but will not be able to cope with the specialized language that musicians often use nor be able to read or write music. This in turn means that many teachers will need to adopt a child-centered approach. With the right support, though, musical savants can thrive in the world of music making just as well as other prodigies do.

References and Further Reading

Cameron, C. (1998). *The Music of Light: The Extraordinary Story of Hikari and Kenzaburo Oe*. New York, NY: Free Press.

Lewis, C. (2008). *Rex: A Mother, Her Autistic Child, and the Music That Transformed Their Lives*. Nashville, TN: Thomas Nelson.

Miller, L. (1989). *Musical Savants: Exceptional Skill in the Mentally Retarded*. Hillsdale, NJ: Lawrence Erlbaum Associates.

Ockelford, A. (2007). *In the Key of Genius: The Extraordinary Life of Derek Paravicini*. London, UK: Arrow Books.

Treffert, D. (2006). *Extraordinary People: Understanding Savant Syndrome* (3rd ed.). Lincoln, NE: iUniverse.

Music and the Brain

17. Contemporary Approaches to the Neuroscience of Music

Karli M. Nave and Erin E. Hannon

You may not realize it, but you know a lot about music, even if you have never had a single music lesson. Music can make you feel sad or happy, it can make you want to move, and it can provide comfort when you feel lonely. When you listen to music you like, you probably find yourself tapping or swaying to the beat. Or when you overhear someone singing, you can tell when they hit a wrong note, even if it is a song you have never heard until that moment. How are you able to do that? Most people know when events are surprising or do not make sense in the context of the music. As soon as complex sound waves enter the ear, the brain begins interpreting them, oftentimes without the listener even being aware that it is happening.

Scientists are still trying to figure out what occurs in the human brain during musical experiences. Recent advances in neuroscience techniques make it possible to examine where in the brain different types of musical responses occur, when they occur, and perhaps even how music is related or unrelated to other aspects of our experience. For example, by studying the brain, scientists can ask whether there are dedicated areas of the brain for processing music. They can also ask whether or not music and language are completely separate in the brain or whether they share some neural circuitry. Have you ever thought about how you know the difference between when someone is singing and when someone is talking? Both singing and speaking are defined by patterns of pitch and rhythm in the human voice; yet, you probably do not usually stop to ask yourself whether someone is speaking or singing. How do you do this? To begin to address questions such as this one, researchers can compare and contrast the way the brain responds to music and to language.

LESION STUDIES

One of the oldest approaches to the neuroscience of music is to study people who have brain lesions. A brain lesion is a region in the brain that has been damaged due to injury or disease. Brain lesions usually occur because of a tumor or a stroke, or they are created on purpose as a part of treatment for a psychological disorder, such as epilepsy. If scientists know the location of a brain lesion, they can compare how a person with such a lesion differs from a person without a lesion. If individuals with brain lesions are worse at a particular ability (such as recognizing a song), it suggests that the damaged area is critical for that ability.

Remember the question about whether music and language are separate? One way to address this question is to see whether people who have damage to language areas of the brain show impaired music abilities. One example of this is Wernicke's area, a part of the brain that, when damaged, tends to result in difficulty understanding language and speaking coherently. If this area of the brain is also responsible for music processing, then people with damage to this area should have trouble with both language and music. However, if this area is not necessary for music, then lesions to this area should impair language but not music. Studies have found that while damage to Wernicke's area usually results in difficulty understanding speech, in most cases, music is spared. In fact, there are two famous examples of a professional pianist with damage to Wernicke's area who could still read music and play the piano as well as a composer who could still create new pieces of music, even though both patients had severe language impairments.

Another way to answer this question is to see whether people with damage to areas involved in music perception also show language impairments. For example, a patient who suffered a stroke had a brain lesion in the left auditory cortex (the brain region responsible for processing sounds), in Heschl's gyrus and the planum temporale, which are specific areas in the auditory cortex. Interestingly, although the patient could still comprehend language, she had severe music perception deficits and was unable to tell two different melodies apart. These findings suggest that, at least to some degree, music is separate from language in the brain.

Brain lesion studies have also revealed that music is not simply processed in one area of the brain. Take the woman from the previous example who had damage to her left auditory cortex and had trouble telling whether two different melodies were different. Interestingly, while she could not distinguish between two different melodies, she could tell whether the songs were happy or sad. This suggests that recognizing a melodic pattern may rely on a different group of brain areas than those involved in recognizing musical emotion. Lesion studies also suggest that many different brain areas on both the left and right sides, or hemispheres, of the brain have various roles in music processing. For example, people who have lesions in both the left and right mesial temporal lobe (important for memory) have trouble learning to play new melodies, but patients with lesions in just the right mesial temporal lobe only have trouble memorizing music, although they can still able to play new melodies if they are given the sheet music to read. These results fit with the idea that music perception engages a complex network of brain areas involved in music perception.

These brain lesion studies provide crucial evidence of at least some of the areas in the brain where music is processed (e.g., the temporal lobe) and also where it is probably not processed (e.g., Wernicke's area). However, this approach is limited only to individuals who have already suffered damage to their brain, and researchers have no control over the extent and specific location of the damage. Because it is not ethical to purposefully damage a person's brain to see how the damage will affect their music perception, researchers use other neuroscience techniques to study responses to music in healthy brains.

FUNCTIONAL MAGNETIC RESONANCE IMAGING (fMRI)

One powerful technique for understanding music psychology is functional magnetic resonance imaging (fMRI). This technique uses a large magnet surrounding the skull to measure blood-oxygen-level-dependent (BOLD) responses in the brain. When neurons (e.g., brain cells) in a particular brain region become active, they need energy, which is supplied via oxygen in the blood. Thus, when a particular brain area is active, blood oxygen levels in that area increase. Researchers can measure BOLD levels while a person listens to music, allowing the researcher to examine how different brain areas are involved in various aspects of music cognition. Unlike lesion studies, which depend on prior damage to the brain area of interest, fMRI can be used to measure brain functioning in healthy individuals.

Based on the brain lesion studies, you might expect that fMRI would reveal increased activation in the auditory cortex when people listen to music, but one of the major insights from recent fMRI research is that there is actually a complex network of brain areas involved in processing music, extending well beyond auditory cortex to all over the brain. This research suggests that distinct areas of the brain are active when listeners are focusing on different aspects of music, such as pitch (degree of highness or lowness of a tone), harmonic chords (simultaneous musical notes, generally producing a pleasing feeling), and key (the group of pitches or scale that form the basis for a song or composition). For example, when listeners are focused on pitch, harmonic chords, or key, there is enhanced activation in the frontal regions of the brain responsible for decision-making and paying attention as well as the thalamic regions, which act as a relay center for motor and sensory information. Similar areas of the brain are active when people hear mistakes in chord sequences and in grammar, suggesting that musical and language rules may rely on the same or similar processes in the brain.

Other studies show that emotional areas of the brain respond to the emotional tone of musical chords. For example, minor chords are what you typically hear in the soundtrack of a scary movie or in a sad song, and major chords are usually used in happy, joyful music. Therefore, it is perhaps not surprising that when people listen to minor chords, their brains show more activation in the amygdala, a brain area that is usually active when people hear or see fearful sounds or images. Similarly, when people listen to music they like, they activate areas of their brain involved in expectation of a reward.

Another important discovery is that music can activate parts of the brain that control movement, which could explain why humans sometimes feel such a strong desire to move when they listen to music with a good beat. Rhythm is any pattern of durations that form a sequence of musical notes. When you hear a rhythm, you often perceive a steady beat that corresponds to those repeating points in time when you would move your feet or your body. The fMRI research has shown that motor areas of the brain are active when participants are simply making judgments about heard rhythmic patterns (such as whether two rhythms are the same or different), especially when the rhythms have a good beat. Importantly, even when people are not moving or preparing to move, increased activity is seen in the supplementary motor area (responsible for preparing to move) and basal ganglia (responsible for motor control). Some propose that there is a network of brain regions, including both the motor and the auditory cortex, that work together to allow people to perceive musical rhythm and beat as well as to dance along to the music.

Without neuroimaging studies using fMRI, scientists would have never discovered the vast network of brain areas involved in music processing. Although fMRI is a very useful tool for studying music psychology, it also has its limitations. On a practical level, fMRI is very expensive to use. In addition, because BOLD responses take a long time to occur in the brain (two or more seconds), fMRI does not allow researchers to ask questions about the responses that occur on a fast time scale (i.e., milliseconds). For example, if a researcher wanted to examine the immediate brain response to a wrong note in a piece of music, fMRI would not be ideal because the response would not show for two seconds. Fortunately, there are other neuroscience techniques that are well suited for examining more immediate brain responses to music.

ELECTROENCEPHALOGRAPHY (EEG) AND MAGNETOENCEPHALOGRAPHY (MEG)

While the BOLD response can tell researchers about the location of activity in the brain, it is an indirect measure of the brain activity itself. This is because the fMRI technique makes the assumption that blood flow is related to neurons firing in the brain. When neurons are active, they operate by sending signals to neighboring neurons through action potentials. In this way, information can be sent from one brain region to another. When action potentials are sent down a pathway of neurons, they give off an electric current. This electric current can be measured at the surface of the scalp using electroencephalography (EEG).

Because EEG is measuring electrical activity directly, it provides precise information about exactly when a brain response occurs. This means that researchers can use it to look at event-related potentials (ERPs). An ERP response can be measured immediately after an event, such as a wrong note. For example, research has shown that a wrong note will produce a larger electrical response than a correct note. This is true whether the note is wrong because it was the wrong pitch or because it happened at the wrong time (e.g., wrong rhythm). This violation of expectation response is shown even when the listener is not paying attention to the music, which makes it possible to measure this response in listeners who are not good at focusing their attention, such as babies or young children. Even newborns show an ERP response to wrong notes in music. The timing of different ERPs can also shed light on the neural processes involved in a complex ability. For example, a wrong note may elicit an earlier response than a wrong chord, which suggests that distinct underlying neural processes are involved in pitch and harmony perception. EEG is much less expensive than fMRI, making it a somewhat more accessible tool for music neuroscience. Because it has very good timing precision and reflects when responses occur, it is ideal for studying musical rhythm. It is not as well suited to detect where in the brain the electrical signal is coming from.

Neuron activity also generates a magnetic field. Consider a magnet: one side is positive, and the other side is negative. Now imagine that you have a single pathway full of neurons. At any given time, the information being sent down the pathway is being transmitted from one neuron to the next neuron. As a neuron passes a message, it becomes the "negative" side of the magnet, and the neuron receiving the message becomes the "positive" side of the magnet. In this way, the electrical activity is creating what is called a *dipole* (a component with a positive and a negative pole separated by a given distance). These dipoles create a magnetic field, which can be measured using magnetoencephalography (MEG). MEG uses sensitive magnetometers surrounding the scalp to measure brain activity. Compared to EEG, with MEG, it is somewhat easier to determine the source of the brain activity being measured.

In music psychology, MEG has been used to investigate not only the timing mechanisms involved in processing music but also the areas of the brain involved. In such research, MEG has been used to determine where violation of expectation responses occur in the brain. For example, while deviations to memorized lyrics cause a larger response in the left hemisphere of the brain, deviations to expected musical notes generate a larger response in the right hemisphere of the brain. MEG studies have also shown that the power (amount of brain activity) of the brain response can match the rhythmic pattern the listener is hearing. MEG provides more information about location of these brain signals than EEG, but it is still less spatially precise than fMRI and more expensive than EEG.

CONCLUSION

Scientists are still just beginning to understand how the brain works, so much is yet to be discovered about how the brain gives rise to musical experiences, feelings, and responses. Research using the combination of different neuroscience approaches described here has revealed a complex network of brain areas involved in musical experience, from areas that respond to sound, to areas that process fear and reward, to areas that govern people's movements. Because music is a complex and meaningful part of the human experience, it provides a good model for studying more general questions about brain organization in other domains of experience. Moreover, by understanding how music is processed in the brains of typical healthy people, music can also be used to better understand what goes wrong when people suffer from brain injuries or disorders. As researchers continue to employ a combination of the approaches discussed here, new neuroscience techniques will continue to develop and enrich the neuroscience of music.

References and Further Reading

Koelsch, S. (2014). Brain correlates of music-evoked emotions. *Nature Reviews Neuroscience, 15*, 170–180.

Patel, A. D. (2007). *Music, Language, and the Brain.* New York, NY: Oxford University Press.

Peretz, I., & Zatorre, R. J. (Eds.). (2003). *The Cognitive Neuroscience of Music.* Oxford, UK: Oxford University Press.

Zatorre, R. J., Chen, J. L., & Penhune, V. B. (2007). When the brain plays music: Auditory-motor interactions in music perception and production. *Nature Reviews Neuroscience, 8*, 547–558.

18. Music and the Brain across the Life Span

Frini Karayanidis, Michelle Kelly, and Michael Nilsson

We used to believe that the human brain developed from infancy up until adulthood but then stopped changing. Although some of the brain's capabilities can decline in older age, we now know that the brain can continue to develop new neural connections throughout our lives. There are countless older adults who show that we are never too old to learn. For example, at ninety-one years, Colette Bourlier was awarded a PhD from the University of Fanche-Compte, France, and at ninety-nine years, Leo Plass graduated from Eastern Oregon University.

THE EVER-CHANGING BRAIN

How does the brain work to accomplish such impressive outcomes? Scientists used to believe that the brain was like a computer that works in a step-by-step way, collecting input from our senses (e.g., sight, hearing), interpreting this input, and generating an appropriate response. For example, the brain might use the visual input from seeing a wallet on the ground to generate a set of thoughts and responses, such as picking it up and looking for its owner. However, new techniques of studying the brain have cast doubts on this stage model of the brain. We now know that the brain works in more complicated ways, with many brain regions working simultaneously and cooperatively through *distributed neural networks* that develop and are continuously refined with each new experience in our lives.

Modern brain imaging techniques, such as functional magnetic resonance imaging (fMRI) and electroencephalography (EEG), are used to identify the areas of the brain that are activated when we complete a task and the moment-by-moment changes in this activity (down to the order of milliseconds (one thousandth of a second)). With the help of these methods, researchers have identified a number of distributed neural networks and characterized how their synchronized activity helps us make sense of information coming into our brain through different senses. For example, when playing the violin in an orchestra, we use our sense of vision (primary visual cortex) to read the music and follow the conductor; we process auditory (primary auditory cortex) information coming from our own playing and from other members in the orchestra; we process haptic (primary somatosensory cortex) information arising from our own hands; and we issue motor commands (motor cortex) to position our fingers correctly and play the right notes. To make music, we need to put together these multiple sources of information and rely on prior learning (for example, how notes on the page correspond to keys on the piano and the sound they produce) to translate this information into our own actions. This prior learning shapes our brain over time and reshapes it with further experience, a process referred to as *neuroplasticity*.

This new realization of the brain as a dynamic organ that changes structure and function throughout our life span has led to an explosion of research seeking to understand how complex activities, such as mastering a musical instrument, are enabled by the brain's *architecture*, its structural and functional organization. In turn, we are beginning to understand how musical expertise brings about immediate as well as long-lasting benefits to the brain. Both active (e.g., playing an instrument, singing, or musical improvisation) and receptive (e.g., music listening) music-based interventions strengthen neural connectivity and induce changes in the brain's gray and white matter in different brain regions. These changes provide benefits that extend into other areas of learning and in social interactions. For example, children involved in musical learning often perform better at core subjects at school (especially mathematics) and show better self-control and emotion regulation than other children their age. Musical expertise can also produce long-lasting neuroprotection; that is, music can protect the brain against the wear and tear of aging and delay the onset of dementia.

HOW DOES THE BRAIN PROCESS AND PRODUCE MUSIC?

Anyone who has learned to read music and play a musical instrument will tell you that it is very demanding. To read music from a score, one must rapidly read complex visual symbols (musical notes) and translate them into a specific set of motor responses, depending on the specific type of musical instrument. For instance, the same symbol on a staff may be translated into pressing one or more keys on a keyboard, maneuvering fingers across strings on the violin, or coordinating breath and finger positions on a flute. Although we continuously complete this process of translating visual input to motor action (feedforward processing from sensory to motor), we also use the higher-order cognitive centers of our brain to control the quality of playing and the tone of the music through a system of feedback loops (see Figure 18.1). For example, we monitor the sound we are producing, identify and correct our errors, retrieve from memory or read ahead the

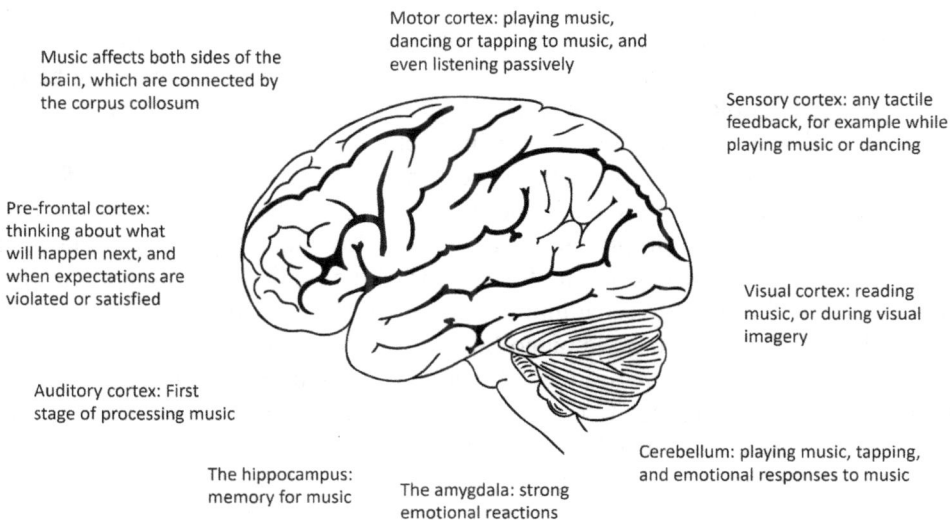

Figure 18.1 Music Processing Is Distributed Throughout Many Brain Areas That Are Organized into Networks.

upcoming notes, respond to visual cues by the conductor, and adapt our timing based on the notes played by other musicians.

These complex processes are enabled by brain networks that connect different areas of the brain with each other. For example, anterior (frontal) brain areas are connected to posterior (e.g., parietal, temporal) brain areas, motor areas of the brain, and subcortical areas (deeper brain regions). These brain *networks*, and the cognitive functions that they support, develop from infancy through childhood and adolescence, reach full maturity in young adulthood, and progressively deteriorate in old age. Although the development of these brain networks is to some degree genetically programmed, the precise pattern and level of maturation of different networks varies between people, depending on their experiences. That is, every opportunity that we have to experience new learning in everyday life (e.g., playing in a band, visiting new countries) influences how brain regions develop and are connected to one another.

MUSIC CHANGES THE BRAIN

Any new learning experience, such as learning a musical instrument, can change brain structure (e.g., the thickness of the gray matter of specific brain structures and the white matter fibers that connect them) and brain function through processes we refer to as *neuroplasticity*. In fact, much of the evidence for neuroplasticity across the life span has come from research examining the effects of music learning on the brain's structure and function. Many scientists now believe that long-term training in music results in core differences in brain architecture, depending on the type of instrument, the age of onset of musical training, and the level of practice across the life span. Moreover, older musicians tend to show better cognitive aging than nonmusicians, suggesting that these changes in brain structure and function protect the brain against wear and tear. However, much of this evidence is correlational because musicians and nonmusicians often differ from each other in other ways. For example, people with extensive music training tend to come from families with higher income, have more education, and perform better at school than people without music training. Nonetheless, as we know that short-term musical training can change the brain's architecture, it is reasonable to assume that long-term intensive training in music is at least partially responsible for the aging-related neuroprotection differences between musicians and nonmusicians.

Even short periods of practicing a musical instrument produce structural changes in specific sensory and motor regions of the brain. For example, the size of areas in the motor cortex that map to individual fingers increases in both brain hemispheres when learning the piano but only in the hemisphere opposite to the hand used to manipulate strings when learning the violin. Although we still do not know exactly how long the effects of short periods of musical training last, we do know that professional musicians have more gray matter volume in sensory and motor areas that are relevant to playing their specific instrument.

More importantly, compared to nonmusicians, professional musicians have greater cortical volume in areas of the brain that are involved in higher-order cognitive functions, including the premotor cortex and the cerebellum (areas involved in planning, preparing, executing, and controlling sequential finger movements), the superior parietal brain (areas that support the integration of information coming from different senses and that guide sequences of movements through their connections with the premotor cortex), and the inferior temporal and ventral prefrontal cortices (areas that translate continuous visual input into motor actions, such as reading into speech). These structural effects are more pronounced in professional than in amateur musicians, suggesting that they are modified by the amount of practice.

Musical practice changes not only the structure of cortical areas but also the strength of the white matter pathways that connect them. The microstructural organization of the brain's white matter (the connections between brain areas) differs between musicians and nonmusicians, and these connections become stronger with more hours of practice in skilled musicians. Differences in the strength of white matter tracts have been shown in the corpus callosum (a thick set of fibers that connects and transfers information between hemispheres), the corticospinal tract (a pathway that transforms motor commands to physical action), and long fiber tracts that transfer information from sensory to association areas (feedforward pathways) and back again (feedback pathways).

These changes in brain structure are accompanied by changes in the way that musicians' brains process information. Musicians' brains are more sensitive to musical sounds, especially sounds that are produced by their class of instrument. That is, pianists' brains show a greater neural response to piano music than to string music, whereas violinists' brains respond more to string than piano music. In fact, even the brains of nonmusicians show some changes in how they process music after only minimal training.

In one study, a group of nonmusicians was trained to play simple piano melodies, and a second control group listened to recordings of these training sessions and identified errors. After training, the groups were tested on their ability to identify errors in pitch and timing in a series of sounds. The group that practiced the piano identified more errors and had stronger brain responses than the control group that just listened to the training sessions. In another study, nonmusicians were trained to play a familiar simple melody and then their brain responses were recorded while they listened to this same trained melody, or to a different one. The motor networks of the brain showed greater activity when listening to the trained melody as compared to the untrained melody. So, listening to a trained melody activated not only brain areas associated with auditory perception but also the motor networks that had been trained to form these new sound-action associations.

In fact, when highly skilled musicians visualize a well-practiced musical piece (that is, listen to it in their head and try to visualize themselves playing it), fMRI scans show that their brains activate the same visual, auditory, and motor planning areas that are activated when they actually perform that piece. These findings show that the brain networks that help us to play a musical instrument are also activated when we are merely listening to that music or even when we are just imagining it.

EARLY MUSIC MAKING MAY ENRICH BRAIN DEVELOPMENT, COGNITIVE PROCESSES, AND SOCIAL SKILLS

It is hardly surprising that music training can change the function and sensitivity of visual, auditory, and motor areas that are directly involved in music. What is surprising and exciting, however, is that musical training may also improve brain functions that are not directly involved in playing or listening to music. General cognitive skills, such as thinking, reading, math, and attention, all seem to improve in children who take music lessons. Some studies show that early musical training improves early reading skills in prekindergarten children. In addition, children who take music or drama lessons have more developed understanding of emotional prosody, the tone of voice that expresses the emotional content of the speech, and this advantage extends into adulthood. These findings are extremely promising, but we need to be cautious. It is not clear whether these benefits are directly related to the musical training or to the fact that these children are engaged in organized learning activities that are personally and socially rewarding. More work is needed to differentiate between the benefits of music learning and the broader benefits derived from engaging in motivating experiences.

MUSIC MAY PROTECT THE AGING BRAIN

Given that music training is associated with better thinking abilities in children and produces changes in the structure and function of the adult brain, it stands to reason that music may protect the brain in older age. As our body ages, so does our brain, resulting in less efficient sight, hearing, memory, and problem-solving. Age-related hearing decline is especially important. Many older people find it difficult to understand speech, especially in noisy environments, and this often leads to avoidance of social gatherings and, eventually, social isolation. In fact, hearing loss in midlife is the strongest single predictor of dementia in old age, so maintaining healthy auditory processing into old age may help to delay the onset of dementia.

Lifetime musical instrument playing can protect parts of the brain that are responsible for processing auditory information from the effects of aging. For instance, whereas language skills usually decline with increasing age, older musicians can process speech as quickly as younger listeners. In fact, sustained musical training has been shown to protect the structure and function of frontal brain areas that are involved in problem-solving, planning, and flexible thinking, and to facilitate new neuroplasticity in old age.

CONCLUSION

The human brain changes and develops throughout the life span as we become exposed to complex experiences, such as playing a musical instrument. Music learning produces changes in the structure and function of brain areas that are specific to the type of musical training a musician has experienced. It is possible that musical training benefits the brain not only while you are actually practicing or playing music but also when you are passively listening to music or just imagining it. Musicians' brains are more sensitive to musical sounds. Scientific evidence suggests that musical training can also improve general functions, such as complex thought processes, attention, and short-term memory. These benefits have been shown to occur in childhood, young adults, and old age. However, the existing evidence mainly comes from comparing musicians and nonmusicians (who as a group differ from each other in many ways) or from the results of short-term music training programs. To establish that musical training produces long-term beneficial effects in brain development, aging, and recovery from trauma, we need to run systematic longitudinal studies that measure differences in brain and cognition between musicians and nonmusicians over long periods of time. Finally, as the brain remains "plastic," or changeable, throughout life, taking up an instrument in older adulthood may be an effective, enjoyable, and nonmedicalized way to protect the aging brain or even reverse early age-related damage.

References and Further Reading
Doidge, N. (2007). *The Brain That Changes Itself: Stories of Personal Triumph from the Frontiers of Brain Science*. New York, NY: Viking.

Levitin, D. (2020). *This Is Your Brain on Music*. New York, NY: Plume.

Särkämö T. (2018). Music for the ageing brain: Cognitive, emotional, social, and neural benefits of musical leisure activities in stroke and dementia. *Dementia*, *17*(6), 670–685. https://doi.org/10.1177/1471301217729237

19. Tone Deafness

Barbara Tillmann and Anne Caclin

Do you know someone who cannot sing in tune, who cannot detect wrong notes when someone else sings or plays music, or who has difficulties recognizing a familiar tune without lyrics? This person may have a condition known as *tone deafness*, a deficit in music perception (resulting from impaired processing of pitch, rhythm, etc.) and production (e.g., singing). It is thus distinct from the more frequent phenomenon of "bad singing," where only production is affected but not perception. An alternative terminology refers to this phenomenon as *amusia*. This labeling indicates that there is a problem with "music" in a way similar to the terminology of *aphasia* or *apraxia* (indicating a deficit with language or movement, respectively).

Being tone-deaf, or amusic, can be caused by lesions in the brain following a stroke or brain injury; this is then referred to as *acquired amusia*, meaning that the person did not have difficulties in music processing before the accident that damaged the brain. It can also be a secondary deficit in other pathologies, such as in patients with aphasia. Studying acquired amusia can inform us about involved brain regions, potential associations between deficits, and potential dissociations. Double dissociations are particularly interesting. For example, one patient shows a deficit in music processing but intact language processing, while another patient shows the reverse pattern, that is, a deficit in language processing but intact music processing. This can also be observed for the processing of specific musical features, such as rhythm, meter, pitch, timbre, and the like. However, cases of pure double dissociation are rather rare, and patients most often show combined deficits.

In contrast to acquired amusia, tone deafness can also exist since birth, and this is referred to as *congenital amusia*, with *congenital* referring to the hypothesis of potential genetic origins. In the following, we will discuss this type of tone deafness in more detail. It has been known about for a long time (in 1878, a report described a man who showed these music processing deficits), but it has attracted systematic research only over the last decade.

The research domain investigating music processing and particularly its deficits has been growing recently, in part because of the development of a testing battery (the Montreal Battery of Evaluation of Amusia). Testing a large group of people (i.e., a population) with this battery has led to normative scores or norms (that is, scores that a "normal," nonamusic individual should obtain) and thus a calculation for cutoff scores. When someone performs worse than these cutoff scores, the individual can be diagnosed as amusic. Having this testing tool for a research community allows for a homogenous definition and is useful for working together on the understanding of this phenomenon.

CONGENITAL AMUSIA

In contrast to cases of acquired amusia, congenital amusia cannot be explained by cerebral lesions; the brain seems to be rather intact. Research investigating this phenomenon has also controlled for other obvious reasons; for example, congenital amusia cannot be explained by hearing impairment, by missing exposure to music in childhood, or by cognitive, attentional, or social deficits. Indeed, congenital amusia can occur in individuals with high intellectual capacities and young people with intact hearing who have followed, or tried to follow, music classes in childhood. The prevalence of congenital amusia has been estimated at 2–4 percent of the population.

The term *congenital* indicates a link to the hypothesis that this deficit is present from birth and may have a genetic origin. Recently, case studies with children have been reported. To investigate the potential genetic causes, research has studied either twins or entire families, allowing for the calculation of a risk factor to be amusic (or not). For example, in the families of an amusic individual, 39 percent of the first-degree relatives may also show amusia, but this is the case for only 3 percent of the first-degree relatives in families of the control participants (nonmusicians without amusia). Interestingly, this frequency of occurrence is comparable to the frequency of occurrence of other cognitive dysfunctions, such as specific language impairment, which is contributing to categorize congenital amusia as a neurodevelopmental disorder. Note that while some findings provide evidence for a potential genetic origin, for now, no potentially involved gene or gene combinations are known for being responsible for this disorder. Nevertheless, studying this phenomenon provides a unique opportunity to investigate the potential interaction between genetics, environment, and behavior.

A MUSICAL HANDICAP

Amusics' difficulties in music perception and performance (including singing) stand in strong contrast to the musical competences of young infants and of non-musicians. Indeed, various research has shown that nonmusician individuals have acquired knowledge about the musical structure of their culture just by mere exposure to music in everyday life, and they can process sophisticated tonal structures and functions, even though they may not be able to explicitly label or verbalize them. Music is ubiquitous in our lives, and having a deficit in processing music can create social difficulties for the affected individuals. Note that in contrast to the pleasure evoked by music for most of the population, some amusics indicate that music sounds like a foreign language or does not make any sense to them, and they rather prefer avoiding exposure to music. Isabelle Peretz, a main researcher in this domain, has thus referred to this condition as a "musical handicap." For example, amusic individuals may not understand some social situations, such as sharing emotional pleasure evoked by music or laughter raised by a mistake in a pupil's concert, or they may even encounter difficulties in their work environment. For example, when internal and external telephone calls are indicated by two different melodies, amusic individuals will have trouble recognizing the tones and thus have difficulty in knowing how to answer the phone (that is, with a simple "yes" for internal calls or the full name of the firm and a "Good morning, how can I help you?" for external calls).

DEFICITS IN DISTINGUISHING AND MEMORIZING TONES

Research has shown that the main impairment lies in the processing of the pitch dimension (pitch height distinguishes tones that sound high versus low). The first data have shown that amusic individuals have difficulties in discriminating whether two tones are the same or different. They need bigger differences between the tones to actually distinguish them. Indeed, while it is relatively easy for non-musician (nonamusic) individuals to distinguish two notes that are one semitone a part (that is, two adjacent keys on the piano keyboard), some amusics need two or even three semitone differences. As the semitone is a frequent distance between tones in tonal music and has even structural functions, one can make the hypothesis that this pitch discrimination deficit can lead to impaired music processing and impaired tonal knowledge acquisition.

However, as some amusic individuals also show normal pitch discrimination capacities, more recent research has shown that congenital amusia may mainly be linked to impaired memory for tones. For example, amusic individuals may be able to compare two tones when these are separated by a short silence (e.g., less than one second), but they are impaired to do so when the silence is increased to three or five seconds. Note that this delayed comparison remains easy for nonamusic individuals.

The weakness of amusics' short-term memory can also be seen with their stronger sensitivity to interference: When they have to memorize a couple of tones and other tones are presented during the delay (instead of a silence), they fail more easily in the task than do control participants who are not amusic. These various findings suggest that the memory traces of the tones are impaired or at least less stable than in normal nonamusic individuals. This also fits with some of amusics' subjective reports: amusics indicate that they "try to hold on the melody, but it just vanishes and disappears." The deficit can affect the three main phases of memory—encoding, storing, and recall—and research suggests that it is present starting with the encoding, that is, with the creation of the memory trace.

CAN THE IMPAIRMENT BE SEEN IN THE BRAIN?

Even though amusic individuals do not have any lesions in the brain, neuroimaging methods have allowed revealing very fine differences in the amusic brain in comparison to control brains. These subtle differences can be observed both for anatomical correlates as well as for functional correlates (that is, measuring the brain activity when participants have to do a given task, such as comparing melodies presented in pairs). These brain differences cannot be observed when only a single brain is analyzed. They can only be observed when groups of amusic individuals are compared to groups of nonamusic individuals who are matched in terms of age, sex, educational level, and musical training.

The findings have revealed anomalies in a cerebral network comprising areas in the frontal cortex and the temporal cortex as well as the connections between these structures. The impaired frontotemporal network is mainly observed in the right hemisphere. This hemispheric asymmetry is in agreement with neuroimaging data reported for music processing in the brain of nonamusic individuals. Different brain imaging techniques have provided converging evidence for anatomical abnormalities in congenital amusia for the inferior frontal gyrus (a gyrus in the frontal cortex that has been observed to be involved in tasks requiring short-term memory and structure processing, in particular for pitch) and regions in the temporal cortex that are dedicated to auditory processing. In these areas (and their connectivity), functional abnormalities have also been observed, that is, when participants are listening to and memorizing short melodies: amusic individuals show weaker activation in frontal areas than control participants, and the responses in the temporal auditory areas during the encoding of tones in short-term memory are delayed in comparison to the controls. Investigating the amusic brain thus provides insight into the potential reasons of their musical disorder and also informs us about the cerebral networks underlying music processing.

IS THE DEFICIT SPECIFIC TO MUSIC OR CAN IT ALSO CREATE DIFFICULTIES IN LANGUAGE PROCESSING?

In light of amusics' deficit in musical short-term memory, it is important to verify that these individuals do not have a general cognitive deficit that affects their memory performance. First reports on amusia have run extensive neuropsychological testing batteries to show that these individuals were not cognitively impaired. In addition, short-term memory for words was tested with the same experiment as for the tones: amusics first listen to a sequence of words (instead of tones), followed by a silence of three seconds, and then a second sequence of words, and they indicate whether the two sequences were the same or different. Results confirmed that the amusic individuals do not show any deficit for this task with verbal material.

Pitch-related information is not only relevant for music but also for speech processing. Speech is modulated in pitch to communicate the speakers' intention or emotion, which is referred to as *intentional* or *emotional prosody*. Changes in pitch indicate whether a sentence is a question (i.e., pitch goes up at the end of the phrase) or a statement (i.e., pitch goes down at the end of the phrase), and they also contribute to expressing the speaker's emotional state (e.g., there are bigger pitch variations in a sentence pronounced by a happy person than a sad person). In tonal languages, such as Mandarin or Thai, pitch information can also modulate the semantic meaning of a word (e.g., *ba* with a falling pitch means "father," but with a rising pitch, it means "to pull").

Despite their difficulty in pitch processing, amusics do not complain about speech perception difficulties in everyday life. This may be partly due to the use of other acoustic cues, such as intensity or duration changes as well as the semantic information of the context or information related to the situation. However, within a controlled experimental setting, some research has shown that amusics are also impaired in processing pitch-related information in the speech signal. These findings together with data about the involved neural correlates contribute to our understanding about how the brain processes musical and verbal information. They suggest that some of the neural networks are shared for their processing.

IMPAIRED ACCESS TO CONSCIOUSNESS

For various populations, and in particular for patients, previous research has shown that the brain is able to process some information on an implicit, unconscious level, even though deficits are observed in tasks that require explicit and conscious judgments. One well-known example is that patients with brain lesions who report perceiving (consciously) only in one part of their visual field, but nevertheless implicitly (unconsciously), can locate a visual object and grasp it appropriately by estimating its size.

For tone deafness, the pitch processing deficits were mostly observed with explicit investigation methods that required direct judgments on the tones. Some recent data show that the amusic brain can process some pitch information at an implicit level (without consciousness). For example, while amusics fail to detect mistuned tones in melodies, their brains show evoked-related potentials reacting to the mistuned tones, as revealed by electroencephalography (EEG) measurements. Perhaps related to these observed spared implicit processing capacities, amusics are able to provide some preserved judgments about musical emotions and report a feeling of familiarity evoked by music, suggesting that famous musical pieces are even stored in the long-term memory of the amusic brain.

CONCLUSION

Investigating impaired music processing, whether acquired or congenital, helps to understand not only the deficits and the reason for the deficits, but it also provides further information about normal brain functioning as well as links between music and language processing (for example, is a given deficit specific to music or does it also affect language processing? Are the involved neural correlates specific or shared?).

Research investigating the phenomenon of tone deafness and its related disorders is still a developing area with numerous open questions. Some findings suggest that there is not one type of tone deafness but different types. Some amusic individuals are impaired in the processing of pitch but not rhythm, others experience the reverse (arrhythmia or beat deafness), and some are impaired in both. Some still like music, but others only tolerate, avoid, or even hate music. Very recently, the phenomenon of *musical anhedonia* was described, where music perception is intact (as opposed to in amusia) but there is a complete loss of music enjoyment. Current research continues investigating amusia, which also allows for studying genetic bases related to music processing.

Understanding the deficits in tone deafness as well as revealing potential implicit capacities will also allow for the development of potential training or rehabilitation programs that aim to decrease the deficit, ideally in childhood. In the meanwhile, studying this phenomenon and communicating about it to the general public will also diminish stigmatizing or excluding tone-deaf individuals. Some personal reports of amusics reflect that their condition of tone deafness can actually lead to unpleasant situations. For example, a child who fails in a music class may be punished by the music teacher, ignoring the condition of congenital amusia, even though the child puts forth their best efforts to respond to the expectations of the teacher.

References and Further Reading

Bigand, E., & Poulin-Charronnat, B. (2006). Are we "experienced listeners"? A review of the musical capacities that do not depend on formal musical training. *Cognition, 100*(1), 100–130. https://doi.org/10.1016/j.cognition.2005.11.007

BRAMS. (n.d.). *Online test.* https://www.brams.org/en/onlinetest. This Website provides an online screening test used by the team of I. Peretz.

Omigie, D., Müllensiefen, D., & Stewart, L. (2012). The experience of music in congenital amusia. *Music Perception: An Interdisciplinary Journal, 30*(1), 1–18. https://doi.org/10.1525/mp.2012.30.1.1

Peretz, I., Ayotte, J., Zatorre, R. J., Mehler, J., Ahad, P., Penhune, V. B., & Jutras, B. (2002). Congenital amusia: A disorder of fine-grained pitch discrimination. *Neuron, 33*(2), 185–191.

Tillmann, B., Albouy, P., & Caclin, A. (2015). Congenital amusias. *Handbook of Clinical Neurology, 129*, 589–605. https://doi.org/10.1016/B978-0-444-62630-1.00033-0

Tillmann, B., Hirel, C., Lévêque, Y., & Caclin, A. (2017). Musical connections: Music perception and neurological deficits. In R. Ashley & R. Timmers (Eds.), *The Routledge Companion to Music Cognition* (pp. 225–236). New York, NY: Routledge.

Tillmann, B., Peretz, I., Bigand, E., & Gosselin, N. (2007). Harmonic priming in an amusic patient: The power of implicit tasks. *Cognitive Neuropsychology, 24*(6), 603–622. https://doi.org/10.1080/02643290701609527

Vuvan, D. T., Paquette, S., Mignault Goulet, G., Royal, I., Felezeu, M., & Peretz, I. (2017). The montreal protocol for identification of amusia. *Behavior Research Methods, 50*, 662–672. https://doi.org/10.3758/s13428-017-0892-8

20. Music and Language

Meagan Curtis

Music and language are similar in many ways. They can both be produced by the human voice and are built from the same basic properties of sound. They also both unfold over time, and the groups of individual sounds (tones, words) combine to form larger units of meaning (melodies, sentences). They are both viewed as social signals, communicating information and evoking responses in those who hear them. They are used universally, although their evolutionary history is not easy to untangle.

Scientists have been grappling with the classic chicken-and-egg question for quite some time: which came first in human evolution? Did music and language evolve at the same time? Did both systems have an important biological function for our evolutionary ancestors? Language may have been crucial for communicating information about predators or food sources, but what was the function of music?

Most scientists agree that humans are unique in the animal kingdom in possessing highly complex systems of language and music. Of course, many non-human species also produce sounds that have some of the properties of music and speech. Whales and songbirds for instance, produce vocalizations that exhibit some, but not all, of the characteristics of music. And some species seem to enjoy music—the Internet abounds with videos of dancing cockatoos. Rhesus macaques use different vocal sounds to communicate about the quality of food, and vervet monkeys use different alarm calls to distinguish between different types of predators. But none of these species are able to string a series of words together in a rule-governed way, an essential feature of language that allows us to represent the relationships between agents, actions, and objects. Only humans have developed full-blown linguistic and musical systems, and the human brain has evolved to support both systems, often using the same brain areas.

Music and spoken language are characterized by rapidly changing patterns of sound. In music, pitches are combined to form melodies, whereas in language, phonemes—the smallest meaningful units of speech—are combined into words, which are, in turn, combined to form sentences. The way these elements are combined to form larger units of meaning is referred to as the *grammar* of music and language.

Although sentences are very different from melodies, the brain seems to process music and spoken language in similar ways. This similarity is perhaps not surprising. After all, for both music and language, the brain must analyze a continuous stream of incoming sound, recognize individual elements (such as words or notes), and represent the relationships between those elements for meaning to emerge.

SHARED ELEMENTS

Music and spoken language are built from the same basic elements of sound: pitch, timing, and timbre. We will consider each aspect of sound in turn.

Pitch is generally conceptualized according to height. Although most musical systems use discrete pitches, most spoken languages tend to use pitch on a continuum. When someone speaks, the pitch of their voice rises and falls rapidly while producing the sounds of their language. The following exercise illustrates this difference. Sing the word "oh" for one second. You probably noticed that you used only one pitch and held that pitch steady until you were done singing. Now try speaking the word "oh" as if someone just pleasantly surprised you with an adorable puppy. What did you notice about the pitch of your voice as you spoke this word? You probably noticed that it changed rapidly. These rapid pitch changes are typical of speech, whereas sustained pitches are more commonly used in music. It can be argued that precise pitch perception is more important for processing music than language because of the use of precise tuning systems in music and the lack of such systems in language.

Both music and language involve patterns of pitch that unfold over time. In music, we refer to these patterns as *melodies*. In language, we refer to them as *prosody*. People generally do not attend closely to the prosody of speech because words often dominate our experiences of speech. (An example of prosody without words can be found in *Peanuts* cartoons, in which all adults "speak" in indecipherable words, making prosody the most prominent feature of their speech.) However, the brain processes prosody automatically and extracts information that may not necessarily be communicated by the words being spoken. For instance, the emotional state of the speaker is largely communicated by prosody, as is sarcasm. Prosody also helps us differentiate between statements and questions.

The same brain systems that enable us to perceive melodies are also thought to be important for the perception of prosody. This is evident when we consider case studies of individuals with pitch perception deficits. For instance, approximately 4 percent of the population has *amusia*, a condition that is more commonly referred to as *tone deafness*. People with amusia do not process pitch in a typical way, resulting in an impaired ability to recognize familiar melodies and a general lack of enjoyment of music. People with amusia also exhibit impaired perception of prosody, suggesting that pitch perception in language and music relies on some of the same brain areas.

Timing plays important roles in language and music. Both forms of sound unfold over time, so our ability to process each relies on having the ability to represent overall temporal properties, such as the speed of the music or speech, as well as the timing of individual elements relative to other elements. In spoken language, our ability to hear the difference between similar consonants, such as *b* and *p*, is due to a small difference in timing. To hear these differences, humans need to process timing differences on the order of milliseconds—that is, just a few thousandths of a second. Timing also helps us process the properties of sentences, drawing our attention to words that are emphasized through timing.

Timbre is a perceptual characteristic of sound that is related to the distribution of sound energy. It enables you to easily differentiate between the sounds of a piano and guitar, between different speaking voices, and between countless other types of sounds. In language, concentrations of sound energy enable listeners to differentiate between vowel sounds.

LANGUAGE AND MUSIC IN THE BRAIN

The perception of pitch, timbre, and timing poses different processing challenges for the brain. Pitch and timbre are perceptual features that reflect the frequency distributions of sound. Thus, the brain needs specialized systems for representing frequency information and recognizing familiar patterns. On the other hand, the brain also needs to represent timing on a millisecond scale. Brain imaging data suggest that the auditory cortex in the right hemisphere is more specialized for processing pitch and timbre, and the auditory cortex of the left hemisphere is more specialized for processing rapid temporal changes, though both hemispheres are involved in processing language and music to some extent. It has been proposed that these lateralization differences may stem from the importance of rapid temporal processing in the perception of language and the need for fine-grained pitch discriminations in the perception of music.

EXPECTATIONS IN MUSIC AND LANGUAGE

Musical systems generally have rules for organizing and combining units of sound, just as languages have rules for combining words into phrases and sentences. Lifelong exposure to music and language enables the brain to effortlessly learn the rules for organizing elements of sound (such as pitches and words) into longer phrases. Most people are able to recognize when a musician plays the wrong pitch, just as most people are able to detect errors in grammar (for instance, "My dogs likes cookies"). This demonstrates knowledge of the cultural rules for constructing phrases. These rules vary according to the specific language or musical system, but the same brain areas are used to track the overall phrase structures in language and music.

As the brain processes incoming sounds, it generates expectations for what words or musical elements are likely to occur next. These expectations are generated from the brain's automatic ability to apply the rules of the language or musical system to incoming information. This also makes these brain areas good at detecting rule violations. In fact, we generally only become aware of our expectations when they have been violated—that is, when we hear something unexpected.

Broca's area, a left hemisphere structure in the inferior frontal gyrus, is involved in tracking incoming musical and linguistic information. This area of the brain is thought to represent how the different elements of sound are related (i.e., who did what to whom), generate expectations for what should come next, and detect rule violations. Damage to Broca's area often results in a condition called *Broca's aphasia*, which impairs one's ability to produce words and to combine words together into grammatical sequences. Research has indicated that individuals with Broca's aphasia generally also have a difficult time processing the "grammar" of music; they are unable to generate expectations about what musical elements should come next and have an impaired ability to detect musical rule violations. This suggests that the brain relies on the same set of neural areas to process rules in language and music.

CAN MUSIC COMMUNICATE IDEAS?

Although the primary function of language is intuitively communication, the primary function of music is much less clear. Language can designate ideas that are incredibly specific, whereas music communicates ideas that are often less precise. On the other hand, music can convey some basic emotions, such as happiness, sadness, and fear, with a high degree of agreement between listeners. However, listeners may have a difficult time labeling musical emotions beyond these basic categories, as music can convey and evoke feeling states for which we have no words.

Beyond emotions, music does have some ability to communicate ideas, but it does not seem to do so with the same level of recognition accuracy that language does. Some of this communication occurs via acoustic similarity with sound-producing objects. For instance, a high-pitched lilting melody played by a flute may remind a listener of a bird because of its similarity to a bird call. Similarly, a high pitch that is sustained or repeated over and over may evoke the concept of fear due to its acoustic similarity with the vocal alarm calls produced by many species, which tend to have a high pitch. Threatening entities, on the other hand, may be communicated through the use of instruments that produce low pitches (as in the movie *Jaws*, where a low-pitched motif is used to represent the presence of the shark). Large animals tend to produce low-pitched vocalizations due to their relatively large vocal cords, and large animals tend to pose a threat to smaller animals.

The power of music to communicate specific concepts has been confirmed by research demonstrating that music can evoke a neural response associated with linguistic meaning. When the brain encounters words that are unpredicted by their context, such as encountering the word "bear" after seeing the words "bed," "pillow," and "blanket," it evokes a specific electrical response a split second after seeing the word. This electrical response is called the *N400*. There are many other types of electrical responses that occur for other reasons. Interestingly, the N400 electrical response is not evoked by unexpected events in general (such as an unexpected sound) but is specific to unexpected concepts. Scientists have now established that this same electrical response can be evoked by music. These findings suggest that music does evoke meaning in the brain.

BENEFITS OF SHARING BRAIN STRUCTURES

The partial neural overlap for the processing of language and music has some interesting potential benefits. In particular, some researchers believe that skills gained in music can transfer to language abilities, and vice versa. Their argument is that musical training should result in improved perception of pitch, timing, and timbre, which should enhance the perception of these properties of language. They also point to the fact that children who have musical training are less likely to have reading impairments than those without musical training. This benefit is thought to occur because musical training enhances the perception of timing, which helps children distinguish between similar language sounds (such as *d* and *t*). The ability to differentiate between similar sounds helps children learn to associate these sounds with the correct letters as they are learning to read, which reduces the overall incidence of reading impairments. Musical training also benefits pitch perception, which may help individuals better recognize aspects of speech that are carried by pitch, such as the emotional state of the speaker.

Musical training also seems to benefit the perception of speech in noisy environments, such as a party or a noisy restaurant. It can be challenging for young individuals to understand what someone is saying in a noisy environment, and that challenge only increases as we age and our hearing declines. However, musical training helps preserve that ability. Older adults who have had musical training earlier in life are better able to understand speech in noisy environments than older adults who have not had any musical training. It is possible that musical training helps one attend to the stream of sound and that it may also help with auditory pattern recognition.

The neural overlap between music and language is also useful in therapeutic contexts. One of the most compelling uses of these shared neural structures occurs in Melodic Intonation Therapy (MIT), which is a therapy utilized to help stroke patients recover their ability to speak. Damage to Broca's area can result in Broca's aphasia, an inability to speak. However, individuals with Broca's aphasia are generally still able to sing, as long as there is no damage to the right hemisphere of the brain. The right hemisphere brain structures that enable one to sing can be trained to support language, as these areas seem to be specialized for the types of processing challenges that are common to music and language. MIT involves teaching individuals with aphasia to sing the linguistic phrases that they wish to speak. Over the course of months of intensive therapy sessions, individuals are taught to speed up the singing, and at a certain point, the "singing" begins to sound like speech. Brain scans of individuals who have completed MIT generally show increased activity in the right hemisphere when the individuals are speaking, suggesting that the right hemisphere structures that enable singing have learned to support speech production.

CONCLUSION

The ways in which music and language overlap in the brain—as well as the ways in which they do not—are still being explored. This research may hold the key to developing a greater variety of therapeutic approaches to treating language disorders with music—and perhaps vice versa. It may eventually help scientists solve the mystery of the evolutionary history of these two uniquely human systems, potentially elucidating why these cognitive capacities are so complex and important for the human species.

References and Further Reading

Kraus, N., & Anderson, S. (2014). Music benefits across lifespan: Enhanced processing of speech in noise. *Hearing Review, 21*(8), 18–21.

Mithen, S. (2006). *The Singing Neanderthals: The Origins of Music, Language, Mind, and Body.* Cambridge, MA: Harvard University Press.

Patel, A. D. (2010). *Music, Language, and the Brain.* New York, NY: Oxford University Press.

PART 2

Psychological and Social Implications of Music

Music and Identity

21. Defining Ourselves through Music

Karen Burland

Music inhabits a special place in our twenty-first-century world. It is difficult to find spaces where there is no music. It is present in the background as we socialize in public spaces, and you only have to look around at people traveling to school or work to see that many of us opt to listen to music using personal devices. Indeed, accessing all genres of music from around the world is easier than ever before. Televised singing competitions such as *The X Factor* have become part of our everyday conversations with others, and experiencing live music events is commonplace—whether we attend in person or watch online. What this demonstrates is that music is part of our everyday lives, and it likely plays a role in how we define ourselves and our relationships with others.

Think about when you meet someone for the first time. How do you describe yourself and your likes and dislikes? You might tell the person that you work at a university, play the clarinet and saxophone, enjoy running, and have two children. This immediately reveals that work, music, exercise, and family are an important part of how you perceive yourself and how you want to be perceived by others; these are different identities that contribute to an overall sense of who you are—a sense of self. Our sense of self consists of multiple identities, and these align with the various roles we hold in society, for example, as a high school student, a son or daughter, a musician, or an athlete.

We can also have a *musical* identity that relates to our activities as a performer, composer, listener, or music fan. We understand what these roles mean for our sense of self through our self-concept that helps us to understand who we are through observing and evaluating our behaviors; by understanding the behaviors associated with particular roles; by interpreting other people's expectations, responses, and behaviors toward us; and by considering whom we hope to be in the future. There are three key ideas here. The first is that our identities are not fixed; they change over time. The second is that our ideas about our future self help us to evaluate who we are now and motivate behaviors that will help us to achieve our goals. And the third idea is that our identities are socially determined.

Consider the last class test you took. How did you feel immediately after the test was over? How did you feel once you received your grade? How did you feel once you found out how your classmates had performed?

Comparing ourselves with others offers a way to evaluate our own performance, and we use that information to develop an understanding of our "student" identity—either that we exceeded our own (and perhaps others') expectations or that we still have some work to do. Achieving a disappointing grade can influence our feelings of self-worth—our self-esteem. Our comparisons with similar others and their comments about our abilities or appearance, for example, have a significant impact on our self-esteem and can affect our motivation to continue with particular activities. One way to retain positive self-esteem is through our association with groups of people who have a positive image; associating with the qualities of an in-group, and rejecting those of an out-group, helps us to develop favorable identities (this is known as *social identity theory*).

LISTENING AND CONNECTING WITH OTHERS THROUGH MUSIC

Think about the music you most enjoy. How do you identify with the artist and the musical style? How frequently, and when, do you listen to music? Do you discuss music with your friends or family? How can you tell what music your peers like?

Music listening is a regular activity in our everyday lives and tends to accompany other activities, such as tidying up, doing homework, or traveling, which suggests that listening to music serves some useful functions—whether the function is to relieve boredom or tension or is a distraction from effortful tasks. Music listening can also play an important role in identity formation, which typically occurs during adolescence. Adolescents have been found to spend a lot of time listening to music, preferring to listen to popular and dance music (rather than classical or folk music) because it fulfills emotional needs, offers enjoyment, and creates the right external impression: the choice to listen to pop or dance music relates to the desire to be seen as fashionable or cool and therefore provides a way to create a positive self-image that connects with an in-group—pleasing friends and consequently reducing loneliness. Music becomes a "badge of identity" that can influence elements of behavior, dress code, and friendship groups.

Experiencing live music as an audience member also offers opportunities for connecting with others and can also help us to define ourselves. Think about the last time you went to a live music event. What did you go to see? In what kind of venue did the event take place? Who did you go with? What did you enjoy most about the experience?

When people choose to go out to watch live music, they usually see a favorite artist or band, hear a preferred style of music, or go because they like a particular venue. They may also choose to attend because they know people who are going or because they think it will be a good social occasion. Live music events are usually an opportunity to be surrounded by like-minded people and, like the friends shown together in photo 21.1, can allow us to confirm aspects of our musical identity. For example, we might confirm our in-group identity by observing and interacting with similar people (e.g., taking note of their dress or behavior), or we may meet new people through the shared musical interest. Being in close proximity to the performers and seeing the music being created in the moment may strengthen personal identification with the music or the artist and may mean that we begin to perceive ourselves as active participants in the event or the musical community, particularly as we join in by singing, dancing, cheering, or clapping. Being part of

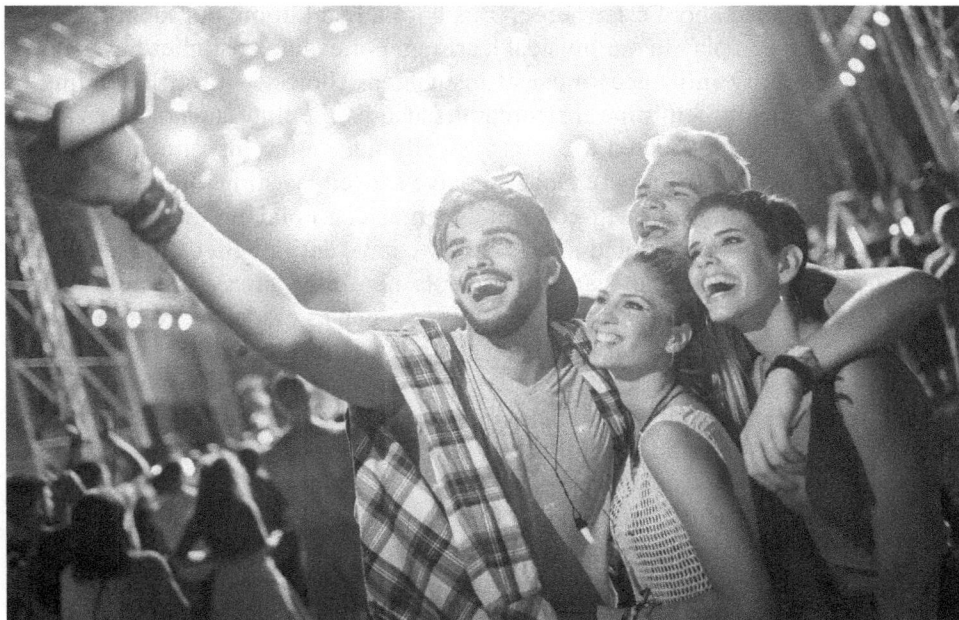

Photo 21.1 Happy Friends Taking Selfie at Music Festival. (© Nd3000/Dreamstime.com)

a live music event is not necessarily defined by being physically present in the venue during the performance; we can watch live performances online or follow what is happening on fan websites where we can connect with other members of the community—the in-group. And let us not forget that, after the performance, we review the event online, share photographs, and publicly identify that "I was there."

Listening to music at home or at live events connects us with others and helps us to feel part of a community; it also allows us to understand ourselves better and to evaluate who we are and what is important to us by comparing ourselves with other music listeners or fans and by reflecting on the importance and value of music to us in our everyday lives.

MAKING MUSIC

Do you play an instrument or sing? Do you write your own music? Do you play in a band or orchestra? Have you previously played but decided to give up? Think about how you first became interested in music and what has motivated you to develop your interest or to stop learning.

Starting to Learn: Music in School

The factors that influence our musical development have been widely researched and include aspects of social influence, motivation, practice, and learning styles (which you can read about elsewhere in this book). In addition, our identities have an important role to play in our musical learning. For example, studies have shown that gender identity influences musical instrument choice, with girls tending to select stereotypically feminine instruments (such as the flute, piano, and violin), while boys are more attracted to stereotypically masculine instruments (such as the guitar, drums, and trumpet). Once we have started learning, our beliefs about the roots of our ability (our self-concept as a musician) play an important role in determining our motivation and progress. If we have entity beliefs (the belief that musical ability is fixed and that some people naturally have more ability than others), we tend to prioritize and value outcomes such as grades or external recognition. If we have incremental beliefs (believing that musical ability is malleable and can improve with practice and effort), value is attributed to hard work, effort, and the process of learning. This has important consequences for our resilience when we are learning and can influence whether we persevere when we do not perform as well as we would like.

The context of learning also has an important role to play. It has been argued that if schools offer inclusive musical experiences and actively promote musical participation, then children will more likely have positive musical identities. A positive and inclusive musical context at school or home can foster incremental beliefs that influence our musical identity; the vital ingredients for musical learning are therefore dependent on our beliefs that musical activity is worthwhile and offers personal satisfaction, that it is supported and shared by significant others (such as teachers, parents, peers), and that our personal skills and resources will enable us to progress and succeed.

Making Music as Adults

Self and identity play an important role in the decision (or not) to pursue a career and to do so successfully. For aspiring professional musicians, music becomes a vehicle for self-expression, providing an emotional outlet not often offered by other activities. It is also central to self-concept, as it helps musicians to understand and evaluate themselves—whether that is positively or negatively. For example, in one of my studies, an aspiring professional musician said, "Because it's such a big part of me, I kind of see myself through the music. So if I'm doing well, then that's good, and when I'm not doing well, then that's terrible." Finding new hobbies provides a break from music once it becomes the focus of working life, and this protects the self (our self-esteem) against the potentially negative psychological impact of the tumultuous transition into the music profession.

The perceived fit between a particular career (a possible future self) and our awareness of ourselves and our values is also important. Some musicians decide that they do not want to become professional musicians because their image of the profession does not match their self-concept. For example, one of the participants in my research said, "There's just no certainties at all, and the rejection is just so hard, you know, if it is your life. That for me would be impossible, you know; I have to have stability." The interaction between our different identities and our overall sense of self is a complex one: our musical identity serves as a mode of self-expression, as a means to evaluate and define the self, and ultimately as a motivator for (or against) behavior.

Most people do not seek a professional performance career, but music is still an important part of whom we perceive ourselves to be. Making music with other people connects us to a community of like-minded people who are interested in developing musical skill while also having fun. The regular rehearsals provide a means of escape from the pressure of work, a way to express emotion, and sometimes an opportunity to feel motivated and enthusiastic about a different challenge that helps us to learn something new about ourselves. One of my research participants described his musical activities as being "at my core . . . I feel very much a three-part person split between . . . education, music, and the family. I really feel that, and that's sort of driving me throughout the three of them probably." Musical participation can provide a way to evaluate and moderate our different identities; with society's recent focus on how we can support and promote psychological well-being, greater understanding of musical identities may help to explain music's potential value and importance in this arena.

CONCLUSION

Music provides numerous ways for us to define ourselves—whether we are a performer, a composer, an avid fan, or a listener or a professional or an amateur. Our musical identity is just one of many identities that combine to create who we are—our self. Creating and listening both provide opportunities for us to express ourselves, to explore our emotions, and to feel a sense of belonging within a community. Our musical identity interacts with our other identities. For example, when we have negative experiences at school or work, our musical identity provides a reminder that we have other skills; it offers a way for us to express our emotions, to take comfort in another aspect of our lives, and to escape from those difficulties, even if for a short while. Our musical identities provide a way for us to connect with others, to join communities of people with similar interests, and, in so doing, to confirm our identities or to develop them further. There is a danger in assuming that the prevalence of music in everyday life means that it is, by default, something special and unique; it is music's capacity to allow us to express ourselves, to release and regulate emotion, to connect us to others and provide a sense of belonging, to help us represent ourselves externally to others, and to understand ourselves internally that ultimately means that music is a vehicle through which we define ourselves and our identities.

References and Further Reading

Burland, K., & Davidson, J. W. (2002). Training the talented. *Music Education Research, 4*(1), 121–140.

Burland, K., & Pitts, S. E. (Eds.). (2014). *Coughing and Clapping: Investigating Audience Experience*. Farnham, UK: Ashgate.

MacDonald, R., Hargreaves, D., & Miell, D. (Eds.). (2017). *Handbook of Musical Identities*. Oxford, UK: Oxford University Press.

North, A. C., & Hargreaves, D. J. (1999). Music and adolescent identity. *Music Education Research, 1*(1), 75–92.

Tajfel, H., & Turner, J. C. (1986). The social identity theory of intergroup behavior. In S. Worchel & W. G. Austin (Eds.), *The Psychology of Intergroup Relations* (pp. 7–24). Chicago, IL: Nelson-Hall.

22. Music and Cultural Identity

Alex Chilvers

Music is inseparable from any definition of *culture*. Throughout history, music has been influenced and shaped by geographical location, traditional behaviors and practices, and political events. Over time, however, we have come to understand that the relationship between music and culture goes both ways. Culture shapes music, but music also shapes culture. As the world evolves and we become more interconnected than ever before, we have greater opportunities to influence our own cultural identity through the musical choices we make and the communities we engage with.

MUSIC FROM THE PEOPLE: FOLKLORE STUDIES AND ETHNOMUSICOLOGY

Western thinkers in the late eighteenth century, led by the philosopher Johann Gottfried Herder, believed that musical practices provided a window into the cultural identity of a community. In other words: a community formed in a specific geographical location, and unique musical traditions and styles emerged from that community. Music was specific to a community's needs: it enhanced their unique rituals and even accompanied them while they worked. Musical styles were shaped by the physical materials that were available for the construction of instruments. Passed down from one generation to the next, each community's music was as unique as the daily lives of the people who had created it. It was also deeply embedded in their lives.

Folklore is a term that refers to the music, art, and various other belief systems that evolve within a community across multiple generations. By Herder's definition, it is the fundamental essence of a community. In the nineteenth century, folklore became a defining feature of a nation. In the eyes of many, this cultural definition of a nation was more meaningful than political or geographical definitions, as borders were constantly being redrawn. Furthermore, it allowed for the romantic notion that a community's unique spirit would survive as long as care was taken to study and document its folklore. As Europe rapidly industrialized in the nineteenth century, and boundaries between different cultural groups were increasingly blurred, folklorists from the cities went rural and commenced the task of cultural preservation.

Ethnomusicology is the study of music in its cultural contexts and can be considered a descendent of folklore studies. Herder was a German philosopher with Eurocentric ideas, and nineteenth-century folklorists were primarily concerned with preserving European cultures. Yet, music is recognized as a human universal. A *human universal* is a feature that has been common to every single human society throughout history (other noted universals include emotions, the use of tools, the existence of families, and, oddly enough, a wariness of snakes). With so much world music to study, folklorists with an adventurous streak began studying the musical traditions of non-Western communities. They did so by physically traveling to these communities and transcribing performances of their music (while always keeping a safe distance from snakes). Referred to today as *ethnomusicologists*, such people continue to study and document music in its many diverse cultural contexts.

Importantly, the music preserved by folklorists in nineteenth-century Europe did not merely end up gathering dust on library shelves. Folk music soon began to infiltrate the concert hall. A significant number of composers, working independently in different parts of the world, took inspiration from the musical traditions of their native lands. While some were certainly motivated by the desire to preserve cultural traditions, many were responding to a separate crisis that had spread throughout late nineteenth-century musical circles. It was thought by many that all art music was basically starting to sound the same. Composers were bound to a system of structural rules that, having originated in Viennese classicism, was now considered the universal musical language. Many felt trapped by these rules, and the diversity found in folk music presented a possible means of escape.

MUSICAL NATIONALISM

Composers across Europe (particularly outside the Western centers of Germany, France, and Italy) increasingly took advantage of the growing popular interest in folklore. For example, the Czech composer Bedřich Smetana (1824–1884), Russia's Mily Balakirev (1837–1910), and the Norwegian Edvard Grieg (1843–1907) all became pioneers of respective national musical styles that relied heavily on native folk melodies and thus celebrated specific cultural identities. The emergence of this trend among nineteenth-century Polish composers is particularly fascinating. To begin, Poland disappeared entirely from the map in 1795 and did not return until after World War I. Having held its place in Central Europe for approximately eight centuries, its territory was divided up by three surrounding empires—Russia, Austria, and Prussia (Germany)—and Poland ceased to exist for well over a century.

Despite this crisis of cultural identity—or perhaps because of it—efforts to document Polish musical traditions were particularly comprehensive during this time. Oskar Kolberg (1814–1890) was solely responsible for publishing twelve thousand songs collected from all around the former territories of Poland. Thereafter, composers of Polish ethnicity were equipped with the distinctive material that would allow them to pay creative homage to their cultural heritage. In pioneering a national style reliant on Polish folklore, composers sought to not only break free from the norms of classical style but also to demonstrate their support for a reunified Polish state. Furthermore, they saw themselves as following in the

Photo 22.1   Chopin Monument. (© Pepe14/Dreamstime.com)

footsteps of one of the most internationally renowned composers of the Romantic era: Frédéric Chopin (1810–1849). The son of a French father and a Polish mother, Chopin lived most of his adult life in Paris. Many of his works directly allude to the Polish folk dances he heard growing up in Warsaw (where the monument, shown in photo 22.1, stands today), and after his death, he become an unwitting poster boy for Polish nationalism. By presenting him as being in touch with that all-important pure essence of the Polish cultural identity, folk music, nineteenth-century nationalists constructed the patriotic image that continues to resonate today.

National anthems also became commonplace in European countries during the nineteenth century. Adopted as a means of unifying a politically defined community, much like a national flag, these songs were particularly intended for use on ceremonial occasions (a practice that continues today). Although folk influences are evident in some Western national anthems, and much more so in those of Asian countries, most tend to follow similar generic musical patterns. The specific patriotic messages embedded in the lyrics of an anthem tend to be of most significance, with emphases placed on a country's military history, natural beauty, or collective resilience. As such, national anthems do tend to match the agenda and priorities of the ruling class, and we have already acknowledged that the political definition of a nation sometimes fails to capture the cultural reality. You will thus find no mention of the ancient cultures of Australia's indigenous people in that country's anthem. Indeed, the ability of a single anthem to speak to the diversity of backgrounds and experiences that exist within the borders of a nation is highly questionable. Nonetheless, when Poland did regain independence after World War I, the national anthem that finally reunited its people—and that also happened to take the form of a traditional folk dance—delivered a message that would have resonated with most: "Poland Is Not Yet Lost."

MUSIC FOR THE PEOPLE: SOCIALIST REALISM

In the twentieth century, borders continued to be redrawn, and a new empire emerged in Europe: the Union of Soviet Socialist Republics. The Soviet Union, or USSR, provides an important example of the ways in which cultural identity can be used to oppress, rather than inspire, musicians. Soviet ruler Joseph Stalin recognized that a community's identity was expressed in its music and art, and he placed great importance on the creation of new works. However, he insisted that the primary aim of any such works be to inspire loyalty toward his Communist government. Furthermore, music and art had to be within the grasp of all citizens— not just the artistic elite. "Socialist realism" became the official artistic policy in Russia and the Soviet states as well as a number of neighboring countries ruled by Communist governments loyal to Stalin (including Poland, Czechoslovakia, and Hungary). This policy forced composers to write folk-infused, uncomplicated music that could be used as political propaganda.

By this time, the national trends among composers elsewhere in Europe had largely died out. With the planet recovering from the devastation of two World Wars, "nationalism" had become a dirty word. In response to Germany's role in World War II under the leadership of Adolf Hitler, modern composers were staunchly committed to distancing themselves from the Germanic tradition of Classical and Romantic music. Some of the most radical innovations in the history of Western art music were occurring just as socialist realism was being enforced back in the USSR. Most significant of all was serialism—a compositional approach that replaced traditional tonality with an almost mathematical treatment of tones. Serialism was soon adopted (at least fleetingly) by almost every respected composer in the West, and its guiding philosophy conflicted with those ideals laid out by Stalin. Soviet composers caught experimenting with the new style were swiftly punished. Even scores and recordings from the West were strictly forbidden.

To work without ending up on the government's blacklist, Soviet composers were essentially forced to adopt an old-fashioned style. Under socialist realism, artistic identity was thus suppressed by a narrow definition of cultural identity, and this was again driven by the belief that music provides a window into the cultural identity of a community. Here, however, that belief was combined with Stalin's idea that a community's music must be entirely self-serving. That combination led to a situation in which cultural identity was strictly controlled.

MUSIC WITHOUT BORDERS

The world we inhabit today is more interconnected than ever before. Globalization has led to a rapid increase in migration, and people inevitably take their music with them. Physical migration is no longer even necessary for the spread of culture: we are all part of a global village connected by the Internet. Just like the industrialization of eighteenth- and nineteenth-century Europe, this can be perceived as a threat to the purity of cultural traditions. There are many communities today who therefore continue to celebrate folklore in various ways. An annual folk festival in rural Slovakia, for example, allows a native group to maintain a sense of collective identity in an ever-changing world, while a weekly singalong of Celtic tunes at an Irish pub in Sydney helps expats maintain some form of contact with their heritage and distant homeland.

Rather than considering it a threat, however, we can view cultural globalization as an opportunity for integration and cross-cultural collaboration. Musicians are creative, and the creative mind is receptive to the influence of unfamiliar cultures. The music of today is testament to this phenomenon. Listeners barely flinch on hearing the United States' Jay-Z rapping over British producer Panjabi MC's Indian tumbi riff or Sweden's Tove Lo singing in duet with the American Nick Jonas to the accompaniment of West Indian steel drums. This current state of popular music raises questions that challenge past notions of the relationship between music and cultural identity. For instance, which specific community is represented by the music just described? And how do we make sense of a white woman from a small seaside town in Australia who changes her name to Iggy Azalea and makes her fortune as a Los Angeles-based rapper?

Modern theorists have begun to think about the relationship between cultural identity and music as more fluid and bidirectional. Cultural identities are neither permanent nor tied to a specific place, and music can no longer simply be seen to reflect preexisting identities. Instead, music is a medium through which we can construct our own cultural identity. Folk festivals in Slovakia and Irish pubs seventeen thousand kilometers from Dublin are not sites of spontaneous expressions of a people's essence. Yet, they are indeed social settings for individuals to reaffirm their sense of identity and make meaningful contact with their cultural history. The power lies in the act of coming together and making music rather than in the music itself.

Specific musical sounds (such as those provided by the tumbi or steel drums) cannot be inextricably attached to singular cultural identities. They can, however, become valued symbols of a community's identity. Herder would perhaps argue that the hip-hop sound is a reflection of the African American community and that Iggy Azalea is a mere mimic. However, we may also need to make sense of the ever-changing community that is built around the hip-hop genre. It is a community with foundations in particular geographical centers, but its members are also reached via the radio and the Internet. Clearly, the modern exchange of music cannot be contained by boundaries of nationality, race, or any other traditional marker of cultural identity.

CONCLUSION

Musical activities are social activities. When you engage with music, you engage with other human beings. Whether rehearsing in an orchestra, improvising in a jazz trio, or singing carols on a street corner, music making brings people together. If you go out to see a band play, you share that experience with everyone in the room. Even if your sole contact with the musical world is through an online streaming service accessed in the privacy of your own home, there are real people responsible for the creation of the tracks you stream and, perhaps more importantly, there is likely a very large community of real people listening along with you.

Your cultural identity is formed by the social groups to which you belong. Therefore, whether you are a professional musician or an occasional listener, the music that you engage with influences that identity. It is you who decides which ensembles you join, which artists you support, and which playlists you stream. In this way, music allows you to shape your own identity. Certain kinds of music are closely associated with particular communities formed along ethnic lines, and this should indeed be respected. Yet, history shows that music cannot be controlled by borders, and the communities it creates are never fixed.

References and Further Reading

Bohlman, P. V. (2004). *The Music of European Nationalism: Cultural Identity and Modern History*. Santa Barbara, CA: ABC-CLIO.

Haynes, J. (2012). *Music, Difference and the Residue of Race*. New York, NY: Routledge.

Kennedy, V., & Gadpaille, M. (Eds.). (2017). *Ethnic and Cultural Identity in Music and Song Lyrics*. Newcastle upon Tyne, UK: Cambridge Scholars Publishing.

Whiteley, S., Bennett, A., & Hawkins, S. (Eds.). (2004). *Music, Space and Place: Popular Music and Cultural Identity*. Ashgate Popular and Folk Music Series. Aldershot, UK: Ashgate.

23. Gender Bias in Music History

Martin W. B. Jarvis

Any discussion of music and identity would be incomplete without considering the relationship between music and gender. Most striking about this relationship is the scarcity of women in the recorded canon of Western music. Virtually all the so-called great composers are men. We celebrate the remarkable music of composers such as Bach, Mozart, Beethoven, Chopin, Brahms, Wagner, Tchaikovsky, Debussy, and Mahler, but we rarely stop to ask, where are the female composers? Did female composers exist? If so, were their contributions discouraged, suppressed, or ignored?

Even within the past fifty years, the popular music industry has remained largely male dominated, with women underrepresented in mainstream popular music. Popular female musicians tend to get less radio airplay, and they attract lower earnings than their male counterparts. However, at least there are female role models for young girls, with highly successful musicians such as Beyoncé,

Madonna, Taylor Swift, Lady Gaga, Pink, Adele, Joni Mitchell, and the Spice Girls. Centuries ago, there were few female role models at all.

This chapter will provide an overview of the manner in which recorded history has represented the contributions by women to music. Two case studies will be described. They are the stories of two female musical prodigies associated with two very great musical names: Anna Magdalena Bach, the second wife of Johann Sebastian Bach, and Marie Anne Mozart, the elder sister of Wolfgang Amadeus Mozart.

THE BEGINNING

The recorded history of womens' contribution to Western music begins with Hildegard von Bingen (1098–1179). Hildegard was a German Benedictine abbess and a writer, composer, philosopher, Christian mystic, visionary, and polymath. We know about Hildegard's contribution to the musical canon mainly because she was a person of independent significance. Being a nun and an abbess, she was not associated with any males who, under the law of the time, could claim rights to her intellectual property. Consequently, this kept Hildegard von Bingen in obscurity.

Why is this so important? Well, until the latter part of the twentieth century, females in Western civilization were effectively chattel—the property of a male. The period of the Renaissance to the modern era (roughly 1400 to 1900) was a period when religion was very influential and a dominant social force. The prevailing religious point of view was that it was a woman that had caused man's fall from grace in the Garden of Eden, when Eve disobeyed Adam and ate the apple of the tree of knowledge of good and evil. From that religious perspective, women were to be subservient to their husband's authority. Indeed, in some societies, a woman was considered the property of her father before marriage and the property of her husband after marriage.

During this period, a female had no physical or financial property and no intellectual independence. Any education a female might have received focused only on knowledge that supported her goal of marriage. However, even in those circumstances where status and money brought some influence, it was still unacceptable for a young woman to try to improve herself. The fact is that during this period, men considered women as intellectually inferior.

MASCULINE VERSUS FEMININE

This concept of the feminine being inferior to the masculine led to the idea that certain musical devices are less important than others. As musical metaphors, a feminine cadence is one that falls on a weak beat of a bar; the second subject (or second theme) of a sonata form movement is feminine, whereas the first subject (the main theme) is the strong male theme.

None of what has been said so far is meant to imply that females were not directly involved in playing, singing, and composing music throughout that period. Rather, recognition of a female's musical output under their own name was simply not possible. Therefore, publishing was not an option for a woman. This is why the famous author Amantine-Lucile-Aurore Dudevant, née Dupin (1804–1876) wrote under the male pseudonym George Sands, and Mary Ann Evans (1819–1880) published under the name George Eliot.

As every lover of Jane Austen knows, playing music in the home was an important social accomplishment for females of a certain class in society; however, it was also not socially acceptable for females to perform in public. As far as music composition was concerned, females were likewise restricted to compositions for domestic consumption only. This has led to the view that females did not compose prior to the late nineteenth century. As a result, many of the talented female musicians and composers of previous times have been hidden from the history of music. Thanks to researchers such as Mary Mageau, we now know the names of a great number of female composers from the eighteenth century, even if their music does not receive public exposure.

THE CASE STUDIES

We now come to the two case studies of Anna Magdalena Bach and Marie Anne Mozart. The contributions to music of both these female musical prodigies have effectively been lost to music history solely because of their gender. To lift the veil on their lost contributions, the manuscripts associated with their famous family names have been analyzed using scientific forensic handwriting examination.

Anna Magdalena Bach

Relatively little is known of Anna Magdalena Bach (née Wilcken; there are various spellings of her name). She was born on September 22, 1701, at Zeitz, a small Thurigian city, and was the second wife of Johann Sebastian Bach. It is very probable that Bach recruited Anna Magdalena for the work he completed for Prince Leopold of Anhalt-Köthen in the Köthen court, Germany. When one considers the social context of the first quarter of the eighteenth century, it is remarkable that Anna Magdalena appears in the records of the court as a professional musician. She was employed as the "Singer to His Highness the Prince" and as a "Chamber Musician." Evidence suggests that she was probably a violinist, and from the level of the salary she received from the court, it is likely that she was very highly regarded as a musician. She was paid somewhere around 300 Thalers per year, as compared with 400 for Johann Sebastian, so there is a clear indication that she was extremely musical. Some have argued that the reason Anna Magdalena received such a large salary was because she was such a fine singer; singers of her caliber were highly prized at the time. However, there is no evidence to support this argument.

In the written records, there are a few mentions of Anna Magdalena continuing to perform professionally after she married Johann Sebastian; she did up to 1725 for certain and possibly 1729. References to her in any form from the period are very limited, and it is impossible to say with any certainty what she did musically for the remainder of her time with Johann Sebastian.

So, what exactly was her contribution? The forensic examination of many manuscripts attributed to Johann Sebastian Bach has provided strong evidence that Anna Magdalena was involved in the composition process of a number of his works. Those works include the violin sonatas and partitas, the aria that forms the basis of the so-called *Goldberg Variations*, and the first prelude of the *Well-Tempered Clavier*. Further, she was probably the principal author of the six Cello Suites.

Given the fact that many world-leading forensic handwriting experts have seen the evidence from the forensic research over a period of many years, and with no challenge to the research conclusions, we could be tempted to assume that this is now an accepted position. Unfortunately, the Bach scholarly world is still very much a male-dominated environment, and the idea that a female who was not a Bach by blood could compose such fabulous music is still unacceptable! Bach scholars are happier with the idea that Anna Magdalena was simply a copyist and prefer that she not be part of Bach's compositional narrative.

Marie Anne Mozart

The second case study is Marie Anne Mozart (also known by her nickname "Nannerl"). Marie was born in Salzburg, on July 30, 1751. She was nearly five years older than her brother, Johannes Chrysostomus Wolfgangus Theophilus, who is usually referred to as Wolfgang Amadeus Mozart. It is generally believed that when Nannerl was around seven years old, her father, Leopold, started to teach her how to play the keyboard, probably the harpsichord—although it is also possible that she may have been taught to play on the somewhat newer invention of the fortepiano, the precursor of the modern pianoforte. Nannerl soon demonstrated that she was a very gifted performer on the keyboard.

In 1759, Nannerl received a notebook for her music studies from her father. On the front cover she wrote,

> Pour le
> Clavicin ce Livre
> apparteint pour Mademoiselle
> Marie Anne Mozart
> 1759

These handwritten words would end up providing the forensic evidence that Nannerl signed many music manuscripts originally attributed to Amadeus. In Nannerl's music notebook, there is also evidence that she may have been a composer. Indeed, she may have inspired her younger brother, Amadeus, to learn to play the keyboard by composing brief Minuets and Marches for Amadeus to play. However, although it is known from Amadeus's letters that Nannerl composed, it is also known that their father strongly objected to Nannerl's aspirations as a composer, and he refused to allow her to have composition lessons.

From the age of about eleven years old, in 1762, until she was eighteen, in 1769, Nannerl had a very successful career playing music for the aristocracy and royalty in the courts of Europe performing alongside her younger brother. As she toured

Europe as a keyboardist with her family, young Nannerl wowed audiences in Munich, Vienna, Paris, London, The Hague, Germany, and Switzerland. So brilliantly did she perform that her father wrote in a letter in 1764, "My little girl plays the most difficult works which we have . . . with incredible precision and so excellently. . . . What it all amounts to is this, that my little girl, although she is only twelve years-old, is one of the most skilful players in Europe." Leopold is quoted as saying she was "virtuosic," "a prodigy," and "a genius." There is little doubt that in at least the first three or four years of the Mozart family tours of Europe that she was the star, not Amadeus. However, from 1769 onward, because she had reached a marriageable age, she was no longer permitted to show her artistic talent on travels with her brother. She then had to remain at home in Salzburg with her mother until a suitable husband could be found. She also remained at home with her father when Wolfgang visited Paris in 1778, the year their mother died.

The usual reason given for the termination of Nannerl's stellar performing career is that her father thought it was improper for a young woman to be seen on the concert stage once she was of a marrying age. However, a more believable reason for the removal of Nannerl from public performance was surely that Leopold recognized that, given the social conditions at the time, Amadeus was the one most likely to gain full-time employment as Kapellmeister (the leader or conductor of an orchestra) rather than Nannerl, despite her talent. Consequently, Leopold needed Amadeus to shine, so Nannerl had to cease performing in public.

Evidence to support this proposition comes from the fact that Nannerl received several suitors. One such suitor was Franz Armand d'Ippold, who was a captain and a private tutor. Nannerl was in love with him, but they did not marry. One possible reason is that Leopold denied permission for Nannerl to marry because he needed her at home to look after him after his wife died in Paris. Apparently, Amadeus attempted to persuade Nannerl to stand up against their father's wishes, but to no avail.

Leopold finally gave his approval, and on August 23, 1783, Nannerl married and settled in Saint Gilgen, Austria. Her husband, Von Berchtold, had been twice widowed. He already had five children from those two marriages, and through the course of their marriage, Nannerl bore him three more children. Nannerl died on October 29, 1829. Fortunately for her, she did not die in poverty, unlike her brother. She left a fortune that, at least in part, may have lawfully belonged to Wolfgang Amadeus.

As was the case with Anna Magdalena and Johann Sebastian, Nannerl was probably involved in the compositions of her brother, Wolfgang Amadeus. Unfortunately, Nannerl and her sister-in-law, Constanze, destroyed letters and manuscripts that might have exposed these contributions. However, there are certain indicators that suggest her direct involvement.

MATTERS OF HANDWRITING

Curiously, a forensic examination of various manuscripts, ostensibly written by Wolfgang Amadeus Mozart, reveals that there are clear examples where the name

"Mozart" is written in the hand of his sister, Nannerl, and not in the hand of Amadeus! For example, figure 23.1 shows the name "Mozart" written by Nannerl, even though the signature is found on a manuscript attributed to Amadeus.

Figure 23.1 The Name Mozart in Nannerl's Hand.

Amadeus typically wrote his surname like the example in figure 23.2.

Figure 23.2 The Name Mozart as Written by Wolfgang Amadeus.

What does this imply? Well, it indicates that Nannerl was writing on manuscripts attributed to her brother. This presents questions: Why did she do this? Did she really compose famous works attributed to her brother, Wolfgang Amadeus Mozart? We may never know for sure, but it seems quite possible that she may have composed some of the music on those manuscripts.

CONCLUSION

What lessons regarding music and gender can we take from the lives of these very talented women? One lesson is that there were few opportunities for female composers at the time. However, such opportunities are gradually increasing today. Composers such as Elena Kats-Chernin in Australia and Sally Beamish in the United Kingdom can finally take center stage, and female prodigies such as pianist and composer Emily Bear in the United States and Alma Deutcher in the United Kingdom have the opportunity to shine. Alma, at age ten, had already completed her second opera, *Cinderella*; it was performed to sold-out houses in Vienna at the end of 2016. Her first opera, *The Sweeper of Dreams*, was written at the age seven. Comparisons are always difficult, but it is worth mentioning that even Amadeus Mozart did not complete his first opera until the age of twelve!

With the recognition of great composers such as Alma Deutcher and Emily Bear and the huge success of popular female musicians such as Beyoncé, Madonna, Lady Gaga, and many others, one can only hope that the twenty-first century will bring an end to gender bias in the music industry.

References and Further Reading

Beer, A. (2016). *Sounds and Sweet Airs: The Forgotten Women of Classical Music*. London, UK: One World Publications.

Jarvis, M. (2011). *Written by Mrs Bach*. Sydney, NSW, Australia: HarperCollins ABC Books.

Jezic, D. (1994). *Women Composers—The Lost Tradition Found* (2nd ed., E. Wood, Ed.). New York, NY: Feminist Press.

Leonard, M. (2017). *Gender in the Music Industry: Rock, Discourse and Girl Power.* Aldershot, UK: Ashgate.

24. Music and Social Class

Graeme Smith

Can the music that someone listens to tell us about the type of person he or she is? Are people who listen to classical music typically more upper class or intellectual than people who listen to rap music? The concept of *class* refers to a person's sociocultural background and is sometimes divided into categories such as working class, middle class, and upper class. Many people consciously or unconsciously make assumptions about the class of a person simply based on the music he or she listens to. What should we make of this?

The Italian musicologist and popular music scholar Franco Fabbri relates a thought-provoking and amusing story. The van carrying him and his avant-garde rock group Stormy Six is stopped by a French policeman, who, after asking their occupation, follows up with a question: *"Quel genre de musique?"* ("What kind of music?").

Fabbri reflects that the answer he and his fellow musicians give to this question can have consequences, and he points out that, at the time, "the question is extremely serious, and we know well enough what it implies: if the reply is 'classical music,' there should be no problems, but we can easily imagine the reaction of the gendarme to responses like 'hardrock' or 'reggae'—a breathalyser for the driver and a general search of the minibus." But he adds, "Obviously a gendarme who is really well prepared would not even have to ask the question. He would already be in a position to decipher the various indications (of what kind of music): clothes, haircut, reading matter, behaviour, etc." (Fabbri 1982, pp. 131–132).

It is widely accepted that certain "types" of people like, consume, play, or identify with certain "types" of music. In this chapter, we will consider the extent to which such assumptions are true and why people make such choices about their music.

SOCIAL INFLUENCES ON MUSICAL PREFERENCE

In our modern, complex, urban society, we may think that we exercise freedom of choice of music, but our "free" choices are influenced by social factors. Research in the sociology of music has examined influences of gender, class, ethnicity, and age on the ways people relate to music. One common form of investigation asks people about their favorite types of music. In Australia, such a study, conducted over two decades ago, unearthed many interesting results and tried to make sense of them.

This study asked over two thousand Australians detailed questions about their cultural consumption: their tastes in art, sport, entertainment, recreation, and the like. For music, they asked what music they liked, disliked, or knew something

Table 24.1   Preferred music genre by gender and social class (percentages who liked a genre)

Music Genre	Women	Men	Professionals	Manual Workers
Easy listening	25.6	18.2	20.8	19.8
Rock	12.4	19.8	10.8	18.3
Top 40 pop	17.5	11.6	10.7	15.2
Country and western	7.0	11.1	3.2	15.6
Classical	7.2	8.4	18.5	2.9
Light classical	9.1	4.6	7.7	3.9

about. The researchers also recorded gender, age, ethnicity, and occupation of participants, from which they divided people into six social classes, from, for example, manual laborer to business owner or higher professional. The research resulted in a book, *Accounting for Tastes: Australian Everyday Cultures*.

The study sought answers to how choices of cultural consumption and cultural activity were linked to social divisions. To illustrate some of the findings, table 24.1 shows an analysis of some of the responses to some favored music genres by gender and two of the social class groups.

CULTURAL CAPITAL

The researchers organized their investigation around the theoretical approach of an important French sociologist, Pierre Bourdieu. Bourdieu had carried out similar research in France in the 1960s and 1970s and published his findings in the influential book *Distinction*. He argued that cultural choices not only reflect someone's social background but are also part of the way hierarchies of social power are maintained. Thus, he looked at the ways participating in "high-status" cultural practices such as classical music or appreciation of gallery art were enthusiastically favored by the upper classes. He argued that these choices were part of privilege and power, and the knowledge and ability associated with these choices he described as "cultural capital."

His study found many ways in which music choices were particularly potent in this process. Yet, Bourdieu's France has been widely recognized as a strongly class-stratified and "snobbish" society that accords a great deal of power and respect to traditional high culture. The Australian research asked how applicable these concepts were to other societies.

Let us look at what the Australian cultural consumption survey discovered about music preferences. It found that classical music was a favorite genre of 18 percent of professionals but only 2.9 percent of manual workers. If this were medical research, the "risk" of liking classical music for professionals was about six times that of manual workers. Conversely, country music was favored by only 3.2 percent of professionals but 15.6 percent of manual workers. The genre of light classical was selected by 14 percent of managers, 7.7 percent of professionals, and

3.9 percent of manual workers. Other occupational class groups had their own patterns of differences. Women and men distributed their choices differently.

To explain such differences, we can fall back on a number of theories. For example, there is clear evidence that people tend to like the music of their youth. This would go some way to explaining age stratifications. Differences may be reinforced by peer identification—there may be perceptions that some genres are "our music" rather than that of others. Thus, in making choices, people not only have an idea of what they like but also what others like and how they would like to identify themselves through their music.

Many researchers have emphasized that these differences in tastes and choices lay out a hierarchy of *cultural status* that is a direct parallel to hierarches of *social status*. That is, "highbrow" and "lowbrow" musical genres are preferred by higher-class and lower-class participants, respectively. Bourdieu and others argue that where highbrow genres are likely to be abstract and intellectualized in nature, lowbrow genres are direct, down to earth, and simple. If musical tastes have similar patterns to social structure and roles, these are described as "homologous."

The *cultural homology* approach, with its "highbrow" and "lowbrow," seems to be based in ideas of officially sanctioned high culture. Perhaps these may be dated. Does classical music, for example, still hold its traditional value as a marker of taste and intelligent discernment? Some argue that those with social power now increasingly seek more complex and diverse cultural expressions rather than merely participating in and displaying highbrow culture. A new alternative model of "elite cultural omnivorism" has arisen. This model suggests that those with social power now tend to make musical choices not limited to exclusive highbrow genres but show a breadth of taste and inclusive broadmindedness.

OMNIVORES AND UNIVORES

The cultural omnivorism theory was developed by the American sociologist of culture Richard Petersen. Analyzing the music preferences given in some American surveys, he argued that high cultural capital now tends to be associated not (just) with highbrow musical forms but with breadth of taste. Thus, a cultural consumer with this broad taste would be called a "cultural omnivore." Conversely, lower cultural capital is now associated with the limited tastes of a "univore."

His study analyzed musical choices in surveys. Using the framework of a cultural hierarchy of "highbrow/middlebrow/lowbrow" genres, the highbrows among the participants were those who liked opera or classical music, and this group was compared with the rest. It was found that these highbrows tended to like a wider range of genres than the others. They were thus described as "cultural omnivores." To add a historical dimension to the analysis, from 1982 to 1992, this phenomenon of the high-status omnivore seemed to be on the increase. Peterson linked this to the rise of the new "administrative-managerial" class, whose social power rests not in specific knowledge but on flexibility and cultural breadth. This argues that musical taste differences are not about *what* one consumes but *how* one consumes.

Since then, much research in this area has been dominated by these two hypotheses. The cultural homology theory maintains that there are consistent preferences for different genres of music between different classes. The upper-class/lower-class hierarchy is mirrored in a similar ranking of music genres. The preferred genres have certain affinities with the groups who choose them and in some sense reflect their status in life.

In contrast, the cultural omnivore theory suggests that class is manifested not in specific genres of music but in restriction or in the breadth of taste and in the modes of music consumption and use. Although some results of investigations have favored one or the other of these theories, the debate and the research continue.

For example, a recent Canadian research project lead by Gerry Veenstra used a telephone survey of about fifteen hundred people, randomly selected to represent the broader population, and asked them to score their likes and dislikes of a list of genres. As is typical of this sort of research, the authors then used various statistical techniques to look for patterns of likes and dislikes and to see what links there were with social characteristics. The study supported the homology thesis, in that the genres that were liked and disliked were strongly differentiated by class. For example, the highly educated liked choral, classical, folk, jazz, and opera, whereas those with less education liked big band, country, disco, easy listening, golden oldies, and rap. Wealth, rather than education, divided up the genres in fairly similar ways, but there were some differences. The wealthy tended to like big band, blues, classical, jazz, musical theater, and opera, whereas country, folk, and heavy metal were favored by the poorer respondents. However, although there were differences in the number of genres people said they liked, which would point to a type of musical omnivore, there was no evidence that this sort of breadth of taste was linked to higher-class positions.

But different results emerged from a British-based study of cultural consumption using the same sort of investigation of cultural consumption as the Australian Everyday Cultural Consumption project discussed above, with quantitative survey responses that were probed further with in-depth interviews. Although the sort of pattern of musical omnivorousness that it found was not limited to upper classes, it was found to be strongest in the professional classes, with the combination of relative wealth and education. Here it seems the tendency to cultural broad-mindedness was useful to those who needed to be flexible and inventive in their lives. The researchers argued that there are different kinds of omnivores, and those who might, for example, find values in intellectually engaging music might love avant-garde art music as well as heavy metal but despise Andre Rieu. Others would find different kinds of broad-mindedness to enhance their own self-esteem and sense of their place in society (Bennett et al. 2009).

Other research has suggested that musical omnivorousness is most commonly found among those most deeply engaged in music, the musically educated and skilled, either through formal or informal training. Thus, musicians and skilled performers are able to appreciate expertise in many genres, and, conversely, univore taste may be a marker of lower musical, if not general, education.

In many circles, to claim "eclectic" taste in music carries with it some social cache, indicating the high status of omnivorousness. Other research indicates that much claimed "omnivorousness" may be more restricted than it will admit, and if we concentrate on musical dislikes as well as likes and ask the omnivores more detailed questions about their tastes, they show only a limited amount of tolerance.

Clearly, the debate is not settled, and it remains an area for research. It can be argued that the conclusions of some studies are based on simplistic and limited data. Nominating a favorite genre may be too restrictive as a tool of investigation and does not take into account the depth of involvement or commitment to different types of music or musical activity. To get a sense of how research in this area is carried out, it would be valuable to construct a questionnaire to investigate these theories and trial it on a number of people. We may then get a sense of the degree of the effect of class on music choices and also see the ways in which this sort of knowledge is investigated. How do objective tick-the-box survey methods compare with structured in-depth interviews?

CONCLUSION

There is no doubt that musical choices are strongly linked to social differences. However, the ways these links are created remain the subject of much research and perhaps, more importantly, lead us to ask what these links tell us about music and society. Is music to be celebrated for bringing people together, or might it not also be used to maintain social privilege and power and to keep people divided? Or, is this musical difference perhaps a part of maintaining a lively and diverse society?

The sociology of music extends beyond questions of taste and preference. Research such as that discussed above leads to investigations of what music means to us and how we use it in our lives to entertain us, comfort us, and challenge us and to tell ourselves who we are. These uses are not created by individuals but within the patterns of social relationships and structures in which we live. Without such a context, music would have no meanings. The sociological study of music helps us to unravel how these meanings are created.

References and Further Reading

Bennett, T., Emmison, M., & Frow, J. (1999). *Accounting for Tastes: Australian Everyday Cultures*. New York, NY: Cambridge University Press.

Bennett, T., Savage, M., Silva, E., Warde, A., Gayo-Cal, M., & Wright, D. (2009). *Culture, Class, Distinction*. Abingdon, UK: Routledge.

Bourdieu, P. (1984). *Distinction: A Social Critique of the Judgment of Taste*. Cambridge, MA: Harvard University Press.

Fabbri, F. (1982). What kind of music? *Popular Music, 2*, 131–143.

Peterson, R. A., & Kern, M. R. (1996). Changing highbrow taste: From snob to omnivore. *American Sociological Review, 61*(5), 900–907.

Veenstra, G. (2005). Can taste illumine class? Cultural knowledge and forms of inequality. *Canadian Journal of Sociology, 30*(3), 247–279.

Music and Personality

25. Personality and Listeners

Tuomas Eerola and Jonna K. Vuoskoski

Imagine yourself at a party organized by a friend of a friend. At some point in the evening, you happen to glimpse familiar band names on her laptop screen; it is the playlist for the evening and her roster of favorite artists. You feel that you suddenly know the host a little better, and you have a sense that she probably has been to the major festivals and is generally pretty outgoing and open-minded. You strike up a conversation about one particular band you spotted in her collection and soon confirm many of your initial assumptions. Now imagine yourself boarding a plane and observing that the man sitting next to you is wearing a T-shirt with graphically violent images and tour dates of the death metal band Cannibal Corpse written on it. Will this information shape the small talk you might have with him?

Just like in all matters of taste, music preferences tend to vary greatly from one person to the next. In fact, it is a commonly held belief that an individual's music preferences can reveal meaningful information about their personality to others. Indeed, research has shown that people often use their music preferences to communicate information about their personalities to strangers. But what makes us like the music that we like? And what explains this seemingly strong association between the kinds of music we like and the types of people we are? Research has found that there is a consistent pattern of associations between our personality traits and the kinds of music we enjoy listening to. These findings suggest that music can function to both reflect and reinforce aspects of our personalities, self-views, and values. This chapter will introduce you to the key concepts from personality psychology, and it discusses the links between personality traits, music preferences, and music listening habits.

WHAT IS PERSONALITY?

Individuals differ from each other in terms of their patterns of thought, emotions, and behavior, and personality traits are one way of describing and measuring these individual differences. Psychologists studying personality have discovered a set of measurable traits that vary across all people. One of the most widely accepted ways of describing personality is the so-called Big Five personality theory. According to the Big Five theory, people's personalities can be described using five broad trait dimensions: extroversion, neuroticism, agreeableness, openness to experience, and conscientiousness. The important thing to note is that these traits are understood as continuums—dimensions ranging from low to high—rather than categories. Extroversion, for example, can be seen as a continuum ranging from introversion (being reserved, reflective, and self-absorbed) in the low extreme to extroversion (being outgoing, sociable, and talkative) in the high extreme. Neuroticism, on the other hand, is understood as the tendency to experience negative emotions, such as anxiety, worry, and tension. Someone with low neuroticism is emotionally stable and rarely anxious or worried, while someone with high neuroticism often experiences negative emotions.

Agreeableness is characterized by kindness, tender-mindedness, trust, and modesty, and people scoring high in agreeableness are often better able to control their anger in social situations. Openness to experience can be described as the tendency to be imaginative and curious, to have wide interests, and to appreciate arts and music. For example, people who are highly open to experience tend to experience more "chills" or "shivers down the spine" when listening to music. Finally, conscientiousness is associated with high self-discipline and goal-directed behaviors, such as planning and organizing. Research on these Big Five traits has shown that they remain relatively stable across an individual's life, and very similar traits can be found in different cultures across the world. However, differences in language and the words used to describe personality in different cultures pose some challenges to the cross-cultural study of personality. Importantly, personality traits have been associated with almost all forms of human activity, from academic achievement and partner selection to what music we like, and even how we tend to move on the dance floor.

PERSONALITY AND MUSIC PREFERENCES

When people are asked which of their preferences or activities would give the best insight into their personal qualities, music and hobbies tend to be chosen over films, books, food preferences, or clothes. In fact, this assumption is also supported by evidence from experiments, where psychologists have tested whether the information conveyed through music preferences can be reliably picked up by other people. This work has demonstrated that the personality traits of listeners can be reliably identified by other people based solely on their music choices. Even more remarkable is that this link seems to be stronger in the case of music compared to almost any other form of information about hobbies or preferences.

But what is it about music that conveys meaningful information about personality? Is it related to the genre of the music or perhaps to the content of its lyrics or its emotional expression? Or does it all boil down to the music's actual sonic qualities, such as its tempo, loudness, or instrumentation? Eminent personality psychologists had already started to address these questions in the early 1950s. In a study published in 1953, Raymond Catell and Jean Anderson asked groups of American students whether they liked music examples representing diverse styles—all performed by a professional pianist. They found striking links between the students' personality traits and their music preferences, such as extroverts preferring examples with more pronounced rhythmic qualities. Over the next three decades, numerous links between liking specific types of music and particular personality traits were reported. For instance, preference for "exaggerated bass" was linked with extroversion, and liking rock music was associated with sensation seeking and reckless behavior (such as speeding, shoplifting, and drug use). In later studies, people's music preferences were no longer measured using actual music excerpts;

instead, questionnaires were used to ask whether they liked different musical genres. This was an important distinction that enabled broader characterization of music and made large-scale studies on the topic easier and more efficient.

People often define and describe their musical tastes in terms of preference for specific genres (such as rock, pop, or classical). However, what constituted "rock" in the 1960s compared to rock in the 1980s or today is of course not quite the same thing. Consequently, researchers exploring these preference patterns have realized that it is more meaningful to describe musical qualities in a broader fashion (encompassing multiple genres in each category) rather than measuring preferences for individual genres or sonic features. As a result, researchers Peter Jason Rentfrow and Samuel Gosling defined a small number of general music preference categories. For instance, classical music, jazz, and folk music can be described as *reflective and complex* music styles, whereas genres such as rock, heavy metal, and alternative rock might be labeled as *intense and rebellious*. Pop and country can be characterized as *upbeat and conventional*, and soul, rap, and dance fall into the *energetic and rhythmic* category. The actual genres belonging to these four categories have been updated several times, but their overall characteristics have remained fairly similar.

Once the relevant music preference categories have been established, the links between personality and these categories can be investigated simply by collecting information about people's music preferences and personality traits using surveys. A common pattern observed in such surveys is that there is an overall correspondence between particular personality traits and the preference for certain musical categories: people who prefer to listen to *reflective and complex* musical styles (classical, jazz) tend to score high in openness to experience, and those who prefer *upbeat and conventional* styles of music tend to have higher scores in extroversion and agreeableness. These links show that a person's music preferences tell us something about their personality. In other words, if you know the music that an unknown person likes, whether extreme metal or classical piano music, you might be able to correctly guess their dominant personality trait. However, it should be acknowledged that the association between music preferences and personality, though reliable, is not very strong, which is not surprising given our personalities are related to more than just the music we like. An individual's music preferences are shaped by many other factors besides personality—such as their musical environment, past listening experiences, and the music preferences of their friends—and so the relationship between personality and music preferences is never straightforward. In other words, we can find broad overall correspondences between personality and music preferences when we look at large groups of people, but an individual's music preferences alone cannot tell you everything about their personality.

PERSONALITY AND MUSIC LISTENING

A more useful way of looking at the broad correspondences between personality and music preferences may be to view personality traits as tendencies to behave in certain ways across a variety of situations, reflecting differing motivations and psychological needs. Music listening occurs in many different situations and contexts in everyday life, and several studies have shown that music has the ability to fulfill many different functions and goals. Indeed, it is not surprising that people with different personalities also tend to use music for different functions and in different situations.

For instance, people who are extroverted (and by definition enjoy interacting with people) are action-oriented and have high energy levels in social situations. Similarly, music played at parties and clubs is often energetic and loud, inviting people to dance and join in. Extroversion is not only linked to a preference for upbeat, energetic, and rhythmic musical styles but also more generally to the tendency to use music as a background for other activities. It may be that extroverts mainly prefer music that best fits with their desire for social interaction, helping to maintain a high energy level.

On the other hand, jazz ballads and classical music—the *complex and reflective* musical styles preferred by people with high openness to experience—have sonic qualities that invite more solitary, inward-turned reflection. These musical characteristics enable listeners to contemplate and savor the aesthetic experiences that the music evokes, fitting well with highly open people's appreciation for complexity, beauty, and new experiences. In sum, one potentially fruitful way to understand the correspondences between personality traits and music preferences is to consider the different uses and functions afforded by different types of music.

Another helpful way of understanding the link between listeners and music preferences relates to emotions. Emotional tendencies are actually very central to the Big Five personality traits; extroversion is associated with the tendency to experience positive emotions, while neuroticism is associated with negative emotionality. Highly agreeable people are compassionate and less anger-prone, whereas those scoring high in openness to experience appreciate aesthetic emotions. This pattern is also reflected in people's music preferences: extroverts tend to like happy-sounding music, while agreeable people like happy- and tender-sounding music but dislike scary-sounding music. In other words, people tend to like music that somehow reflects or reinforces their personality traits.

Research has also shown that personality traits influence the kinds of emotions listeners experience when listening to music. For example, people who score high in openness to experience tend to experience more intense pleasure when listening to music, which is reflected by physiological reactions such as chills or shivers down the spine. In addition, empathy (a trait outside the Big Five framework) has been associated with more intense emotional reactions to music—especially sad music. It is thought that empathic people respond to emotional music in the same way as they respond to the emotions of other people: through empathy, they experience the same emotions as they perceive in the music (e.g., they feel sad when listening to sad music). However, even though empathic people feel sad when listening to sad music, they also enjoy listening to sad music more than people with low empathy.

CONCLUSION

People's music preferences tend to broadly reflect and reinforce their personality characteristics. However, it is important to keep in mind that personality only explains a very small portion of an individual's music preferences; our music preferences are always the product of a complex interaction between our personality traits, musical experiences, and cultural and social environments. For example, people often convey their musical preferences through clothes (e.g., band shirts) or hairstyles or by sharing their favorite music on social media. In these instances, individuals project an image of themselves to others, defining their identities and the (sub)cultural groups they belong to. In this way, music preferences serve an important function, especially in adolescence, when people are forming their identities and discovering the kinds of people they are.

Our personality traits also influence the type and intensity of emotions that we experience when listening to music. Since our musical preferences are closely intertwined with the emotions that music evokes in us (and emotional tendencies form an important part of our personalities), emotions are crucial to understanding the links between personality traits and music preferences. In fact, it may be that our music preferences are best explained by the fit between particular psychological needs and the types of uses afforded by different kinds of music. Perhaps it could even be argued that the purpose for which an individual typically uses music actually determines the type of music he or she prefers. In other words, the different uses or functions afforded by specific types of music may be what drives the personality-music preference associations that have been observed in research.

One important limitation in the existing research on personality and music preferences is that most studies have used very simple surveys to measure music genre preferences and everyday music listening behavior. However, these short surveys may not accurately capture people's actual music listening habits and preferences. To make matters even more complicated, the rapid development and spread of mobile listening technologies and streaming services has meant that the ways and situations in which music is being listened to has changed drastically within the last ten years. How has our music listening behavior been affected by the fact that many of us are now able to listen to whatever music we want, whenever and wherever we want? A practical solution for future research would be to utilize the mobile technologies (such as smartphones) that people use for music listening to also collect accurate research data about music listening habits and preferences. Such research-targeted smartphone applications have already been developed, and companies providing streaming services also hold vast quantities of data on listeners' everyday music choices. Combining these new sources of information will enable the study of actual music listening behavior in everyday life. These new technologies and research methodologies may hold the key to understanding the patterns of correspondences between music listening habits, music preferences, and personality traits in all their complexity.

References and Further Reading

North, A., & Hargreaves, D. (2008). *The Social and Applied Psychology of Music.* Oxford, UK: Oxford University Press.

Rentfrow, P. J., & Gosling, S. D. (2003). The do re mi's of everyday life: The structure and personality correlates of music preferences. *Journal of Personality and Social Psychology, 84*(6), 1236–1256.

Rentfrow, P. J., & McDonald, J. A. (2009). Music preferences and personality. In P. N. Juslin & J. Sloboda (Eds.), *Handbook of Music and Emotion* (pp. 669–695). Oxford, UK: Oxford University Press.

Vuoskoski, J. K. (2017). Musical preference: Personality, style, and music use. In R. Ashley & R. Timmers (Eds.), *Routledge Companion to Music Cognition* (pp. 453–464). Abingdon, UK: Routledge.

26. Personality and Musicians

Jonna K. Vuoskoski and Tuomas Eerola

It is a common assumption that there is something slightly different about musicians compared to other people; we tend to think that musicians are more creative and that they have something we call *musical talent*. We also tend to assume that they are able to express their thoughts and feelings through their music and that they enjoy performing in front of audiences. Who do you think would be more spontaneous and fun, an electric guitarist in a rock band or a harpsichordist in a chamber orchestra? We tend to have rather specific stereotypes about musicians from different genres (for example, rock musicians versus classical musicians) and specific assumptions about individuals who play certain instruments. But is there any truth behind these stereotypes? Does being a professional musician require certain personality characteristics, or do the years of musical training shape musicians' personalities to a particular direction?

It is useful to understand the motivational drives of those who want to become musicians: what are their reasons and motivations for pursuing music as a career, and what aspects of musicianship do they experience as rewarding? Recognizing the special characteristic of individuals who want to pursue music as a professional pathway can also help to improve the education and support of young developing musicians. Do musicians differ from the average person? Do different types of musicians, whether trumpet players or guitarists, differ from each other? Research on the psychology of music has considered personality differences along with other differences between musicians, such as emotional dispositions, social skills, and the likelihood that they will experience anxiety during a performance.

PERSONALITY CHARACTERISTICS OF MUSICIANS

Personality traits are central for understanding and characterizing individual differences in behavior, emotions, and patterns of thought. One of the most widely accepted ways of describing personality is the so-called Big Five personality theory, which differentiates between five broad trait dimensions: extroversion, neuroticism, agreeableness, openness to experience, and conscientiousness (for more information on the Big Five personality traits, see chapter 25, "Personality and Listeners"). Do musicians differ from the average person in terms of their personality traits, and, if so, how? First, let us consider what it means to be a *musician*. There is no single or easily definable category of musicianship, as the degree of musical training and engagement in musical activities may vary greatly from one musician to the next. For example, some rock musicians may have no formal musical training, but they engage in daily practice and regular performance and have years of informal learning. At the other end of the spectrum, there are highly trained individuals with fifteen or more years of formal musical training who do not work as musicians and only rarely engage in musical activities. Studies investigating the personality characteristics of musicians have tended to focus on those working as professional musicians (either in the domain of classical or popular music) and on music students. Thus, the research findings mainly reflect the personality patterns of professional musicians and of those studying to become professional musicians.

Being a professional musician poses conflicting demands on an individual's personality characteristics. On the one hand, becoming a proficient musician requires hours and hours of solitary, focused practice on a daily basis, which is something that introverts (individuals with low extroversion) thrive in. On the other hand, an important part of being a professional musician is performing in front of large audiences, which is a situation in which highly extroverted people feel more comfortable. These diverging requirements may attract individuals with very specific personality characteristics, but they can also have detrimental effects on the long-term well-being of professional musicians.

Broadly speaking, most musicians can be roughly characterized as "bold introverts." Bold introverts are unlikely to be the life of the party, loudly telling stories to the entire room, but instead have an inner confidence in themselves and in what they are doing. In other words, they are independent, detached, and self-sufficient but not serious or shy. While introversion helps with sustaining the extended periods of solitary practice, it can also make individuals more prone to feelings of anxiety (see the section on personality and performance anxiety later in this chapter). Interestingly, research has found that self-discipline and sustained interest in music are more important than actual musical aptitude or musicality in determining successful musical attainment in childhood. Indeed, introversion is a beneficial trait from this perspective because it supports the long hours of concentrated practice required. Musicians also tend to be more open to experience than the general population, meaning they are imaginative and curious and appreciate variety and aesthetic experiences. In contrast, people who are not open to experience can seem closed-minded because they are not receptive to new ideas or experiences.

One way of gaining a better understanding of the links between personality and musicianship is to look at how these links develop over time and whether you can see similar patterns in music students as well. For example, individuals who enroll for musical training tend to have higher scores in openness to experience to begin with, but they also tend to have better-educated parents. It is difficult to tease apart the causal relationships here; in other words, it is difficult to establish whether those with high openness to experience are more likely to undertake musical training or whether both musical training and openness to experience are related to a third factor, such as the parents' education level. In any case, it is probably safe to say that those individuals who carry on studying music tend to be interested in learning and gaining new experiences in general.

Unsurprisingly, musicians have also been found to be more creative and prone to divergent thinking and sensation seeking compared to the general population. These observations align well with the stereotypes regarding people working in the creative sector. But working as a musician may also require an aptitude for interacting fluently with other people (musically and otherwise) as well as an ability to effectively express a variety of different emotions. Indeed, it has been established that musicians tend to have strong social and interpersonal skills, and some studies have also found that musicians score higher in emotional intelligence and empathy compared to the average person.

PERSONALITIES OF DIFFERENT KINDS OF MUSICIANS

The broad personality characteristics outlined in the previous section apply mostly to classical musicians (or classical music students), as they have been the target of investigation in most studies looking at personality and musicianship. However, musicians working within popular music genres such as rock and pop are somewhat different, partly because the genres themselves carry certain cultural norms (such as different performance and practice conventions) that have different implications for personality characteristics. Overall, research has found that, compared to the general population, rock and popular musicians tend to score higher in neuroticism and openness to experiences and lower in agreeableness and conscientiousness. Interestingly, rock musicians have been found to be more extroverted than classical musicians, probably reflecting the difference in the relative importance of performance versus solitary practice in the two genres. Concerts and interaction with audiences plays a bigger role in popular music genres, while long hours of solitary practice form the core of a classical musician's work. Due to these different emphases, introverts and extroverts are perhaps attracted to different genres and to different aspects of music making.

So far, this chapter has reviewed the personality differences between musicians and nonmusicians and between classical and popular musicians. But what about musicians playing particular instruments or composers, conductors, or music teachers? There certainly exist some well-established personality and gender stereotypes in terms of instrument choice in the domain of both classical and popular music, but are these stereotypes also reflected in the actual personality characteristics of string and brass players in orchestras, for example? Research has found that string players tend to be more introverted, and brass players and percussionists tend to be more extroverted. This pattern fits well with the typical roles of these instrument groups in symphony orchestras, where individual brass and percussion players have more prominent roles than string players, who are part of larger sections. String instruments can also be considered technically more demanding, requiring longer periods of solitary practice. However, it is difficult to establish whether people's personalities affect their instrument choice or whether playing a particular instrument shapes an individual's personality to a direction determined by the typical roles and demands attached to that instrument.

The typical personality profiles of composers and music teachers follow similar intuitive patterns. Composers, for instance, have been found to be the most introverted of all musicians, whereas music teachers are even more extroverted than the general population. These differences reflect the varying roles and forms of musicianship. While there is considerable variation within any given category of musicianship, it may be that musicians have gravitated toward their preferred professional practice—be it composers, ensemble musicians, soloists, or educators—because of the way these tasks fit with their natural ways of engaging with others.

PERSONALITY AND PERFORMANCE ANXIETY

Most professional musicians have experienced some level of performance anxiety while performing, and it has been estimated that 25–35 percent of professional musicians suffer from severe performance anxiety that impairs their work and well-being. Importantly, certain personality traits—namely neuroticism and introversion—are associated with an increased sensitivity to performance anxiety. As discussed in chapter 25, neuroticism is a personality trait associated with an increased tendency to experience negative emotions such as worry and anxiety. Thus, it is not surprising that neuroticism is also associated with the tendency to experience performance anxiety in musical performance situations. The link between introversion and performance anxiety relates back to the dual conflicting demands of musicianship: On the one hand, introversion helps with sustaining focus during the long hours of practice, but on the other, it makes individuals more prone to experience performance anxiety in concert situations.

Introversion is not associated with negative emotionality or anxiety-proneness per se, but it is associated with an individual's capacity to tolerate external stimulation. Extroverts are outgoing and sociable, and they thrive in environments with high levels of stimulation. For example, many extroverts find it easier to concentrate when there is noise or music in the background, as it helps to raise their arousal levels. Introverts, on the other hand, find it easier to focus in silence, and they are easily disturbed by background noise. Psychologists think this is due to introverts and extroverts having differing levels of optimal arousal; extroverts need more stimulation to raise their arousal levels close to optimum, whereas introverts are easily overstimulated. In the context of musical performance, the performance event can be considered a highly stimulating situation. Because extroverts are able to tolerate higher levels of stimulation without becoming overstimulated (and might even perform better as the result of increased arousal levels), they often experience performance situations as positive and exciting. Introverts, on the other hand, can easily exceed their optimal levels of arousal in such situations, and overarousal can have negative effects on their performance. However, the level of optimal arousal also depends on the demandingness of the task at hand. The more demanding the task, the lower the optimal level of arousal is (and vice versa). For example, if one is performing a very familiar and easy piece of music, the level of optimal arousal would be higher than in the case of a very difficult, complex piece of music.

While personality traits such as neuroticism and introversion are associated with the tendency to experience performance anxiety, the most important contributors to music performance anxiety are self-esteem and self-efficacy. Self-esteem refers to an individual's overall attitude toward (and respect for) oneself, and self-efficacy reflects an individual's beliefs about their abilities and capabilities. Research has found that the self-esteem of musicians and music students is directly linked to how well they perform in their work and studies, suggesting that musicians may find it difficult to separate their self-image from their musical abilities. Low self-esteem and low self-efficacy are associated with high performance anxiety, but it is not clear whether low self-esteem leads to anxiety or whether anxiety causes low self-esteem. It may be that high anxiety leads to a poorer performance in concerts, which again leads to lower self-esteem, for example. In any case, it would be beneficial for musicians' and music students' health and well-being if professional music training involved more effective performance coaching and learning about strategies to mitigate negative performance anxiety.

CONCLUSION

The average personality profile of musicians and music students tends to differ from the general population. Moreover, different types of musicians often have distinct personalities related to the type of music or instruments they play and the type of musician they are, whether a performer, teacher, or composer. While cause-and-effect relationships are difficult to establish when it comes to personality and other individual differences, it is most likely that people's personalities influence their motivation to seek out certain kinds of musical activities in the first place (and thus their hobbies and career pathways). Conversely, it seems unlikely that engaging in certain musical activities can actually change one's personality. However, there is also emerging evidence showing that musical training may have a positive effect on certain social traits, such as empathic ability. Thus, while musical activities and careers may be particularly attractive to certain types of people, it may also be that musical activities reinforce and shape their individual characteristics to a certain extent.

References and Further Reading
Hallam, S. (2009). Motivation to learn. In S. Hallam, I. Cross, & M. Thaut (Eds.), *The Oxford Handbook of Music Psychology* (pp. 285–294). Oxford, UK: Oxford University Press.
Kemp, A. E. (1996). *The Musical Temperament: Psychology and Personality of Musicians*. Oxford, UK: Oxford University Press.

North, A., & Hargreaves, D. (2008). *The Social and Applied Psychology of Music*. Oxford, UK: Oxford University Press.

Wilson, G. D., & Roland, D. (2002). Performance anxiety. In R. Parncutt & G. McPherson (Eds.), *The Science and Psychology of Music Performance: Creative Strategies for Teaching and Learning* (pp. 47–62). Oxford, UK: Oxford University Press.

27. Who Likes Sad Music and Why?

Sandra Garrido

A scan of the song charts around the world at any given time is likely to reveal a number of popular songs that will probably draw a tear from the listener. People love to have a good cry over a song. This is quite paradoxical given that, in general, people prefer to avoid things that make them feel sad. In fact, emotion theorists classify *sadness* as a negative emotion, and negative emotions are often understood as evolutionary motivators to avoid things that are harmful or unhelpful. Just as we tend to avoid foods or substances that make us feel physically unwell, we also tend to stay away from situations or people that cause us emotional distress. Why, then, do we enjoy sadness in the case of music?

In fact, not everyone enjoys sad music, and those who do tend to enjoy it or be attracted to it for different reasons. The reasons why we listen to sad music are related both to our personality and to the psychological functions that sad music can fulfill. Even what we *perceive* as sad differs from person to person and may differ from day to day for a single individual.

In cultures all over the world, there are similarities between the way sadness is expressed in music and the physical changes that occur in our voices and vocal tracts when we communicate sadness. For example, people who feel sad tend to speak slowly and with a lower voice pitch and to have less changeability in that pitch than people who feel happier. When a more intense form of grief is being expressed, voices often become higher pitched and louder, use ingressive phonation (or inhaling while vocalizing), or may make a "breaking" sound, which is caused by constriction of the pharynx in the throat. Music often mimics these vocal sounds in expressing sadness or grief, whether through features of the composition itself, instrumental sounds, or the vocal techniques of singers. Thus, much of what we perceive as sadness in music is related to what we have learned throughout our lives about acoustic cues that express sadness.

Our own mood also has an effect on whether a piece of music is perceived as sad. Sadness is generally understood to be a low-arousal or low-energy emotion. However, more positive emotions, such as peacefulness, reflectiveness, or calmness, are also low energy. Emotion theorists say that the distinction between positive low-energy emotions such as peacefulness and negative low-energy emotions such as sadness often lies in whether we personally perceive the circumstances in which the emotions are experienced as positive or negative. For example, music that is slow and calm may be perceived as sad if the individual listening to it is in a sad frame of mind. On the other hand, someone who is feeling peaceful and relaxed may perceive the same piece of music as simply expressing beauty or serenity.

HOW WE USE MUSIC TO MANAGE MOOD

In addition to influencing whether we perceive a particular piece of music as sad, our mood has an influence on the types of music we listen to. Mood management theory argues that all of our choices in relation to media, such as the music we listen to, the movies we watch, or the books we read, are designed to help improve our mood, if we are feeling low, or to sustain a good mood, if we are already in one. The evidence seems to support this, with several studies showing that we generally do seem to prefer to listen to music that makes us feel happy.

However, it is well known that when people feel sad, they often like to listen to music that matches how they feel. It appears that doing this can actually improve their mood in the long run as well. Although the music may cause the listener to feel sad at first, certain psychological benefits can be achieved that ultimately cause some listeners to feel better. Among the benefits that can be obtained from listening to sad music are venting negative emotions (catharsis), feeling connected with other people who are experiencing the same thing as us, or reflecting on and making sense of life events. The types of benefits we are most likely to obtain from listening to sad music are closely related to our personality, and so some of the personality traits that are most closely associated with enjoying sad music are discussed in more detail below.

PERSONALITY AND A LIKING FOR SAD MUSIC

Research has demonstrated that people with particular personality traits are more likely to be attracted to sad music than other people and to use it in particular ways. For example, *absorption* is the capacity to become so deeply engrossed in something we are doing that we are unaware of the passage of time or things that are going on around us. Becoming profoundly absorbed and detached from the world around us for a time is a healthy process that can help us to cope with stress. The temporary suspension of self-awareness involved in absorption can also help us to reach peak states of mental performance known as *flow*. When we are in a state of flow, our mind feels sharp and alert, or we feel what people sometimes call "in the zone." Elite athletes, professional musicians, and other people who are the top performers in their fields, often report experiencing flow in their work. Because absorption enhances our daily functioning and our ability to adapt to stress, the brain appears to reward experiences of absorption by activating pleasure systems when we become deeply engaged in activities to this extent.

Many people with strong capacities for absorption are often attracted to sad music. Several studies have shown that people with high capacities for absorption seem to be able to just enjoy the emotional journey of listening to sad music without this being an unpleasant experience in the way that sadness would usually be if triggered by real-life events. In effect, the listener detaches from the negative aspect of sadness and is able to become absorbed in and to enjoy the emotional stimulation and beauty of the music.

Openness to experience is another personality trait that seems to be connected to liking sad music. Openness is one of the traits included in the Big Five personality model, which holds that just about all human characteristics can be covered by the five traits of extroversion, openness, conscientiousness, neuroticism, and agreeableness. The Big Five personality model is often used in psychological research to understand the basis for differing human behaviors, including the different ways people respond to music. People with high scores in openness tend to be imaginative, are easily moved by the arts, are attentive to their inner world and feelings, enjoy variety, and are intellectually curious. They are also more likely to experience absorption, as discussed above. People with high scores in openness to experience often have intense responses to sad music and usually enjoy it more than other people.

Music that is categorized as *sad* often has a broad range of emotional expression. For example, the music may start sad and melancholy, become intensely passionate in the middle, and then resolve with a sense of peacefulness at the end. Because people with high scores in openness to experience usually like variety and to experience a whole range of emotions, it is often this emotional changeableness that they enjoy rather than just the experience of sadness alone. Listening to sad songs gives them a chance to experience a whole array of different emotions in a short time and in a context that does not have real-life consequences.

Another important characteristic that is related to liking sad music is *empathy*. Empathy is the capacity to imagine how someone else is feeling, or being able to put oneself "in the other's shoes" and to feel what that person is feeling. Many scholars think that empathy involves the activation of *mirror neurons*. A mirror neuron is a nerve cell in the brain that is switched on when we observe someone else performing a particular action. The neuron activated is the same one that would be activated if we were performing the action ourselves. For example, if we see someone else kicking a ball, the neurons that would be activated if we were kicking the ball ourselves are triggered. In the same way, when we see someone else smiling, the neurons in our brain that would be activated if we were smiling are stimulated simply by seeing someone else smile.

To some degree, mirroring or mimicking these behaviors in our brain, even if we do not physically perform them, actually makes us feel as if we were doing them ourselves. Thus, seeing someone else smile makes us feel like smiling, which can cause us to feel a little happier, and seeing someone cry can make us feel a little bit like crying, which can cause us to feel a bit sadder. In the same way, it seems that hearing sadness being expressed in music can activate the same neurons that would be triggered if we were expressing this sadness ourselves. Thus, we feel empathy for the feelings being expressed by the singer or by some imaginary person that we may unconsciously picture behind the music, and we feel a little bit sad ourselves in response to that.

Rather than avoiding music that makes us feel empathetic and sad, however, the evidence shows that people who are strongly empathetic or prone to experiencing the emotions of others are more likely to be attracted to sad music than other people. Why is that? Well, like absorption, empathy is a healthy capacity to have from an evolutionary perspective. Empathy allows people within a group to be able to understand the emotions of others, respond to the needs of others, and take steps to protect the group as a whole from things that could be damaging or harmful.

Imagine our ancestors in prehistoric times when language was not as developed as it is today. Communication of emotions and needs likely took place using facial expressions and body language as well as vocal cues, such as the tone of voice and the speed and urgency of vocal sounds. If one member of the group was sad because of something harmful that had happened, the whole group would benefit from knowing what had happened and from taking steps to protect the group from further harm from the same source. Thus, empathy promotes social bonding between members of a group and causes individuals in the group to stick together and look after each other. Therefore, the capacity for empathy is an evolutionarily adaptive trait that has helped the human race to survive. Again, its usefulness to human survival ensures that the brain will reward empathetic behavior and make it feel pleasurable when we do it. Listening to sad music gives people an opportunity to use and exercise their capacity for empathy, even when there are no real-life events causing the sadness. Although what is experienced is a negative emotion, the brain makes it feel pleasurable for some people because of the way it activates the capacity for empathy.

Another psychological benefit that we can get from listening to sad music is the opportunity to engage in self-reflection. *Reflectiveness* is a psychologically healthy trait that is an inclination toward self-analysis, or thinking about and questioning one's own feelings and experiences. Reflective people are often good at dealing with their emotions because self-reflection can help people to go through processes such as cognitive reframing (finding more positive ways to view their experiences), problem-solving (thinking of solutions to difficult situations), or acceptance (learning to tolerate an unchangeable situation). Listening to sad music provides an opportunity for people to engage in self-reflection, and so it helps them to cope with negative emotions they may be experiencing. Thus, people with high scores in the personality trait of reflectiveness are often more attracted to sad music than other people.

A trait that is related to reflectiveness but has very different outcomes is *rumination*. Rumination, in the original sense of the word, refers to the way cows and other animals regurgitate and rechew partially digested food. In psychology, it refers to thought patterns that are mostly involuntary in which a person "rechews" negative and pessimistic thoughts in a repetitive way. It is similar to reflectiveness in that it involves concentrating on thoughts about the self, but the difference is that rumination does not help individuals to feel better about their experiences or to get over their difficult emotions. Whereas a reflective person will focus on finding solutions or ways to understand their situation that make it easier to deal with, a ruminative person focuses on all the negative aspects of their situation and, therefore, tends to feel much worse afterward. In fact, rumination is closely associated with clinical depression. People can find it very difficult to switch off these negative thoughts because of the chemical imbalances in the brain that can occur during episodes of depression.

People with strong tendencies to rumination also tend to listen to sad music a lot. In fact, when people are feeling depressed, they are likely to increase their music listening, particularly listening to music that reflects how they are currently feeling. However, it seems to be the case that this is not always pleasant for the individual or beneficial for their mental health. The processes described above by which people can obtain numerous psychological benefits from listening to sad music seem to malfunction in the case of ruminators and people with depression because of the negative thought patterns that are triggered when listening to sad music. However, it seems as if the brain often keeps rewarding the behavior on some level, and so depressed people may keep listening to sad music over and over, even though it is not helping, until they obtain professional psychological assistance to develop more helpful patterns of thinking. Interestingly, experimental evidence has shown that even though people who are depressed seldom feel like listening to upbeat, happy music, listening to music that communicates a positive message or that connects them with happy memories whether that music is happy or sad sounding, can often be more effective for improving their mood than listening to music with negative themes.

CONCLUSION

Personality has a big influence on whether we perceive certain music as sad, how we respond to it emotionally, and whether we enjoy listening to it. People with certain personality traits, such as absorption, empathy, openness to experience, and reflectiveness, may enjoy listening to sad music while obtaining certain psychological benefits from doing so. However, the processes that enable us to benefit from listening to sad music often backfire in people with clinical depression; they may end up feeling worse after listening to sad music.

References and Further Reading

Garrido, S. (2017). *Why Are We Attracted to Sad Music?* Cham, Switzerland: Palgrave Macmillan.

Garrido, S., & Schubert, E. (2011). Individual differences in the enjoyment of negative emotion in music: A literature review and experiment. *Music Perception, 28,* 279–295.

Garrido, S., & Schubert, E. (2015). Music and people with tendencies to depression. *Music Perception, 32,* 313–321.

Huron, D. (2011). Why is sad music pleasurable? A possible role for prolactin. *Musicae Scientiae, 15,* 146–158.

Vuoskoski, J. K. (2015). Music, empathy and affiliation: Commentary on Greenberg, Rentfrow, and Baron-Cohen. *Empirical Musicology Review, 10,* 99–103.

Vuoskoski, J. K., Thompson, W. F., McIlwain, D., & Eerola, T. (2012). Who enjoys listening to sad music and why? *Music Perception, 29,* 311–317.

28. Violence and Music

Kirk N. Olsen and William Forde Thompson

Themes of violence are commonplace in all forms of media. The daily news is riddled with stories of murder, death, and destruction. Television and cinema are constantly pushing the boundaries of acceptable depravity. Popular video games allow players to inflict violent acts on other gamers through online multiplayer experiences, and music with lyrics that describe rape and murder is readily accessible through online platforms such as Spotify and YouTube. Exposure to violent media has the potential to desensitize people to violence and normalize its existence in society. It is not surprising, therefore, that research on the psychology of media violence has spent a great deal of resources investigating how exposure to such violence affects how people think, feel, and behave. In this chapter, we will discuss one of the most understudied domains of media violence: music with violent themes.

VIOLENCE IN MUSIC

Violence is defined by the World Health Organization (2019) as "the intentional use of physical force or power, threatened or actual, against oneself, another person, or against a group or community, that either results in or has a high likelihood of resulting in injury, death, psychological harm, maldevelopment, or deprivation." In visual media such as television, cinema, and video games, acts of violence such as those captured in the World Health Organization's definition can be seen and even controlled. Music, on the other hand, is primarily an auditory experience; we hear music rather than see music. Of course, it is true that viewing a live music performance can enhance the listening experience. In some cases, musicians even act violently while they perform (e.g., rock musicians burning or smashing their guitars and drumkits; Nirvana and Jimi Hendrix are noteworthy examples). Nevertheless, violence in music is primarily conveyed through the description of violence found within lyrical content.

Music with violent lyrics is not common when compared to the majority of Western music, but it is increasing. The proportion of music with violent themes rose from almost nonexistent in the 1960s to approximately 10 percent in 2010. The genres that are most associated with violent messages include rap music and extreme metal music, such as death metal. Violent rap music was largely popularized through the gangsta rap movement of the 1990s. It is often characterized by a recurrent drumbeat with strong emphasis on fast-spoken vocals. Not all rap is about violence, but some rap music is explicitly violent and may even glamorize murder, violence toward women, and substance abuse. Extreme metal music, such as death metal, is characterized by loud, distorted guitar playing, fast "blast-beat" drumming, and screaming or growling vocalizations that depict extreme acts of violence. Cannibal Corpse—the most successful American death metal band— has released multiple albums in the American Top 40 Billboard charts and sold over two million units worldwide. Some examples of their song titles are "Relentless Beating," "Hacksaw Decapitation," and "She Was Asking for It." In arguably their most popular song, "Hammer Smashed Face," Cannibal Corpse lead singer George "Corpsegrinder" Fisher writes in intimate detail about a hypothetical murder experience:

"Eyes bulging from their sockets
With every swing of my mallet
I smash your f— head in, until brains seep in

through the cracks, blood does leak
distorted beauty, catastrophe
Steaming slop, splattered all over me"

Lyrics such as these have alarmed parental, community, and lobbyist groups, who blame such music for violent crimes and sometimes even want the music banned. There is no doubt that the lyrical themes push the boundaries of censorship laws: Cannibal Corpse had their music banned for periods of time in Germany, Australia, and Russia. Yet, such lyrics are commonplace and enjoyed by millions of fans across the world, and there is also no definitive evidence that violent music actually *causes* fans to behave violently.

Lyrical content undoubtedly represents the most direct and explicit way to convey violence in music, and for this reason, the phrase "violent music" is best restricted to music with lyrics that unambiguously depict acts of violence. But what about the nonlyrical sounds from musical instruments and the screaming or growling quality of the vocals? Can these sounds successfully convey violence or aggression when violent lyrics are absent or unintelligible?

CAN MUSIC *SOUND* VIOLENT?

People are afraid of what they do not understand, and *fear of the unknown* can apply to music. Early in the history of rock and roll, some people who were unfamiliar with the genre called it "noise." This reaction inspired the AC/DC song "Rock and Roll Ain't Noise Pollution." More recently, extreme metal music has been described as having an "aggressive" sound, and it is interesting to consider whether this description simply reflects a lack of familiarity with the genre or whether there is a legitimate case to be made that extreme metal has an aggressive sound. Take death metal, a genre that is characterized by instrumental and vocal sound qualities (timbres) with unnaturally low fundamental frequencies (pitch) and high levels of distortion, roughness, and intensity (loudness). Distortion has the effect of creating a "harsh" sound quality rather than a "clean" sound quality (consider the difference between an electric guitar and an acoustic guitar). Roughness has a similarly harsh effect on vocalizations and determines whether someone has a "hoarse" or "croaky" voice.

In the environment, sounds that contain these acoustic features tend to be found in auditory warnings—for example, animal growls that communicate threat and elicit fear in potential prey. There is now evidence showing that these acoustic features are found in human growling vocalizations that are commonplace in violent death metal music. When the loud and distorted electric guitars are combined with these vocalizations, nonfans of death metal experience the music as a scary, gruesome, and intense wall of noise that leaves them feeling threatened, fearful, and distressed. It seems that death metal musicians have harnessed specific aspects of sound in their music that taps into primal responses that can be traced back to ecological foundations.

Having explained why music may sound aggressive and even violent, we now discuss the characteristics of those who listen to violent music, how listeners experience this music, and how such experiences affect thoughts, feelings, and behaviors.

CHARACTERIZING FANS OF VIOLENT MUSIC

It is commonly believed that fans of extreme metal music are angry people, and the enjoyment of violent music must indicate a psychological dysfunction and antisocial lifestyle. Research investigating these types of claims study specific characteristics of fans of violent music and compare those with nonfans of violent music. Characteristics may include personality traits, mental health, and capacity to empathize with others. The most common measure of personality is the Big 5 personality inventory that considers five dimensions: extroversion (outgoing, energetic, talkative), agreeableness (friendly, compassionate, cooperative), conscientiousness (disciplined, dependable, cautious), neuroticism (tendency toward anxiety, shyness, self-doubt), and openness to experience (creative, curious, preference for novelty). Mental health is commonly measured using questionnaires that indicate whether someone is currently experiencing depression, anxiety, or stress, or has a predisposition to do so, and empathy can be measured by presenting scenarios to participants (e.g., someone acting aggressively to another person) and asking whether the participant sympathizes with the aggressor or the victim.

The findings from a range of studies in music psychology have shown that fans and nonfans of violent music have quite similar personality characteristics. Where differences are reported, they are often very small. For example, one study in Australia showed that a group of forty-eight fans of death metal were fractionally lower in agreeableness and conscientiousness than a group of ninety-six nonfans. However, their findings also showed that fans of violent music do have the capacity to show empathy for people in need, and this capacity is similar to nonfans. There is some evidence that people with mental health issues such as depression or anger occasionally gravitate toward violent music, perhaps because the music and its associated community of fans fulfill psychological needs that are not met in mainstream society. However, there is no evidence that listening to this music *causes* mental health problems. Rather, there is mounting evidence that violent music can actually function to reduce feelings of depression or anger in fans.

The majority of research investigating how listeners respond to violent music has focused on the potential for negative outcomes. This is understandable, as it is in the community's best interest to predict and minimize the occurrence of tragic violent events. But what does the scientific evidence say? Does exposure to violent music lead to negative outcomes such as aggression and violence?

ARE THERE NEGATIVE OUTCOMES FROM LISTENING TO VIOLENT MUSIC?

There are three key areas of research on the possible negative outcomes of exposure to violent music. They are studies that measure music's effect on aggressive thoughts, feelings, and behaviors. One of the key issues in these studies is whether violent lyrics or nonlyrical aggressive musical sound can elicit negative outcomes. Death metal music often has explicitly violent lyrics, and the musical sounds contain a range of aggressive signals that gives the music an aggressive or violent "feel." That is, an aggressive sound provides a backdrop for explicitly vio-lent lyrics. It is intuitive to predict that an aggressive sound may affect a listener's emotional state (feeling angry) and physical arousal (feeling energized). Lyrics, on the other hand, are explicitly violent and may elicit aggression-related thoughts in addition to feelings of emotional and physical arousal. The scientific evidence suggests that violent lyrics and aggressive sounds in music can both increase the propensity for *nonfans* to think aggressively and feel energized and hostile. How-ever, these effects tend to last for very short periods of time and in the context of a laboratory experiment, so it is unclear whether they translate to real-world situa-tions outside of laboratory conditions.

One way that researchers can investigate the effects of violent music on aggressive behavior is the "hot sauce" method. Here, listeners are presented with violent music for a period of time, and then researchers ask participants to indicate how much hot sauce they would like to give to the next participant, having been told that the next participant strongly dislikes hot sauce. The idea is that if exposure to violent lyrics causes listeners to feel aggressive, they might choose a greater amount of hot sauce than someone who is not feeling aggressive. Researchers have found that people who are exposed to violent lyr-ics in heavy metal, rap, and rock music exhibit greater levels of aggression (more hot sauce) than those who are exposed to music that does not contain violent lyrics. The question of how these results relate to more serious aggres-sive behavior is important to consider. At present, there is no clear evidence that people who listen to violent lyrics become more aggressive in the real world.

Some studies have addressed whether there are long-term effects of violent music that last beyond the hour usually needed for a laboratory experiment. Results have shown that over a two-month period, greater exposure to violent music was associated with an increased propensity to feel aggressive and a higher incidence of reported aggressive behaviors. However, as with many associations, it is impossible to say whether the increased exposure to violent music *caused* the increase in aggression. It could be that some other factor led to an increase in aggression as well as an increase in exposure to violent music.

It is clear that music with violent lyrics can elicit short-term increases in aggres-sive thoughts, feelings, and even behavior within a laboratory setting. When lon-ger time periods are considered outside of the laboratory, it is unclear whether violent music causes negative outcomes. Many fans of music claim that listening to violent music can help them deal with difficult feelings, so it could have a thera-peutic benefit.

Some research on violent music has only considered the effects of music on nonfans and has demonstrated that there are negative consequences of listening to violent music. However, given that nonfans neither enjoy nor listen to violent music in their day-to-day life, it is not surprising that they report negative feelings after listening to this music. To address this problem, more recent research has focused on the experience of fans of violent death metal, and this has shown that fans can actually benefit from listening to violent music.

ARE THERE BENEFITS FROM LISTENING TO VIOLENT MUSIC?

Research suggests that fans of violent music may derive psychological and social benefits from listening to their preferred music. One study measured emotional experiences after participants listened to a range of death metal music. Fans of death metal experienced empowerment, joy, and even peace after listening to violent death metal music. In contrast, the typical nonfan experienced tension, fear, and anger after listening to the same music. Furthermore, fans reported using violent music to regulate their mood. For example, they reported that the music helped them discharge negative feelings and revive themselves when they were feeling tired or worn out. One fan described his experience listening to death metal by stating that the music "makes me feel energetic when I'm down, and when I'm angry it brings me to a dark place internally so that I can work through these feelings." Another fan stated that the music "releases a lot of negative emotions and stress and focuses your attention on something you enjoy." The violent lyrical content in death metal may also function positively to enhance fans' identity and feelings of belonging by defining clear social boundaries between in-group (fans) and out-group members (nonfans). Such boundaries function to deter nonfans while simultaneously increasing social bonds between fans within the death metal community.

CONCLUSION

Why is it that some people can appreciate violent music and experience positive outcomes, whereas others cannot? A full understanding of the enjoyment of violent music needs to incorporate explanations at multiple levels of analysis that include biology, psychology, society, and culture. At the biological level, specific acoustic features in violent music may elicit chemical changes in the body that underpin feelings of positive energy and power reported by fans and tension, fear, and anger reported by nonfans. At a psychosocial level, violent music may enhance fans' well-being through mood regulation and an increased sense of identity and belonging that comes from close-knit bonds with other fans. At a cultural level, depictions of extreme violence in death metal are appreciated by fans for crossing implied censorship lines that further reinforce the community's sense of identity outside the mainstream music culture.

References and Further Reading

Olsen, K. N., Thompson, W. F., & Giblin, I. (2018). Listener expertise enhances intelligibility of vocalizations in death metal music. *Music Perception, 35,* 527–539.

Thompson, W. F., Geeves, A. M., & Olsen, K. N. (2018). Who enjoys listening to violent music and why? *Psychology of Popular Media Culture.* Advanced online publication. http://dx.doi.org/10.1037/ppm0000184

Thompson, W. F., & Olsen, K. N. (2018). On the enjoyment of violence and aggression in music. *Physics of Life Reviews, 25,* 128–130.

Warburton, W. (2012). How does listening to Eminem do me any harm? What the research says about music and anti-social behaviour. In W. Warburton & D. Braunstein (Eds.), *Growing Up Fast and Furious: Reviewing the Impacts of Violent and Sexualised Media on Children* (pp. 85–115). Annandale, NSW, Australia: Federation Press.

World Health Organization. (2019). *Definition and typology of violence.* Accessed January 14, 2019. https://www.who.int/violenceprevention/approach/definition/en.

Music and Ritual

29. Maternal Songs as Bonding Rituals

Sandra E. Trehub

Mothers throughout the world sing to infants in the course of providing care. Each mother sings in a manner that is unique in some respects but similar in other respects to mothers from the same culture. The differences across cultures are striking, reflecting different attitudes and practices about infant care. Infants are a receptive audience for maternal singing, not only because of their keen perceptual abilities but also because of their motivation for musical engagement. In light of the important role that music plays in the lives of adolescents and adults, it is not surprising that maternal singing—the main source of musical exposure for infants—has noticeable effects on infant attention and emotion. More surprising and important, perhaps, are its implications for the mother-infant relationship and for infants' social and emotional development more generally. It seems reasonable to consider maternal songs as bonding rituals because of their similarity to other rituals and their consequences for participants.

MUSIC LISTENING SKILLS IN INFANCY

Infants are remarkable in their perception of auditory patterns, especially musical patterns. They can detect subtle changes in the pitch or duration of a single note in a melody. In general, however, they focus on global melodic patterns rather than individual pitches or durations. Like adults, they recognize a melody when it is transposed or shifted to a different key or pitch level. For example, "Twinkle, Twinkle Little Star" or any highly familiar song is recognized regardless of its starting pitch. Similarly, infants recognize specific rhythms (e.g., **dum** da da **dum dum**) when presented at different tempos or rates (e.g., faster or slower). Infants are also sensitive to the beat of rhythmic music. By about five months of age, they move rhythmically to rhythmic music, which can be considered a precursor to dancing. Such rhythmic movement, although precipitated by music, is not synchronized with the music. In fact, moving to the beat of music is not usually evident until about four years of age.

Infants have distinct music preferences, just as adults do. They prefer vocal music to instrumental music, which may be linked to the biological significance of the human voice. They also prefer temporally regular music (i.e., music with a predictable beat) to irregular music. They prefer familiar music to unfamiliar music, and by twelve months of age, they prefer unfamiliar music in a familiar style (e.g., Western) to music in an unfamiliar style (e.g., non-Western). Also of interest is their preference for emotive song renditions over more neutral renditions, even as newborns, suggesting an inborn preference for positive vocal tone. At one time, infants were thought to prefer higher-pitched to lower-pitched singing. It has become clear, however, that their pitch preferences are context-dependent. For example, they prefer higher-pitched renditions of play songs, which emphasize their lively, playful quality, and they prefer lower-pitched renditions of lullabies, which emphasize their soothing quality.

Infants' memory for music is exceptional, especially for vocal music. After at-home exposure to musical recordings for one or two weeks, infants recognize the melodies when they are presented at the same pitch level or at different pitch levels (transposed). When the melodies are vocal rather than instrumental, they also remember the original pitch level of the melodies. Moreover, when five-month-old infants are exposed to a novel song at home for one or two weeks and have no further exposure to it thereafter, they recognize the song several months later. In fact, they distinguish the original song from another song with the same lyrics and rhythm, which indicates that they remember the melody itself.

The context of listening also influences infants' interpretation of music and their memory for that music. At times, adults bounce infants while they listen to music. The pattern of such bouncing—on every second beat or every third beat—influences how infants perceive and remember the music. Moreover, the songs that mothers sing have short-term as well as long-term consequences for infants.

MATERNAL SINGING: CONTEXTUAL FACTORS

In developing countries, mothers remain in almost constant physical contact with infants, carrying them throughout the day—in slings with infants against the front, back, or side of the mother's body—and sleeping with them at night. In general, mothers in developed countries maintain much less physical contact with their infants. However, they engage in more face-to-face interaction with infants who are safely ensconced in various devices—high chairs, bouncers, or swings—until they are moved to separate areas for sleep. Perhaps it is no surprise that the predominant songs for infants in high-contact cultures are lullabies, and the predominant songs for infants in low-contact cultures are play songs.

Although it is common to think of musical experiences as auditory events, infants' musical experiences are typically multimodal events. For infants in high-contact cultures, maternal lullabies are typically accompanied by the warmth of the mother's body and her movement because her singing often occurs while performing chores at home, in the fields, or elsewhere. Infants in such cultures remain with their mother at all times, resulting in incidental exposure to a wide range of music in the community, including religious songs, work songs, dance songs, and mourning songs. By contrast, the face-to-face performances in low-contact cultures are accompanied by distinctive facial expressions (i.e., considerable smiling while singing) and often by observable body movement, such as side-to-side swaying or rhythmic head nodding. Although these infants have limited contact with the wider community, they have periodic opportunities for overhearing recorded music intended for their parents.

Despite cross-cultural differences in the manner of caregiving, mothers in all cultures are committed to the well-being of their infants. Nevertheless, there are various short-term consequences of high rates of holding and carrying infants, such as increased infant sleep duration and decreased fussing or crying. Different caregiving practices arise from different societal values, such as collectivism and interdependence in high-contact societies versus individualism, independence, and self-reliance in low-contact societies.

Attitudinal differences across cultures are reflected in the ways in which mothers put infants to sleep. In so-called carrying cultures, infant sleep is unscheduled, unfolding naturally and incidentally as mothers go about their usual activities. On occasion, however, mothers sing lullabies to accelerate sleep. What is invariant, however, is the mother's presence during the infant's transition to sleep. In contrast, mothers in low-contact societies that value independence expect infants to fall asleep on their own within a number of months after birth. Such societies have witnessed an unprecedented demand for costly professional guidance in "infant sleep training." Common do-it-yourself alternatives involve commercial sleep machines or smartphone apps designed for use with infants. Such devices emit nature sounds (e.g., rain, ocean), artificial sounds (white noise, simulated vacuum cleaner), or recorded lullabies that promise to deliver infant slumber without parental intervention.

MATERNAL SINGING: DESCRIPTIVE FEATURES

Research to date has largely focused on Western societies and therefore on play songs. What has emerged is that mothers (and fathers) sing to infants at a higher pitch level, slower tempo, and with a warmer vocal tone than when singing the same songs in other contexts (e.g., informal, self-directed singing). Naïve listeners evaluate the versions sung to infants as more loving than the versions sung in other contexts. The presence of an infant seems to be necessary for eliciting fully expressive performances from parents. For example, parents are unable to produce equally emotive renditions when they attempt to reproduce such performances in the infant's absence. In fact, mothers' performances are less expressive or loving than usual when the infant is present but obscured from view (e.g., curtain between mother and infant). The quality of maternal performances seems to depend critically on as yet unspecified feedback from infants (e.g., wide-eyed attention, focus on singer's face) that confirms their engagement with the performer or performance. Also notable is mothers' almost constant smiling face while singing to infants, in contrast to their intermittent smiling when talking to infants.

Although mothers know the tunes and lyrics of several children's songs, they sing the same few songs over and over again to their preverbal infants. When asked why they sing those songs rather than others, mothers claim that these are the infant's favorites. In fact, mothers are highly confident about their reported order of infants' preferences—this one liked best, that one next, and so on. No doubt, infants' song preferences are influenced by how frequently mothers sing specific songs. Whether mothers realize it or not, they are the primary drivers of children's musical preferences until children can make their own music-listening choices. In general, mothers sing conventional children's songs to infants. The melody of "Twinkle, Twinkle Little Star" ranks high among maternal selections

Photo 29.1   Baby Ryan and His Father. (Photo by Sheryl Seidman. Used by permission)

in English-speaking and non-English-speaking countries across wide geographic areas. Some mothers compose unique songs for their infants, and they sing their own compositions frequently. Fathers who have limited familiarity with children's music sing pop songs or folk songs to their infants, personalizing the lyrics by incorporating the child's name and other child-specific information (see photo 29.1).

Remarkably, mothers perform their songs for infants in a highly stereotyped manner, typically singing specific songs at the identical pitch level and tempo on different occasions. Those performances, which feature stereotyped visual as well as auditory gestures, have parallels with rituals in various cultures, religions, or cults where the form of a behavior sequence (e.g., ritual hand washing, ritual chant, prayer, or dance) is more critical than its apparent function (e.g., achieving clean hands, spiritual communion). Although rituals are present universally, they differ in form from one culture to another. There are similarities, however, in their broad function, which is to foster cohesion or belonging with others who perform such rituals.

Maternal play songs are dyadic rituals, rather than group rituals, that promote bonding or cohesion between those who perform the rituals (mothers) and those for whom they are performed (infants). These songs are memorable and meaningful for mother and infant, evoking feelings of warmth, comfort, security, and connection. There is no indication that maternal lullabies are performed in the ritualistic or stereotyped manner of play songs. Moreover, unlike play songs, they promote disengagement (e.g., sleep) rather than engagement (e.g., mutual attention) and social cohesion.

FACTORS THAT COMPROMISE MATERNAL SINGING

Although mothers typically sing to infants several times a day, adverse circumstances can diminish the quality or quantity of such singing. For example, mothers with postpartum depression are less motivated to sing to their infants, and the singing that occurs lacks the vigor, positive emotion, and ritual nature of typical maternal singing. In other words, their songs do not function as bonding rituals, as they do for nondepressed mothers. Other adverse circumstances, such as poverty and infant prematurity, elevate maternal stress levels and impede maternal caregiving, including singing rituals. For example, prematurely born infants often remain hospitalized for several weeks after birth, limiting opportunities for maternal interaction. Even after discharge, such infants remain at elevated risk for health and cognitive problems, and their mothers are at risk for anxiety and depression. A number of ongoing initiatives are aimed at enhancing opportunities for mother-infant interaction and maternal singing in neonatal intensive care units.

CONSEQUENCES OF MATERNAL SINGING: ATTENTION

Infants in the newborn period and thereafter exhibit preferences for songs performed in the maternal style (i.e., infant-directed (ID)) to those performed informally in self-directed style, which is consistent with inborn preferences for emotionally positive vocalizations. Audio recordings of ID speech (i.e., speech in the maternal style) are as effective as recordings of ID singing for capturing infant attention, but multimodal maternal singing is more effective than multimodal speech for maintaining infant attention and reducing distress. Undoubtedly, the ritual nature of maternal singing, as opposed to more variable maternal speech, contributes to its efficacy in regulating attention and emotion.

CONSEQUENCES OF MATERNAL SINGING: EMOTIONAL AND SOCIAL REGULATION

Live multimodal singing by the mother affects infants' level of arousal, perhaps promoting optimal arousal levels—raising arousal when it is low and lowering it when it is high. When researchers induce distress in ten-month-old infants by having mothers become unresponsive to infants after a period of playful interaction, infants become highly aroused and visibly upset, trying repeatedly but unsuccessfully to engage their unresponsive mother. When mothers resume play with infants by means of multimodal singing or talking, infants' arousal levels, negative vocalizations, and frowning decrease more rapidly when mothers sing to infants than when they speak. In fact, crying infants are transformed into smiling infants soon after mothers initiate their ritual songs. Presumably, those rituals signal dyadic identity, evoking memories of comfort and pleasure and distracting infants from their distress.

Songs that mothers sing regularly become especially significant, even when sung by others. For example, five-month-olds are prepared to engage socially with an unfamiliar woman after she sings one of the mother's songs but not if she sings a song heard equally often from a musical toy. By fourteen months, infants offer help to others in need. The extent of their helpfulness is influenced by the adult's previous behavior. For example, fourteen-month-olds offer more help to an unfamiliar adult who previously moved in synchrony with them (i.e., precisely in time) than to an adult whose movement was out of synchrony. If an unfamiliar woman sings one of the mother's songs, fourteen-month-olds subsequently offer more help than if she sings an unfamiliar song. By performing a maternal song or bonding ritual, even if performed imperfectly, the unfamiliar woman exhibits her potential suitability or trustworthiness as a social partner—someone who is similar in some respects to the child's mother.

The onset of independent singing typically occurs between the first and second birthdays. At that time, infants produce songs that their mothers sing most frequently. Despite their familiarity with songs of their favorite TV characters (e.g., Dora), they choose to sing their mothers' songs—their bonding rituals—rather than other familiar songs. As singers, they have new and effective means of emotional self-regulation. Singing one of the mother's songs evokes pleasant memories of mother-infant interactions, easing the stress of separation at bedtime, ameliorating distress, or enhancing pleasure. As toddlers spend increasing time outside the home, whether in daycare or other settings, they affiliate with children who know the songs that they know or who like the songs that they like. Their social choices have parallels to adolescents' and young adults' consideration of music preferences when evaluating peers as potential social or romantic partners.

CONCLUSION

Singing to infants is part of the maternal caregiving repertoire in every region of the world. Maternal singing is characteristically multimodal—involving sight, touch, and movement as well as sound. The specific combination of multimodal components in a specific culture reflects the traditions and values of that culture. Maternal play songs can be considered rituals because of their stereotyped performances, which are repeated with minimal variability. Like other rituals, bonding or social cohesion is the principal function of these songs. Maternal songs also function as critical caregiving tools because of their efficacy in promoting sleep, ameliorating distress, regulating mood, and guiding social interaction.

References and Further Reading
Mehr, S. A., Song, L. A., & Spelke, E. S. (2016). For 5-month-old infants, melodies are social. *Psychological Science, 27*, 486–501.

Sole, M. (2017). Crib song: Insights into functions of toddlers' private spontaneous singing. *Psychology of Music, 45*, 172–192.

Trehub, S. E., & Cirelli, L. K. (2018). Precursors to the performing arts in infancy and early childhood. *Progress in Brain Research, 237*, 225–242.

Trehub, S. E., Plantinga, J., & Russo, F. A. (2016). Maternal vocal interactions with infants: Reciprocal visual influences. *Social Development, 25*, 665–683.

30. Music and Ecstatic States

David M. Greenberg

A powerful effect of music is that it can lead to elevated states of consciousness. One such state is an *ecstatic state*. Ecstatic states are temporary mental and emotional states that involve a sense of increased connectedness to other people or one's surroundings. It is important to note that ecstatic states are different from trance or hypnotic states. Whereas an ecstatic state implies elevated consciousness or heightened awareness, a trance state implies a loss or lack of consciousness or awareness, as in hypnosis. Ecstatic states imply consciously gaining new insights about the self and environment, whereas trance or hypnotic states imply a loss of sense of self.

Ecstatic states have been documented for thousands of years, and although states of ecstasy can occur in many different contexts, they are often associated with religious experiences. This remarkable effect on consciousness means that listening to or playing music can be a *spiritual* activity, whereby music seems to connect us with something that is greater than ourselves. People of faith may report that they feel closer to God; others may report that the music connects them with nature or gives them a deeper understanding of the universe.

A common theme across religions from East to West is the involvement of music and ecstatic states in spiritual practice. Many religious texts, including those dating back thousands of years, provide deep insights about the role of musically induced ecstatic states. Particularly when it comes to mystical elements of religion, ecstatic states play a large role in the connection between music and spirituality. These beliefs and practices remain in prominent use today, and they offer detailed explanations about the psychological and healing effects that music has on the body and mind.

This chapter explores the beliefs and practices of inducing ecstatic states across several religions and spiritual orientations, including Judaism, Sufism, Hinduism, and Shamanism. The chapter culminates with an exemplary but brief case study of an influential musician who used ecstatic states to achieve spiritual transcendence. It will be shown that there is a common musical and psychological process that occurs across religions to create a sense of spiritual transcendence. Specifically, it will be shown that two musical devices, repetition and improvisation, are used to induce an ecstatic state. The musically induced ecstatic state then acts as a container to facilitate a more profound experience of spiritual transcendence. This process is displayed in figure 30.1.

Figure 30.1 The Process of Achieving Spiritual Transcendence Through Music.

JUDAISM

Judaism is a religion steeped in music. Music is a central component to religious celebrations, rituals, and prayer, and the Torah (i.e., the Five Books of Moses of the Old Testament) is read in Hebrew each week using a musical pronunciation called *trope*. Many visual depictions of Tzaddikim (a Jewish righteous person) include ecstatic dancing. These depictions contrast other spiritual practices, such as Buddhist monks who are often depicted in silence and stillness. Musical activity in service of spirituality has been an integral part of the history of Judaism. It is said that the Jewish prophets used music to induce a higher state of consciousness and the mood state necessary to receive prophesy.

Kabbalah is an ancient tradition that includes mystical interpretation of Jewish texts. Chassidism is a form of Judaism that draws heavily on the ideas of the Kabbalah. Central to the worship of Chassidism is the *nigun*. A nigun, in the most traditional sense, is a wordless melody that is repeated over and over again. The melody can be simple or complex, and although nigunim (the plural form of nigun) can be sung alone, they are typically sung in groups to increase their effect. Nigunim are traditionally sung without instruments, although more contemporary musicians have begun to add harmonic, rhythmic, and melodic instruments. The repetition of a nigun can induce an ecstatic state that is experienced communally, often invoking dance and movement. This was taken to an extreme by one Chassidic group that was moved so deeply by the nigun that the members would "swirl in summersaults from great ecstasy" (Pinson 2000, p. 94). Here, the musical ecstasy was driven by the repetition of the nigun sung over and over.

SUFISM

Sufism is the mystical sect and practice of Islam. Similar to Judaism, music is a central component to spirituality for Sufis, and they believe that music connects humans to upper spiritual dimensions. Inayat Khan, who brought Sufism to the West, wrote, "The Sufi . . . names music Giza-I-ruh, the food of the soul, and uses it as a source of spiritual perfection" (Khan 1923, p. 76). In a similar way to how rabbis describe how musical ecstasy can enable a person to "jump" or "skip" beyond intellect to experience higher spiritual dimensions, Khan wrote, "The consciousness by the help of music first frees itself from the body and then from the mind (Khan 1923, p. 77).

Using music as a vehicle to experience spiritual transcendence is a central feature of the spiritual practice of Sufism. Sufis' musical practices often use repetition and improvisation as a musical device. At a Sufi Dhikr ceremony, prayer includes repetition, such as repeatedly chanting a devotional single word or phrase. The chanting is sometimes accompanied with side-to-side head movement. During the ceremony, Sufis form circles (e.g., concentric) and move step by step to their left while chanting and praying. At times, an individual will step to the middle circle and pray or sing devotionally (sometimes using improvisation) with word and wordless melodies. The ceremony includes whirling dervishes who spin in circles toward the left with their heads tilted and arms slightly raised (movements are to the left so as to lead with the heart). During these rituals, the repetition of the chanting along with the repetition of the circular movements create a circular effect that induces a state of ecstasy and, as Khan said, achieves a higher state of spiritual awareness.

HINDUISM

In Hinduism, like Judaism and Sufism, music is a key component of spiritual practice. The Bengali saint Paramahansa Yogananada, who brought Hinduism to the Western world, said that vibrational sound is the most powerful force in the universe. As Yogananda (1974) detailed, singing can lead to an elevated state of consciousness referred to as "God-realization" by attuning to the vibrations from devotional singing to the "cosmic vibration" (Yogananda 1974).

Mantras, although now pervasive across religious and spiritual practices, were first composed by Hindus thousands of years ago. They consist of a syllable, word, or phrase that is chanted repeatedly. These mantras contain both melodic and rhythmic elements. Some mantras have explicit meaning, but others are simply sound patterns. Mantras can be practiced individually or in a group. They are often used within the context of meditation or devotional prayer and have an emotive or spiritual effect that is intended to create a transcendent experience for the practitioner. Therefore, mantras can be considered to be the Hindu counterpart of Jewish nigunim.

An extension of the mantra is *kirtan*, which is a musical form that features call-and-response. Kirtan means "narrating" in Sanskrit and is considered to be a form of chanting. Typically, the leader(s) sing a spiritual or religious phrase that is then repeated by a separate group of individuals. This call-and-response pattern is performed repeatedly, inducing a state of ecstasy. Kirtan often features instruments, including the harmonium, tablas, mridanga, and kartals. As with the practices of Judaism and Sufism, kirtan uses repetition as a musical device to induce an ecstatic state.

SHAMANISM

Shamanism is an ancient practice that involves using altered states of consciousness to interact with other people, the environment, and the spiritual world. The altered state is achieved through different methods, including music. A prominent method is drum circles, which involves at least three individuals and includes percussion instruments in African, Native American, or South American cultures (e.g., djembes and congas). During a drum circle, there are one to several rhythmic sequences that are repeated over and over, producing an ecstatic effect. At times, one of the participants may improvise while the other members continue with the same rhythm, providing a musical grounding for the improviser to freely explore musically. Here, the repetition of the percussive rhythms facilitates a container with which the participants can achieve a heightened state of spiritual awareness.

Ecstatic states cannot be discussed without noting movement and dance. Ecstatic dance, which has been documented for thousands of years, is a communal event in which a group of individuals come together to dance freely (i.e., entirely improvised) for hours at a time. A more structured form of ecstatic dance was developed by Gabrielle Roth, who, after studying with psychologists (including influential gestalt therapist Fritz Perls) and shamans, developed the 5Rhythms movement, which has become internationally known. 5Rhythms is a dance practice that involves meditative movement that increases a sense of creativity and connection. In 5Rhythms, like in ecstatic dance, a group of individuals come together for an improvisational dance to music. However, in the case of 5Rhythms, the music and dance is structured across five successive rhythms: flow, staccato, chaos, lyrical, and stillness. These five rhythms are intended to bring an individual to experience the range of human emotion and to achieve a heightened state of conscious awareness. Though repetition can play a prominent role in the dance, improvisation is the key element that put an individual in touch with one's inner self and an ecstatic state.

CASE STUDY

Many influential musicians throughout history have fused spirituality with their music: Johann Sebastian Bach included an acknowledgment for the "glory of God" at the end of his compositions; The Beatles spent significant time in India to study meditation, and the great twentieth-century saxophonist John Coltrane used both improvisation and repetition to induce spiritual transcendence. Coltrane was one of the first in the jazz idiom to incorporate spirituality and music from the East into jazz. His musical intensions were largely of a spiritual nature. He said, "I'd like to point out to people the divine in a musical language that transcends words. I want to speak to their soul" (Porter 1998, pp. 78–79). Coltrane also stated toward the end of his life that the majority of his music was a prayer to God.

In describing his improvisations, Coltrane wrote, "I'll try to build things to the point where this inspiration is happening again, where things are spontaneous and not contrived. If it reaches that point again, I feel it can continue—It's alive again" (Porter 1998, p. 229). Coltrane was known to improvise continuously for an hour or more at a time (in comparison, the typical jazz musician might improvise for three to five minutes during any particular song). Coltrane was known to have ecstatic experiences while performing, which can be heard and seen in video recordings of his music. The audience also experienced ecstasy during his performances, as he could evoke spontaneous reactions from the audience that were

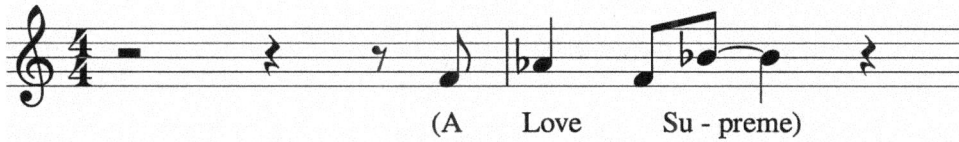

Figure 30.2 Motif That Is Repeated Musically and Vocally in "Acknowledgement" from John Coltrane's *A Love Supreme.*

akin to primal screams. The transcendent spiritual experiences felt by the listener from both Coltrane's live and recorded music has been well documented. There is even an African Orthodox Church in San Francisco that reveres Coltrane as a saint and revolves its services around his album *A Love Supreme.*

In addition to improvisation, Coltrane often used repetition as a musical device. To the untrained ear, it may not sound like repetition, but through his improvisations, Coltrane would repeat an idea and modulate it in a variety of ways. One explicit use of repetition is from the first part of the four-part suite of *A Love Supreme* called "Acknowledgement." In the piece, Coltrane plays the "A Love Supreme" motif repeatedly. This motif is notated musically figure 30.2. Coltrane repeats the phrase thirty-seven times and in all musical keys, indicating that "God is everywhere" (Porter 1998, p. 242). This is followed by the musicians chanting, "A Love Supreme," to the same melody. This repeated motif is in many ways similar to the nigunim from Judaism, chants from Sufism, and mantras from the Hinduism.

CONCLUSION

This chapter explored different routes to ecstatic states through music and their connection to spiritual transcendence. It highlighted practices from Judaism, Sufism, Hinduism, and Shamanism and showed how the use of repetition and improvisation during prayer can facilitate ecstatic states that lead to spiritually transcendent experiences. The chapter culminated with an exemplary case study, showing how John Coltrane used improvisation and repetition in his music as a device for spiritual transcendence. These diverse spiritual practices share remarkable similarities, and their use for psychological and spiritual growth warrants attention from the fields of music psychology and music therapy for future research.

References and Further Reading
Khan, I. (1923). *Mysticism of Sound.* London, UK: Pilgrims.
Pinson, D. (2000). *Inner Rhythms: The Kabbalah of Music.* Northvale, NJ: Aaronson.
Porter, L. (1998). *John Coltrane: His Life and Music.* Ann Arbor: University of Michigan Press.
Roth, G. (1992). *Maps to Ecstasy: Teachings of an Urban Shaman.* Novata, CA: Nataraj Publishing.
Yogananda, P. (1974). *Cosmic Chants.* Los Angeles, CA: Self-Realization Fellowship.

31. Music and Rites of Passage

Jane W. Davidson and Stephanie Rocke

Music has a rich association with cultural traditions linked to key changes in our lives. These changes are often referred to as *rites of passage* and include birth and infancy, the transition from childhood to adulthood, love and heartbreak, and marriage and death. This chapter explores how music can augment rites of passage and their associated ceremonies and events across cultures and time.

BIRTH AND INFANCY

The arrival of a baby is one of the most significant events in human experience. In this context, music is found to have a variety of purposes. It can be a tool for managing childbirth, assisting with bonding infant and caregiver, forming part of birth ceremonies, and supporting infant care.

Although a baby's arrival is a time of great joy, childbirth itself can be highly stressful. Relying on scientific evidence that certain types of rhythms, harmonies, and melodies can help the woman relax, playing music with these features has been found to reduce the stress of labor. For example, music with a slow pulse tends to reduce heart rate, and this can help to calm the mother and even those with her as supporters.

Music can also influence hormone releases. Hormones are substances produced in the body that are transported in the blood to stimulate cells or tissues into action. In childbirth, the release of these hormones can be counterproductive, but when music is played, the hormone produced in stress-provoking situations can be greatly reduced because the listener focuses on the music and is distracted from the stressor.

In addition, according to gate control theory, loading an individual's nerve pathways with music information restricts other messages, such as pain signals. This means that listening to music can also help to reduce the experience of pain. In a situation such as childbirth, which can be both stressful and painful, women are increasingly encouraged to use their favorite playlists to aid them through the experience.

In some traditional African cultures, each mother is given a unique birth song that is sung by both parents when planning the baby. Later, other female members of the community learn the song so that it can be sung while the mother is giving birth. It is the first sound that greets the child, its familiarity forming a sonic bridge between life in the womb to life beyond.

In traditional Indian Hindu family contexts, special songs are sung by women at different stages of pregnancy and at birth. The lyrics of these *sohar* give the woman information about what to expect to reduce her anxieties. Immediately after the baby is born, loud noises are made with conch shells and metal plates to announce the baby's arrival and ward off evil spirits. Songs are also sung to celebrate the new arrival.

Singing to infants is an internationally enjoyed and common cultural practice. Infants are most typically exposed to lullabies as sleep-inducing songs. Play songs, by contrast, are used with slightly older babies to entertain and teach and are lively and fun. Thus, two types of songs can be used to create different effects on infants. Some developmental psychologists argue that singing to infants is an interactive process that strengthens mutual feelings and bonds between caregivers and infants in a continuous feedback loop.

In all cultures, music is strongly associated with birth and infancy. This acknowledges music's power to relieve and empower mothers, calm or energize infants, strengthen bonds between caregivers and infants, and express the joy of the community when a new life is introduced to the world.

COMING OF AGE AND THE TRANSITION FROM CHILDHOOD TO ADULTHOOD

Coming of age is a rite of passage that varies immensely between cultures. For some, it is aligned with puberty and so will often occur at around fourteen years of age. For others, it may be tied to the society's legal definition of adulthood, which is often eighteen or twenty-one years of age, and associated with certain rights, such as the rights to vote, marry, or drink alcohol in a bar.

In societies structured according to traditional tribal order—that is, based around traditions of common heritage, descent, language, culture, and ideology— the coming-of-age rite most often takes place at puberty. This tradition recognizes that once puberty is reached, certain adult roles, including reproduction, are possible. Rites contribute to social stability by enforcing communal beliefs and authority systems and often include music, song, and dance. Specific songs are used to educate young people about local customs and traditions, gender roles, and sexual knowledge.

In other contexts, performances invoke spiritual or mystical conditions that transcend everyday experience to signify the special transformation of the individual. In the Okrika tribe in Nigeria, girls aged fourteen to sixteen are taught traditional songs and are encouraged by older women to sing them at the riverbank at dawn for several days in succession. In so doing, it is believed that the girls detach themselves from romantic feelings for water spirits, freeing them for human romance.

In Judaism, a ceremonial bar mitzvah (for boys) or bat mitzvah (for girls) is held when the child reaches twelve or thirteen years of age. In this coming-of-age context, the child often chants the relevant week's *haftarah*—a text from the prophets— as well as the blessings before and after it. Their participation in this leadership role symbolizes their initiation into Jewish traditions as young adults.

With globalization, many of these traditional rituals are changing, sometimes removing the significance of the coming-of-age transition entirely. In fact, coming-of age ceremonies worldwide are increasingly being replaced by birthday celebrations. These often include dancing to live or recorded music and commonly include the singing of "Happy Birthday," which is the most recognized song in the English language, and many other languages too. This song is a growing international choice, revealing that once a tradition is created, it can develop over time, especially where conditions such as digital media support its dissemination.

ROMANTIC LOVE AND HEARTBREAK

Romantic love and the heartbreak associated with lost or unrequited love are concepts that are found in all cultures. The links between love and music may have an evolutionary basis. Among birds, for example, song helps to attract a partner. Thus, music may have played a role in mate selection and courtship across human evolution.

Romantic love is a phenomenon common to all cultures, yet history shows that it has been given varying degrees of value according to context. In Europe, notions of romantic love may have been developed and fostered to motivate people to attach themselves to a single mate, enabling a stable environment in which to perform parenting duties. In other societies, marriages have been arranged based on other criteria, some believing love to be the outcome of a good match and others finding love to be irrelevant. In modern Western societies, the association of music with romantic love is evident in the expression "they're playing our tune." Once established as personally significant, the "tune" is frequently used to memorialize the couple's love experiences. In one survey, it was found that 60 percent of couples have a particular song that defines their relationship, a "couple-defining song."

In another survey, people were asked what song they might choose to listen to on a first date. The majority of respondents selected a favorite upbeat rock or pop song in the major key. Only one-third of participants selected a song because it was "romantic," indicating that this was not an expected attribute of first dates for the majority.

Songs of heartbreak are also found all over the world but appear to be particularly prevalent in societies where there is less freedom to pursue romantic relationships. In the 1990s, a study comparing Chinese love songs with those of the United States showed that Chinese love songs are more likely to predict negative outcomes and heartbreak. Research evidence shows that many people experiencing heartbreak choose to play sad music, anticipating it will offer emotional release and aid the healing process. In addition, the results of an Australian survey showed that a higher proportion of respondents chose songs from the singer-songwriter or folk genres than was the case for the first date. Typically involving a single artist playing an acoustic instrument, such songs convey an intimate tone that seems to invite self-reflection and reappraisal of the situation, both acknowledged steps on the road to recovery for loss.

In matters of the heart, music has two main uses. First, it invokes emotional responses that heighten joy or relieve sorrow, and, second, it can take on a symbolic and commemorative quality when a couple decides a particular piece of music is "our tune."

MARRIAGE

Weddings are key life rituals that signify couples' changed status. Weddings typically have three discrete phases: preparatory rituals, a marriage ceremony, and the activities that follow. In each phase, music is likely to form a key component.

Preparatory rituals often acknowledge the imminent change to the couple's living arrangements. For example, the female relations of Bulgarian brides knead dough while singing fertility songs. In other places, brides sing traditional laments while leaving the parental home. In modern Western societies, hen (bachelorette) and buck (bachelor) parties often use erotic music and dancing to signify the end of single life for the bride and groom, respectively.

Processions are commonplace in most marriage traditions. In fifteenth- and sixteenth-century royal European weddings, a band of loud instruments often accompanied the bride and her entourage into the city of the groom. In non-Islamic Egyptian wedding processions, guests walk to a distinctive rhythm called *zaffa* with a dancer leading the bride. In modern Western-style weddings, the "Bridal Chorus" from Wagner's opera *Lohengrin* is a firm favorite. In all cases, the music is joyful, loud, and communal.

In many cultures, tradition dictates the type of music performed during the marriage ceremony. However, in modern Western weddings, the couple often selects personally significant music. Research indicates that contemporary songs are preferred in most instances, but Mendelssohn's triumphant-sounding "Wedding March" is the most popular choice to accompany the couple leaving the ceremony together once the marriage is complete. This conventional choice, and that of the "Bridal Chorus" for the bridal arrival, show how old traditions can work well with otherwise highly individualistic choices.

Postceremonial celebrations often feature feasts and dancing. In seventeenth-century Russian noble weddings, toasts were accompanied by trumpet fanfares. In many traditions, circle dances have been common. Somalian females take turns dancing in the middle of a circle of other females; Swedish males encircle the groom and take turns dancing with him; and Ashkenazi Jews dance to klezmer music while encircling the married couple, who are held up on chairs. In each case, music is used to heighten the sense of joy and celebration.

Following the feast, further rituals may be enacted. In ancient Greece, singers accompanied the bride and groom to the nuptial chamber, and in traditional Hindu weddings, singers welcome the bride to her new home. In Sudan, musicians sing at the bride's door, requesting permission for the groom to enter.

Of all the life stages, weddings arguably involve the most diverse array of feelings. These feelings are reflected in wedding music and lyrics that range from consoling and instructive to celebratory, aspirational, and joyous.

DEATH

Death rituals acknowledge the grief of the bereaved, offer sympathy and support, and often include a life celebration. Within communities that believe in an afterlife, ceremonies include prayers directed at one or more gods or spirits. Rituals span several days and include announcing the death, preparing and viewing the body, commemorating the deceased, and placing the body in its final resting place.

Bells and drums commonly announce death in tribal cultures, and songs, with or without musical instruments, are typically employed in funeral ceremonies across all cultures. In large-scale Roman Catholic funerals, a requiem by a famous composer may be performed by a chorus and orchestra, while Orthodox Christian funerals and those of many Jewish and Islamic faith traditions only feature the human voice.

A type of lament called a *dirge* is common to most cultures and can help mourners release feelings of grief through tears, chest-beating, and other physical actions. The dirge is usually sung or chanted but may be purely instrumental. For example, the long slow notes and heartrending melody of a Scottish *pibroch* played by a lone bagpiper provokes strong emotional responses in listeners.

In many cultures, rituals are gendered. In Ghana, Akpafu women perform a dirge to mark the boundary between two forms of existence—that of the material world and that of the spirits. In Georgia, laments are improvised around the coffin by several female neighbors, each singing an individual but harmonizing melody. Through their singing, these Orthodox Christians hope to assist the soul's passage to heaven.

In Lebanon, Muslim males and females gather separately, and ceremonies may involve hired specialist performers. Men are guided into controlled displays of emotion by a male poet-singer, and women are led by a female dirge-singer, whose stamina and ability to invoke outpourings of grief are of greatest importance.

Some deaths are celebrated with joy. In rural Chile, a child's death may be exalted because their innocence grants them the status of an angel. A celebratory fiesta atmosphere is created through singing and dancing. In Ghana, the Akpafu express elation over a natural or "good" death through "talking drums." In Christian ceremonies, uplifting hymns that speak of heaven reinforce a belief in God's love and power, reminding the bereaved that life after death is blissful for the faithful.

Many funeral traditions also celebrate life. Akpafu honor the deceased's best attributes through their dirge selections, and modern Western services often include songs or other music of personal significance to the deceased.

In one of the surveys described above, people were asked what music they would want played at their own funeral or that of a loved one. Younger people selected popular music, whereas older adults showed a greater tendency to favor instrumental or classical music. Regardless of genre, most respondents preferred music that expressed positive emotions and memorialized the joy of their lives and relationships.

Rituals associated with death acknowledge music's psychological and social powers to relieve the physical and emotional manifestations of grief. The therapeutic release that music provides helps mourners process their loss and reestablish the emotional equilibrium that facilitates their return to everyday life once the ceremonies conclude.

CONCLUSION

Across cultures, people have established rituals to mark transitions and important life events. Whether ancient or newly established, rituals are carefully designed to create an atmosphere in which emotions can be expressed in accordance with communal expectations. By forming bonds that create a sense of belonging, ceremonies ground participants and give meaning to life. Although modern science is gaining an understanding about how music interacts with brain activity and neurochemical systems to produce rich emotional responses, rituals associated with key life stages across all cultures reflect an intuitive understanding of music's power to enable and enhance appropriate emotional responses and to capitalize on this potential.

References and Further Reading

Davidson, J., & Garrido, S. (2014). *My Life as a Playlist*. Perth, WA, Australia: University of Western Australia Publishing.

DeNora, T. (2000). *Music in Everyday Life*. Cambridge, UK: Cambridge University Press.

Dissanayake, E. (2006). Ritual and ritualisation: Musical means of conveying and shaping emotion in humans and other animals. In S. Brown & U. Voglsten (Eds.), *Music and Manipulation: On the Social Uses and Social Control of Music* (pp. 31–56). Oxford, UK, and New York: Berghahn Books.

Garrido, S., & Davidson, J. W. (2019). *Music, Nostalgia and Memory: Historical and Psychological Perspectives*. London, UK: Palgrave Macmillan.

32. Music and Death

Amy Clements-Cortés

Death is part of the life cycle. We are born, and we will die. When our body processes (i.e., breathing and heartbeat) shut down and stop functioning, we die. There are many ways in which a person may die, and a variety of issues may contribute to the dying process. These include things such as accidents, illness, natural aging, murder, suicide, and the environment. The way death has been viewed has changed over the course of history, such as attitudes toward death and even simply being able to speak about death openly. That being said, music is something that has had an important and constant role in death rituals before, during, and after the death of a person. The topics of death and grief are also prevalent themes in a variety of music and song lyrics. Further, songwriting may be a useful method for discussing and talking about death. Death and music are part of every life, and as you will learn, there are connections between the history of death and music.

DEATH AND MUSIC HISTORY

In almost every society in history, there has been a large shared belief that there is life after death. Of course, this does not mean all persons believe in life after death; rather, it is a prominent, long-standing belief. Also, religion has been the typical avenue through which people have searched for meaning and coping with death. Other professionals who provide information about mourning and funerary connections include anthropologists and sociologists, and psychologists have focused on how persons respond on an individual level to death. This includes a fear of dying and the unknown, bereavement, grieving, and processing these emotions. This ties into music, as music has roles in how people process grief and die.

Ancient Cultures (Sixth Century BCE–Fifth Century CE)

In the ancient Egyptian society, there was a strong belief in the afterlife. The evidence for this can be seen in pyramids, artifacts, writings, and monuments that reflect the belief that the soul continues to remain after a person dies. Music during this time was a large part of religious ceremonies and was even present at the pyramids and tombs. Evidence is displayed in the paintings and the drawings that portray music and dance as well as writings on tombs sharing chants or songs.

Music also played a significant part in death rituals and funeral processions in ancient Greek and Roman societies. For example, Apollo was a Greek god who demonstrated an association and connection between healing, music, and death. Interestingly, he was also known as a god that could bring plagues and illness. The association between music and medicine is long standing. The philosopher Pythagoras, in ancient Greece, is an example of a person who was connected with healing and music. Also, the Roman theologian and philosopher Boethius put forth the idea that the body and soul were balanced by harmony.

Moving on to ancient India, drummers performed characteristic rhythms when a death was declared, and these were heard in the village where they played as well as other villages nearby. Chanting for the intention of helping a person who has died in moving on to the afterlife is discussed in the Tibetan Book of the Dead. A number of musical compositions have also been created based on this book, including: "Bardo Thödol" by Erik Bergman and "When I Was Done Dying" by Dan Deacon. As you can see from these examples, music was clearly part of death and dying and was connected to the soul and spirit.

Medieval Times (Fifth–Fifteenth Centuries)

The majority of music that was created in European medieval times had to do with godly and spiritual beliefs. The themes of many compositions were about a person's soul and heaven. Music was an integral part of religious events, and this included funerals. In fact, the church used music to convey beliefs and ideology. One example of this is the medieval chant and prayer known as "Dies Irae" ("Day of Wrath"), which is for the souls of those who have died.

According to Philippe Aires, a historian who has extensively studied death in European societies, during the twelfth century, death was seen as being natural as well as unavoidable. Death was accepted at this time, and as the church had significant influence over people, death was something that people thought a lot about. People also worried about their life after death to such a degree that was almost more important than living in the present.

It was not until the 1300s when attitudes toward death changed as a result of the plague. There were also shifts in the music and culture. Unfortunately a lot of music that was played by persons who were in lower classes and considered uneducated was not written down and therefore has not been preserved. The music that did make it into the history is that of educated persons, the majority of whom were working in the church. There were more changes in music during the fifteenth to nineteenth centuries. Although death continued to be represented in music compositions, music was no longer solely being composed for the church.

Initial Modern Times (Fifteenth–Nineteenth Centuries)

Progressing into modern times, the death theme was not only for funerals and rituals surrounding death but also part of music compositions in the nonspiritual arena. Requiems are masses that are performed to honor and commemorate the person who has died, and music composed for observing the death of a person takes its roots in this style. A number of classical music composers wrote requiem masses, including Johannes Brahms and Wolfgang Amadeus Mozart, and the term *requiem* does apply to both secular and religious music that is connected to death, mourning, and bereavement. At this time, other classical music composers wrote a number of compositions for death and funerals. Examples of this are Chopin's "Marche Funèbre" and the "Dead March" written by Handel. Of course, the world of opera was also portraying dramatic deaths in its plots at this time, and the music therefore reflected this drama and emotional expression. Other composers began following a new tradition—creating legacies with their music for people to remember them after they died.

Twentieth and Twenty-First Centuries

Philosophers during the twentieth and twenty-first centuries had debates over how people should react to death. The famous philosopher Martin Heidegger studied how death and the knowledge that we will die influence people's approaches and thoughts on how they can live and accomplish goals and specific achievements knowing that they may die before having the opportunity. Another view was held by Jean-Paul Sartre, who affirmed that meaning in life could not be provided by looking at death. He further advocated that death and life were things that were beyond a person's control, and that life was in fact silly or irrational. He even went on to say that suicide was the way that a person could bring some control into their life. It seems fitting that musicians were introducing dissonant and atonal music during this time, perhaps in a response to the way society was changing because of industrialism, technology, and individualism.

Two significant world events, World War I and II, had an impact on the view of death. With so many people dying, death became more taboo to speak about, and people were more fearful. In health care, with medical advancements, more people were dying in hospitals, whereas people had previously died in their homes with family and friends around them. By the mid–twentieth century, in the United States, the percentage of people dying in hospitals exceeded 50 percent, and it is the common place for people to die even today, although there are many strides

Photo 32.1   World War I and II Memorial. (© Dawnyh/Dreamstime.com)

made to help people remain at home as long as possible if desired when their conditions become palliative.

In the music world, the composer Frank Martine created nine pieces about death from a number of viewpoints to help people to understand the finality of life on earth. Music has also been composed as a reflection or remembrance of death, much like the sculpture shown in photo 32.1 that depicts a memorial of the deaths in World War I and II. Death was portrayed in a darker and more negative light in pop and rock music of the late twentieth and early twenty-first centuries. There is even a musical genre known as death metal, which incorporates heavy metal, that came onto the world stage in the 1980s. Grunting, snarling, and growling are features of this style of music. Themes presented in death metal music are religion, nature, violence, Satanism, and horror.

Unfortunately, because of drug dependence, many popular musicians have died young due to drug overdoses as well as accidents and even assassinations as a result of gang involvement. Popular music started to be linked to dying young, and so musicians began focusing on writing tribute songs for musicians and other famous persons who had died. One example is Elton John's "Candle in the Wind," which he wrote to memorialize Marilyn Monroe, a famous and popular actress.

MUSIC TO FACILITATE LAMENTING AND MOURNING

Expressions of deep grief, known as laments, and mourning, which is the expression of sorrow following a person's death, are rituals that help people to put some closure to death and to process their feelings. Mourning rituals to aid the bereavement process often include the use of both vocal and instrumental music, which can be selected based on religious beliefs or associations with the person, society, and culture. Specific musical practices for funerals include laments, elegy, doina, endecha, threnody, and dirge. This music is selected to assist those mourning but also to help the dying person in their transition to the next place or state of being.

Singing hymns is a common practice in the Christian faith, and the organ is often used to accompany the singing. Increasingly, a keyboard or piano is replacing the organ in these settings or being used along with other band instruments.

Ululation, which is a wailing or howling vocal sound, is used in African and Middle Eastern cultures at funerals and weddings to express emotions. This expression is long lasting and often includes higher pitches. Monks chanting scripture are commonly included in Buddhist services alongside the use of trumpets, flutes, and gongs as a way to assist the person who has died to reach heaven. In Zambia, men often engage in a crying sound called *kukhuza*, and the cry of women is *chitengelo*, which is a loud, high-pitched mourning expression. *Kudinginyika* is the most mournful cry expressed; it affirms that someone has died. These cries are heard throughout the villages and include unique rhythms and syllable combinations.

Bagpipes are an instrument typically used in Irish and Scottish funeral customs to assist in comforting mourners and honoring the person who has died. In Western cultures, many song choices are used from the popular music genre from the past fifty years. Some examples are "Oh Danny Boy" and "You Raise Me Up" (made popular by Josh Groban).

THE USE OF MUSIC IN THE DYING AND GRIEVING PROCESS

Because music is prevalent in all cultures, it is part of our daily lives and is included in many daily practices. Therefore, it is a natural fit to include music as part of the dying process. For persons who are actively dying, music can assist them with overall symptom management, reducing pain, increasing motivation, connecting to identity, and facilitating relaxation. Music therapy is a practice that is increasingly being included and offered to persons who are dying. Often, a music therapist not only works with the person dying but also the family and friends accompanying the person to help with physical issues as well as to provide a holistic therapy addressing spiritual, emotional, psychological, and social concerns. The therapist may also work with persons to assist the grieving process and even to create a musical legacy. There are many music therapy techniques that can be implemented, ranging from more passive to more active practices. Examples include singing, songwriting, improvisation, guided imagery, musical autobiographies, and life review.

For family and friends who are in bereavement, music and music therapy also provide a number of benefits. Once again, songwriting and composing music can be a way to recognize the person who has passed and to remember them in a special way. These songs can then be included in funerals, tributes, and memorial services or celebrations. Music therapists use techniques such as improvisation, instrumental playing, group music therapy, composition, and music listening to help people address emotional and spiritual issues they may be facing after someone has passed away or during the grieving process. Lyric analysis is another important technique that can help initiate a conversation about feelings that are very difficult to express. People can find comfort and connection to the lyrics of songs that reflect how they are feeling at present.

Music thanatologists are another discipline of specialists who work with the dying by providing harp and voice music to assist the emotional, spiritual, and physical needs of the person who is dying, as well as their family and friends. Their music is prescriptive to some extent in that it is implemented to respond to the symptoms present at the time they provide the intervention.

CONCLUSION

Today's society seems to be more accepting of a growth of spiritual and cultural beliefs and awareness, and so religion, while still important in how death is approached and viewed, is less dominant than in previous times. The way a person approaches death and thinks about it in forming an opinion is related to identity and "making meaning" in life. There is still a prominent fear of death for many, and at the same time, with medical advances, people are living longer. On the flipside of this is a growing awareness of providing palliative care to the dying and also providing physician-assisted dying support to those enduring suffering and extensive pain at the end of life. Different parts of the globe have made more strides in this area than others; however, the topic is central to health care professionals working with the dying, and there is large debate on the value placed on both life and death.

With a multitude of religious beliefs and cultures, issues surface for educators, health care workers, and theologists, as death may be seen as a part of life for some and as a final stage for others. Complicating things further, there are differing beliefs about an afterlife and, for some, reincarnation. There is no doubt that the way death is viewed will continue to change along with society, and it will be interesting to see how the music corresponds and is impacted by those views.

References and Further Reading

Clements-Cortés, A., & Klinck, S. (2016). *Voices of the Dying and Bereaved: Music Therapy Narratives*. New Braunfels, TX: Barcelona.

Kastenbaum, R. (2006). *The Psychology of Death* (3rd ed.). New York, NY: Springer.

Kellehear, A. (2007). *A Social History of Dying*. Melbourne, VIC, Australia: Cambridge University Press.

Kerrigan, M. (2007). *The History of Death: Burial Customs and Funeral Rites, from the Ancient World to Modern Times*. Guilford, CT: Lyons Press.

Meagher, D. K., & Balk, D. E. (Eds.). (2013). *Handbook of Thanatology: The Essential Body of Knowledge for the Study of Death, Dying, and Bereavement* (2nd ed.). New York, NY: Routledge.

Music and Belief

33. Religion and Music

Eric S. Strother

Music has played a role in the ritual and practice of every major religion in recorded history. The impact of religion on human society has also led to a wealth of imagery and mythology that is recognizable and meaningful for those in society, and that musicians and other artists draw from to add meaning and connections for their audiences.

THE RITUAL USE OF MUSIC

Each of the world's major religions has had a history of musical expression. The Dharmic religions of India, most notably Hinduism and Buddhism, have integrated music from their beginnings, with many of their sacred texts describing not only the use of music but also prescribing methods for creating it.

In Judaism, music was abundant in the Temple period, with a choir of singers and a twelve-instrument orchestra leading worship, but following the destruction of the Temple by the Romans, Jewish leaders declared that all singing and musical performance should be banned until the Temple was restored. Over time, however, the ban lost its force as law, and music now abounds in Jewish life.

The place of music in Islam has been controversial for centuries and remains unresolved. Some Muslims believe Muhammad forbade the use of music for religious or secular purposes, and so they have proclaimed it *haram*, "forbidden." Others cite the presence of songs in the Koran as permission to use music in worshipping Allah.

Christianity also has a varied history of musical practice. The simplicity of chanting in the early church gave way to more complex songs performable only by trained professional singers. The Protestant Reformation of the sixteenth century returned worship music to the congregations, although the nature of that music was still in dispute. Jean Calvin's branch of Protestantism restricted worship music to the unaccompanied performance of the Psalms. Martin Luther's version, which dominates most Protestant worship today, consisted of hymns based in folk and popular song styles. This approach has also led to the development of gospel and contemporary Christian music, which is largely based in popular musical styles.

Despite these differences, there are some commonalities in these traditions. One of the most common forms of sacred music is chanting, or the intonation of sacred texts, mantras, and prayers. Many religious traditions share this musical approach, and there is a wide variety of methods and approaches for religious chanting.

In Dharmic religions, most chanting involves recitation, or mantras—words, syllables, phonemes, or groups of words believed to hold psychological or spiritual power. The earliest mantras are found in the Hindu sacred texts known as the Vedas. The most familiar mantra to those outside these traditions is the intonation of the syllable "Om." In some forms of these religions, such as Tibetan Buddhism, many of the chants are complex recitations of portions of sacred texts. The International Society for Krishna Consciousness, also known as the Hare Krishna movement, focuses on chanting the Sanskrit names of God. In fact, the name *Hare Krishna* is derived from its most prominent chant.

Jewish chanting is commonly associated with the cantors in the synagogues. The florid chant known as *hazzanut* was first introduced in Europe in the seventh century and was used for the cantillation of Scripture, the recitation of prayers, and eventually hymns. Few of these chants have fixed melodies, with most cantors using melodies of their own creation or derived from common melodic patterns from their geographic regions.

The most recognizable form of Islamic music for non-Muslims is the *adhan*, or call to prayer. This ritualistic invitation is intoned five times a day by a muezzin. Traditionally, the recitation was performed from the minaret of the mosque, but in most modern practice, it is simply broadcast from loudspeakers mounted to the minarets. There is no fixed melody for this recitation, but there are rules to which the muezzin must adhere while intoning.

With the spread of Christianity throughout Europe, distinct chant melodies and traditions developed around the celebrations of the office and the mass. To unify the liturgy of the church, Pope Gregory the Great began the work of revising and simplifying the liturgy and creating a uniform body of liturgical chant for the whole Catholic Church. This body of chant is generally referred to as Gregorian chant, even though it was not fully codified until the late eighth century under the rule of Charlemagne and Pope Stephen II.

Regardless of the methods and traditions, chanting is a means of spiritual discipline and a path to spiritual development. Recent research shows that chanting may also have benefits for the practitioner's physical and mental well-being, including improving concentration, stimulating brain activity, improving cognition and memory, and reducing stress.

Hymns and other songs of devotion are also common in most religious traditions. These songs are generally viewed as additions to any formal liturgy and are typically meditations on the attributes of the divine, or songs of prayer to the deity. These songs serve to create an emotional bond between the adherents of a religious system and its deity or deities. It is a way of giving the intellectual theological concepts a root in the heart of the believers.

In Hinduism, devotional songs tend to fall into one of three categories: bhajan, kīrtana, or aarti. Bhajan is an umbrella term for religious songs without a specific purpose and is typically connected to the Bhakti movement, which focuses on devotion to concepts built around particular Hindu deities. As there is no specific function for these songs, they have no prescribed form or rules for performance. Kīrtana songs are narrative songs that convey spiritual or religious ideas and legends. They are performed as accompanied call-and-response style chants, and performances sometimes incorporate dancing and audience participation. Aarti songs are sung in connection with the aarti lamp lighting rituals. The most common aarti is *Om Jai Jagdish Hare*, which is dedicated to all deities.

. The earliest codification of what is thought of as modern Jewish musical practice occurred with the composition of liturgical poems knowns as *piyyutim*. Cantors sang these songs to melodies specified by the poem's writer or sometimes created by the cantor himself. Musically, the melodies of these songs were often modified and augmented by the melodies of other music to which the singers were exposed.

Islamic devotional songs also take many forms. One of the most common are the *nasheed*, which are unaccompanied moral songs. Other songs include monophonic songs of devotion and praise to Allah and Muhammad. One sect of Islam, the Mevlevi Sufis of Turkey, are famous throughout the West for their use of chanting and rhythmic dancing as a form of *dhikr*, Islamic devotional acts, earning them the nickname "whirling dervishes." These are accompanied by songs called *Ayin*, which are vocal songs accompanied by Turkish classical instruments, particularly the reed flute known as the *ney*.

In Christian traditions, devotional songs date to the earliest musical practices as ornaments to the liturgy. As Protestantism moved away from Catholicism, many Protestant sects began adopting hymns as their primary music. In many cases, these hymns were collected into books called hymnals for congregational use. In the American Southeast during the late nineteenth century, revival spirituals developed in the camp meetings of the Second Great Awakening. These were initially transmitted orally and typically used a refrain form, or call-and-response, to make transmission easier. In the postrevival period, many of these songs found their way into hymnals or other songbooks for congregational singing.

Some types of music that are not specifically considered "sacred music" have also been informed by and rooted in religious writings and teachings. Many of the classical and traditional musical practices of the world's cultures have roots in the religious traditions of those cultures. The Honkyoku of Japan are pieces of shakuhachi flute music that were introduced by Zen Buddhist monks in the thirteenth century, the ragas and talas of Indian classical music are rooted in Hinduism's Vedic literature, and the klezmer music of Eastern European Jews was based on the cantorial music of the synagogues.

RELIGION AS A CULTURAL MARKER IN MUSIC

Religion also appears as a cultural marker and a symbol within nonreligious music. A *cultural marker* is any aspect of a society that is used to display the values of that society and create a sense of identity for its members. Because dominant religious practices are an integral part of culture, the use of religious language, symbolism, and imagery within nonreligious music is a tool for conveying meaning within a society. So, for instance, when the nineteenth-century French composer Hector Berlioz included the "Dies Irae" chant melody in the fifth movement of his *Symphonie fantastique*, the pervasive presence of Catholicism in France made possible the connection to the liturgical "day of wrath and judgment" meaning of the chant, even though it was used in a nonliturgical context.

Traditional music frequently carries references to religion, particularly the devil. In the blues, the imagery of the devil is a representation of the hardships of life. The familiar trope of the musician selling his soul to the devil is symbolic of the idea that the bluesman's songs are born out of difficulty and hardship. Likewise, in Anglo-Celtic folk music, some fiddlers and other traditional musicians attribute the origins of some of their tunes, or even their ability to play their instruments at all, to an appearance from the devil. The devil is also used as a warning sign for deviations from social norms and societal order, as in the ballad "The Farmer's Curst Wife," in which the devil takes a farmer's troublesome wife. When the devil gets her to hell, she proceeds to kill several of the devil's imps until they beg the devil to get rid of her. The song is often used to chastise women for deviating from their assigned social roles.

Stories from the Bible and other sacred texts also serve as metaphors within other bodies of song. One of the most prominent examples is the use of the Exodus narrative in American slave songs. For instance, the narrative of the liberation of the Israelites from captivity in Egypt and the hope for freedom in the Promised Land serves as a parallel to the plight of the slaves themselves and their hope for freedom in songs such as "Go Down, Moses," "Deep River," and "Sweet Canaan's Happy Land."

Religious imagery also figures into popular styles such as heavy metal and hip-hop. Heavy metal bands frequently use references to religion to situate themselves within society as well as create an antithetical position to that society. References to "Satan" and "the devil" serve to symbolically reference forces of chaos and disorder within a society with a Christian understanding of these figures. One striking example of this is Norwegian black metal. When the black metal wave developed in the early 1990s, many of the bands and musicians adopted imagery, language, and personas that rejected organized religion, particularly Christianity, and embraced theistic Satanism—actual "devil worship" rather than the symbolic use of Satan espoused by the atheistic Satanism of Anton LaVey and the Church of Satan. Most of these musicians now claim that the Satanism was more of a gimmick to provoke people, stir up fear, and create an image that was hostile to the values of mainstream society. Many of them believe the Christianization of Norway was largely responsible for destroying Norway's unique culture, so by advocating Satanism as an inversion of Christianity, they believed they were fighting for a resurgence of a distinct Norse culture. Some even embraced Old Norse paganism as a means for recalling a romanticized Viking Age. These "Viking metal" bands incorporated references to the Norse pantheon and imagery and symbolism associated with Vikings and the Old Norse into their music.

In the 1990s, some hip-hop artists began to adopt the image of Jesus as a symbol for their life and struggles. In 1996, the cover rapper Tupac Shakur's final studio album, *The Don Killuminati: The 7 Day Theory*, featured artwork showing Shakur hanging from a cross, symbolizing that he had been "crucified" by the media and that this album would be a sort of artistic resurrection. Likewise, the video for Nas's 1999 song "Hate Me Now" features the rapper wearing a crown of thorns and carrying a cross through an angry crowd shouting and throwing rocks at him, and the cover of his 2005 album *Street's Disciple* shows a recreation of da Vinci's *The Last Supper*, with Nas in the place of Jesus. In these ways, the image of a crucified Christ is representative of the persecution—real or perceived—from the media and other artists that these rappers feel. It is also accompanied by the promise of a "resurrection," whether through some sort of vindication in the media or the continuation of their popularity and fan support.

Other rappers took their Jesus references a step further and adopted the moniker for themselves. In 1998, former Wu-Tang Clan rapper Ol' Dirty Bastard, who was going by the name "Osiris," announced that he was going to be called "Big Baby Jesus." Since then, Slim Jesus and several rappers named Black Jesus have entered the hip-hop scene. In 2000, Jay-Z began openly referring to himself as "Young Hova," which he claims is a reference to God (Jehovah) and the idea that he is the "god of rap," and in 2013, Kayne West proclaimed that the name of his album *Yezzus* was a reference to his "god name." The adoption of names that reference divinity is often viewed as an example of the braggadocios nature of rap music, but it also connects to the tradition within rap of adopting honorifics such as "master," "king," and "boss" to assert the artist's position at the top of the genre. Adopting names that identify them with Jehovah or Jesus is a way of signifying within a culture dominated by Christianity that they are the supreme figure in the field that no one can ever surpass.

CONCLUSION

The synergistic relationship between religion and music has existed since the beginnings of these forms of human expression and understanding. Music has given religion a means of expressing, transmitting, and preserving its principles and experiences, whether through the chanting of sacred texts or the creation of hymns and other songs of devotion that reflect the personal experiences of their composers. At the same time, religion has given music, by way of the culture at large, a body of imagery and a set of stories and characters from which to draw, and that are generally recognizable and meaningful to audiences.

References and Further Reading

Hoffman, L. A., & Walton, J. R. (1992). *Sacred Sound and Social Change: Liturgical Music in Jewish and Christian Experience*. South Bend, IN: University of Notre Dame Press.

Pinn, A. B. (Ed.). (2003). *Noise and Spirit: The Religious and Spiritual Sensibilities of Rap Music*. New York: New York University Press.

Rabinovitch, I., & Klein, A. M. (1952). *Of Jewish Music: Ancient and Modern*. Montreal: Book Center.

Shiloah, A. (2001). *Music in the World of Islam: A Socio-Cultural Study*. Detroit, MI: Wayne State University Press.

Thite, G. U. (1997). *Music in the Vedas: Its Magico-Religious Significance*. Delhi: Sharada Publishing House.

34. Music and Lyrics

Jeanette Bicknell

People in all cultures that we know of set words to melodies, and sing. The presence of words (lyrics) set songs apart from other musical forms, and the need to communicate words separates singers from other musicians. There was singing before there was writing, musical notation, or musical instruments. There may have even been singing before there was human language. We do not know what the first "songs" sounded like. They may have originated in threats howled in imitation of an animal's cadence or perhaps in a mother's reassuring syllables, crooned and repeated until a lilting melody took shape. Music with lyrics raises different questions than music without words. These include the communication of language, the contributions that melody and rhythm can make to verbal meaning, and the nature of performance, sincerity, and artistic truth.

SONGS AS COMMUNICATION

One function of singing is the communication of a text. To what degree, if at all, a singer is permitted to change or embellish song lyrics depends on the expectations held within a particular culture or musical style. Many traditional songs exist in numerous versions due to the fact that they were passed along from singer to singer before being written down. Each new singer may have changed, omitted, or added words, whether on purpose or inadvertently. For example, the traditional American folk song "Go Tell Aunt Rhody" also exists in versions with aunts Nancy, Patsy, and Dinah.

Song texts are shaped by the demands and limitations of oral communication. This is clearest in traditional songs (including children's songs, lullabies, spirituals, ballads, work songs, and blues songs), but it is also evident in more recent music. Song texts usually feature repetition (of single words, lines, or verses) and redundancy (with the same idea conveyed several times and in a variety of ways). The repetition in the children's song "She'll be Coming 'Round the Mountain" is easy to see:

> She'll be coming 'round the mountain when she comes.
> She'll be coming 'round the mountain when she comes.
> She'll be coming 'round the mountain,
> She'll be coming 'round the mountain,
> She'll be coming 'round the mountain when she comes.

Subsequent verses follow the same pattern: "She'll be driving six white horses when she comes" and so on. An example of redundancy is found in Lady Gaga's song "Born This Way" from 2011. Not only is the title phrase itself featured repeatedly, but the theme of self-love and self-acceptance is expressed many times in different ways in lines such as "There's nothing wrong with loving who you are" and "Just love yourself and you're set."

Traditional song lyrics tend to reflect the concerns of the community in which they are sung. Their themes are the topics, feelings, and events that would have been of interest to many performers and listeners. These include the vagaries of love ("My Bonnie Lies over the Ocean"), the hardship of life ("Sometimes I Feel Like a Motherless Child"), personal salvation ("Swing Low, Sweet Chariot"), and important historical or cultural happenings ("Battle Hymn of the Republic," which is linked with the American Civil War). We can see similar concerns reflected in today's popular music. Other traditional songs enable or accompany functions that were important to many members of the community. For example, calming or entertaining children, facilitating the rhythms of shared work, marking important occasions, and accompanying dance.

Traditional song lyrics had to be accessible to most members of the community if they were to be appreciated and shared widely. Similarly, today's mass media popular songs must be accessible to their intended audience if they are to be commercially viable. This, combined with the features of repetition and redundancy, means that song texts convey a low density of information. Song texts are not a good means for conveying complex or intricate ideas. However, the same qualities of repetition and redundancy mean that song lyrics are a good method for helping people learn and remember relatively simple concepts. For example, there are songs to help children learn the alphabet, the books of the Bible, and simple routines.

SONG MEANING

Singers communicate words, but that is not all they do nor all they are expected to do. Rather, singers use words, as well as other means, to communicate and share meaning. Songs are music, not texts, and we cannot talk about song meaning while we limit ourselves to the meaning of song lyrics. To understand songs as meaningful communication requires thinking about the relationship of music to words, the act of singing, the nature of performance, and the role of an audience.

In the simplest songs, lyrics are set to a single melody. (Think of a group of friends singing "Happy Birthday" in unison.) More complicated musical forms may add layers of vocal harmony. (Think of a barbershop or gospel quartet singing different parts without instrumental accompaniment.) In other musical forms, a different instrumental melody or rhythm accompanies the melody of the lyrics. This is what happens in many "classical" music and jazz standards. For example, in the art songs of Franz Schubert, the piano part does not just echo and support the singer but is of musical interest in its own right.

Song lyrics, song melody, and instrumental accompaniment may all be similar in style and expressive character. For example, this is what happens when a sad-sounding melody accompanies sad lyrics and the sad tune and slow rhythm reinforces the sadness of the words. Alternatively, the emotions expressed by the lyrics may be contrasted by the song melody, by the instrumental accompaniment, or by both. The example most often mentioned here is from Christoph Gluck's opera *Orfeo ed Euridice* (1762). The aria "I Have Lost My Euridice" is Orfeo's lament for his dead wife. However, the sad words are set to an inexplicably jaunty tune. A contrast between the expressive character of the words and the melody of a song (say, a sad-sounding melody for happy lyrics, or vice versa) may be a failure on the part of the composer or songwriter, or it may not. The contrast may reinforce the impact of words or music, or it may be heard as ironic, or it may make us question what we thought we had understood, either about the words or about the music.

To add another layer of complexity, a performer may choose to sing a song in a way that is inconsistent or at odds with the song's overall expressive character. That is, a singer can make a sad song sound cheerful, or a happy song can be simplified and slowed down until it becomes dirge-like. Again, a singer may choose a performance style that seems inconsistent with what the song seems to communicate for artistic reasons. Barbra Streisand, the beloved American singer and songwriter, startled her fans when she recorded the normally cheery "Happy Days Are Here Again" slowly and sadly. And Nina Simone, the great African American jazz singer, is known for her snappy, up-tempo version of the bluesy song "Mood Indigo."

The meaning of a song, then, is not in its lyrics, in its music, nor in some relationship between them. Unlike novels or films (and like some poetry and plays), songs are meant to be performed. The meaning of a song extends beyond the meaning of its lyrics. That is, the meanings of songs are not fully disclosed until they are performed, and performance implies an audience.

Song meaning emerges from the patterns of interaction among the song, the performer, and the audience. For example, singers perform differently for hometown fans than they do for unfamiliar audiences, and they perform differently in large and small venues. Typically, and other things being equal, the smaller the audience and the venue, the more intimate the atmosphere. Audiences, for their part, may respond differently based on their expectations of the venue, the music, and the performer. The audience at a big city classical music recital comes to a performance with a different outlook than the audience for a cover band in a bar, and those venues make some responses appropriate and others not so much. The audience at an open mic night, where most performers will be amateurs, responds differently than an audience who has come with the expectation of hearing professionals. And audiences take different meanings from song performances depending on their own personal histories and cultural background. Songs found meaningful and attractive in adolescence may evoke a reaction of "What did I see in that?" in later life. The appeal as well as the meaning may now be opaque.

TRUTH IN SONGS

Are music lyrics a type of fiction? Sometimes it is obvious that song lyrics are telling a fictional story. The Eagles, who were responsible for some of the biggest hits of the 1970s, never did check into a place called the "Hotel California" and find that they could not leave, as recounted in their song of that name. With apologies to songwriter Jim Croce, there never was a bad man named "Leroy Brown," meaner than a junkyard dog, frequenting the South Side of Chicago.

However, assessing the truth value of song lyrics is more complicated than might be expected. A performance of a song carries with it demands and expectations that vary according to culture and musical genre. Some musical genres place a high value on personal self-expression, and artists in these genres draw on their personal history in their songwriting and singing. Audiences expect them to convey some form of emotional, if not literal, truth. For example, hip-hop artists who rap about killing rivals or dealing drugs but hail from middle-class or comfortable backgrounds may be criticized by fans as being "posers."

However the demand that singers be "truthful" in their performances raises a paradox. On the one hand, everyone involved understands that professional singers are performers and that a performance is a special kind of event that, by its very nature, has elements of artificiality. On the other hand, at least some audiences in some musical genres desire and expect sincerity from performers, and they are disappointed when they perceive elements of insincerity.

A musical performance is a social interaction with a specific set of conventions that vary according to time, place, and culture. Singers and their audiences have different roles to play, and both recognize this. For example, performers are usually physically separated from audiences. Audiences do not typically go on stage to share the performance space or sing along with the performance, except in special circumstances, and then only when they are invited. Depending on the type of performance, audience members may speak to one another, but listeners do not usually try to start conversations with performers. The social conventions surrounding vocal performance are occasionally violated, of course. However, if they break down completely, the event in question is no longer a performance but something else.

So, why should listeners expect singers to be truthful or sincere? It comes down to two reasons. First, there is the nature of songs as communication. In singing, the medium of communication is the human voice. The presence of a human voice means that a song can feel like a personal communication, even when the listener is just one of many in a crowd or hears a recording made in a different time and place. When communication is not genuine—or when it is not perceived as such—relations can be damaged. Insincere communication, such as a reluctantly given apology or a disingenuous compliment, can be sources of friction and can even end relationships.

Second, audiences are influenced by the powerful social norm of reciprocity. This means that human beings tend to—and are expected to—treat others in ways commensurate with how they have been treated. When fans feel genuine emotion and enthusiasm for performers and music, it is only natural that they want these feelings to be sincerely returned. Fans want to feel that the singers they admire are just as eager to perform for them as they are to listen. They would be disappointed to get the impression that performers are just "doing their job" or "in it for the money." Audiences want singers to be genuinely enthusiastic and to communicate something of their true selves. (Although, at the same time, their more rational selves likely know or suspect that singers and other performers cannot possibly feel all the emotions they project in performance each and every time they perform. If they did, their work would be too difficult and draining.)

CONCLUSION

Music with lyrics continues to be an important component of nearly every musical genre. People all over the world take great pleasure in listening to music with lyrics and in singing themselves. The prevalence and continued significance of vocal music raises the question of why the practice of singing has survived and even thrived. Singing is not a particularly efficient means of communication when compared with speaking. Singers convey meaning, but not in a manner that is straightforward or necessarily obvious.

One possibility is that the answer to the question, "Why sing?" connects in some more fundamental way with the possibilities of the human voice and the desire for recognition. People sing and respond to vocal music because it is a way of asking for and receiving acknowledgment from others of one's standing as a human being with basic dignity, as an equal to others in this regard, and as worthy of respect.

References and Further Reading

Bicknell, J. (2015). *Philosophy of Songs and Singing: An Introduction*. New York, NY: Routledge.

Bicknell, J., & Fisher, J. A. (Eds.). (2013). *Song, Songs, and Singing*. Hoboken, NJ: Wiley-Blackwell.

Booth, M. W. (1981). *The Experience of Songs*. New Haven, CT: Yale University Press.

Mithen, S. (2006). *The Singing Neanderthals: The Origins of Music, Language, Mind, and Body*. Cambridge, MA: Harvard University Press.

Sparshott, F. (1997). Singing and speaking. *British Journal of Aesthetics, 37*(3), 199–210.

35. Music and Advertising

Kirk N. Olsen and William Forde Thompson

Background music is used for many purposes in our day-to-day life. We often listen to music while studying, entertaining guests, or just relaxing on our own. Music creates a mood that subtly influences how we feel. In many situations, we control the choice of music to ensure it has the outcome we desire, whether to energize, relax, contemplate, or celebrate. But background music is also used in contexts where we do not have control over the music. Television commercials, retail stores, and restaurants often use music as a device to influence our thoughts, feelings, and behaviors. In all such cases, music is used to help advertise a product or service. The goal of using music is to influence potential consumers by increasing their positive attitudes toward a brand or service, thereby increasing the revenue potential of their business, whether that business is the sale of clothing, tourism, computers, or food. In the field of behavioral economics, such techniques are sometimes referred to as "nudges," defined as strategies that subtly influence the behavior and decision-making of people without actually enforcing or prohibiting options.

But does it work? Does music have the power to change the way we think and feel about brands and services or to manipulate us into spending money? This chapter will address key questions regarding the impact of music on consumer behavior. We begin by discussing general effects of music in advertising and then consider how music can influence consumers' experiences with products, brands, and services.

THE USE OF MUSIC IN ADVERTISING

The main purpose of advertising is to promote or sell a product, service, or idea by using persuasive messaging. Music that accompanies an advertisement can enhance this process in a number of ways. For example, positive attitudes and preferences toward a product can be enhanced when music facilitates a positive mood or reaction within the listener. One of the ways of achieving this effect is to present music that comprises characteristically positive and uplifting features, such as "happy" music composed in a major key and a fast tempo. Potential consumers are repeatedly bombarded with an association between the product and positive music, and an unconscious process of associative conditioning takes place. Neural connections in the brain are changed by this repeated exposure, and our attitude toward the product gradually becomes positive, thereby increasing the probability that we will be paying customers.

Another way that music can enhance the message of an advertisement is by making it more memorable. If people forget the core message in an advertisement, then the marketing strategy is less likely to succeed. Here, the congruency or fit between the music and the goals of the advertisement becomes important. One study presented listeners with two versions of radio advertisements for five different products, such as an energy drink. For each product, one advertisement presented music that was consistent with the marketing goal (e.g., fast-tempo music paired with the energy drink), and another presented music that was inconsistent with this goal (e.g., slow joyful music paired with the energy drink). Memory for the product was better when the advertising music was congruent. Familiarity of and preference for the music are also key for increasing memory for products. Listeners enjoy and remember familiar music and are likely to remember advertisements that contain familiar music.

From these examples, we see that carefully chosen background music in advertising can influence listeners' thoughts and feelings about certain products. But what about the act of consuming? Can music influence people when they are actively involved in consumer environments such as retail stores, cafés, and restaurants? We now move from the context of consumer advertising to consider key questions in the context of consumer behavior.

CAN MUSIC LURE PEOPLE INTO CONSUMER ENVIRONMENTS?

Not surprisingly, people are more likely to approach a retail environment when they enjoy the background music than when they do not enjoy the background music. Interestingly, the complexity of the music can also influence whether people approach and remain in a retail environment. One study played pop music with three levels of complexity, defined as the extent to which the music was erratic and difficult to predict. The researchers counted the number of times people walked within one meter of an information stall that played the music in the background. A moderate level of complexity in the music elicited an average of ten visits every ten minutes, significantly more than when highly complex music was played (three visits every ten minutes) or when no music was played (four visits every ten minutes). In other words, moderately complex music is most effective at attracting people to a desired location and has the greatest chance of enticing potential customers into a place of business.

Having enticed customers to visit a store, café, or restaurant, can music extend the duration of their visit? It turns out that customers stay longer in a retail environment when background music is present. Moreover, the tempo and loudness of background music play a role in influencing the speed at which customers complete their shopping or gastronomic experience. Music that is slow reduces the speed of supermarket shopping by 15 percent relative to conditions where fast music is presented. In the same way, soft music slows down supermarket shopping, whereas loud music speeds it up. Similar effects have been observed when people are eating food at a restaurant. Researchers have shown that restaurant and café customers tend to eat more slowly when slow-tempo background music is played relative to fast-tempo music. Familiar background music also results in customers staying longer than when unfamiliar music is played.

Music can not only extend (or limit) the duration of stay but also change our perception of time. Upbeat and loud music tends to make people feel that more time has passed than actually has passed, whereas time passes more quickly when slow and soft music is playing. This finding has important implications for waiting times, such as those experienced in medical waiting rooms and supermarket queues, where customers find themselves having to endure long waits to access services or purchase products. Retailers can reduce customer frustration by ensuring slow and soft music is played in the background to minimize the perception of long waiting times.

CAN MUSIC INFLUENCE HOW MUCH MONEY CUSTOMERS SPEND?

The quest to increase spending is the holy grail of consumer marketing. Business owners need to make a profit, and if simple atmospheric features such as background music can lead to an increase in customer expenditure, then profits will increase with minimal cost to the business owner. Research suggests that the presence of background music increases expenditure relative to silence, but the tempo and loudness of the music are important. One study showed that shoppers who experienced slow background music spent 33 percent more money than those who experienced fast-tempo music. Furthermore, the presence of slow background music in a restaurant can increase profits because customers tend to purchase additional courses or rounds of drinks. One explanation for these findings is that people linger in the presence of slow-tempo music, and while they are there, they spend money. These findings can be used by retailers and restaurateurs to help choose the most appropriate music for certain situations. In busy periods when high customer turnover leads to high profits, fast and loud music is ideal. People are there to make a purchase, and fast and loud music will encourage rapid decisions and fast turnaround to the next customer. At times when clientele is lacking, slow and soft music may be optimal, as it can extend the duration of a customer's visit, leading to additional purchases.

Along with tempo and loudness, the style or genre of music also affects consumer spending. Research has shown that restaurant customers spend more money when classical music is played in the background than when pop music is played or when there is no music. Why does classical music influence spending? One possible reason is that classical music is associated with affluence and sophistication, so when this genre of music is played in the background, customers feel more affluent and spend more money by purchasing additional items that they normally would not buy. Another possibility is that classical music tends to be slower and softer than pop music, and customers tend to stay longer when classical music is playing.

CAN MUSIC INFLUENCE PRODUCT CHOICE AND SATISFACTION?

Music can influence the choices that we make and our satisfaction with that choice. However, these effects rely on a good fit between the music and the product. Take the purchase of wine. In one study, either classical music or pop music was played to customers in a wine store. Customers who heard classical music purchased more expensive wines than customers who heard pop music. That is, customers gravitated to wines that best fit the style of the music. Classical music is associated with affluence and sophistication, whereas pop music is not.

Another study investigated whether the presence of stereotypical French or German music might influence customers' decisions to purchase French or German wine. As predicted by the "musical fit" hypothesis, customers bought French wine five times more than German wine when French music was presented. A similar effect of smaller magnitude was observed for the pairing of German wine and German music. Interestingly, customers seemed unaware that the music influenced their purchasing behavior. Thus, music not only affects the way people think and feel about products through advertising, but it can also influence the consumer choices that people make; customers are often unaware that they have been manipulated in this way.

Music can also affect consumer satisfaction once a product choice has been made. Multiple studies have shown that the presence of background music in retail settings increases consumer satisfaction. However, the benefit of music depends on the age of the customer: people under fifty reported greater satisfaction when shopping with slow-tempo pop music, whereas people over fifty reported greater satisfaction when shopping with environmental sounds or instrumental music. Familiar music was most important for the younger age group.

PSYCHOLOGICAL EXPLANATIONS FOR THE IMPACT OF MUSIC IN ADVERTISING

What are some psychological explanations for these effects? Four mechanisms have been identified: physiological arousal, priming, emotional response, and control. First, music has a direct impact on listeners' physiological state of arousal. Heightened arousal can manifest as an increase in heart rate, breathing rate, sweating, blood pressure, and other physiological measures. Loud or fast-tempo music has been shown to elicit greater arousal than soft or slow music. Indeed, high arousal is one of the main reasons why fans of high-intensity music, such as rock or heavy metal, enjoy it so much. Customers may spend less time in stores when listening to fast or loud music because high-arousal states motivate people to move quickly and with purpose, rather than in a slow and contemplative manner. Many people also do not enjoy it when a high state of arousal has been imposed on them, and so they tend to remove themselves from the situation as quickly as possible.

Second, music has the ability to prime thoughts and associations within a listener. In other words, music taps into networks of association that have developed over the course of one's life experience. When classical music is played in a wine store, it can prime the listener to feel more affluent because of previously learned associations between classical music, sophistication, and affluence.

Third, music has a strong influence over our emotional experiences. Music interacts with emotions for many reasons: by triggering our most personal memories, toying with our expectations, encouraging us to move in time with it, and stimulating our imagination. When it is used in advertising, music elicits powerful emotional responses that influence whether people feel positively or negatively about products, brands, and services.

Fourth, researchers have determined that a feeling of choice or dominance over a music-listening situation predicts how much an individual enjoys that experience. When music is imposed on us, we tend to like it less than when we have selected the music and controlled our own experience. With the increasing use of personal listening devices, customers often choose whether or not they listen to in-store music or continue to listen to their own music through headphones. The element of choice adds another layer of complexity to the role of background music in consumer psychology.

CONCLUSION

Music in advertising influences people's attitudes, feelings, and behaviors toward products, brands, and services. The impact of music is especially powerful when the music aligns with the product goals or brand message, whether to energize customers, relax them, or make them feel sophisticated. In consumer environments such as retail stores, cafés, and restaurants, the mere presence of music influences the amount of time people stay in an environment, the amount of money they spend, and their overall satisfaction with the experience. Structural features of music such as tempo and loudness play an important role. Background music that is slow and soft encourages customers to spend more time and money than background music that is fast and loud. Classical music also encourages greater expenditure because of its association with affluence and sophistication. All such influences, however, are somewhat dependent on the age of the customers and their familiarity with the music being played. For this reason, businesses need to know their target market and select advertising music accordingly. If the right music is selected, it can interact with psychological mechanisms such as arousal, priming, and emotion in a way that benefits the business owner by influencing the experience of customers.

References and Further Reading

Garlin, F. V., & Owen, K. (2006). Setting the tone with the tune: A meta-analytic review of the effects of background music in retail settings. *Journal of Business Research, 59,* 755–764.

Krishna, A., Cian, L., & Sokolova, T. (2016). The power of sensory marketing in advertising. *Current Opinion in Psychology, 10,* 142–147.

North, A. C., Hargreaves, D. J., & Krause, A. E. (2016). Consumer behavior. In S. Hallam, I. Cross, & M. Thaut (Eds.), *The Oxford Handbook of Music Psychology* (2nd ed., pp. 789–804). Oxford, UK: Oxford University Press.

Roschk, H., Loureiro, S. M. C., & Breitsohl, J. (2017). Calibrating 30 years of experimental research: A meta-analysis of the atmospheric effects of music, scent, and color. *Journal of Retailing, 93,* 228–240.

36. Music and Healing Rituals

Gemma Perry and Vince Polito

Many cultures around the world believe that music can be used for healing. When music is used in this way, it is usually part of a ritual or religious event that is highly significant to the culture in which it is found. Global traditions have used music in rituals to cure illnesses, enhance spiritual development, prevent future diseases, and treat psychological disorders. Ritualistic uses of music for healing typically take the form of chanting. Chanting is a type of singing that is usually performed in groups, is often repetitive, and can have symbolic or narrative meaning. In most contexts in which chanting occurs, ritualistic music is treated with an attitude of reverence, as there are often strong beliefs about its religious or spiritual effects. In many cultures, chanting is considered a spiritual practice that can facilitate healing and assist practitioners to enter deep states of meditation.

MUSICAL BELIEFS AND TRADITIONS

Beliefs about the effects of music and its power to heal vary from culture to culture, and different traditions use music in a range of ways to bring about change in people's lives. Common to all such traditions, however, is a strong association between participation in musical ritual and positive psychological and physiological benefits.

Native Americans

Musical rituals are an important part of many traditional Native American cultures; however, there are diverse languages, beliefs, and ceremonies across these traditions, and chanting practices vary considerably from tribe to tribe. Native American people commonly use singing and chanting in a range of rituals as a form of prayer. Rituals may incorporate sounds from within nature as well as instruments, such as drums and rattles, along with ceremonial dance. Songs are used to invoke elements of the natural and spiritual worlds, to offer promises, and to ask for guidance and healing. There are specific ceremonies for healing sickness, connecting to spirit beings, performing initiations, restoring harmony in relationships, growing crops, hunting, changing weather patterns, and expressing gratitude to nature. It is believed that songs sung in a sacred setting can be heard by ancestors and nature spirits and that these can offer inspiration, fortune, and healing.

Indigenous Australians

Indigenous Australians lived in Australia for thousands of years prior to the arrival of Westerners. There are hundreds of distinctive indigenous cultures and languages across the continent. Indigenous Australians use music rituals such as chanting to connect to the land and the spirit world to calm the mind, maintain social health, and strengthen community. It is believed that chanting ceremonies, along with sacred objects and body painting, put individuals and groups in direct contact with the ancestral world. According to these traditions, ancestors can take natural forms, such as rocks, trees and rivers, so these chanting practices are also a way for people to connect with country. Connecting to country can be a difficult concept to understand for non-indigenous people; but is fundamental to indigenous identity and does not just refer to the land, but also to family origins, culture, language, and spirituality. It emphasizes the interdependent relationship between the people, nature, and ancestors.

Indigenous Australians encode and pass on detailed cultural, geographic, and historical traditions in chants known as *song lines*. These songs are vital for survival in this tradition because they provide a means of traversing the vast landscape. Navigating the land through song is done by chanting stories that record pathways across the country and the sky. By singing these songs in sequence, people can navigate the land, finding water, food, and protection from the environment. These songs are also used together with neighboring communities for sacred ceremonies and trading. This makes music a fundamental part of Indigenous Australian culture, promoting connection with other tribes in the country and strong social bonds.

Music is also used in Indigenous Australian cultures for healing. Elders of the tribe learn particular sacred songs that are believed to have healing properties for their family group. These songs can only be sung by initiated men or women and are used to treat sickness and disease or to counteract evil influences.

Islam

Islam is one of the major world religions; the followers of this faith are called Muslims. In the Islamic tradition, prayers are chanted daily as a reminder of an individual's connection and surrender to God. These chants have gestures to accompany them, such as bowing down or placing the hands by the side or in front of the chest. There are five daily calls to prayer, which are a reminder for people to connect with God by chanting devotional phrases. These prayers are said to invoke the ninety-nine attributes of God, which are qualities such as peace, kindness, and justice. Focusing on these qualities assists the person chanting these prayers to feel God's love and compassion.

The regularity of this activity means that this musical ritual is a highly learned and natural activity for practicing Muslims. This ritual is also a way of strengthening community bonds, as people often gather in mosques, promoting social connection through coordinated behavior and the common interest of bringing their awareness to religious and spiritual beliefs.

Buddhism

Buddhism is the main religion of many countries in Southeast Asia; however, it is sometimes said to be a philosophy rather than a religion. It emphasizes that everyone has the capacity to reach *enlightenment*, which is believed to be a state of consciousness beyond the disturbances of the mind and the ego. There are two basic principles of Buddhism: the interdependent nature of all things and the practice of nonviolence, which is the behavior that stems from the belief system that nature is interdependent.

Although there are many different Buddhist traditions, chanting is a common practice. Chanting is used as part of formal religious rituals and also as a tool to prepare the mind for meditation. Chanting in Buddhism typically takes the form of reciting sections from Buddhist sacred texts, known as *sutras*. In some Buddhist traditions, repetitious chanting is used to focus awareness entirely on a spiritual symbol. Buddhists believe that these symbols can enhance the effects of chanting and have positive influences on their lives.

Buddhism also acknowledges many psychological benefits of chanting, and it is believed that the practice can heal, protect, and increase emotional stability, patience, inner strength, and peace. In Buddhist traditions, ignorance, attachment, and hatred are said to be the three poisons of the human psyche, and chanting is believed to be one of the practices that can eradicate these disturbances of the mind, which is said to lead to enlightenment.

Hinduism

Hinduism is the most common religion of India and Nepal. Hindus worship many different deities, depending on social traditions, location, and family history. These deities are all representative of qualities that are present within the universe. Similar to Buddhist traditions, Hindu chanting practices are believed to lead to peace and liberation from disturbances of the mind. Hindus believe that devotional practices, such as chanting sacred sounds, called *mantras*, can bring physical and psychological healing.

Chanting in Hinduism can be directed toward specific deities, which each have specific characteristics or traits. Different rituals are designed to worship particular deities, each with their own sounds, chants, and associated symbology. By chanting to deities in this way, it is believed that these spiritual forces can intervene and influence the lives of the chanter. For example, families may engage in chanting ceremonies for healing, strength, abundance, clarity, or overcoming worldly desires. These chanting ceremonies often occur in temples along with other practices, such as fire ceremonies, the washing of an idol, and offerings of fruit and flowers. Other musical practices within Hinduism involve call-and-response chanting in groups, whereby someone leads the chanting and a group responds. This method of chanting, called *kirtan*, is often associated with a spiritual concept or deity. Kirtan can be quite ecstatic and is often accompanied with body movements, such as dancing and clapping.

Secular Western Culture

Chanting has also made its way into some aspects of Western culture and popular music. George Harrison, of the Beatles, included chanting from various traditions in his songs. One example is in "My Sweet Lord," in which he sings, "Hare Krishna, Hare Rama," from the Vedic tradition, and "Hallelujah," which was originally from the Hebrew Bible and is now used in Christian prayer. Chanting also sometimes takes place in quasi-ritualistic settings among large crowds of people at emotionally charged events, such as sporting contests. In these settings, chanting may be used as a way of building group identity at the national level (e.g., "U-S-A, U-S-A") or more locally through chants or songs associated with specific sporting teams.

In summary, chanting and musical rituals are widely used across many different cultures. Although the specific sounds and musical practices may differ, there are also some striking similarities. In most cultures, ritualistic music involves repetition and group participation. Also common across cultures is the belief that music can provide psychological and physiological benefits, such as healing, personal and spiritual development, and social connection.

WHAT DOES SCIENCE SAY?

Do these beliefs and claims about the effects of chanting practices make sense from a scientific perspective? Although many of the specific beliefs associated with musical rituals refer to spiritual concepts outside of the realm of science, it is possible to investigate the effects that musical practices such as chanting have on physical and mental processes. It turns out that it is not just a coincidence that so many traditions use chanting for spiritual and psychological development. There is growing scientific evidence showing that chanting can reduce stress, alleviate depressive symptoms, improve attention, increase altruism, alter neurology, and even induce altered states of consciousness. Despite the many different traditions that use chanting in various ways, there are some fundamental commonalities in chanting practices that can lead to physiological and psychological changes. Some of the mechanisms that explain why and how chanting works are outlined below.

Breathing

A direct consequence of chanting is that making rhythmic sounds affects the physiology of breathing. The regular pattern of inhalation and exhalation influences the parasympathetic nervous system and can promote feelings of relaxation. These altered breathing patterns have been found to occur across traditions. In one study, Italian researchers found that chanting a Roman Catholic prayer (*Ave Maria*) and a Buddhist mantra (*Om Mane Padme Hum*) had the same effect on breathing. Both chants slowed breathing to six respirations per minute, a rate that has been found to have positive effects on respiratory and cardiovascular functioning. Respiration at this slower rate also reduces stress and increases heart rate variability, which is useful for the management of cardiovascular disease.

Vocalizing sounds that create slow rhythmic breathing also directly influences the vagus nerve. When the vagus nerve is engaged, a stress hormone called *cortisol* decreases. High levels of cortisol can lead to serious health issues, such as chronic stress, depression, or panic disorder. In this way, practices such as chanting that can help maintain lower levels of cortisol can be beneficial for overall health and well-being.

Focused Attention

Chanting can also influence the mind by decreasing the frequency of ruminative or negative thoughts. This occurs by focusing attention exclusively on the sound that is being chanted. Research has found that by mindfully chanting and focusing the mind on a single sound or phrase, an individual is better able to monitor thought patterns. This can encourage disengagement from automatic thoughts and lead to a reduction in uncontrolled mental content, such as mind wandering. Practicing focused attention on a sound or phrase is an effective method of increasing mindfulness. This can lead individuals to become better at recognizing thinking patterns and observing them rather than becoming emotionally involved in thoughts, which could otherwise result in distress. Increasing the capacity for focused attention in this way can be particularly useful for improving self-regulation to better manage habitual thought patterns.

Synchrony

Chanting typically involves making highly coordinated sounds in a social setting. The predictable, repetitive, and rhythmic quality of this type of music often results in highly synchronized behavior. Also, when people make music together, individuals become very focused on matching the sounds they are creating with those around them. This closely coordinated, synchronized behavior can facilitate community bonding by creating a sense of social connection that promotes cooperation. These shared experiences also increase prosocial attitudes and decrease feelings of loneliness and isolation. In particular, research has also shown that making synchronized musical sounds in groups leads to increases in altruism and can also improve the ability of groups to solve problems together.

The predictability of rhythm and repetition helps individuals to synchronize together with musical sounds. This predictability is also part of what makes music enjoyable and enhances its capacity to alter mood. Chanting in a social setting has reliably been shown to elevate positive emotions and decrease depressive symptoms. For example, research has found that group singing can influence neurochemistry by reducing levels of cortisol and adrenocorticotropic hormones, which leads to a reduction in stress.

Altered States of Consciousness

In many traditions, chanting is used as a ritual tool that may lead participants to experience an altered state of consciousness. An altered state can occur when a specific environment or activity changes a person's perception and cognition in dramatic ways. In many ritual settings, the environment is quite extreme; there is often a reduction in some aspects of sensation (e.g., darkness, limited movement) but with a very pronounced emphasis on intense, repetitive chanting (sometimes also accompanied by loud drumming, bright fires, and other extreme perceptual stimuli). In these states, an individual may feel overwhelmed by positive emotions and at one with others, nature, or the entire universe. Other common experiences of these states include feelings of alertness, timelessness, intense focus, increased self-awareness, and improved attention. These states can also have a longer-term healing effect on the individual. Following the experience of an altered state, individuals often describe a shift in perspective toward feeling more connected with others and with nature. Research has found that these changes can result in better health and well-being as well as persisting improvements in behavior and attitudes.

Expectations

In addition to the direct physiological and social impacts discussed so far, there is another important way that chanting and musical rituals can lead to changes in psychological functioning. People's expectations about the rituals they perform may themselves have an effect. Musical rituals typically involve religious or spiritual mythologies that lead to beliefs or expectations. For example, a Hindu praying to the elephant god, Ganesha, may strongly believe that this deity will remove some problem that he or she has been facing in life. This expectation may make the person feel more relaxed and confident after chanting, and this change in emotional state will then influence their subsequent behavior. In this way, the act of chanting leads to psychological changes that occur due to changes in a person's beliefs.

Engaging in musical rituals can also strengthen social norms and customs that shape behavior. For example, a Buddhist who joins in a community chanting ritual takes part in a highly specific social interaction that may have a focus, for example, on compassion and loving kindness. In addition to explicitly chanting words related to these themes, participants may be expected to enact these qualities in their interactions with others during the ritual. In this way, a person's beliefs and expectations about appropriate ways to behave are reinforced subtly and directly by taking part in the musical ritual. The combination of social expectations and the effect of taking on ritual roles can lead to beliefs that strongly impact participants' subjective experiences of the effects of these musical practices.

CONCLUSION

Music is an intricate part of highly meaningful rituals for many cultures around the world. In traditional settings, these rituals can have a wide range of purposes, including trying to cure disease, traversing challenging landscapes, transcending ordinary states of consciousness, strengthening communities, or healing the sick. In all these cases, music and chanting are believed to be an important tool for causing change in people's lives.

Although many of the specific cultural beliefs associated with ritualized music cannot be directly tested by science, there is growing and reliable evidence that chanting can have physiological and psychological impacts. By changing breathing patterns, chanting affects the parasympathetic nervous system to encourage relaxation, reduce stress, and improve cardiovascular functioning. By providing a clear and repetitive target for focused attention, chanting can increase mindfulness and improve self-regulation of thoughts. By providing strong social cues for synchrony, chanting can increase cooperation and feelings of connectedness. By triggering subtle and more profound alterations in a person's conscious state, chanting can have a lasting positive impact on attitudes. By providing a rich cultural context, chanting in ritualized settings can establish strong patterns of belief that train and influence positive behaviors. Understanding the mechanisms by which music engenders positive change across diverse cultures will point the way forward to a more complete science of music.

References and Further Reading

Bernardi, L., Sleight, P., Bandinelli, G., Cencetti, S., Fattorini, L., Wdowczyc-Szulc, J., & Lagi, A. (2001). Effect of rosary prayer and yoga mantras on autonomic cardiovascular rhythms: Comparative study. *British Medical Journal, 323*(7327), 1446–1449. https://doi.org/10.1136/bmj.323.7327.1446

Newberg, A., D'Aquili, E., & Rause, V. (2001). *Why God Won't Go Away: Brain Science and the Biology of Belief.* New York, NY: Ballantine Books.

Newberg, A. B., Wintering, N. A., Yaden, D. B., Waldman, M. R., Reddin, J., & Alavi, A. (2015). A case series study of the neurophysiological effects of altered states of mind during intense Islamic prayer. *Journal of Physiology Paris, 109*(4–6), 214–220. https://doi.org/10.1016/j.jphysparis.2015.08.001

Norton, K. (2016). *Singing and Wellbeing: Ancient Wisdom, Modern Proof.* New York, NY: Routledge. https://doi.org/10.4324/9781315740065

Portman, T. A. A., & Garrett, M. T. (2006). Native American healing traditions. *International Journal of Disability, Development and Education, 53*(4), 453–469. https://doi.org/10.1080/10349120601008647

Music and Social Bonding

37. Lullabies

Tonya R. Bergeson

Imagine a newborn infant, just a few days old. What does the life of this newborn look like? Does it depend on where the infant lives? The newborn is likely spending the majority of time sleeping and the remaining time eating and grooming, such as taking baths and having their diaper changed. Moreover, the newborn depends entirely on caregivers to provide the food, care, and shelter necessary for survival, and can only communicate their needs by crying. Now fast-forward two years. The infant is now transitioning into toddlerhood, exploring their world by walking around and handling objects, and beginning to communicate with caregivers by using language in addition to cruder means, such as crying or tantrums. In chapter 29, "Maternal Songs as Bonding Rituals," we learned how singing is used to promote strong bonds between caregivers and infants. In this way, singing is a ritual that supports cohesive societies. In this chapter, we consider the specific nature of lullabies and the various effects and functions that they have not only for parent-child bonding, but also for other functions, such as cognitive development, reducing stress, promoting movement, and inducing sleep.

SPEAKING AND SINGING TO INFANTS

What do typical caregiver-child interactions look like during this period of infancy? Most caregivers provide more than just food and shelter for their infants. Parents likely talk to their infants while feeding them ("Here comes the yummy avocado!") or bathing them ("Time to wash your tummy!"), even though their babies do not yet understand the words. Moreover, caregivers typically use a special speech register commonly known as "motherese," "baby talk," or "infant-directed speech" when talking to their infants. This style of talking is higher in pitch, has more ups and downs in pitch (i.e., exaggerated pitch contour), is slower in duration, has more sing-song rhythm, has heightened positive expression, and is far more repetitive when compared to speech directed to adults. In fact, this type of repetition would sound rather silly if used to speak to adults: "Good morning, Susan! That's right . . . good morning! Ah! Good morning, Susan!" Caregivers also sing to their babies, and their songs are similarly higher in pitch, slower in duration, and heightened in positive expression compared to songs that are not sung to infants. The songs themselves are also typically more repetitive than those sung among adults. Finally, the interactions between caregivers and infants are multimodal; caregivers rock their infants to sleep, play peek-a-boo games, and shine with adoration when their babies gurgle, hiccup, or say "mama" or "dada" for the first time.

It turns out that these types of positive interactions are extremely important for child development. Studies of children in orphanages who were provided food and shelter but no positive attention grow up with attachment, cognition, and emotion problems. In fact, many researchers and scholars have proposed that lullabies, songs primarily for infants, are particularly well suited to promote the parent-infant bond because of their soothing, calming quality. It is within this strong social bond that an infant develops *emotion regulation* and *secure attachment.* Emotion regulation is the ability to calm oneself down after experiencing a stressful situation, whereas secure attachment is feeling protected by and cared for by one's caregivers.

Lullabies, which are often related to feelings of tenderness and love, are characterized across cultures by simple musical structure, lower pitch, falling pitch contours, slow tempo, limited changes from soft to loud, and a soothing or calming tone of voice. Lullabies are often sung while rocking or providing calming touch to infants and when putting infants to sleep. Play songs, typically performed for older infants and toddlers, contain higher pitch, large variability in pitch contour, relatively high loudness levels, and quick tempos. In other words, play songs sound "happy" as opposed to "tender." One could imagine singing the same song ("Twinkle, Twinkle Little Star") in two drastically different ways that might result in a lullaby (slow tempo, lower pitch level, soothing voice) or a play song (upbeat tempo, higher pitch level, exaggerated dynamics, energetic performance). Play songs, like lullabies, are sung in multimodal contexts, bouncing to the beat, acting out the words (e.g., moving fingers like a spider crawling up a water spout in the song "Itsy Bitsy Spider"), and smiling.

How do babies respond to lullabies and play songs? It is likely that caregivers would stop singing if their infants cried or fussed during their performances. Instead, infants tend to display positive interest to caregivers' songs and pay greater attention to infant-directed over non-infant-directed performances of the same song. Moreover, the type of song matters. Infants prefer to listen to higher-pitched over lower-pitched versions of play songs, but lower-pitched over higher-pitched versions of lullabies. Infants also prefer fast-tempo versions of play songs, but they show no preference in tempo for lullabies.

Do infants respond differently to lullabies as opposed to spoken motherese? Studies have shown that infants listen longer to "happy" than neutral voice quality regardless of the performance style (spoken or sung), and they will listen just as long to happy-sounding speech as happy-sounding songs. However, when presented with videos of infant-directed speech and singing, infants watch the singing videos for a longer period of time—even if the sound is turned off. This is likely because mothers tend to smile more when singing than when speaking to infants.

MANAGING THE EMOTIONAL LIVES OF INFANTS

The positive and reciprocal dyadic interaction—caregiver smiles while singing to baby; baby watches with positive expression—is important for creating the parent-infant bond. The infant-directed singing attracts the infant's attention, which opens the door to positive communication and the development of emotion regulation. Lullabies, in particular, can be used to soothe infants already distressed or showing signs of stress. In fact, maternal singing has been shown to modulate infant arousal, as measured by cortisol levels. It has been proposed that singing lullabies to babies helps them develop the two skills—attentional control, or flexibility, and arousal modulation—necessary for affect or mood and emotion regulation by synchronizing or matching their emotions to those of their caregivers.

Affect regulation is thought to play an important role in helping an infant develop a secure attachment with a caregiver. Remember that affect or emotion regulation is the ability to shift emotions, for example, calming yourself down after experiencing something stressful. According to attachment theory, first proposed by John Bowlby and Mary Ainsworth, infants learn over time whether their caregivers respond appropriately and in a timely way to their signals. That is, an infant may come to expect their caregivers to sing a soothing lullaby when he or she shows signs of crying. If the caregiver does not respond appropriately time after time (e.g., consistently ignores a crying infant), that baby may not learn to regulate their own emotions and form an *insecure attachment* to the caregiver. On the other hand, if a caregiver consistently picks up a crying infant and tries to calm them down, the baby may eventually learn some of these calming tricks to regulate their own emotions and form a *secure attachment* to the caregiver.

The degree to which caregivers respond in a timely and appropriate fashion to their infants has been labeled *sensitivity*. Several recent studies have linked maternal sensitivity not only to social-emotional attachment between mother-infant dyads, but also to social-cognitive development in children, such as *executive function* and *theory of mind* skills, which are crucial for success in the school-age years and beyond. Executive function is kind of like the control tower of cognition and involves management skills such as the ability to focus attention, the ability to shift attention, and the ability to hold and use items in short-term memory (i.e., working memory). Executive function is involved in planning and organizing a school project or just paying attention to the teacher or standing patiently in line. Theory of mind is the understanding that others have their own thoughts and perspectives separate from your own. Theory of mind is important for understanding others' emotions or perhaps something as simple as taking conversational turns.

The idea that lullabies could help infants develop affect regulation has been largely theoretical until the past few years. Researchers have only recently begun to study whether singing lullabies directly delays or alleviates negative affect or stress in infants. In one study, seven- to ten-month-old infants listened almost twice as long to infant-directed songs in an unfamiliar language than they did to infant-directed speech in that same language before showing signs of stress. Another study measured whether infant-directed speech and singing differentially reduced ten-month-old infants' distress. The researchers measured negative vocal and facial expression as well as infant skin conductance, which corresponds with arousal. Infant-directed singing was more effective than infant-directed speech in reducing negative affect and arousal in the ten-month-olds.

DOES SINGING LULLABIES HAVE ANY EFFECTS ON INFANTS?

There have been several studies conducted on the effects of live and recorded singing on premature infants in neonatal intensive care units (NICUs). Lullabies have positive effects on several physiological measures, such as heart rate and respiratory rate, and have been linked to increased weight gain and sleep, and shortened hospital stays. Critically ill premature infants cry less often and for shorter periods of time after being presented with lullabies during regular nursing interventions. Although live and recorded lullabies result in similar decreases in heart rate and oxygen saturation level, live lullabies result in an even deeper sleep in infants than recorded lullabies.

What is it about the singing that helps alleviate stress more effectively than speech? Keep in mind that infant-directed speech is typically quite melodic and rhythmic, similar to music. However, the melodies and rhythms do not repeat over time in speech in the same way that they do in music. Perhaps infants find the repetition and clear metric pulse soothing. Additionally, caregivers typically pick up infants and rock or bounce them to the beat of the music. This kind of movement stimulates the vestibular system in the infant, which is also linked to affect regulation. Finally, lullabies are not only potentially predictable on a beat-by-beat level, but mothers also sing songs for their infants at similar pitch levels and tempos across performances. This makes the songs themselves not only soothing but also predictable for their babies. Caregivers' soothing, repetitive performances may even enhance their own well-being in a stressful environment.

Some scholars have suggested that music evolved from the exaggerated prosodic features (such as melody and sing-song rhythm) at play in interactions between caregivers and infants. When mothers speak or sing to their infants while changing their diapers or rocking them to sleep, the infants' positive reactions reinforce their mothers' positive affect. In this way, the mother-infant dyads coordinate their emotions and create a social-emotional bond that serves to affiliate a mother with her helpless and dependent offspring. According to one theory posited by Ellen Dissanayake, over larger periods of time, these very early mother-infant interactions may have become "ritualized" into more formalized musical structures with social implications for larger communities. That is, singing and dancing together is one way to increase social cohesion among large groups of people.

A recent series of studies examined the effects of bouncing infants to music in synchrony with others on their social behavior. In one of these studies, fourteen-month-olds were bounced in time with the beat of music while watching an experimenter bounce either in synchrony or out of synchrony to the same beat. After listening and bouncing to the music, the experimenter accidentally dropped an item on the floor. The infants in the in-synchrony group helped the experimenter by picking up the object significantly more often than the infants in the out-of-synchrony group. Thus, it could be the rhythmic synchrony of rocking babies to lullabies that helps promote the caregiver-child emotional bond at even earlier ages.

ARE LULLABIES IMPORTANT FOR HUMAN SURVIVAL?

Let's think some more about this idea of lullabies and evolution. What these theorists are saying is, first, that lullabies are important for protecting defenseless infants, and, second, that lullabies (or at least musical mother-infant vocal exchanges) are the reason we have music at all. These are pretty major claims. If we took away lullabies, what would happen? At first glance, it seems like taking away lullabies may not be that big of a deal. Moms and dads would still probably change diapers and provide food for their babies, right? Wouldn't that be enough? Keep in mind, though, the studies on babies raised in orphanages that showed that babies need positive attention to develop affect regulation and secure attachment.

Okay, so let's add in talking to babies. Moms and dads would still talk to their babies, of course. Ah, but remember that lullabies have qualities that even very musical infant-directed speech does not, such as clear repetition and regular timing. And studies show that singing helps delay and alleviate stress more effectively than speech. Anecdotally, what would dropping lullabies mean for the amount of protective time infants spend with their caregivers? How would this affect later development of affect regulation and emotional attachment or executive function and theory of mind? All these factors together may increase infant and child mortality, even just a little. And over larger periods of evolution, hundreds of thousands of years, these very small changes in mortality can have important effects.

CONCLUSION

Lullabies are more than just sweet songs caregivers across the world sing to their infants. Lullabies carry the potential to soothe and calm young infants—even those with critical illnesses—help infants learn to regulate their own emotions, and strengthen the emotional bond between caregivers and dependent infants, which is a secure foundation for the development of more complex social-cognitive skills.

References and Further Reading

Bergeson, T. R. (2014). Lullabies. In W. F. Thompson (Ed.), *Music in the Social and Behavioral Sciences* (Vol. 2, pp. 657–661). Thousand Oaks, CA: Sage.

Cirelli, L. K., Wan, S. J., & Trainor, L. J. (2016). Social effects of movement synchrony: Increased infant helpfulness only transfers to affiliates of synchronously moving partners. *Infancy, 21*, 1–15. https://doi.org/10.1111/infa.12140

Corbeil, M., Trehub, S. E., & Peretz, I. (2016). Singing delays the onset of infant distress. *Infancy, 21*, 373–391. https://doi.org/10.1111/infa.12114

Dissanayake, E. (2008). If music is the food of love, what about survival and reproductive success? *Musicae Scientiae, 12*(Suppl. 1), 169–195. https://doi.org/10.1177/1029864908012001081

Trehub, S. E., Ghazban, N., & Corbeil, M. (2015). Musical affect regulation in infancy. *Annals of the New York Academy of Science, 1337*, 186–192. https://doi.org/10.1111/nyas.12622

38. Love and Music

Sandra Garrido

Love and romance are found in music from all around the world and from many different time periods, even though the songs themselves and the way love is described may be very different. Studies that have looked at love songs from the 1950s through to the present day report that 70–90 percent of popular music from the charts during those decades were about love.

Music has quite possibly been closely linked to romantic love since prehuman times. Fertility songs—songs performed in ancient rituals designed to guarantee that crops and livestock will be abundant—are about as old as recorded human history. However, examples of songs about romance are found in Sumerian literature dating from around 2100–1800 BCE and on papyri and other artifacts from ancient Egypt.

In fact, many of the features that are found in love songs today can be traced right back to ancient times. Some scholars even argue that love songs have been important forces of social change throughout history. Past musicians and songwriters have had a big impact on how we understand and conceptualize love in the modern day, with many of our contemporary ideas about romance coming from the traditions of the troubadours, or traveling musicians, found in parts of Europe from the eleventh to the thirteenth centuries. Fantasy has been a particularly key element in love songs throughout history, with romantic partners often being described in idealistic terms in song lyrics, and this is no different today.

Why is it that love and music have been so closely linked throughout history? To answer this question, we need to understand more about the biological processes behind romantic love and how music can play a part in these processes.

LOVE AND BIOLOGY

While romance is, of course, linked to sexual attraction, romantic love is different to the sex drive in that it motivates people to attach themselves to a single mate for a long period. The sex drive ensures that the human species will reproduce, but romance motivates people to create long-term relationships, which in turn create a stable environment for the nurturing and protection of children—something that is also important for the survival of the human race.

Given the important evolutionary function of romantic love, our brain is geared to provide powerful motivations to select a mate and remain attached to that person. Neurological studies indicate that when people are deeply in love, the areas of the brain that are responsible for critical thinking become deactivated and the reward systems and pleasure systems of the brain become activated. Thus, being in love can feel much like a natural drug high. When we are in love, the brain produces chemicals such as dopamine, that are deeply pleasurable, motivating us to want more of the person who is triggering the release of such chemicals. This desire to be with the beloved can override normal logical thought processes, causing the individuals to behave less cautiously and rationally than usual.

Just like using drugs, though, when the cause of the dopamine rush is removed, the motivation to regain it becomes even more powerful. Thus, when we are rejected or we lose the object of our love, our desire to be with that individual only increases. Parts of the brain associated with risk-taking become activated, increasing our willingness to take extreme actions to get back the object of our desire. In fact, the brain patterns in rejected lovers can be similar to that of people with obsessive-compulsive disorders, as they are often unable to stop thinking about the individual and previous encounters with that person.

THE ROLE OF MUSIC

One of the key roles that music appears to play in romance is in *enhancing the attraction* of potential partners. Music has likely played a role in enhancing sexual attraction since prehuman times. Charles Darwin argued that for some bird species, song is similar to the brightly colored tail of the peacock in that it is used to help attract a mate. Darwin observed that bird species tended to have either colorful plumage or impressive singing skills, leading him to conclude that they probably served the same function in sexual selection.

Research indicates that music can still serve the function of the peacock tail in human society today. For example, one study in France with three hundred young women found that they were more likely to accept the advances of a young man if he was carrying a guitar case. In some cultures, the link between courtship and music is particularly obvious. For example, in southern Peru, a guitar-like instrument called a *charango*, traditionally must be learned by every young man because it is by playing it that he signals his interest in the object of his affections. There is also considerable biological evidence that music plays an important role in attracting a romantic partner. For example, one neurological study found that when female birds hear the male of their species singing a mating song, similar pathways in the brain are activated as when humans listen to music.

What is it about musical ability that enhances sexual attractiveness? The answer may be closely connected to the whole evolutionary purpose of romance mentioned at the outset of this article, that is, to encourage long-term attachment between mating partners so as to provide a safe environment for the raising of offspring. In fact, this biological motivator lies behind much of what we understand as attraction. For example, females are often attracted to masculine traits that signal the male's potential to act as a protector or provider. Males, on the other hand, are often attracted to female traits that are related to fertility and the capacity to conceive and bear children.

Some of this information about suitability as a potential mate can be gained from the sound of the voice. Low voices, for example, are produced by a large vocal tract, and so the pitch of a creature's voice suggests its size and therefore its capability to protect a mate and any offspring. Humans do seem to be able to accurately predict the physical appearance of an individual from that person's voice. Thus, it may be that the capacity of the voice to suggest physical size or strength is what lies behind the evident evolutionary connection between musical ability and romantic success.

Other studies suggest that the creativity suggested by musical ability may be the evolutionary marker of a potential romantic partner that we find so attractive. Creativity can be a signal of cognitive flexibility, or the ability to think about multiple concepts at the same time or to adapt quickly to new challenges in the environment. One research study found that women are particularly likely to find a penniless artist more attractive than a rich but uncreative man when at peak levels of fertility. It may be that creativity in general, rather than musical skill, is what is attractive in a potential mate given the ability to pass on such genetic traits to future offspring.

Music is also useful for *setting the mood* in romantic situations. The ability of music to create a certain mood is one of the primary reasons that people report listening to music. In general, in romantic situations, we seem to prefer music that creates an intimate tone, slow music, music that is not too dominating of the listener's attention, and music that expresses how we feel. Song lyrics often dramatize a sort of conversation between two lovers, or at least the expression of one person's feelings toward another. The language of song thus provides a way that the listener can express their own feelings toward a love interest.

Does playing romantic music actually increase one's chances of romantic success? Research has demonstrated that romantic music does have an influence on the behavior of the people who hear it. People who listen to a romantic song, for example, are more likely to be receptive to a romantic invitation shortly thereafter. Similarly, playing romantic music in a flower shop has been shown to cause men to spend more money on buying flowers for their beloved.

Another function that music can serve in romantic relationships is in *deepening the bonds* between individuals. In fact, this is likely one of the other key evolutionary functions that music has played in human society. Our taste in music is a very personal thing by which we express much about who we are. We tend to be attracted to people who share the same musical taste as ourselves because musical choices are a way that we communicate our own values and make judgments about how much another individual could fit in within our social world. Sharing information about the music we like is also a way that we build relationships and create a sense of connection between other people.

The act of engaging with music along with other people also strengthens our connections with those people. This is also found in some animal species. A study of the Australian red-backed fairywren, for example, found that bird pairs who regularly sang duets together were less likely to mate outside their pair than others. Similarly, pairs of male and female gibbons also sing a kind of vocal duet as a way of cementing their alliance to each other. In humans, there is evidence that when members of a group join together in drumming to a beat, they behave more cooperatively and helpfully toward other members of the group. On the other hand, when people move together in synchrony to music, research shows that they are more likely to be willing to go along with suggestions from someone in the group to behave aggressively toward someone outside that group. This evidence suggests that making music together or even enjoying music together has the effect of deepening our feeling of connection to the person with whom we share the music.

WHY ARE THERE SO MANY SONGS ABOUT HEARTBREAK?

From ancient love songs to the songs of today, music often contains themes of longing and the pain of unrequited or lost love. When we are happily in love, both men and women like to listen to songs that celebrate the joys of love and romance. However, when things go wrong in our romances, we are usually attracted to love-lamenting music. In other words, we prefer to listen to or to sing songs about love gone wrong when we are experiencing that ourselves. This seems to particularly be the case for men; women seem to prefer to listen to music that celebrates love even when feeling lonely. Why is this?

One reason is perhaps the fact that love is somewhat addictive. Biologically, being in love is much like an addiction in that the craving to be with the person we love becomes even stronger in that person's absence. When the source of the feel-good chemicals released in our brain is gone, we seek other ways to recreate the chemical rush. Music can bring the person we love back vividly to our minds, giving us the feeling that the person is almost with us. So, we often feel like listening to music about love to help us keep a feeling of connection with a loved one who is gone. In much the same way as an addiction, when love goes unsatisfied, our strongest instinct appears to be to listen to music that gratifies the craving for the beloved or for the sensations of love itself. Love songs allow us to fill that need when real relationships are unsatisfying or unattainable. Interestingly, listening to any music that we particularly like causes the release of dopamine, as does being in love, perhaps adding to the rush that the deprived lover is craving. Music can be used to feed private fantasies of an ideal love and to experience love in our imagination when we are lonely or when the realities of love fall short of what we would like.

As well as perhaps compensating for the absence of a loved one, songs about heartbreak really can help us to cope with a broken heart. Listening to songs about other people's heartbreak can make us feel less alone in our emotions. This is perhaps why research has shown that we generally prefer to listen to a singer of our own gender when we listen to love-lamenting music. Sometimes it makes us feel comforted to know that others of our own sex have experienced something similar to us. Listening to songs about heartbreak also gives us a chance to have a good cry and get some negative emotions off our chest. In addition, listening to music gives us a chance to reflect on our experiences, working through our emotions, thinking about solutions, and learning from our past mistakes, all of which ultimately help us to feel better about our experiences.

Of course, for some people, particularly those prone to depression, listening to tragic love songs can just make them get stuck in their feelings of heartbreak. Thus, some people instead prefer to turn to songs that both inspire and renew hope in love, while others turn to songs that express their pain and hurt. It is because of this power of song to help us to recover from a common human experience that love songs, even sad love songs, resonate strongly with so many listeners around the globe.

CONCLUSION

Love songs are found in all cultures, from ancient times until today. In fact, music is linked with love and courtship in several animal species and has likely been a part of the rituals of wooing a mate since prehuman times. Music serves several functions in connection with love: it can enhance the attractiveness of a potential mate, it can be used to set a romantic mood so as to make one's intended love interest more receptive, and it can deepen the bonds between couples. In addition, music serves as a comfort in times of heartbreak, allowing individuals to feel an ongoing sense of connection with a lost love or to process emotions when a broken heart is experienced.

References and Further Reading

Fisher, H., Aron, A., & Brown, L. L. (2006). Romantic love: A mammalian brain system for mate choice. *Philosophical Transactions of the Royal Society B, 361,* 1476.

Garrido, S. (2017). The addiction of love: Sad music and heartbreak. In *Why Are We Attracted to Sad Music?* (pp. 213–232). Cham, Switzerland: Palgrave Macmillan.

Gibson, R., Aust, C. F., & Zillmann, D. (2000). Loneliness of adolescents and their choice and enjoyment of love-celebrating versus love-lamenting popular music. *Empirical Studies of the Arts, 18*(1), 43–48.

Gioia, T. (2015). *Love Songs: The Hidden History.* New York, NY: Oxford University Press.

Guéguen, N., Meineri, S., & Fischer-Lokou, J. (2013). Men's music ability and attractiveness to women in a real-life courtship context. *Psychology of Music, 42*(4), 545–549.

39. Intercultural Relations through Music

Samantha Dieckmann and Jane W. Davidson

Intercultural psychology is a branch of social and cultural psychology that considers the attitudes and behaviors that emerge when people from distinct ethnocultural origins come into contact with each other. This domain of psychology involves acculturation, intercultural relations, and intercultural competence. Acculturation considers changes that occur within each culture in response to cross-cultural contact and is shaped by the extent to which each group wants (and is able) to maintain its heritage culture and identity and the extent to which intergroup relationships are sought. In the context of migration, these factors determine what strategies are adopted by migrant communities and the host society to deal with change.

There are several acculturation theories in psychology. The dominant fourfold theory, outlined in the tables below, is attributed to John W. Berry. Table 39.1 shows how migrant communities can integrate or assimilate into or separate and marginalize themselves from their host society. Correspondingly, table 39.2 shows how the host society can adopt one of four strategies: multiculturalism, melting pot, segregation, or exclusion.

While acculturation focuses on what occurs *within each group* as a result of cross-cultural contact, intercultural relations considers the *space in between.*

Table 39.1 Acculturation strategies of ethnocultural groups outlined in John W. Berry's fourfold model in the context of migrant minority groups

Acculturation Strategies of Ethnocultural Groups	Heritage Culture and Identity	Relationship Sought with Larger Society
Integration	Migrant community maintains heritage culture and identity	Relationship sought between migrant community and larger society
Assimilation	Migrant community does not maintain heritage culture and identity	Relationship sought between migrant community and larger society
Separation	Migrant community maintains heritage culture and identity	No relationship sought between migrant community and larger society
Marginalization	Migrant community does not maintain heritage culture and identity	No relationship sought between migrant community and larger society

Table 39.2 Acculturation strategies of larger society outlined in John W. Berry's fourfold model in the context of migration

Acculturation Strategies of Larger Society	Heritage Culture and Identity	Relationships Sought with Other Communities
Multiculturalism	Larger society supports maintenance of heritage cultures and identities	Relationship sought with other communities
Melting pot	Larger society does not support maintenance of heritage cultures and identities	Relationship sought with other communities
Segregation	Larger society supports maintenance of heritage cultures and identities	No relationship is sought with other communities
Exclusion	Larger society does not support maintenance of heritage cultures and identities	No relationship is sought with other communities

Concerns include prejudice, an issue that affects how people associate with "different" others, and intercultural competence, an individual's capacity to communicate and behave appropriately during cross-cultural interactions. Businesses, universities, and schools use psychological tools to measure their employees' or students' intercultural competence and provide training for the skills, knowledge, values, and behaviors required to operate in a globalized and culturally diverse world.

We know that continued globalization, diversification, and immigration contribute to a society's creativity and growth across several spheres of life. For example, cross-cultural contact can result in financial, social, and cultural innovation and development. However, some research findings suggest that neighborhoods with high levels of cultural pluralism (in which several ethnocultural communities reside) demonstrate lower levels of trust, civic attitudes, altruism, and community cooperation. Therefore, it is important not only for individuals but also for community groups to develop intercultural competence. As most modern societies are made up of various ethnocultural communities, broad-scale intercultural competency is required to achieve social cohesion. A cohesive society is characterized by inclusivity and equity, in which all members have access to civic participation, high living standards, and opportunities for upward mobility. In such societies, everyone works together toward all members' survival and well-being.

THE ACCULTURATION OF MUSIC: HOW MUSIC CHANGES UPON CROSS-CULTURAL CONTACT

From the mid–twentieth century onward, ethnomusicologists—researchers who study music, emphasizing its social and cultural contexts and meanings—studied how cross-cultural contact changes musical practices. In 1955, Alan P. Merriam hypothesized that music is more likely to undergo significant changes upon culture contact when the original music types share characteristics. He demonstrated this through analyzing the music of two groups: Flathead music (i.e., the music of the Confederated Salish and Kootenai Tribes of the Flathead Nation, indigenous peoples of North America), and music from the Congo, in Africa (Merriam studied the country when it was known as Belgian Congo). When comparing the music of the two groups, he found that before cross-cultural contact, the Congolese music was more similar to Western music in that it involved harmony, polyphony, and the use of stringed instruments for accompaniment. According to Merriam, the Congolese music underwent more change than the Flathead group's music in response to cultural exchange with Westerners, supporting his theory.

In 1978, ethnomusicologist Bruno Nettl continued Merriam's work. He was interested in syncretism, which he defined as "the results when two musical systems in a state of confrontation have compatible central traits." He looked beyond the music itself to also consider the motivations that determine whether or not groups choose to adopt elements from other musical cultures. Nettl argued that, in the context of non-Western music traditions, attitudes to change and the resulting musical behaviors are determined by how much members of a non-Western society want to keep their traditional culture intact and how much they are willing to adopt Western cultural systems. (Although categorizing musical traditions as "Western" or "non-Western" is an outdated practice, these terms were commonly used at the time.) There are clear parallels between these determining factors and those in the model of acculturation psychology described in the previous section (tables 39.1 and 39.2). Nettl constructed his own "typology of processes" to describe several responses that non-Western societies had to the arrival of Western music (e.g., through colonization) in the twentieth century (table 39.3).

Table 39.3   Selections from Bruno Nettl's (1978) typology of processes

Abandonment	Musical traditions are completely lost or abandoned.
Impoverishment	Musical traditions are impoverished, whole components lost or replaced by Western counterparts.
Diversification	Musical traditions originally from different regions are brought together into a single context.
Consolidation	Musical traditions originally from distinct regions are recontextualized to create national musical traditions.
Reintroduction	Musical traditions return to their place of origin after being developed elsewhere (e.g., African music that migrated to the United States during slavery).
Preservation	Musical traditions are protected and maintained through conscious isolation from cross-cultural contamination.
Exaggeration	Musical traditions are presented in exaggerated forms to cater to notions of "exotic" cultures.
Modernization	Western-compatible musical properties are adopted into musical traditions for the musical system's survival.
Westernization	Elements of Western music are incorporated into musical traditions and are then considered central, regardless of how (in)consistent these elements are with the musical tradition as it existed before contact.

In 1981, Margaret Kartomi extended Nettl's work on non-Western responses to Western music in the twentieth century, developing a system that applies to various types of culturally pluralistic societies and intercultural encounters. Some of her categories, such as *musical impoverishment*, strongly resembled Nettl's typological processes, but others were less familiar. The most remarkable distinction is in Kartomi's inclusion of *musical compartmentalization*, in which individuals in a multicultural society absorb the musical styles of several ethnic groups (including their own) throughout childhood.

Kartomi critiqued the term *acculturation*. Her concerns with the term included that it has ethnocentric undertones; it suggests there are pure, isolated cultures that exist before cross-cultural contact (when all musical traditions are continuously changing); and it focuses on "parent" music rather than the music actually being studied (the "offspring" music).

DEVELOPING INTERCULTURAL RELATIONS, INTERCULTURAL COMPETENCE, AND SOCIAL COHESION THROUGH MUSIC

The notion that music has the power to transform situations of intercultural conflict is widespread in popular culture. Justin Bieber, Pope Benedict, Henry David Thoreau, and Ella Fitzgerald have all publicly commented on music's capacity to bring people together. The supposed "power of music" is even celebrated in music itself, as in the lyrics of Mac Davis's "I Believe in Music" ("Music is the universal language, and love is the key") and Rihanna's "Don't Stop the Music" ("Don't stop the music. The world will keep turning if you use it. . . . Music like love floating in the air"). Popular musicians use their records and live performances to encourage peace building and charity, as with Michael Jackson's "Heal the World," John Lennon's "Give Peace a Chance," or Arianna Grande's 2017 One Love concert.

There are many examples of music ensembles intended to demonstrate the creative and social power of making music across boundaries. These include the West-Eastern Divan Orchestra, made up of young musicians from across the Middle East, and Yo-Yo Ma's Silk Road Ensemble, which showcases musicians from dozens of nationalities and music traditions. Although there were many other contributing factors, the story of the famous 1914 Christmas truce between German and British soldiers during World War I suggests that carol singing played a key role.

Claims about the power and universality of music can be oversimplified, and it is important to remember that music can be used not only to bring people together but also to reinforce what divides them in the first place. Although carol singing may have played a role in the 1914 Christmas truce, there are numerous other examples across the world and throughout history of music being used in war to heighten aggressiveness and inspire violent behavior. During the Vietnam War, American soldiers are known to have "pumped themselves up," readying themselves for combat using rock music. Even away from the battlefield, governments and political sects use music to disseminate propaganda, spreading divisive messages about cultural nationalism or ethnic superiority. Music can stimulate people's attitudes and behaviors toward war as well as peace.

Although there is nothing inherently peaceful about music, research has found that music works on a psychological level to strengthen social connection and feelings of affinity. Researchers have shown that when two or more people play music together, the level of togetherness they feel is mirrored in how they interact musically. Playing music together directs our attention outside of ourselves, as we need to focus on the actions, intentions, and physical and emotional states of our music collaborators to play together successfully. These skills—being able to identify and tap into other people's emotional states and the capacity to respond sensitively and appropriately—are also central to the empathy. We know that both empathy and music combine knowing and feeling, and researchers have shown how musical interaction can enhance the capacity for empathy and other positive social-emotional skills.

Some researchers think that musical group interaction goes beyond empathy. This is because empathy involves the ability to respond to and approximate someone else's feelings, maintaining a separation between the individuals involved. Music facilitates a process of intersubjectivity through which performers share emotions, intentions, and experiences, and the boundary between the people playing music together becomes blurred. Have you ever sung in a choir or perhaps in a sports stadium and not been able to tell which voice was yours? A performer's perception of such music reflects a merging process, as it becomes difficult to distinguish one part from another. However, the key question becomes, is music being used to bond people that already consider themselves to be alike, or is it being used to bring people together who consider each other foreign or even threatening?

Using music to develop positive intercultural relations or social cohesion is not simple. In some places, music is considered dangerous, and some genres and tunes are associated with particular political viewpoints. For example, some tunes played in the flute bands of Northern Ireland are so strongly connected with the long conflict between Republicans and Loyalists that whistling them has resulted in violence. In other contexts, singing or playing music is considered religiously forbidden. However, what constitutes "music" differs across cultures. Many languages do not have a specific word for *music* or do not separate music from dance or other related practices. To claim that music is universal does not account for the various ways that musical practices are conceptualized across the world. Nevertheless, singing, dancing, and instrumental playing are important in communities of all ethnocultural groups and religions, as people everywhere use these practices to lull their babies to sleep, celebrate significant life events, and in rituals of mourning. Thus, music can and has been used to great effect when developing empathy, positive intercultural relations, and social cohesion.

CONCLUSION

This chapter introduced the field of intercultural psychology. Of specific relevance is the concept of acculturation, which has been criticized as well as accepted by scholars. This idea has been used as a basis to discuss cross-cultural contact and the grounds on which intergroup relationships are built. Referring to music, key studies have served as examples of how music is maintained, developed, and merged as a result of different cultural contacts. It has also been shown that while music can be used to stir people to conflict, its capacity for developing social connectedness and its widespread significance in communities across the world reveal its potential to enhance a range of social-emotional skills to positively affect intercultural cohesion.

References and Further Reading

Bergh, A. (2007). I'd like to teach the world to sing: Music and conflict transformation. *Musicae Scientiae, 11*(2), 141–157.

Berry, J. W., Poortinga, Y. H., Breugelmans, S. M., Chasiotis, A., & Sam, D. L. (2011). *Cross-Cultural Psychology: Research and Applications* (3rd ed.). Cambridge, UK: Cambridge University Press.

Cooper, D. (2010). Fife and fiddle: Protestants and traditional music in Northern Ireland. In J. M. O'Connell & S. E.-S. Castelo Branco (Eds.), *Music and Conflict* (pp. 89–106). Champaign: University of Illinois Press.

Jones, P. M. (2010). Developing social capital: A role for music education and community music in fostering civic engagement and intercultural understanding. *International Journal of Community Music, 3*(2), 291–302.

Kartomi, M. J. (1981). The processes and results of music culture contact: A discussion of terminology and concepts. *Ethnomusicology, 25*(2), 227–249.

Laurence, F. (2015). Music and empathy. In O. Urbain (Ed.), *Music and Conflict Transformation: Harmonies and Dissonances in Geopolitics* (pp. 13–25). London, UK: I. B. Tauris.

Merriam, A. P. (1955). The use of music in the study of a problem of acculturation. *American Anthropologist, 57*(1), 28–34.

Nettl, B. (1978). Some aspects of the history of world music in the twentieth century: Questions, problems, and concepts. *Ethnomusicology, 22*(1), 123–136.

Rabinowitch, T.-C., Cross, I., & Burnard, P. (2013). Long-term musical group interaction has a positive influence on empathy in children. *Psychology of Music, 41*(4), 484–498.

Sam, D. L., & Berry, J. W. (Eds.). (2016). *The Cambridge Handbook of Acculturation Psychology* (2nd ed.). Cambridge, UK: Cambridge University Press.

Walsh, M. J. K. (2015). Mama's boys, celtus, and the troubles in Northern Ireland. *Rock Music Studies, 2*(1), 46–60.

40. Music as Social Grooming

Jacques Launay

The term *grooming* refers to any act of tidying, cleaning, or brushing oneself or another individual, for example, brushing one's hair or cleaning one's teeth. *Social grooming* is said to occur when such behaviors function to create and reinforce social connections with other individuals. For example, chimpanzees are known to spend time cleaning other chimpanzees, and chimps that groom together seem to develop a special bond. Although listening to music is very different from brushing one's teeth, some theorists have observed that, for humans, music can function in the same way as social grooming in other primate species. Making music together can result in people feeling closer to one another. Thus, music has been described as a form of social grooming.

Music and dance are performed socially in every human culture around the world—from dancing in a nightclub in Sydney to ceremonial fertility rituals among the Kassena of northern Ghana. The prevalence of group music making suggests it may have some important function for human society. It is hard to trace the evolutionary origins of music, but it is likely that music and dance were performed in social settings by ancestral species that existed long before modern humans. This has led to the suggestion that group music making may serve the important function of making people feel more socially bonded to one another. This would have benefited early human species because more socially connected species can survive better.

This chapter will introduce social grooming, which helps primate species to develop social bonds, and the biological mechanisms that cause the formation of these social bonds. It will then discuss some recent evidence that suggests that human music making can have the same biological effects as social grooming in other primate species. It is possible that music and dance are human behaviors that developed to serve a functional purpose in helping us maintain close communities when we started living in very large groups.

PRIMATE SOCIAL BONDING

Humans are a primate species, which means we are in the same family of animals as chimpanzees, gorillas, and monkeys. Although we are very different from these other species in some ways, we also share many similarities. Unlike herding animals (such as cows), primates tend to have quite complicated social relationships and will often have group leaders and other members of the group with lower status. This social structure is useful because it makes it easier for the group to make difficult decisions. However, this structure can also lead to conflict. For example, if a low-status member of the group wants to gain higher status, he or she may start to fight with other group members to gain this status. This conflict can cause problems for the group, particularly if there is a large number of individuals who want to obtain higher status.

It is generally beneficial to live in a large group because this means the group has more individuals to look out for predators and more help with hunting. This means that primate species are more likely to succeed in large groups. However, having a larger group also means there is more potential for conflict between group members; therefore, larger groups need some ways to stop this conflict from occurring. Some group members are less likely to fight one another, and it is possible to form some closer relationships between individuals through social grooming. Social grooming is the process of individuals cleaning one another by picking pests off each other's skin. Although this may serve some hygienic purpose, it also appears to have a strongly social effect for primates. In most primate species, it seems that social grooming is used to maintain something similar to friendship and therefore may reduce the chance that there will be conflict between group members.

Studies into the biology of social grooming show that it can lead to the release of endorphins. Endorphins are a natural painkiller, generally released as an adaptive response to physical injury, and can lead to positive emotions and euphoria. In primates, it has been shown that endorphin levels are higher after social grooming. It is likely that the positive emotions associated with this endorphin release help individuals feel more socially bonded with one another and less likely to behave negatively toward each other in the future. In humans, it has also recently been shown that light touch may release endorphins. This suggests that our ancestors may have also used grooming as a way to encourage social bonding.

Across all primate species, social bonding is important for maintaining functional groups. Comparing across several different species, it is possible to see that social grooming is often used to maintain these social bonds. However, larger groups may have trouble with the amount of grooming required, and humans in particular may have had to develop other ways to maintain social connections.

HUMAN EVOLUTION AND SOCIAL BEHAVIOR

Humans are one of the most social species on the planet. Our civilizations can only exist because we have developed the ability to communicate and exchange ideas. Through language, we are able to pass on ideas from generation to generation and change the physical environment around us by using technology. As part of this evolutionary process, we have started living in much larger groups than any other primate species. In the same way as every other primate species, there would have been advantages to our social living, such as better support from predators, more help with hunting, and better exchange of ideas. It has been argued that while our species was adapting to living in larger groups we would have also been developing larger brains.

The social brain hypothesis argues that the development of large brains in humans is linked to the increase in our average group size. The parts of the brain that deal with complex decision-making and organizational skills are called the *frontal lobes*. In humans, the frontal lobes are very large in relation to the rest of the brain. Our large frontal lobes allow us to deal with more complex problems and decision-making than most other species. The social brain hypothesis argues that the most complicated problems we can manage are those associated with other humans. To interpret the actions of other people and to react to these actions we may have needed to develop much larger frontal lobes than other species. But what evidence shows that frontal lobes grew to deal with our larger groups?

By comparing brain sizes in different primate species, it has been possible to identify a direct relationship between the expansion of the frontal lobes and the size of social group. Different species live in different sizes of groups, so it is possible to compare the average group size of a species with the size of its members' brains. This comparison shows there is a direct relationship between group size and the size of more recently developed parts of the brain. There are likely to be a number of pressures that led to the development of larger brains, but social living may have been an important part of this.

Using the comparison of brain size and group size, it is possible to calculate the group size that humans are best able to live in, before we lived in a globalized civilization. This calculation suggests we should be able to live in communities of around 150 people. This is the number of people we should be able to live with in a close community and the number of people that we can remember information about and talk to on a regular occasion. The relevance of this number has been supported by studies investigating the number of Christmas cards people send, the number of Facebook friends people interact with, and the size of hunter-gatherer groups.

A group size of 150 would have come with a high risk of group conflict and would have required a way of maintaining positive social connections with all individuals within a group. There are not enough hours in the day to physically groom that number of individuals regularly, so our ancestors would have had to find a new way to maintain the social connections within their groups. It has been proposed that group music making could have been the behavior that allowed this large group bonding in the same way that social grooming works for other primate species in smaller groups.

MUSIC AS SOCIAL GROOMING

At some stage in evolutionary history, our ancestors would have started living in groups that were too large to maintain relationships through social grooming. They would have then needed a new kind of behavior to maintain social connections with large numbers at the same time. This behavior would ideally be something that could be performed in large groups and lead to the release of endorphins. This would allow the behavior to have the same effect as social grooming but for the whole group of 150 people instead of just working between two individuals at a time. It has been suggested that group music and dance could have been the behaviors that had these effects. We know that group music and dance can happen in large groups of people, and recent evidence suggests that they may lead to the release of endorphins.

At the point in history that music started, there would not have been any recordings, and the earliest forms of music are also unlikely to have involved any specialized instruments. This means that we have no clear evidence about very early human music and can only guess that it could have involved singing, which may have been accompanied by rhythmic movements (e.g., clapping, stamping, banging objects together). Any movements would have been rhythmic and in time with the music, so they would have seemed like a kind of dance.

In many cultures, dance still accompanies most musical performance, and this suggests that musical sounds and movements are generally very closely linked to one another. The combination of music and dance is sometimes called *musicking*. The concept of musicking is useful in thinking about music and dance as inherently intertwined rather than thinking of them separately, as we often do in many Western cultures in the twenty-first century.

Musicking is a physical activity that involves movement as well as hearing sounds and interacting with other members of a group. It has been suggested that this combination may lead to the release of endorphins. Endorphins are known to be responsible for "runner's high", which is the sense of elation that people who run often feel. The physical activity involved in musicking could therefore also lead to the release of endorphins. To investigate this possibility, recent studies have looked at the influence of movement during musicking on pain thresholds. Endorphins are a painkiller, so increases in the pain threshold are thought to indicate a release of endorphins.

One study looked at whether synchronized dance movements could lead to the release of endorphins. People were asked to dance together in groups of three people. Some groups of participants were asked to do the same dance movements at the same time, and others were asked to do different dance movements. There were also groups who made big movements that required a lot of physical effort, and some groups made small movements that did not require much movement. Researchers took pain threshold measures before and after they danced together, which showed that more physical effort and more synchronized movements led to a greater change in pain thresholds. More effort and synchronization also caused people to report feeling socially closer to one another afterward. This provides some evidence that synchronized dance, which requires physical effort, can lead to the release of endorphins and also cause social bonding. The discovery of this connection supports the argument that group music making may be a form of social grooming.

Another recent study looked at singing in groups of people. It was designed to discover whether social bonding can happen in a very large group of people when they are making music together. This is important because our ancestors would have needed an activity that allowed groups of 150 people or more to experience endorphin release and social connection at the same time. The study looked at choirs that generally rehearse in groups of twenty to eighty people. It measured pain thresholds and looked at how socially close people felt to one another before and after these small group rehearsals. People who had sung together reported feeling socially closer to each other and also showed an increase in pain thresholds, suggesting a release of endorphins.

The researchers then visited a rehearsal where 220 people all sang together at the same time and measured pain thresholds and social closeness to the group before and after singing. They found that after the singing there was a similar increase in pain thresholds and a similar increase in reports of connectedness compared to the small group rehearsals. This suggests that music making can lead to endorphin release and social bonding on a large scale. This evidence also supports the argument that group music making can be a way for social grooming at a distance, without the need for physical touch.

There is still emerging evidence in this area and the need for more detailed analysis of endorphin release during music making. It is likely that there are other chemicals that are involved in the social bonding effects people experience during musicking, and there is a need to understand these processes better in the future.

CONCLUSION

Group music making can act as a form of social grooming that leads to the release of endorphins. Endorphins have the effect of making people feel more positive, and this causes a type of friendship to form between different members of a group. Whereas many primates establish social bonds through individual grooming, humans live in much larger groups than other primate species and need some other way to experience a sense of connection with their social group. Group music making and dance may perform this role. Perhaps that is why making music and dancing together are such good ways to break the ice in a social situation and also to help us feel connected to our friends.

References and Further Reading

Dunbar, R. I. M., & Shultz, S. (2017). Why are there so many explanations for primate brain evolution? *Philosophical Transactions of the Royal Society B: Biological Sciences, 372*(1727), 20160244.

Machin, A. J., & Dunbar, R. I. M. (2011). The brain opioid theory of social attachment: A review of the evidence. *Behaviour, 148*(9–10), 985–1025.

Nummenmaa, L., Tuominen, L., Dunbar, R., Hirvonen, J., Manninen, S., Arponen, E., . . . Sams, M. (2016). Social touch modulates endogenous μ-opioid system activity in humans. *Neuroimage, 138*, 242–247.

Small, C. (1998). *Musicking: The Meanings of Performing and Listening*. Hanover, NH: University Press of New England.

Tarr, B., Launay, J., Cohen, E. E. A., & Dunbar, R. I. M. (2015). Synchrony and exertion during dance independently raise pain threshold and encourage social bonding. *Biology Letters, 11*(10), 20150767.

Weinstein, D., Launay, J., Pearce, E., Dunbar, R. I. M., & Stewart, L. (2016). Singing and social bonding: Changes in connectivity and pain threshold as a function of group size. *Evolution and Human Behavior, 37*(2), 152–158.

PART 3

Impact and Applications
of Music

Music and Emotion

41. Why Is Music Emotional? Theories of Music and Emotion

Steven R. Livingstone

Is music emotional? Many would answer, yes, of course it is! But why is music emotional? In this chapter, we will explore the role of emotion in music and review the science helping us to understand the effect of music on our brains, bodies, and minds.

With the advent of recording and playback technology, music has made its way into nearly every aspect of daily life. Today, you can hear music while at a parade, a cultural or religious ceremony, on the drive to school, at the shopping mall, at a football match, or even while on hold on the phone. Music plays an intimate role in people's lives, and music is ranked among the top ten activities that people find pleasurable. The ubiquity of music, combined with its ability to evoke pleasure, highlights the capacity for music to communicate *emotional meaning*. This quality makes it an ideal accompaniment to circumstances in which an emotional backdrop is desirable. This capacity is used to great effect in film: the blaring trumpets of *Star Wars* is triumphant; the alternating pattern of two notes in *Jaws*, E and F, evokes feelings of terror and powerlessness; and the celesta in the *Harry Potter* films fills us with mystery and curiosity.

Take a moment to think about how music has played a role in your own life. Is there a song you like to play when you are feeling sad? Do you have a playlist for getting energized to work out? What music makes you smile and feel good? What lullaby did your parents sing to you? Does your national anthem fill you with pride? While every person's connection to music is unique, it is likely that music has some form of emotional association in your life.

PSYCHOLOGICAL MODELS OF EMOTION

Before outlining specific theories of music and emotion, it is helpful to first review general theories of human emotion. As we will learn, specific theories of musical emotion often use elements of the following general theories.

Emotion and Cognition

Plato wrote in the *Republic* (380 BCE) that the human mind is composed of three main elements: reasoning, emotion, and desire. This view separates emotion from reasoning and motivation and has influenced many subsequent theories of the human mind. Several recent theories highlight the importance of *appraisal* in emotional response, which is similar to Plato's concept of "reason." Following an event or situation, your appraisal of the situation—how relevant and significant a situation is to your life—determines your emotional response. For example, it is a beautiful warm day, and you are out swimming in the ocean. Suddenly, you see a shark swim by your legs. Immediately, you "appraise" the situation as dangerous, which causes an emotional response and bodily reactions, such as increased heart rate, trembling, and a feeling of fear. This fear, in turn, motivates you to swim to shore.

Descartes's Primary Passions

In his work *Passions of the Soul* in 1649, René Descartes explored the connection between mind and body. Descartes used the term *passions* to describe experiences that are now commonly called *emotions*. Here is the basic problem: thoughts are not physical. How do thoughts, which are intangible, interact with your body, which is physical? Today, we understand that connection a lot better because of the work of neuroscientists. But five hundred years ago, it was a major sticking point and was called the *mind-body problem*. To address this problem, Descartes described the concept of passions as animal spirits produced in the blood that were responsible for the physical stimulation that causes the body to move. We would later learn that these spirits function like the body's central nervous system. Descartes outlined six primary passions: wonder, love, hate, desire, joy, and sadness.

Darwin and the Evolution of Emotion

A few hundred years later, in 1871, Charles Darwin shook the scientific world with his theory of evolution, proposing that our heritable (genetic) characteristics change over successive generations due to environmental and sexual pressures. Darwin believed that our emotional expressions, such as smiling when happy and scrunching our face in disgust, were selectively developed for the goal of communication. He concluded that all humans should share these universal expressions of emotion, regardless of culture or language. Like Descartes, Darwin outlined six basic emotional expressions: anger, fear, surprise, disgust, happiness, and sadness. Darwin's ideas received strong support in the mid–twentieth century when scientists discovered that individuals in remote preliterate cultures could accurately identify emotions conveyed by the facial expressions of people outside their cultural group.

Dimensional Models

Basic emotion theorists believe that each emotion involves a distinct state; however, others suggest that emotions fall on a continuum within a multidimensional space. These dimensions commonly include valence and arousal; *valence* refers to the positive or negative dimension of experience, and *arousal* is the degree of energy that is driven by the body's autonomic nervous system. Think for a moment about what it is like when you are feeling happy. Most people would describe happiness as a positively valenced state ("good") and often arousing (causing increased

alarmed   excited

afraid

astonished

angry

annoyed   delighted

frustrated

high arousal

happy

displeasure   pleasure   pleased

content

miserable

serene

depressed

calm

bored

low arousal

relaxed

tired   sleepy

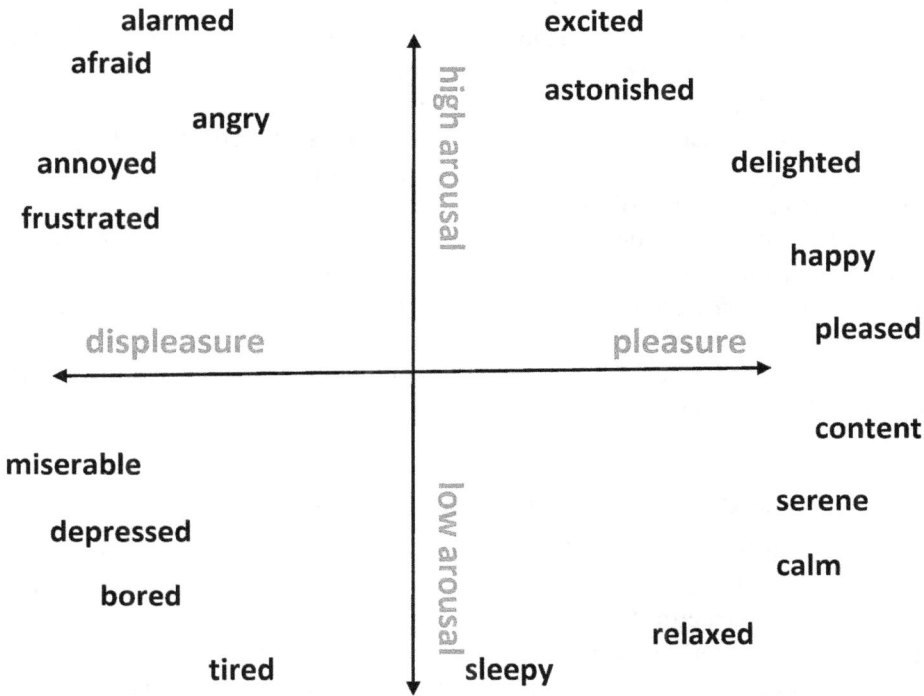

Figure 41.1   A two-dimensional representation of emotion. The horizonal axis represents valence, with negative on the left-hand side to positive on the right-hand side. The vertical axis represents arousal, with low energy at the bottom to high energy at the top. Common emotions words are placed within the space according to their arousal-valence levels. For example, "delighted" has both positive valence (right-hand side) and high energy (top), so it can be found in the top-right corner of the space.

heart rate and elevated sensory awareness). In contrast, sadness is generally thought to be negatively valenced ("bad") and lacking in energy. A two-dimensional representation of emotion can be seen in figure 41.1.

Dimensional models contrast with basic emotion models. Basic emotion theorists believe that each emotion is discrete, and different emotions arise from separate neural and physiological systems. In contrast, dimensional theorists view all emotions as points on a continuum that arise from common and interconnected neural and physiological systems.

THEORIES OF MUSIC AND EMOTION

What properties of music make it sound emotional? Can we identify features of music that are associated with communicating and eliciting emotion? Beginning in the twentieth century, scientists began theorizing about why music is so emotional.

Music as a Language of the Emotions

One popular theory is that music contains a vocabulary of sounded features that are associated with emotion. Composers draw upon these features to capture and convey the desired emotions. In effect, music is a "language of emotion," with a vocabulary that consists of melodic intervals and musical patterns that represent different feelings. For example, an ascending major third was said to express "an outgoing, active, assertion of joy," while its minor counterpart was characterized as "expressive of an outgoing feeling of pain—an assertion of sorrow, a complaint, a protest against misfortune."

An important consequence of this theory is that it made for testable predictions. There now exists significant evidence that major thirds are perceived as more "joyful" than minor thirds, but it seems unlikely that music all around the world communicates emotion in the same way.

Contour and Convention of Musical Emotion

Another influential theory argued for two sources of connection between music and emotion. First, many features of music, such as tempo, mode, and melodic patterns, have a "structural resemblance" with human behaviors that are expressive of these emotions. These features are called the *contour* of music. For example, a descending pitch might resemble a human sigh and have a similar emotional connotation. As another example, a slow tempo in music might resemble the slow walking pace of a sad individual and, hence, will also sound sad. Aside from these "natural" connections with emotion, there are also learned associations between music and emotion. These associations have no natural connection with human behavior and are therefore called *conventions*.

Music Sounds the Way Emotions Feel

The two previous theories argued that music can represent specific emotions. Other theorists reject this position, proposing that there is only a similarity between the structure of feeling and the structure of music. These characteristics of music are shared with human feeling, such as "patterns of motion and rest, tension and release, agreement and disagreement." However, music has no specific vocabulary of emotion; it is only capable of representing qualities of emotion. Although this theory remains popular, it does not outline how musical feelings can be measured. As such, there have been no direct attempts to empirically test the hypothesis.

Music Toys with Our Expectations

An influential theory from 1956 proposed that the emotional power of music lies in the expectations it creates in listeners. These expectations are learned through exposure to the musical works of our culture. For example, most of us have heard the ascending major scale (*do–re–mi–fa–sol–la–ti* . . .). You were probably expecting it to end with the upper *do*. The failure of this musical sequence to resolve as expected may have created a sense of unresolved tension within you. When listening to music, emotions are induced through the violation, delay, or confirmation of our expectations. Violations elicit arousal through activation of the autonomic nervous system, a control system in the body that largely acts unconsciously and regulates functions such as heart rate, digestion, and respiration.

This theory proposed that music can evoke arousal in listeners, but it rejected the notion that music can convey or evoke basic emotions (e.g., happiness or sadness). Another implication of this theory is that our expectations must be culturally learned. Recent evidence supports this position; typical musical expectations are not exhibited by young children (five years old) but later develop by age nine. The theory of musical expectations has gone on to inspire more recent accounts of the relationship between music, emotion, and our expectations.

A Fleshed-Out Model of Expectations

A more recent theory revisited the role of expectations in our emotional response to music. This refreshed theory identified five expectation-related components: imagination, tension, prediction, reaction, and appraisal. These components happen one after another when listening to music that affects our expectations. The first two mechanisms capture feelings that occur prior to an expected or unexpected musical event. With *imagination*, music motivates us to behave in a way that increases the likelihood of future beneficial outcomes. Next comes *tension*, which prepares us by adjusting our arousal and attention to match the level of uncertainty and importance of the event's outcome. The last three components describe responses that occur after the (un)expected musical event has passed. After the musical event comes *prediction*, which produces brief periods of positive and negative feelings that encourage the formation of accurate expectations. Then follows *reaction*, a rapid knee-jerk response to address possible worst-case scenarios by acting to immediately protect us. Finally, the event ends with an *appraisal*, a conscious assessment of the outcome of the event on our physical self. Collectively, these five components describe the time line of our emotional response to music that toys with our expectations.

Multiple Sources

The theories we have reviewed so far have mainly focused on the connection between musical sound and emotion. However, other theorists have sought to understand the sources of these emotions in the brain and body. Many researchers acknowledge that there is no single reason why music makes us feel emotional; it is likely the result of many interacting systems. Identifying these systems may help us to understand not only what aspects of music elicit an emotional response but also *why* these emotions occur.

One recent theory identified eight sources for our experience of musical emotionality. These included: brain stem reflexes, rhythmic entrainment, evaluative conditioning, emotional contagion, visual imagery, episodic memory, musical expectancy, and aesthetic judgment. *Brain stem* responses reflect our most primitive brain mechanism, preparing us for fight-or-flight reactions at a moment's notice. Our brain stem responds to sudden, loud, rapidly approaching, or dissonant sounds, and this occurs whether these sounds are present in music or the general environment. Horror films have long used the startling power of loud music to great effect, eliciting shrieks and causing audience members to jump out of their seats.

Rhythmic entrainment occurs when a powerful external rhythm in the music influences our internal bodily rhythm (e.g., our heartbeat), which gradually adjusts toward and locks in to a common periodicity. The adjusted heart rate can then spread to other components of emotions. Independent research has shown that listeners' heart rates and breathing may synchronize to the music, and that this periodicity can be affected by the beat of the music. For example, the presence of a strong pulse in electronic dance music (e.g., crunk, trap, techno, dubstep) has been shown to increase heart and breathing rates in listeners.

Evaluative conditioning, also known as Pavlovian, or classical, conditioning, occurs when an emotion is evoked by a stimulus simply because that stimulus has often been paired with other positive or negative stimuli. For example, a piece of music may always play when your favorite TV show begins (e.g., "I'll Be There for You" from the show *Friends*). Over time, through repeated pairing, the music alone will eventually arouse happiness, even in the absence of the show.

Emotional contagion happens when we perceive the emotional expression of the music and mimic, or copy, this expression internally. For instance, the music may have a sad expression, as indicated by a slower tempo, lower pitch, or softer sound level, that in turn induces sadness in the listener.

Visual imagery occurs when we conjure up inner images in our mind (e.g., a beautiful sunset) while listening to the music. Research has long considered imagery as a trigger for emotions, with different feelings elicited by different images (e.g., a sunny, sandy beach versus a dark, wet basement).

Episodic memory occurs when music evokes a memory of a past emotional event in our life. For example, a song played at a funeral, when heard years later, may remind you of that day and evoke intense feelings of sadness.

Finally, *aesthetic judgment* accounts for "appreciation emotions" when we enjoy a piece of art (e.g., admiration, awe). These judgments involve a set of personally subjective criteria we believe make the piece good or enjoyable art.

CONCLUSION

There are a wide range of theories that attempt to account for our emotional responses to music. While not all theorists believe that music can induce emotions in listeners (cognitivists), there are many others who do (emotivists). An appealing part of the last three theories reviewed is that they provide a wide range of mechanisms to account for the scope and depth of musical emotion. Being relatively new theories, research is actively ongoing to better understand how these models account for our emotional responses to music.

References and Further Reading

Cooke, D. (1959). *The Language of Music*. London, UK: Oxford University Press.

Descartes, R. (1989). *Passions of the Soul*. Indianapolis, IN: Hackett. (Original work published 1649)

Huron, D. (2006). *Sweet Anticipation: Music and the Psychology of Expectation*. Cambridge, MA: MIT Press.

Juslin, P. N., & Vastfjall, D. (2008). Emotional responses to music: The need to consider underlying mechanisms. *Behavioral and Brain Sciences, 31*, 559–575.

Kivy, P. (1981). *The Corded Shell: Reflections on Musical Expression*. Princeton, NJ: Princeton University Press.

Lazarus, R. S. (1991). *Emotion and Adaptation*. New York, NY: Oxford University Press.

Meyer, L. B. (1956). *Emotion and Meaning in Music*. Chicago, IL: University of Chicago Press.

Scherer, K. R. (1984). On the nature and function of emotion: A component process approach. In K. R. Scherer & P. Ekman (Eds.), *Approaches to Emotion* (pp. 293–317). Hillsdale, NJ: Lawrence Erlbaum.

Zajonc, R. B. (1980). Feeling and thinking: Preferences need no inferences. *American Psychologist, 35*, 151–175.

42. Contemporary Research on Music and Emotion

Emery Schubert

Have you ever wondered why music can make us feel exhilarated or calm, moved or blown away? Our understanding of how emotion in music works has changed considerably in recent times. Many researchers no longer believe that emotions are just subjective, irrational, and too variable to measure. In this chapter, you will learn about some of the recent major developments in understanding emotion in music, particularly in terms of how emotions are measured, what happens in the body and brain during a musical emotion experience, and in what other ways music evokes emotions in the listener.

DO PEOPLE RATE THE EMOTION OF A PIECE OF MUSIC CONSISTENTLY?

Major advances in music and emotion research have taken place over the last century, and contemporary research on music and emotion owes much to the work of research conducted almost one hundred years ago. As early as the 1930s, Kate Hevner, a pioneer of modern research on emotion and music, showed that people often agree on the emotion that a particular piece of music expresses (e.g., happy, sad, fearful). One of the reasons researchers have been able to delve into more detail about emotion in music is because of the development of new ways of measuring emotional responses. In early approaches, listeners were sometimes asked to write down the emotion they noticed after listening to a piece of music (called *self-report*). Kate Hevner adopted a similar method. She presented listeners with various adjectives from a collection of emotion words, which she had previously grouped according to similarity of meaning. For example, the words *sad* and *mournful* were presented as part of one group, whereas *happy* and *joyous* were presented as part of another group. In the case of the two groups of words just mentioned, they can be placed opposite one another on the response sheet because each group has emotional meanings opposite to one another, one negative and the other positive.

Hevner found that certain qualities of music were consistently associated with these word clusters. Happy words were typically picked to describe music that was faster, higher pitched, and in the major mode, whereas sad words were typically picked to describe music that was slower, lower pitched, and in the minor mode. Contemporary researchers would say that the first group of words have a positive emotional valence, and the second group of words have a negative emotional valence. *Valence* refers to the continuum of emotional experience that extends from positive to negative, regardless of whether an emotion is high energy or low energy. In Western culture, songs composed in a major mode (e.g., "Oh, Susannah," "This Land Is Your Land," "Alouette") tend to have an emotional valence that is more positive (happier) than songs composed in a minor mode (e.g., "Greensleeves," "My Funny Valentine," "House of the Rising Sun").

DIMENSIONS OF EMOTIONS AND RATING SCALES

More recent findings have shown that emotions can be organized around a number of *dimensions*. We have already seen how Hevner implicitly understood this, with the awareness of positive and negative emotion word clusters. The other commonly used dimension is referred to as *arousal* (which is similar in meaning to *activity* or *energy*), and it is distinct from the valence dimension, making it a useful one. High-arousal emotions involve high physical activity or high internal stress, such as *exhilaration* and *anger*. Music that is loud and fast tends to be described as having high arousal. Notice that music that has high arousal can have either a positive or a negative valence. For example, exhilaration is a positive emotion, whereas anger is a negative emotion; however, both have high arousal. Serenity and sadness, on the other hand, are both low-arousal emotions, but one has a positive valence and the other a negative valence. Music that is slow and soft is associated with low-arousal emotions.

BEYOND VALENCE AND AROUSAL IN MUSIC

The valence-arousal view of emotion implies that all of our emotional experiences can be boiled down to just two basic dimensions. Can this simple view account for all the emotional responses that we have to music? Valence and arousal do not seem to capture the powerful experiences that we often feel when listening to music. Since the 1990s, different ways of describing our emotional experiences to music have been proposed. One alternative was proposed by the British researcher John Sloboda. He argued that self-reports of emotional experience are very subjective and hard to verify, so a more objective way to measure emotional responses to music is to focus on the physical responses that are triggered by music, such as crying, goosebumps (piloerection), tingles down the spine, and a feeling in the pit of the stomach. Much research has been done on goosebumps and tingles down the spine using related words for physical responses to music, such as *thrills* and *chills*.

Thrills and chills are sometimes described by the French word *frisson* (pronounced "free sawn"). But these emotional experiences can be hard to pin down. They can be highly individual and subjective. Music that produces chills in one person does not necessarily produce chills in another person, even when the very same passages of music consistently evoke them for the first person. It is as though music contains the *potential* to elicit a thrill or chill in the listener, but something, perhaps sufficient familiarity, is required of the listener to be able to unlock this emotional power. As an example, in the forty-second bar of the Sanctus of Gabriel Fauré's *Requiem*, Op. 48, a flowing, stepwise, conjunct melody and connected *legato* notes with violin obbligato changes to a louder section with articulated rhythm and the entry of French horns playing octave leaps. This change can be experienced as being powerfully emotional and producing frisson. Not everyone will experience frisson in response to this change, however. Perhaps an emotional response will only occur in people who are familiar with the piece or style of music.

PHYSIOLOGICAL AND NEUROSCIENTIFIC RESEARCH

So far we have looked at verbal self-report responses to music reported by the listener. There are nonverbal ways researchers have used to measure emotions in response to music. Physiological measures, such as measures of heart rate, respiration (breathing) rate, and skin conductance, have been reported since the end of the nineteenth century. Typically, these physiological measures are closely connected with the arousal dimension previously discussed. For example, a high heart rate is associated with high arousal, and so fast and loud music is more likely to increase heart rate than soft and slow music. But this finding is complicated by people who report high-arousal states, such as joy or excitement, even when there is no increase in physiological measures of arousal, such as heart rate. Indeed, joyous music, although "feeling" like a high-arousal emotion, can lead to a corresponding reduction in heart rate.

Brain science (the study of how the brain works, sometimes called *neuroscience*) is also making progress in understanding why music causes listeners to feel emotional. Brain science researchers such as Stefan Koelsch point out that it is unusual for a brain structure to have a single function, such as the musical emotion center. Instead, many regions of the brain work together, with experiences such as joy associated with brain activations that are distributed across many locations of the brain. The precise brain structures that are involved in a particular emotional state can sometimes differ across individuals, depending on their hereditary and autobiographical background. However, some brain regions, such as the amygdala and the hippocampus, are almost always involved in strong emotional responses to music.

BRINGING THE RESEARCH TOGETHER: BRECVEMA

How do we come to feel emotions in response to music? Over the last decade, the Swedish researcher Patrik Juslin has drawn a number of ideas and data together into a broad-based multiple mechanism understanding of this matter. As shown in table 42.1, he proposed eight ways that music triggers emotional experiences. He called these eight different ways *mechanisms* to emphasize that they probably involve different mental operations. The collection of these mechanisms is referred to using an acronym that is formed by the first letter of each mechanism: B-R-E-C-V-E-M-A. Each mechanism is explained in table 42.1.

Humans can quickly and automatically adjust to many changes and situations in the environment without thinking. Such behaviors are called *reflexes* and are thought to also occur in response to music. The brain stem is a part of the brain that is involved in processing the environment for these reflexive reactions. Musical features such as loudness can create emotional responses through the raw signal of the music directly affecting the listener with this automated reaction. Think of a piece of music that is very soft and then suddenly becomes very loud. This point in the piece may well create a strong emotional charge in the listener. Juslin refers to this kind of emotional process as the "brain stem reflex" (row 1 of table 42.1).

Table 42.1   **BRECVEMA model of how emotion is communicated by music to the listener**

Mechanism Name	Description
(1) Brain stem reflex	A hard-wired response to simple acoustic features such as extreme or increasing loudness or speed
(2) Rhythmic entrainment	A gradual adjustment of an internal body rhythm (e.g., heart rate) toward an external rhythm in the music that affects the listener's emotions through proprioceptive feedback
(3) Evaluative conditioning	A regular pairing of a piece of music and other positive or negative stimuli leading to a conditioned association
(4) Contagion	An internal "mimicry" of the perceived voice-like emotional expression of the music
(5) Visual imagery	Inner images of an emotional character conjured up by the listener through a metaphorical mapping of the musical structure
(6) Episodic memory	A conscious recollection of a particular event from the listener's past, which is triggered by a musical pattern
(7) Musical expectancy	A response to the gradual unfolding of the syntactical structure of the music and its expected or unexpected continuation
(8) Aesthetic judgment	A subjective evaluation of the aesthetic value of the music based on an individual set of criteria

Source: Juslin, Barradas, Ovsiannikow, Limmo, & Thompson (2016).

The *rhythmic entrainment* mechanism (row 2) is perhaps the least obvious of Juslin's mechanisms because it refers to physiological and musculoskeletal (the body frame) locking in to the beat of the music (i.e., entraining with the music). Examples of *rhythmic entrainment* are dancing and marching, and these often involve groups of people entraining (dancing, marching, etc.) simultaneously. Changes in heart rate and movement as a result of such music and the social setting in which these movements occur can alter one's emotions through feeling of oneness, communion, or emotional bonding. Some researchers have even referred to dancing as a kind of emotion (not just a stylized series of human movements, which is the regular definition of dancing).

Evaluative conditioning (row 3) refers to the connection between the music and the emotion occurring through the regular previous pairing of musical features with a particular message, such as sad music frequently being in the minor mode and causing other newly heard music in the minor mode to also sound sound sad. The pairing has occurred so frequently that the listener may not be aware of the reason for why the music sounds sad. It just does.

The *contagion* mechanism (row 4) is a special mechanism because it suggests that musical emotions can "leap" from the music into the listener; The listener, without consciously trying, "catches" the emotion that the music appears to portray. The mechanism is special because it relies on the idea that the music can act like a sentient being (a human or some other animal) that can be understood by the listener: The music "tricks" the listener into capturing its emotion.

If a piece triggers a sensation or memory that is visual, that sensation may produce the emotion. For example, if a piece of music evokes the visual memory of a painting, and that painting makes the listener feel joyous, then the emotion is triggered by the *visual imagery* mechanism (row 5). Research by Robina Day and William Thompson has demonstrated that people frequently experience visual images when listening to music, and these images can be linked to the processing of emotions.

If the music triggers a memory of an event in the past when the music was first heard, then the emotion generation can be described as *episodic* (row 6). Here, the music triggers the event or episode of that person's life when the event and music first occurred together. Lovers may hear a piece of music and feel an emotion such as nostalgia because the piece was heard when they first fell in love, an experience that has been referred to by British psychologist John Booth-Davies as "darling they're playing our song."

Another way emotion is communicated is based on the automatically learned expectations one develops by listening to music within a culture. If one frequently hears a perfect cadence across many pieces within a style of music, the arrival of such a cadence will lead to its expectation. If the expectation is fulfilled, satisfaction may result, and if it is disrupted (e.g., an interrupted cadence), surprise may be experienced. Emotions generated by musical structures in this way are referred to the as *musical expectancy* (row 7).

The final mechanism, *aesthetic judgment* (row 8) may be thought of as the overall emotional evaluation that is felt as the result of a powerful, moving, and energizing live performance, for example.

CONCLUSION

Emotional response to music can be measured in many different ways. It can be measured by self-report using lists of fairly simple emotion words, or rating scales, with the latter being more common in recent years. However, we also saw that researchers have developed interest in more powerful, aesthetic emotions, such as chills and thrills, which are harder to pinpoint because they are difficult to reproduce in laboratory-based experiments. Brain scans have also been used to identify parts of the brain that are active during emotional experiences to music. The development in recent years of the BRECVEMA mechanisms provides an important, comprehensive resource explaining how emotion is evoked in the listener through music. Researchers are now building an increasingly sophisticated scientific picture of how it is that music can produce various emotions.

References and Further Reading

Huron, D. (2006). *Sweet Anticipation: Music and the Psychology of Expectation.* Cambridge, MA: MIT Press.

Juslin, P. N. (2019). *Musical Emotions Explained: Unlocking the Secrets of Musical Affect.* Oxford, UK: Oxford University Press.

Juslin, P. N., Barradas, G. T., Ovsiannikow, M., Limmo, J., & Thompson, W. F. (2016). Prevalence of emotions, mechanisms, and motives in music listening: A comparison of individualist and collectivist cultures. *Psychomusicology: Music, Mind, and Brain, 26*(4), 293–326. doi:10.1037/pmu0000161

Koelsch, S. (2014). Brain correlates of music-evoked emotions. *Nature Reviews, 15*(3), 170–180. https://doi.org/10.1038/nrn3666

Sloboda, J. A. (1991). Music structure and emotional response: Some empirical findings. *Psychology of Music, 19*(2), 110–120.

43. Music as Emotion Management

Katrina Skewes McFerran

Do you find it easier to will yourself to happiness or is it more effective to choose music that you know will make you happy? Some people believe that the inherent qualities of music affect our emotions in predictable ways, helping us to manage how we are feeling by choosing the right piece of music. Others believe our preexisting associations with particular songs fill those pieces with emotional meaning; memories are triggered by the music and provoke emotions, sometimes unexpectedly. This distinction strikes at the heart of causation: which is more powerful, you or your music? The answer to this question suggests very different strategies for using music for emotion management.

MUSIC INFLUENCES EMOTIONS

If music has a powerful influence on our emotions, we should be able to reliably draw upon particular qualities of music to help us with emotion management. This means identifying which emotions are problematic and deciding how they should be regulated. Music can then be selected to match the initial problematic emotion as well as the desired emotion, and a musical journey can be taken that gradually transitions from one to the other. This does not suggest music can be taken like a drug to rid oneself of problematic emotions, but it can be used to match and meet emotional needs and then to inspire more positive emotional experiences. Consider the following scenario.

Sula felt very sad after the loss of her beloved grandmother. She decided to use music as a way of making herself feel better. She tried playing positive music with energetic tempos, exciting melodies, and upbeat rhythms. However, she found these difficult to tolerate because they did not match the way she was feeling and were difficult to relate to. She then decided to listen to music that matched her mood, with a slower tempo, poignant melodies, and harmonic progressions that are less predictable and more melancholic. She initially cried, but then, after one or two songs, she felt a sense of relief and a lightening of her mood.

Sula then selected some songs that are still touching but pick up the tempo a little, with a bit more emphasis on energetic drum sounds and more upbeat melodies. This type of music no longer felt jarring because her need to have her sadness validated had been addressed. She began to tap her foot and drum her fingers along with the songs.

Sula then remembered that she needed to do some chores and chose songs that increased her energy level to accompany the vacuuming. The songs had predictable "four on the floor" drumbeats and bouncy melody lines. She soon found herself moving backward and forward in time to the music as she moved between different rooms. By the time she was finished, she felt energized, despite having done chores, and decided to call a friend to see whether she wanted to catch up later that day.

This example illustrates the application of a music therapy principle called the *iso principle*, where "iso" means equivalent or the same. This principle was originally applied by Ira Altschuler in the late 1940s when he experimented with using Western classical music to help psychiatric inpatients manage their moods. This was the first experiment to identify how music has a more powerful effect on emotions when it is first used to match and validate those that are prominent and only then to gently draw people toward a preferred emotion.

However, it is still unclear whether it is the qualities of the music that have been most powerful or the associations that people have with music. Although Altschuler used classical music from his own collection, the therapeutic impact is more effective when we use our preferred music in creating emotion management playlists. This is because people are less likely to listen to music that they do not like and are more motivated to listen when it is their favorite music. Although Western classical music is often regarded as particularly useful because of the complexity and careful construction of compositions, it is not always popular. Similarly, a heavy metal fan may prefer to construct playlists of metal music that canvasses a wide array of emotional experiences and musical parameters, but people who are not familiar with the genre would be unlikely to be motivated to use this playlist.

MUSIC AFFORDS EMOTIONAL RESPONSES

Another way music can be used to manage our emotions is understanding that our individual associations with music are more powerful than the qualities of the music itself. In this scenario, your personal circumstances are considered to be highly influential, and both emotions and music are understood as experiences that occur in context. Rather than trying to control individual emotions as though we are conducting a scientific experiment in a lab, a contextually sensitive approach allows for existing music preferences and associations. In this way, we can manage our emotions by identifying which songs trigger problematic emotions and then consider how to, first, acknowledge those difficult emotions and, second, move on to songs that are associated with the preferred experience. The example from above would be revised to look more like the following (note: Sam's gender identity is unknown, and I have used the plural pronoun in this example to avoid binary language).

Sam was feeling very sad after the loss of their beloved grandmother. Sam decided to use music as a way of coping with their emotions. Sam usually has music playing on shuffle and had noticed that some of the songs triggered their grief when they began to play. This often caught Sam by surprise and had been disconcerting on occasions when it happened in public. Sam decided to construct a playlist that would use these songs more intentionally and labeled the playlist "Grandma." As Sam looked through the list of songs in their library, they added those associated with sad feelings about losing their grandmother into the Grandma playlist. Sam then thought about which songs had positive associations, particularly those that their grandmother had also heard or enjoyed.

Sam ended up with around ten tracks that were then carefully organized to start with the one that triggered the strongest and saddest emotional reactions and progressed toward those that evoked less powerful feelings, ending with songs that seemed to provoke a smile and were associated with positive memories. Sam used the playlist intentionally, often choosing to listen when at home alone and sometimes beginning from the third or fourth track to avoid connecting with the saddest emotions. Sam also noticed that the songs no longer caught them by surprise when they played unexpectedly, and so Sam was better able to understand the emotional responses and manage them accordingly.

This example illustrates intentional programming with a focus on appropriating the affordances of music. Theorists from sociology, such as Anthony Giddens, suggest that music is one of many cultural resources that can be used to bring about change. This emphasizes the agency of the individual who is using music, as in the example above. This is different than believing that particular elements of the music, such as a minor key or a slow tempo, are what provokes different emotions. Even though particular musical qualities suggest specific emotional states, the individual's preferences, historical associations, and the conditions under which the person is listening will also be influential.

MENTAL HEALTH AND WELL-BEING

One of the most powerful contextual influences is our current state of mental health. Research has shown that the way you use music can differ depending on whether you are well or unwell. Our ability to make decisions about how to use the power of music is shaped by our state of mind. For example, it is quite common for people who are struggling with depression to choose music that increases their tendency to ruminate rather than choosing music that distracts them from the cause of their concern. Even if you have used music effectively to energize or soothe yourself in the past, this capacity may be more limited when your mental health is poor because it influences decision-making. A number of studies have shown how many people intuitively use music to make themselves feel better without needing to be conscious of their reasons for choosing a piece of music. Suvi Saarikallio's studies of Finnish youth have revealed a range of different mood management strategies with music, including using music for entertainment, revival, diversion, solace, mental work, discharge, and strong sensations. However, if your mental health is compromised, music listening habits that were once helpful can become unhelpful without your even realizing it. The following scenario illustrates this point.

Abdul had always loved hip-hop music and found it empowering to listen to his preferred genre. He was happy to listen to a range of artists that had successfully transitioned into mainstream pop listening, but he particularly enjoyed local Aussie hip-hop that addresses issues such as racism and sustainability. At the age of fifteen, Abdul experienced his first episode of serious depression and was briefly hospitalized for feeling suicidal. In the months leading up to that time in the hospital, he had been particularly focused on three hip-hop songs and often listened to one song on repeat for up to three hours. The song he listened to mostly talked about the pain of losing someone you loved and wanting to join that person in heaven. Abdul's grandmother had died one year earlier, and he often thought of his grandmother in heaven as he listened to the song.

Without thinking about it consciously, Abdul had hoped that feeling so bad while he listened to the song on repeat would eventually help him to feel better; he expected to get some relief from the cathartic aspects of listening. This had worked for him in the past, and hip-hop music had been helpful in shifting his mood to a more positive frame when he was feeling negative. But the same songs were not helpful anymore, and Abdul did not notice that he often felt worse after listening, and sometimes a lot worse.

While in hospital, Abdul worked with a music therapist who asked him about his music listening habits and particularly focused on how he felt after listening. As Abdul began to reflect on this, he noticed how his feelings while listening had changed. Together with the therapist, he developed a playlist labeled "Grieving" that included many of his favorite songs. He carefully considered which ones were now associated with feeling worse and which ones he could use to feel better. He organized them so that the first songs matched his sad emotions but then the list moved toward more positive songs with themes of resilience and survival. Abdul also started noticing when he played songs on repeat. Sometimes he would let himself wallow in difficult feelings, but at other times, he would choose not to listen and tried to make himself do something active instead. Over time, he began to use music as a resource to manage his emotions rather than unconsciously reinforcing difficult emotions and felt that this was helpful during difficult times. He continues to be a massive hip-hop fan.

Being aware of how you might use music differently depending on your state of mental health is critical. This idea still relies on the notion that we are active agents who can use music as a resource for change. It acknowledges that particular types of music are more likely to suggest particular emotions, but personal preferences and associations are also very powerful influences. The question of whether you are using music in healthy or unhealthy ways needs to be consciously contemplated. The following are questions that have been found to be useful in studies of young people:

- How often do I feel happier after playing or listening to music?
- How often do I use music to escape really hard feelings?
- How often do I relate more to my favorite lyrics than to what my friends have to say?
- How often does music give me an excuse not to face up to the real world?
- How often does music give me the energy to get going?
- When I try to use music to feel better, how often do I actually end up feeling worse?
- How often does sharing music with my friends make me feel part of the group?
- How often do I listen to songs over and over, even if it makes me feel worse?
- How often does music help me to express who I am?
- How often is it hard to stop listening to music that connects me to bad memories?
- How often does music lead me to do things I should not do?
- How often does music help me to relax?
- When I listen to music, how often do I get stuck in bad memories?
- When I am feeling tense or tired in my body, how often does music help me relax?
- How often do I hide in my music because no one understands me and it blocks people out?
- How often does music make me feel bad about who I am?
- How often does music help me to connect with other people who are like me? (Saarikallio, McFerran, & Gold 2015)

Your answers to these questions will reveal whether you are using music to feel better or worse and, in knowing that, whether we want to make any adjustments. Note that it does not suggest that any particular kind of music is better or worse than another. Nor does it imply that you will always use music in the same way.

CONCLUSION

When we use music for emotion management, it requires ongoing evaluation. The emotional experience of listening to the same piece of music can change over time and in different situations, particularly when we are struggling with poor mental health. Interestingly, we rely on music most when we are feeling worst, so the value of being conscious of how you are using it effectively doubles. Next time you listen to a piece of music to work with, or avoid, difficult emotions, take a moment to see how you feel afterward. Do you feel better or worse?

References and Further Reading

DeNora, T. (2003). *After Adorno: Rethinking Music Sociology.* Cambridge, UK: Cambridge University Press.

McFerran, K. S. (2016). Contextualising the relationship between music, emotions and the wellbeing of young people: A critical interpretive synthesis. *Musicae Scientiae, 20*(1), 103–121.

McFerran, K. S., & Saarikallio, S. (2013). Depending on music to make me feel better: Who is responsible for the ways young people appropriate music for health benefits. *The Arts in Psychotherapy, 41*(1), 89–97. https://doi.org/10.1016/j.aip.2013.11.007

Saarikallio, S. (2008). Music in mood regulation: Initial scale development. *Musicae Scientiae, 12*(2), 291–309.

Saarikallio, S., McFerran, K. S., & Gold, C. (2015). Development and validation of the healthy-unhealthy uses of music scale (HUMS). *Child and Adolescent Mental Health, 20*(4), 210–217.

44. Music and Emotion across Cultures

Emery Schubert and Marco Susino

Some people believe that music is a universal language. Is this true? Can a piece of music express or evoke emotions when played to someone from a culture where that music is not part of the culture? We know that music can make us feel emotional for different reasons, and many of these reasons can be traced to a particular psychological mechanism. Some mechanisms may well be universal, meaning that anyone in the world is likely to experience an emotion in response to music in this way. For example, a sudden loud sound tends to trigger a visceral alarm response at the level of the brain stem—called a *brain stem reflex*—and this mechanism is likely to be universal. But other mechanisms are more dependent on cultural and individual experiences such that the emotional experience of music may differ from person to person, school to school, street to street, and country to country.

Music can induce an emotional experience while we listen to it. Sometimes we feel joyful, energetic, empowered, nostalgic, or sad while we are listening to music. Other times music does not seem to affect us emotionally, even though it may have an emotional connotation. Have you ever listened to music that seems to be sad but that did not make you feel sad or music that is supposed to be happy but left you cold? Such examples illustrate that music can communicate an emotion without actually making us feel that same emotion. Because most cross-cultural research has focused on the communication of emotion through music, this will be our focus in this chapter. There are also interesting questions to be asked about whether emotional *experiences* of music differ around the world.

Researchers have wondered about the extent to which emotion in music is communicated across cultures and, more specifically, the extent to which the same emotion is experienced when listening to a music composition regardless of culture. Such research attempts to question the age-old aphorism "music is a universal language." In this section, you will learn how emotions are communicated cross-culturally by music, which emotions are best communicated, and the difference between *cultural cues* and *psychophysical cues* used in communication via music.

WHICH EMOTIONS CAN BE COMMUNICATED ACROSS CULTURES BY MUSIC?

Emotions of sadness and happiness tend to be communicated more or less universally by music, regardless of how different the culture of the music is from the culture of the individual listener. For example, a team of researchers led by Thomas Fritz conducted an experiment by playing music to an isolated village of Mafa people (in Africa). The Mafa people were shown pictures of faces displaying three emotions: one face was happy, another sad, and a third expressed fear. The participants listened to an extract of Western music and pointed to one of the faces. The extracts varied in several aspects of music structure, including mode (major or minor), tempo (the pace of the music), pitch, and rhythm so as to portray one of three target emotions. The results of the study showed that Mafa people with no exposure to Western music still recognized the emotions portrayed by music in a way that was similar to Western listeners.

Does this really mean that some emotions, in particular sadness and happiness, can be communicated universally by some music? Actually, it is important to note that the Mafa people chose the correct emotion more often than if they had just guessed, but they certainly did not choose the typical Western listener's emotion all the time. This result means that people can perceive glimpses of an intended emotion in unfamiliar music from another culture, but their performance is hampered by a lack of familiarity with the culture associated by Westerns with the music. Familiarity with music from one's own culture must provide additional cues that were missing for the Mafa people who participated in this study.

WAYS OF COMMUNICATING EMOTION IN MUSIC

The cue-redundancy model was put forward by Laura-Lee Balkwill and William Thompson to explain why people from one culture can partially, but not fully, appreciate the emotional connotations of music from another culture. A cue is a piece of information that links to or triggers (with or without conscious effort) another piece of information. One example is when the cue occurs naturally, such as a high pitch in a piece of music indicating happiness, and that link occurs regardless of cultural norms. This is called a *psychophysical cue*. Another example is when a cue is formed through cultural convention, such as learning that music in the major mode is happy by frequently hearing music in the major mode that is also happy within a particular culture. That is, some cultures

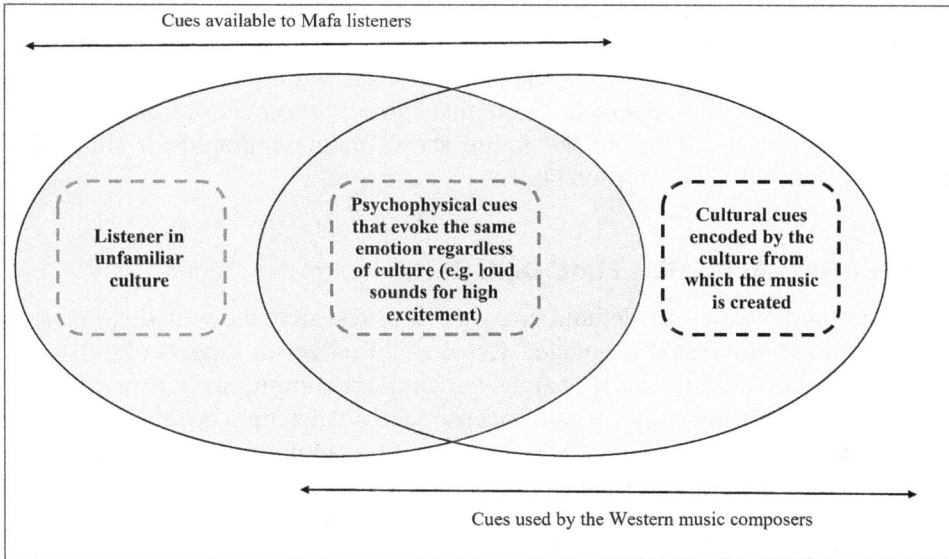

Figure 44.1 Schematic representation of emotion in music from the perspective of one culture (Mafa in this case) when the music was created in another culture (Western). *Source:* Balkwill and Thompson (1999).

will not share this association. In those other cultures, the major mode does not cue happiness. The major mode is therefore a *cultural cue*.

The Mafa people could not use Western cultural cues when making their judgments about Western music, but they could still perceive the intended emotions to some extent. According to the cue-redundancy model, music communicates emotions through psychophysical cues (musical features) and cultural cues, as shown in figure 44.1. An individual not accustomed to a style and culture of music may use psychophysical cues to assess the emotions of the music rather than the cultural meanings that come to be associated with that music in its culture of origin.

The figure shows how combinations of cultural and psychophysical (musical feature) cues explain similarities and differences in emotional responses to music based on the cue-redundancy model. The model shows how emotion in music partly depends on cues expected from music of the listener's culture in addition to musical feature cues. And so, the listener may not notice or understand some of the cues encoded by the other culture. In the figure, the dashed-line boxes depict the separation of these different kinds of cues. In the example, cues are used by Mafa listeners (boxes on the left, covered by the darker ellipse) to understand the intended emotion in Western music. Note that, for the Mafa listeners, their cultural cues are not shared with the Western cultural cues, and so those cues do not help to decode whether the music is happy, sad, or some other emotion that a Western listener notices. The Western listeners, on the other hand, understand emotions based on the features in the boxes on the right, covered by the lighter ellipse. Notice also that if the Mafa listeners are agreeing with the *intended* emotion for Western ears, but there is no cultural interaction between the two groups (Western and Mafa), then the bulk of the cues conveying emotions must be the psychophysical cues (the overlapping region of the two ellipses). In that case, the two ellipses should have a much larger overlapping region, and the middle box will be wider. In other words, psychophysical cues can convey emotions cross-culturally and possibly universally. Note that some cultural cues of even two distant cultures may overlap, but the figure shows them separated for simplicity. (Based on Balkwill & Thompson (1999).

UNIVERSAL AND MULTIMODAL CUES

The cue-redundancy model and cross-cultural research show us that music is only partially a universal "language." Evidence of universal aspects of music are also present in the nonmusical channels of musical communication of emotion. Although Western cultures are well accustomed to listening to music through sound recordings, this can be thought of as a cultural anomaly. Under normal (cultural and historical) circumstances, music is played or sung by people, and may also be danced to, and as a result is usually accompanied by signals from visual and even physical (kinesthetic and haptic) sensory channels. Several researchers have pointed out that music, under normal circumstances, is multisensory. This means that the visual and physical gestures that accompany music listening and performing may be divided along the same lines as the cue-redundancy model, and, furthermore, the senses (auditory and visual) may somehow naturally be connected. That is, certain physical and visual cues may naturally go with certain musical gestures, while others may be more culturally specific.

Joyful music is associated with particular movements (such as jumping for joy) that are distinctly different from other emotions, such as sadness (where a sad song would be performed with more crooning, introverted, less mobile physical poses). There is evidence that musicians do link emotions conveyed in the music with physical expressions. In 2009, Steven Livingstone and colleagues asked listeners to continue singing a song that they were listening to with music expressing emotions of sadness, happiness, or no explicit emotion. The participants were wired up with motion capture devices so that their facial expressions could be monitored. Motion capture devices are able to continuously record the position a person is in while that person is moving, store the position-related information on a computer, and reproduce the movements for later analysis by researchers—similar techniques are used by animation companies such as Pixar.

The researchers found that, even though not specifically instructed to do so, facial expressions made by the participants were commensurate with the emotion they were mimicking. For example, they spontaneously tended to smile when the music they were about to sing was expressing a happy emotion. David Huron has argued that when we produce signals for communicating with others, it is useful to maximize the clarity of the signal by presenting it in several sensory modalities. An angry animal may puff itself up to look larger and make bigger (deeper and louder) sounds to communicate its intentions (emotions, if you like). Synchronized, multisensory signaling is therefore an important part of cross-cultural communication. We just need to be conscious that this signaling will only be part of the answer as to how music and its sensory counterparts communicate emotion.

CULTURAL CUES

The cue-redundancy model described above has been expanded and modified to provide increasingly sophisticated explanations of cross-cultural communication of emotion in response to music. The "imperfect" cultural cues of emotions across cultures appear to be influenced by the degree of familiarity the individual has with the musical style in question. For instance, in a study conducted in 2019, we found that when a listener is reasonably, but not overly, familiar with a music style, the listener applies an emotional stereotype (an overly simple, usually unconscious) judgment of the music. That is, familiarity with cultural cues can help people make a good guess as to the intended emotional meaning portrayed by the music, but in some cases, that guess may be incorrect. As an example, if people have learned that death metal music is often violent, they may assume all death metal music they hear is violent. This assumption is a form of emotion stereotyping. Stereotypes can be correct, but not always.

Where do these stereotyped emotions come from? In the case of anger and death metal, media has an important role to play. Historically, there have been numerous occasions when new musical styles overturn tradition and are seen as threatening to the establishment. In the 1950s, rock and roll received similar views as death metal and hip-hop have since the 1990s and still do. Whether music can be said to cause people to acquire and act out violent (and other) emotions is debatable. But recent research has started to identify the source of emotion stereotyping that the music appears to convey.

Apart from the media and other forms of large-scale communication, there is also the principle of *psychological fit*, where one kind of stimulus tends to go well, or fit, with another. When given a choice of what kind of food to eat, people will choose Indian food rather than Malay, German, or Italian if Indian music is playing in the background. This kind of subconscious preference for mentally matching music with (in this case) cuisine also appears to occur with music and emotion. Implicit knowledge about Cuban culture, for example, appears to influence the kind of emotion that Cuban music evokes. Cuban culture is stereotyped by some as being romantic. Listeners who have picked up on this cultural stereotype (without conscious effort) will perceive typical Cuban music styles, such as bolero, as expressing emotions of love and romance. If a particular bolero song, such as "Lágrimas negras," composed in the late 1920s by Miguel Matamoros, is heard by a Westerner with limited experience of Cuban music and culture, the Westerner may make a stereotyped romantic judgment of the emotion the music expresses, even if that individual understands the Spanish lyrics, which are in fact about loss and contemplation of suicide.

CONCLUSION

Is music a universal language? In this section, we have seen that music is only partially a universal language of emotion because only certain emotions (sadness and happiness, in particular) are well communicated and because only certain musical features are able to communicate these emotions cross-culturally. These cues of emotion can therefore be said to be universal, and, furthermore, they tend to be accompanied by universal emotional communications in the visual sensory mode simultaneously. We have also learned that cultural cues are specific to a particular culture and are probably not able to communicate emotion to cultures unfamiliar with the emotional meaning. Cultures outside those where the music was created are likely to assess the emotion of such music based on psychophysical cues or on other cultural cues, such as by stereotyping, each of which may or may not result in an emotion reported that is commensurate with that reported by the culture for whom the music was originally created. The cultural component, therefore, while not part of the universality of emotion in music, poses interesting questions about how emotion becomes associated with music.

References and Further Reading

Balkwill, L.-L., & Thompson, W. F. (1999). A cross-cultural investigation of the perception of emotion in music: Psychophysical and cultural cues. *Music Perception, 17*(1), 43–64.

Balkwill, L. L., Thompson, W. F., & Matsunaga, R. (2004). Recognition of emotion in Japanese, Western, and Hindustani music by Japanese listeners. *Japanese Psychological Research, 46*(4), 337–349.

Fritz, T., Jentschke, S., Gosselin, N., Sammler, D., Peretz, I., Turner, R., . . . Koelsch, S. (2009). Universal recognition of three basic emotions in music. *Current Biology, 19*(7), 573–576.

Livingstone, S. R., Thompson, W. F., & Russo, F. A. (2009). Facial expressions and emotional singing: A study of perception and production with motion capture and electromyography. *Music Perception, 26*(5), 475–488. https://doi.org/10.1525/mp.2009.26.5.475

Susino, M., & Schubert, E. (2019). Cultural stereotyping of emotional responses to music genre. *Psychology of Music, 47*(3), 342–357. https://doi.org/10.1177/0305735618755886

Yeoh, J. P. S., & North, A. C. (2009). The effects of musical fit on choice between competing pairs of cultural products. *Empirical Musicology Review, 4,* 130–133.

Music and Memory

45. What Is Memory for Music?

Matthew Schulkind

Hearing an old favorite song for the first time in many years is often accompanied by feelings of nostalgia or even specific memories of people or events. These experiences suggest that there is a close connection between music and memory. One could argue that musical memory consists of two different kinds of memory. First, there is the ability to identify familiar melodies. Brief excerpts of a song are often enough for listeners to identify the title and artist. The second kind of musical memory often occurs because music has what psychologists refer to as *mnemonic capacity*. That is, when we hear a familiar song, the music sometimes triggers a memory of a personal experience or event in our lives. A *mnemonic* is something that promotes memory.

Music promotes memory in different ways. Sometimes memory for a song is so powerful that the song gets "stuck" and plays over and over in our head; this experience is often called an *earworm*. Sometimes songs remind us of a place or event from our past; psychologists call these *music-evoked autobiographical memories* (or MEAMs). Hearing music from the 1980s may remind people of high school or college or wherever they were when this music was popular. Many times, hearing a song reminds the listener of its accompanying lyrics. The ability of songs to remind us of texts is often deliberately employed, such as when American children are taught the names of all fifty U.S. states (in alphabetical order, no less) with a song. These experiences are notable not only because of how quickly one can learn a text set to music but also for how long the memory of the song seems to persist. (There are probably many American adults who are still able to sing the U.S. states song many years after initial learning it.)

The rest of this chapter will describe what psychological research tells us about melody identification and how music helps us remember information.

MELODY IDENTIFICATION

Thinking about how we remember melodies immediately introduces one of the fundamental questions in memory research: is memory absolute? If memory were absolute, it would imply that we record every piece of music in perfect or near-perfect detail. *Absolute memory* does not imply that we would never make mistakes: details can be lost over time or if we were not paying attention as well as we thought we were. But, absolute memory does imply that the memory system is designed to store as much specific information as we can. One could wonder, why would our memory system be devised any other way? Why would memory not record as much information as possible? The answer to that question is efficiency. Let's examine an extreme example.

A woman comes home from work at the end of a long day. Unlike her spouse or children, the family dog excitedly greets her at the door. The woman smiles as the dog approaches, easily recognizing her beloved pet. She does so by drawing on past experiences (memories) of what the dog looks like. If memory were absolute, the woman would have separate memories for every time she saw the dog, from all different angles, with all different kinds of lighting and all different hair lengths. That would require a lot of neurons and a lot of computing power every night when she gets home from work. It would be more efficient that she only store the amount of information that she needs to recognize her dog quickly and accurately.

If we apply this logic to music, the question is this: do listeners remember the exact pitch, duration, and timbre of every single note in every single song that they know? This would take up a lot of cognitive capacity that might be better used for other purposes. Or, do listeners recognize melodies based on some kind of abstracted pattern? That is, do people store a "shorthand" representation that retains only the information needed to identify the melody while leaving some information behind?

One approach to addressing this question is with a thought experiment. Imagine or sing aloud a common song, such as "Happy Birthday." Now imagine or sing it faster or slower. Or imagine or sing it at a higher or lower pitch. Or do an impersonation of Lady Gaga or Ed Sheeran singing "Happy Birthday." Would a listener have trouble identifying the fast/slow, high/low, Gaga/Sheeran versions of the song? Probably not. This implies that memory for melody is not absolute: the original pitches, tempo, and timbre are not essential to identify a melody. This is not to say people do not remember any information about these features, only that we can identify melodies that have been transformed in various ways. It should be noted that melody identification may become difficult or impossible if a song is sped up or slowed down, but it takes a very large manipulation for this to happen.

If people do not remember absolute information about melodies, what is remembered? Many psychologists argue that people remember the relationships between notes. A version of "Happy Birthday" that is sung with very high notes can still be identified as long as the pitch relationships between the notes remain the same. A fast or slow version of "Happy Birthday" can still be identified as long as the relative durations of the notes remain the same.

One early model of melody identification suggested that we retain the contour (pattern of rising and falling pitches) and key relationships within a melody; the key is a system for organizing pitches in Western music. This theory was supported by experiments in which listeners were asked to determine whether two melodies played one after the other were the same or different. When either the contour or key relationships of a melody changed, listeners had no problem saying, "Whoa . . . that is different." But the same was not true when contour and key remained the same. Even expert listeners behaved as though they were randomly guessing when they were asked to distinguish two different note patterns that shared the same contour and key relationships.

Still, there is some evidence that memory for some aspects of melodies can be absolute. For example, people are pretty accurate at singing the first note of a pop song that they know very well. This implies that they remember the exact starting pitch of a song. Other experiments have demonstrated similar results for tempo. For example, in one experiment, people were asked to imagine that a well-known song was playing and to tap along with the beat of the version that was "playing" in their head. The tempo of the beats for the imagined song closely matched the tempo of original recordings of that song. This suggests that people also retain detailed information about the timing of popular songs.

It could be that people retain absolute information like this for popular tunes because listeners typically hear one and only one recorded version of that song— Adele's studio recording of 'Rolling in the Deep' is often the only version of that song that most people have heard. Thus, the question of how much absolute and how much relative information is stored in musical memory remains open to further research. It could be that relational properties are remembered when listeners are exposed to many different versions of a melody, but absolute information is retained when listeners hear relatively few versions of a melody.

MNEMONIC CAPACITY OF MUSIC

As mentioned in the opening paragraph, many people believe that music helps us remember things like song lyrics or events from our past. This belief is rooted in people's own experiences, such as learning the fifty U.S. states song. In psychology, this kind of evidence is labeled *anecdotal*. Anecdotal evidence is not "bad," but researchers value experimental evidence over anecdotal evidence because experimental evidence is gained over repeated trials under controlled conditions. As we shall see, experimental evidence can produce data that are inconsistent with anecdotal experience.

Let's start by thinking about how a researcher might obtain experimental evidence to support the idea that music aids memory. The researcher might ask people to remember the same text (the fifty U.S. states) under the exact same conditions but with one small change: one group would be exposed to a musical or sung version of the text, and one group would hear the text spoken. Versions of this experiment have been conducted, and the initial results indicate that music helped memory. The subjects learned traditional North Carolina folk ballads, either sung or spoken, and recalled more of the words when the text was sung. The effect was especially strong when the melody was repeated several times over multiple verses. Thus, it seems that learning the music well helped fuse the song and the lyrics together into a common memory representation.

But, here is where it gets interesting. The goal of an experiment is to isolate one variable (in this case, whether the text was sung or spoken) while holding all other variables constant. Some researchers have wondered whether this was the case for the research described in the previous paragraph. In particular, they wondered whether the presentation time was controlled: that is, were the sung and spoken versions equal in duration? Here is another thought experiment to attempt: record how long it takes to sing a verse of a well-known song and compare that to how long it takes to read the lyrics aloud, without singing. It is very likely that the sung version will be longer than the spoken one. Some notes are sustained when singing, and there are relatively long pauses at the ends of lines; this tends to make the sung version longer than the spoken version.

With this idea in mind, another group of researchers conducted similar experiments while controlling for the duration of the sung and spoken versions of the to-be-remembered texts. These researchers had a big advantage over the researchers that were described earlier. Computers had become more powerful, which made it easier to construct sung and spoken stimuli that did not differ in terms of length or any other variable. When the length of the stimuli was controlled, these experiments demonstrated no difference between sung and spoken versions of the text. Music did not help people learn the words, but at least music does not interfere with learning lyrics. Or does it?

An even more recent study suggests that music actually interferes with learning! In this experiment, the subjects heard a sung text and responded either by singing the words with the same melody or by speaking the words without melody. The subjects recalled more words when speaking than when singing; this suggests that learning the music interfered with learning the lyrics. Conversely, learning the words interfered with learning the music. The researchers who conducted these experiments argued that the music and lyrics of a song are not fully combined in memory, so attention must be devoted to both the music and the words. This makes learning the words and music together more difficult than learning just the words or just the music. A reasonable analogy might be noting that it is harder to do one's chemistry homework while reading a novel than it would be to do either task on its own.

Some people find these data perplexing because they conflict with our anecdotal experiences regarding the mnemonic capacity of music. One way to resolve this conflict is to argue that although music makes texts harder to learn initially, repeated exposure to music helps us remember texts far better than we would without music. How could this be possible? Bear in mind that most people like music and find singing enjoyable (although, Sigmund Freud is reported to have passionately disliked music). Because singing is enjoyable, people tend to rehearse (i.e., sing) more than they might for a spoken text; more practice yields better memory. According to this argument, older adults (e.g., one's grandparents) do not remember songs that were popular when they were young. This is not because songs are unusually memorable, but because they have spent a lifetime singing them again and again. When young people today become grandparents in their own right, they should be able to sing songs that are currently popular, but not necessarily every popular song; only those that were sung often over the years.

Another possibility is that memory for song lyrics is different from memory for texts divorced from music. Typically, psychologists refer to memory for text as *declarative memory*. This is memory for facts and is typically verbally and consciously mediated. Music may be an example of what psychologists call *procedural memory*. Procedural memory is when you demonstrate your knowledge of a skill by doing it rather than talking about it. One example is riding a bicycle. It is difficult to verbally explain how to ride a bike; it is much easier to just do it. The skills that develop by practicing a sport, instrument, or a video game are also examples of procedural memory. It is possible that although singing the words of a song involves verbal memory (declarative memory), this act may still have more in common with procedural memory. That is, starting to sing a song may be like starting to ride a bicycle. The singer or rider does not consciously think about what do to next; instead, the process unfolds seemingly automatically.

CONCLUSION

The scientific study of memory for music has produced some interesting conclusions. Research indicates that music is remembered well over long periods of time. Instead of remembering exact pitches and note durations, we seem to retain a pattern of the relative pitch and timing of notes. Still, listeners do seem to retain some absolute information about familiar melodies, including the exact starting pitch of well-known songs. Music has also been shown to facilitate memory for other stimuli. Music can remind us of autobiographical experiences (e.g., MEAMs) and also affect memory for song lyrics. At early stages in the learning process, music appears to interfere with memory for text, but with repeated exposure and practice, musical texts are recalled better than texts presented without music.

References and Further Reading

Andrews, M. W., Dowling, W. J., Bartlett, J. C., & Halpern, A. R. (1998). Identification of speeded and slowed familiar melodies by younger, middle-aged, and older musicians and nonmusicians. *Psychology & Aging, 13*, 462–471. https://doi.org/10.1037/0882-7974.13.3.462

Dowling, W. J. (1978). Scale and contour: Two components of a theory of memory for melodies. *Psychological Review, 85*, 341–354. https://doi.org/10.1037/0033-295X.85.4.341

Jakubowski, K., Farrugia, N., Halpern, A. R., Sankarpandi, S. K., & Stewart, L. (2015). The speed of our mental soundtracks: Tracking the tempo of involuntary musical imagery in everyday life. *Memory & Cognition, 43*, 1229–1242. https://doi.org/10.3758/s13421-015-0531-5

Kilgour, A. R., Jakobson, L. S., & Cuddy, L. L. (2000). Music training and rate of presentation as mediators of text and song recall. *Memory & Cognition, 28*, 700–710. https://doi.org/10.1080/09658211.2015.1130843

Levitin, D. J. (1994). Absolute memory for musical pitch: evidence from the production of learned melodies. *Perception & Psychophysics, 56*, 414–423. https://doi.org/10.3758/BF03206733

Racette, A., & Peretz, I. (2007). Learning lyrics: To sing or not to sing? *Memory & Cognition, 35*, 242–253. https://doi.org/10.3758/BF03193445

Wallace, W. T. (1994). Memory for music: Effect of melody on recall of text. *Journal of Experimental Psychology: Learning, Memory, & Cognition, 20*, 1471–1485. https://doi.org/10.1037/0278-7393.20.6.1471

46. Music and Studying

William Forde Thompson and Kirk N. Olsen

In various activities of everyday life, music can be heard playing in the background, whether at the supermarket while you shop, in the lobby of an office building as you prepare for an interview, at a social gathering while you chat with friends and make new acquaintances, or while driving your car. The widespread practice of accompanying other activities with background music raises an important question: does music help, hinder, or have no effect on these other activities? An emerging body of evidence suggests that there are subtle yet important effects of background music on other concurrent activities. Understanding the negative and positive consequences of background music can help us to determine whether music is an optimal accompaniment for any task or activity in which we might engage.

THE PROS AND CONS OF STUDYING WITH MUSIC

Many students listen to music while they are studying, completing homework, or preparing for a test. Is that a good idea? The question has no simple answer because there are both positive and negative effects of listening to music, and these effects may depend on one's personality and musical background. On the positive side, music can make an otherwise tedious task more enjoyable, which may motivate students to continue studying for longer periods of time. If a student is feeling stressed about difficult study materials, music can be calming. Upbeat music can improve mood and energy levels, decreasing the risk of fatigue while studying. If you are studying in a distracting environment, such as a busy coffee shop, listening to quiet music through headphones can mask those sources of distraction and replace it with a predictable and enjoyable source of stimulation. Finally, music stimulates the imagination and so can act as a source of inspiration for tasks that involve creative thought.

On the negative side, music is distracting. This is especially true if the music contains lyrics because the verbal information that is expressed by lyrics can interfere with, or become confused with, any verbal information that is being read for comprehension or memorized. If the music is fast and loud or contains a lot of changes, it can capture your attention, pulling your focus away from the academic materials and toward the qualities of the music. Such distraction effects mean that students who listen to music must continuously refocus on the study materials, and they tend to move back and forth between the music and their academic materials, slowing down their progress.

HOW DOES MUSIC AFFECT OUR ABILITY TO THINK?

People sometimes perform better on intellectual tasks while listening to music, but there are some simple explanations for this benefit. These simpler explanations have replaced an earlier view that music has a special power to enhance the human mind because of its intricate or sophisticated structure. According to an explanation proposed in the 1990s, listening to highly complex patterns of music, with their melodies, harmonies, and variations on a theme, helps to tune, or prime, the brain to perform well on other tasks that require people to pay attention to patterns. In other words, listening to "sophisticated" music may put the brain in a sophisticated mode of operating.

This intriguing explanation arose from a 1993 article that was published in *Nature*, one of most prestigious journals in the world, and was widely publicized in the media as the "Mozart effect." The impact of this research was so widespread that it led to a movement in the United States and elsewhere in which parents were encouraged to play Mozart's music to their unborn infants during pregnancy.

In the original research, participants listened to ten minutes of classical piano music by Mozart and then were tested on a skill that required them to use mental imagery to compare visual patterns. The test is called the "paper folding and cutting" task and is a measure of a mental skill called *spatial-temporal reasoning*. It involves folding pieces of paper, cutting a section of the folded paper with scissors, and then trying to imagine what the paper will look like when it is unfolded again. It is a deceptively tricky but interesting task. Compared with people who listened to a verbal relaxation tape or who sat in silence, those who listened to Mozart performed better on this task. The researchers proposed that listening to Mozart, with its sophisticated musical patterns that are continuously being compared to one another, can enhance other intellectual tasks that require people to compare patterns, even if those patterns are not musical patterns but visual ones.

Subsequent to the publication, however, this explanation was largely discounted. Most researchers now believe that listening to music can lead in higher performance on certain mental tasks because (a) music can put people in a better mood, and people work better when they are happy than when they are grumpy or bored, and (b) music can make people feel energetic, and energetic people work better than people who are tired or apathetic. In other words, listening to music can temporarily enhance one's intellectual ability, but there is nothing mysterious or special about music, and you do not need to listen to Mozart or other classical music to get this benefit. Any musical or nonmusical activity that enhances one's mood and energy levels will have the same effect. In one subsequent study, researchers found that school children aged ten and eleven years performed better on a spatial task after listening to a song by the band Blur than after listening to a piece by Mozart or a discussion about research. That is, listening to music that people enjoy is most likely to be beneficial because enjoyable music has the strongest benefits to our mood and energy levels.

THE EFFECTS OF MOOD AND ENERGY ON INTELLECTUAL TASKS

What is it about mood and energy that help people perform better on intellectual tasks? Research suggests that positive mood and high energy each affect mental capacity in different ways. Positive mood tends to enhance our ability to think creatively, measured as the ability to solve problems by thinking outside of the box. People who are in a good mood tend to adopt an open style of awareness that invites multiple and novel ways of considering possible solutions to a problem, including any important decisions that need to be made. This open style of awareness often leads to more efficient and innovative decision-making.

Such benefits not only arise from listening to music, however; they should also occur for any activity that leads to a positive mood. In one study, it was determined that people who were in a good mood after watching a comedic film or receiving a gift were also better at solving problems that require an inventive solution. Therefore, if studying requires that you think inventively, think outside of the box, and be open to multiple possible solutions, it would be advantageous to listen to music that puts you into a good mood.

Along with the cognitive benefits of being in a positive mood, there are also some disadvantages. For example, happy people may be more open-minded, but they also tend to be somewhat uncritical in their thinking. That is, a positive mood can sometimes mean that you are wearing rose-colored glasses and are more likely to agree with weak or superficial arguments than people who are in a neutral or skeptical mood. These results suggest that background music that puts you in a good mood can have both positive and negative effects on studying. Positive music may encourage you to think creatively and make efficient decisions. However, if your studying requires analytic and critical thinking, it may be best to avoid music that makes you so mesmerized with joy that you end up wearing rose-colored glasses.

The effects of increased energy, often referred to in the literature as *arousal*, are somewhat different from the effects of positive mood. Increased arousal mainly tends to enhance the ability to work quickly, sometimes called *speed of processing*, just as one might work quickly after having a cup of strong coffee. This benefit is typically measured in reaction time tasks, including the ability to rapidly search for a particular shape, object, or individual in a complex visual scene. There is a well-known series of British children's puzzle books called *Where's Wally* (or *Where's Waldo* in North America) that requires children to find Wally in a scene that includes hundreds of people. Rapidly detecting Wally is the kind of task that people perform better when they are in a state of heightened arousal.

Not surprisingly, the relationship between arousal and task performance is not straightforward. If you drink too many cups of coffee, your arousal level will be so high that you are unlikely to perform well on any task. That is, arousal can benefit intellectual function up to a point, after which any further increases in arousal hinder performance—a relationship that has been described as an *inverted U*. The detrimental effects of too much arousal are unlikely to occur while listening to music, unless you are listening to very loud, fast, energetic music. Indeed, one study reported that reading comprehension is worse when people listen to fast and loud music than when they listen to music that is softer, slower, or both softer and slower. Presumably, fast and loud music induces a state of arousal that is higher than the optimal level of arousal for reading, and it is likely also more distracting than soft, slow music. The take-home message is that if your studying requires quick thinking and rapid decision-making, especially for routine tasks such as sorting or locating items, then it can be useful to listen to moderately stimulating music that enhances your energy levels but not so much that you are overstimulated or the music is a source of distraction.

When positive mood and arousal are combined, the potential benefits for intellectual tasks are substantial. In one study, a group of students completed a trigonometry test either while they sat in silence or while they listened to classical music. Those who completed the test with music in the background performed better than those who completed the test with no music in the background. Although it is difficult to determine why people performed better while listening to music, it is likely that increases in mood and arousal led to better problem-solving and enhanced speed of processing combined with reduced anxiety. Presumably, the music was also played at a level that was minimally distracting.

It is well known that musical preferences are important to the effects of music on intellectual function, but it is not clear exactly why this is the case. One possibility is that preferences amplify any effects that music may have on our mood and energy levels. Soft and slow music may be calming, but if we also know and like the music that we are listening to, its capacity to calm us is even greater. Another possibility is that *only* music that we like will affect us emotionally. We might listen to highly energetic and joyful music, but if we do not enjoy that music, it may leave us cold and have no emotional impact on us.

MUSIC CAN BE DISTRACTING

Along with the previously described benefits, listening to music can be a source of distraction, so it is important to weigh the benefits that have been described with the potential drawbacks of distraction. In many of the experiments that have been conducted on the intellectual benefits of listening to music, participants listened to music for a period of time, such as seven to ten minutes, and then they were asked to perform an intellectual task in silence. The reason the experimenters turned off the music during the task is because they wanted to evaluate the benefits of music for task performance in the absence of the distracting effects of music. However, when people study while listening to music, the music remains playing throughout their studying such that the net effect of the music is some combination of benefits from changes in mood and arousal mixed with the negative consequences of distraction.

Interestingly, music is only rarely distracting to the point that it interferes with an accompanying task. After all, almost everyone drives in the presence of music: if music were a significant source of distraction, there would probably be many more accidents. People have an amazing ability to experience music as part of the background environment and to allocate their attention to their primary task at hand. Many people experience background music in the way that they experience soft lighting, interesting wallpaper, and artwork on the walls. We might dim the lights and sit in front of the fireplace while reading a novel. These background conditions, like background music, can have a relaxing benefit without significantly distracting us from our book.

However, the *changing-state theory* of auditory distraction suggests that any auditory stimulation that involves abrupt and noticeable changes in acoustic characteristics will capture our attention and become a source of distraction. Whereas wallpaper and soft lighting remain unchanged in our background experience, music typically involves constant changes in its acoustic characteristics, including chord changes, sudden changes in loudness, new textures, and unexpected melodic changes. For this reason, background music that has a fairly consistent texture that minimizes sudden changes, such as classical guitar or piano music, will be less distracting to your study than genres of music that involve sudden unexpected changes.

For some individuals, the presence of music is always distracting. For example, some musicians claim they find it difficult to work or read in the presence of music. They cannot ignore music or treat is as part of the background because they are so used to listening attentively and deeply to it. Personality can also influence the impact of background music on another primary task such as studying. One study showed that extroverted people can perform well on a task in the presence of complex or faster-paced music, whereas introverted people perform better with slower-paced music or no music. In other words, each individual needs to evaluate the costs and benefits of listening to background music while studying to ensure that the benefits outweigh the costs of distraction.

CONCLUSION

Music has both positive and negative effects on studying, depending on the type of music, the nature of that studying, and the musical background and personality of the individual in question. Benefits of background music include enhancement of mood and energy, reduced anxiety, and the capacity of music to mask other ambient sources of distraction, such as environment noises and people chatting. The costs of background music include the fact that music is a source of distraction and may draw attention away from the primary task of studying. Music can also lead to decreases in mood and energy if it is too slow or depressing. All such factors are dependent on the individual who is studying. Most people are remarkably capable of listening to music while engaging in other activities, such as studying, but it is important to consider one's personality and musical background, the nature of the music, and the type of studying that you are doing.

References and Further Reading
Furnham, A., & Stephenson, R. (2007). Musical distracters, personality type and cognitive performance in school children. *Psychology of Music, 35*, 403–420.

Furnham, A., Trew, S., & Sneade, I. (1999). The distracting effects of vocal and instrumental music on the cognitive test performance of introverts and extraverts. *Personality and Individual Differences, 27*, 581–592.

Thompson, W. F., Schellenberg, E. G., & Letnic, A. K. (2012). Fast and loud music disrupts reading comprehension. *Psychology of Music, 40*, 698–706.

47. Earworms

Freya Bailes

Have you ever had the experience of having music stuck in your head? Maybe it is happening to you even as you are reading this page. When music persistently plays in our mind, it is known as an *earworm*. Earworms are characterized by being both involuntary and repetitive. Popular culture tends to portray earworms as necessarily annoying, but music psychologists have shown that earworms can be experienced as neutral or even pleasant. Use of the English term *earworm* has become increasingly widespread and is thought to derive from the German equivalent, *Ohrwurm*. Earworms are common: there are earworm reports from 173 countries—which is a conservative figure as it is based on an analysis of tweets that come from the English-speaking community only—with most people experiencing earworms at least once a week. Earworms are reported to occur for up to one-third of our waking time.

We can think of earworms as being a form of musical memory because they are instances of mentally replaying familiar music. Even when we experience an earworm for music that we have made up ourselves, it is nevertheless a repetition of a memory of our invention. Earworms are one category of what music psychologists have termed *involuntary musical imagery* (INMI). Other forms of INMI include the disorders of musical hallucinosis and musical hallucination. Everyday earworms differ from both of these disorders: when we have an earworm, we understand that the music is imagined and not real, and our earworm music "sounds" dulled in comparison to the vivid sounds of the live music that we physically hear at a concert, for example.

THE SCIENCE OF EARWORMS

Although earworms are a common experience, attempting to undertake their scientific study has only recently begun in earnest. After all, studying earworms is fraught with difficulties. How could it be possible to get inside another person's mind to understand their personal and subjective experience of imagining a form of music that we cannot ourselves hear? Music psychology has responded to this challenge by using a variety of different research methods. The most frequently used are self-report methods, whereby people are asked to report on their experiences. For example, sometimes respondents are interviewed in-depth about their earworms, and at other times, individuals respond to shorter questionnaire surveys. Others have kept earworm diaries, which are particularly helpful because of the information that they can provide about the circumstances in which people experience earworms as well as descriptions of the earworms themselves. Another technique, known as *experience sampling*, extends the idea of observing the conditions during which earworms occur by contacting research participants on their mobile phones at random times of the day as they go about their everyday lives. When a text message cue is received, the respondents are asked to reflect on their current circumstances and to report the details of any music that they happen to be imagining at the time of contact. In this way, we can begin to ask not only what music people imagine but also when, where, and perhaps even why.

Unfortunately, there are limitations to the properties of our earworm experience that we are able to communicate verbally. For this reason, it can be useful to ask people to enact aspects of the music that they are imagining, such as tapping the beat of the earworm. This method has enabled researchers to explore the relationship between the tempo of the music that we imagine and our reported emotional state as we are imagining it. Another method that has been used, a technique known as *data mining*, identifies common patterns of earworm experience as reflected in the thousands of tweets that refer to the phenomenon. Brain scan technology has also been used to investigate earworms in the brain: magnetic resonance imaging (MRI) suggests that there are differences in our brain structure that relate to the INMI experience. Finally, some studies have mixed methods to combine laboratory with real-world research: participants are first subjected to an earworm induction phase by being presented with particularly catchy music in the laboratory before having their subsequent earworms observed by means of experience sampling as they go about their daily lives.

THE MUSIC THAT WE IMAGINE

What music is in your head? Perhaps you are imagining one of the commonly reported earworm songs in recent times: Lady Gaga's "Bad Romance," Kylie Minogue's "Can't Get You Out of My Head," or Journey's "Don't Stop Believin'." The study of earworms has consistently revealed two important contributing factors to the earworm experience: musical repetition and recency. In other words, if you have recently heard a particular song, and the song was repetitive or you have heard it many times, the chances are high that it will transform into an earworm. This finding is in line with general psychology, which tells us that our memory is superior for recent experiences and improves with increased exposure. Music tends to be highly repetitive in terms of its constituent parts, with recurring rhythmic and melodic motifs as well as the regular use of recurring chorus and verse structures. Indeed, jingles and music in advertising regularly exploit the repetitive structures of music, and their repeated and recent presentation through various media is designed to generate earworms, reminding us of the product or service associated with the imagined music. Let's not forget that the very act of experiencing an earworm serves to reinforce both the repetition and the recency of the music, albeit in an imagined form.

A related feature of the music that we imagine is its singability. For example, most earworm reports concern music with a clearly identifiable melody rather than music produced by unpitched instruments. Moreover, melodies with intervals that are easy to sing and that fit within our vocal range allow us to sing along. By singing, we reinforce the repetition and recency of the music and, in turn, raise the likelihood of forming an earworm.

POSSIBLE CAUSES OF EARWORMS

In addition to imagining repeated music that we have recently heard and can readily sing, we might ask what else contributes to the earworm experience. Research is underway to determine whether we *imagine* music at the times when we would normally *hear* that same music. There are anecdotal accounts of words that we happen to hear that then trigger INMI for a song with lyrics that match those words. There are also accounts of individuals imagining music with a beat that matches their walking pace. There is some evidence of an effect of mood congruence between heard and imagined music: people report feeling the same way when they imagine a particular song as when they listen to that same song. Whether we imagine music to regulate our mood in the course of everyday life or whether our mood influences the musical selection of our mental jukebox will need further investigation. Another possible earworm trigger is moving to music. One study shows that when we hum, sing, tap, or otherwise physically move while listening to music, we are more likely to experience a subsequent earworm than when we listen without engaging our motor system.

In addition to our level of physical activity, our level of mental activity also plays a part in when we experience earworms. Some research suggests that when we are engaged in mental activities that are not cognitively demanding, such as going about our daily routine, earworms are more likely to occur. Conversely, tasks that are high in cognitive load, such as working on challenging homework, have also been linked to INMI. It is at these extremes of mental effort (both low and high) that our minds wander, with some research suggesting that mind wandering comes first, leading to the onset of earworms. An alternative perspective would be to view earworms as a form of musical mind wandering in its own right.

INDIVIDUAL DIFFERENCES IN EXPERIENCING EARWORMS

A remarkable finding from experience sampling studies of earworms is the lack of overlap from person to person regarding the specific pieces of music that people imagine, despite the shared musical environments of the study participants, such as songs currently on the music charts or music currently in use in advertising. Indeed, individual differences in earworm experience are common, and these relate to differing degrees of musical engagement, the duration of earworm episodes, the extent of the individual's mental control, and the degree to which earworms are experienced as disturbing or intrusive.

First, studies of individual differences in earworms suggest that rather than our levels of formal musical training relating to the frequency of our earworm experience, it is the extent to which we engage with music more broadly that relates to the way in which we imagine it. Listening to music and singing music are associated with more frequent and longer-lasting INMI episodes. There are also considerable differences in the duration of reported earworm episodes. Some people report a near constant mental soundtrack, which has been variously referred to as a *perpetual music track* or *permanent involuntary musical imagery*. This chronic experience of imagined music differs from the typical experience of earworms as the momentary looping of short musical extracts.

Because earworms are characterized by their involuntary nature, some researchers have asked whether their occurrence may be linked to those aspects of personality that relate to mental control. Indeed, evidence points to higher levels of INMI for individuals who score highly for obsessive compulsion, and other evidence links earworm frequency to high levels of schizotypy (which is a personality trait characterized by low cognitive control). Individual differences also exist in relation to the extent to which we find earworms disturbing. This is reflected in the variation in our ratings of how positive or negative we find our earworm experiences to be. On the one hand, it could be that the popular view that earworms are negative stems from a reporting bias: when we are asked to recall the fleeting experience of having music stuck in our heads, we may primarily recall and report those instances when the earworm was bothersome, having forgotten the unremarkable neutral or positive earworms that passed more or less unnoticed. However, for some individuals, earworms are regularly experienced as intrusive, particularly for those who also experience high levels of other involuntary thoughts and when the emotional response to the music being imagined is negative.

WAYS TO BLOCK EARWORMS

When earworms are intrusive, how can they be stopped? Unfortunately, music psychology is unable to prescribe a solution, but a number of different methods of distracting oneself from the earworm have been explored. The first of these is verbal distraction, based in part on an important theory stemming from research on inner speech (i.e., when we imagine the sound of our voice speaking), whereby imagining vocal sounds such as singing engages our vocal apparatus, despite the sounds being imaginary. In other words, when we imagine music, we imagine not only its sound but also a motor image of how the sounds are produced. Given that earworms primarily concern music that we can sing, it has been suggested that by giving our vocal apparatus an alternative task to do, such as occupying our jaw with gum chewing, the earworm will be blocked. There is some preliminary evidence to support this argument.

An alternative form of verbal distraction reported to be effective by many is to watch TV or engage in conversation. Other forms of auditory distraction, such as listening to different music, may be enough to suppress the earworm, as we have limited mental resources available to process sounds that are both real and imagined at once. Some people also report that seeking out a recording of the earworm music to listen to can be an effective "cure." Finally, because we know that moving in time to music increases its chances of becoming an earworm, we can use our bodies as our own form of sensorimotor distraction by choosing to move to a different beat. Many of these ideas have yet to be properly investigated, which will be important if our understanding of earworms is to mature from anecdote to science.

CONCLUSION

The next time that you become aware of involuntarily imagining repetitive music in your mind's ear, know that you are not alone. Earworms represent a form of musical memory that is frequently experienced and widely reported. Although recency and repetition play the most obvious roles in shaping earworm content, a complex range of factors contributes to when and why we experience earworms. Methods from music psychology have led to an improved understanding of earworm phenomena, highlighting individual differences between us that concern the ways in which we engage with music through listening and singing, aspects of our personality and capacity for mental control, and our emotional responses to the music that we come to imagine. Many questions remain, including whether imagined music functions as a substitute for "real" music—for example, imagining music to regulate one's mood when we do not have immediate access to a recording of that music—as well as how we might effectively banish earworms that have become intrusive.

References and Further Reading

Bailes, F. (2015). Music in mind? An experience sampling study of what and when, towards an understanding of why. *Psychomusicology: Music, Mind, and Brain, 25*(1), 58–68. https://doi.org/10.1037/pmu0000078

Beaman, C. P., & Williams, T. I. (2010). Earworms ("stuck song syndrome"): Towards a natural history of intrusive thoughts. *British Journal of Psychology, 101*(4), 637–653. https://doi.org/10.1348/000712609X479636

Byron, T. P., & Fowles, L. C. (2015). Repetition and recency increases involuntary musical imagery of previously unfamiliar songs. *Psychology of Music, 43*(3), 375–389. https://doi.org/10.1177/0305735613511506

Hemming, J., & Merrill, J. (2015). On the distinction between involuntary musical imagery, musical hallucinosis, and musical hallucinations. *Psychomusicology: Music, Mind, and Brain, 25*(4), 435–442. https://doi.org/10.1037/pmu0000112

Jakubowski, K., Farrugia, N., Halpern, A. R., Sankarpandi, S. K., & Stewart, L. (2015). The speed of our mental soundtracks: Tracking the tempo of involuntary musical imagery in everyday life. *Memory & Cognition, 43*(8), 1229–1242.

Liikkanen, L. A., Jakubowski, K., & Toivanen, J. M. (2015). Catching earworms on Twitter: Using big data to study involuntary musical imagery. *Music Perception, 33*(2), 199–216. https://doi.org/10.1525/MP.2015.33.2.199

McCullough Campbell, S., & Margulis, E. H. (2015). Catching an earworm through movement. *Journal of New Music Research, 44*(4), 347–358.

Müllensiefen, D., Fry, J., Jones, R., Jilka, S. R., Stewart, L., & Williamson, V. J. (2014). Individual differences predict patterns in spontaneous involuntary musical imagery. *Music Perception, 31*(4), 323–338. https://doi.org/10.1525/MP.2014.31.4.323

Williamson, V. J., Liikkanen, L. A., Jakubowski, K., & Stewart, L. (2014). Sticky tunes: How do people react to involuntary musical imagery? *PLoS One, 9*(1), e86170. https://doi.org/10.1371/journal.pone.0086170

48. Music-Evoked Autobiographical Memories (MEAMs)

Amee Baird

Do you have a favorite song that reminds you of a special person or time in your life? Most of us know the feeling of hearing a song and within seconds being transported back in time and remembering something from our past. Music often triggers personal, or autobiographical, memories, and this phenomenon is called *music-evoked autobiographical memories* (MEAMs).

WHAT ARE AUTOBIOGRAPHICAL MEMORIES?

Autobiographical memories are memories about our lives and personal experiences based on a combination of *episodic* and *semantic* memories. Episodic memory is about when and where something occurred (such as knowing that your first kiss occurred at your high school disco when you were thirteen years old). Semantic memory is general knowledge and facts about the world (such as the name of your high school and the person you first kissed).

The experience of MEAMs is common in everyday life, but it has only recently been studied by scientists. The first scientific study of MEAMs was done in 2007 with over three hundred university students who reported personal memories in response to short excerpts of pop music. An example of a MEAM reported in this study that was written in response to "Pieces of Me" by Ashlee Simpson is "I was finishing high school and starting college away from my boyfriend. We talked on the phone a lot." MEAMs occurred in response to 30 percent of songs, and these songs were typically rated as "highly familiar" and associated with positive emotions. The MEAMs were most commonly of a person (usually a girlfriend or boyfriend) or a time of life (such as the high school years), and typical situations were dancing or driving a car. This is not surprising because we often listen to music during those situations. So, the songs that you listen to on your next long road trip or when you are hanging out with your girlfriend or boyfriend may end up being important triggers for your memories of that holiday or person in the future.

MEAMs CAN OCCUR IN PEOPLE WITH ALZHEIMER'S DEMENTIA

People with brain injuries or diseases such as Alzheimer's dementia often have difficulty remembering things, sometimes even their own life history. Music can be an important key to unlocking their past and bringing back memories. The main symptom of Alzheimer's dementia, which is the most common type of dementia caused by Alzheimer's disease, is impaired memory, but memory of familiar music and the ability for this music to trigger personal memories can remain intact. This phenomenon is dramatically shown in the documentary *Alive Inside*, from which there is a famous YouTube clip of Henry, a man with dementia who "comes alive" when he hears one of his favorite songs. MEAMs can occur quickly and involuntarily, that is, without any effort by the person, and they are often very vivid and emotional.

Self-chosen music or a person's favorite songs from their youth (late teenage years or early twenties) are the most effective at triggering personal memories. This period of time is known as the *reminiscence bump*, as it is a time when we have a peak in our autobiographical memories. That is, in people over the age of forty years, there is an increased proportion of autobiographical memories from the ages of ten to thirty years. Many people argue that this is because this is a crucial time in our lives for the formation of our sense of self. We typically have many first experiences during this time, such as our first boyfriend or girlfriend and our first job. Music often plays an important role in our lives at this age; we become fans of certain styles of music or bands and often go to music concerts with friends. It has also been found that songs your parents played during your childhood are strong triggers for personal memories. So, for musical stimuli, there are two reminiscence bumps. One for the songs of your parents' generation and the other from your own youth. In other words, if your parents were fans of the Beatles, you are likely to have personal memories triggered by songs by the Beatles as well as the music you listened to as a teenager. This phenomenon has been called *cascading reminiscence bumps*.

THE POWER OF LOVE SONGS

Songs can also be the key to remembering someone you love. This was the case for Barbara and David, a couple I met while doing research on MEAMs in people with dementia. They first started dating in high school and have now been married for nearly sixty years. Barbara was diagnosed with Alzheimer's dementia five years ago. In the two years before her diagnosis, she showed changes in her cognitive, or thinking, abilities, particularly in her ability to remember things. She would get lost easily, repeat herself in conversation, and lose things, and she had a lot of difficulty finding her way around unfamiliar environments, such as during holidays. Now she has difficulty speaking and often gets confused and upset. Sometimes she does not even recognize her husband, David. She thinks he is an intruder and chases him out of their home. This is called a *misidentification delusion*, and it can occur in people with psychiatric conditions such as schizophrenia or in people with certain types of dementia, including Alzheimer's dementia.

David had no idea how he could make Barbara understand that he was not a stranger. He decided to sing a special song to her that they heard when they first met. It was "Unchained Melody," the last song they danced to on the evening they met. He began singing this to her every day, and eventually "she came back." She now knows who he is and never sends him out of the house. This shows the powerful ability of music to reconnect people through memory.

Many couples like Barbara and David have a special song ("our song") that typically reminds them of a significant event or time in their relationship, such as their first meeting or wedding day. "Our songs" can be considered a special type of MEAM, which in this case is a shared memory for the couple. These songs can be a powerful way of stimulating shared personal memories and associated emotions. "Our songs" can also occur between friends and can strengthen and be a reminder of friendships and cue memories of fun times shared in the past. This phenomenon has been shown in many movies. For example, in *Shaun the Sheep Movie*, the song "Feels Like Summer" plays as you watch how Shaun and his owner, the farmer, grew up together. When Shaun is lost and alone, he hears the song and yearns for his owner. In *Moonlight*, the Oscar-winning Best Picture in 2017, a song triggers long-lost memories of a significant childhood friendship and prompts a man to phone his friend, who then drives a long distance to visit him and confront their shared past. In the animated film *Coco*, the character Coco has dementia, and it is only when she hears a special song that her father wrote and sang to her as a child that she can finally recall her childhood and reconnect with her family. These examples show how MEAMs can revive and reunite relationships.

MEAMs can even occur in people with severe brain injury due to a traumatic brain injury or stroke. They experience MEAMs at a similar frequency as healthy people, and the types of memories triggered by music are also the same. For example, a man with a severe brain injury due to a motorbike accident described this MEAM in response to the song "Bette Davis Eyes": "I bought the song for my wife. I would turn it up if it was on the radio." In response to the same song, his healthy, uninjured wife's MEAM was "listening to music with (him) in the car or at home." In this couple, their MEAMs were often of each other, but his MEAMs were typically less specific than hers. In other words, he would describe a general event (e.g., "going to dances") or a period of life (e.g., "when I was at high school"), while her MEAMS were more specific and contained references to specific events (e.g., "going on a camping trip to Aura Beach, we lit a fire and talked with friends").

Unfortunately, some people with brain injuries do not experience any MEAMs. This can occur if they have damage to parts of the brain that process music, causing *amusia*, or an inability to process the different components of music, such as melody and rhythm. People with amusia can have difficulty recognizing tunes, and if you cannot recognize a tune, it cannot activate a memory. It is like trying to fit a key into a damaged lock: the door will not open. Brain imaging studies of people who have amusia after a stroke have found that this typically occurs after right side brain damage to the temporal and subcortical (deep in the brain) regions.

WHERE ARE MEAMs STORED IN THE BRAIN?

Brain imaging studies have also helped us understand what parts of the brain are involved in our experience of MEAMs. They have shown that when we listen to music, our entire brain is activated. The parts of the brain that control movement, emotions, the feeling of reward, and memories are all stimulated by music. This means that when certain brain areas are damaged or diseased, music can activate other parts that are still working well, and in this way, it can access memories that other types of stimuli may not be able to. In the case of people with Alzheimer's dementia, we know that the disease process usually starts in the temporal lobes of the brain. This part of the brain controls memory, which is why impaired memory is typically the first symptom. The frontal lobes of the brain, however, are typically free of the disease. Brain imaging studies have shown that when people listen to familiar songs and experience MEAMs, the frontal brain regions are particularly active, suggesting that this part of the brain is important in controlling MEAMs. This is why people with Alzheimer's dementia can forget what they did yesterday and the names of their children, but they may still recall the lyrics to familiar songs and experience MEAMs. Their frontal lobes are relatively spared of the disease and allow the survival of their musical memories.

The special relationship between music and memory is not only a result of how our brains respond to music but also due to the nature of music itself. For example, we know that repetition of information helps memory, so the way we listen to music by playing our favorite songs repeatedly and hearing them many times over our lifetime means the songs stick better in our memory. Music is also highly effective at stimulating emotions, and feeling strong emotions such as joy or sorrow can also enhance memory. Music also makes us move in that our whole bodies can respond to music, from tapping of our feet to bobbing our heads. Even body functions that we cannot see, such as our heart rate and breathing, can be affected by music. This whole-body response, or *arousal*, to music can make us more alert, which also helps us to remember things. So, there are many ways in which music is memorable and enhances our memories. In this way, memories of familiar music may be more resistant to brain damage or disease compared with other types of memories. Because the music itself is easily remembered and the emotion and movement-inducing features of music enhance memory function overall, music can activate related memories of the things that were happening in our lives at the time that this music was heard. In other words, your favorite songs are the soundtrack to the movie of your life.

ARE MEAMs SPECIAL?

We know that music is very effective at triggering memories, but is it any better at this than other stimuli? Studies of both healthy people and those with brain injury have found that music triggers more vivid and frequent memories than stimuli such as verbal questions or photos. For example, you would be more likely to recall a memory if you heard a song from your primary school years than if you were asked, "Tell me about something that happened to you during primary school." In recent work with people with Alzheimer's dementia and healthy elderly people, we compared music- and photo-evoked memories using songs that were number one hits and photos of famous events from across the decades. There was no difference in the frequency of MEAMs between people with Alzheimer's dementia and healthy elderly people, but people with Alzheimer's dementia showed a significant decline in the frequency of photo-evoked memories. MEAMs were often about significant people. As predicted, songs from the time of the reminiscence bump (when the people were aged ten to thirty years) were most effective at triggering memories. We also found that objects (such as familiar household items) cued even more memories than music or photos. Further research is needed to understand the nature of the memories evoked by these different stimuli.

CONCLUSION

MEAMs can occur in all of us, even after a traumatic brain injury or in the severe stage of dementia, and they can bring us back to a special person or time in our lives and enhance our sense of self. Despite their common occurrence in daily life, there is still a lot more to learn about MEAMs. For example, why do some people not experience MEAMs? Do MEAMs differ across cultures? How do they occur in natural rather than lab-based environments? Do they change over time? Even though there are many questions left to be answered, we know without a doubt that the relationship between music and memory is special.

References and Further Reading

Baird, A., & Samson, S. (2014). Music evoked autobiographical memory after severe acquired brain injury: Preliminary findings from a case series. *Neuropsychological Rehabilitation, 24*(1), 125–143. https://doi.org/10.1080/09602011.2013.858642

Baird, A., & Thompson, W. (2018). When music compensates language: A case study of severe aphasia in dementia and the use of music by a spousal caregiver. *Aphasiology, 33*(4), 449–465. https://doi.org/10.1080/02687038.2018.1471657

Jacobsen, J. H., Stelzer, J., Fritz, T. H., Chételat, G., La Joie, R., & Turner, R. (2015). Why musical memory can be preserved in advanced Alzheimer's disease. *Brain, 138*(8), 2438–2450. https://doi.org/10.1093/brain/awv135

Janata, P., Tomic, S. T., & Rakowski, S. K. (2007). Characterisation of music-evoked autobiographical memories. *Memory, 15*(8), 845–860. https://doi.org/10.1080/0965 8210701734593

Krumhansl, C. L., & Zupnick, J. A. (2013). Cascading reminiscence bumps in popular music. *Psychological Science, 24*(10), 2057–2068. https://doi.org/10.1177/09567976 13486486

Music and Movement

49. Movement and Music Performance

Andrew Geeves and John Sutton

Whether moving fingers to strum a guitar, arms to bow a cello, or lips to play a trumpet, human movement is essential for the production of musical sound. Without movement, music performance would not be possible. Beyond the physical actions that are necessary to sing or play a musical instrument, musicians often embellish their performances with facial expressions and bodily gestures. These additional, or *ancillary*, movements convey useful information about the personality of the performer and mood of the music, shaping the way in which sound is perceived and the way in which experiences and emotions are shared.

So, music performance hinges on movement produced across a number of levels, including the movements required to make sound (production movement) and the additional movements that occur during performance (ancillary movement). Playing an instrument, communicating and collaborating with other performing musicians, and engaging with an audience all require a musician to move in complex ways that are consolidated through hours of practice and that remain open to dynamic, on-the-fly modification to meet particular environmental demands. After exploring why movement is so important in music performance, this chapter examines the movements that are required for a musician to play an instrument, perform with other musicians, and communicate expressive intent during performance.

WHY IS MOVEMENT IMPORTANT IN MUSIC PERFORMANCE?

To get a sense of the crucial role of both production and ancillary movements in performance, take a moment to bring to mind a favorite music performance. Recollect the performance from beginning to end. Now replay this performance in your mind, but, this time, prevent the musician(s) involved from moving. With this restriction in place, what does your favorite music performance look like? Without movement, the performance will no longer involve sound and will be without the multitude of interactions that transpire between a musician and their instrument, a group of musicians, and the audience and musician(s). Without movement, music performance ceases to exist.

Movement is of central importance to music performance for two main reasons. First, and most obviously, movement initiates the process that results in the production of sound. The processes are frequently mediated by electronic technologies. But for the most part, were it not for a human musician making a movement to strum a string, touch a key, hit a drum, vibrate vocal cords, depress a valve, or push air out through lips held in a particular way, musical sound would not be produced. Instruments rely on human movement to produce sound. In the case of music performance, to generate a sound that is considered desirable for a particular instrument or composition, such movement may need to be especially refined or executed in a way that demands particular intentions and technical skills that must have been finely honed by a musician during hours of practice and rehearsal.

Second, over and above their ties to sound production, the actions involved in music performance provide important information to audience members. When we perceive the actions of a musical performer, it brings to mind the sounds that should result from such actions, and this process can clarify or complement the actual sounds. Imagine, for example, the difference between your experience of a musician who stands motionless while playing lead guitar and one who makes dramatic gestures for every bended note and melodic accent. Such movements can be used to clarify and highlight parts of the music that the performer wants to emphasize, thereby helping to shape the experience of audience members.

THREE TYPES OF MOVEMENT IN MUSIC PERFORMANCE
Playing an Instrument

The fluent playing of an instrument requires production movement to be trained or sedimented into the body via hours of rehearsal over many years. The technical proficiency required for an expert level of music performance has been estimated to require thousands of hours of deliberate training dedicated solely to playing a particular instrument. Many hours of rehearsal consolidate musician movement at a number of levels. The exact way in which this occurs is a topic of hot debate among researchers. As such, there is no one theory that is commonly accepted as providing an adequate explanation for how movement becomes organized through practice.

At a general level, the continual repetition of biomechanical movement is thought to gradually build automaticity, consolidating motor tasks into sequences and skills in procedural memory. It fosters what many musicians think of as a "muscle memory" that frees a musician's attention from being consumed by concentrating on the specific demands of particular movements. As the foundation for a movement repertoire is built and the vocabulary of this repertoire is enlarged, motoric patterns expand to encompass lengthier and more complex combinations of tasks. A musician becomes increasingly familiar with the parameters of their body and the idiosyncratic specificities of the particular instrument(s) that he or she plays. An ever-expanding cognitive road map that organizes and affords a musician access to bodily based movement sequences accompanies the slow acquisition of technical prowess. As motoric technical competency grows, a capacity for attention to be devoted to more expressive, communicative movement is then free to develop.

Imagine, for example, someone beginning to learn the piano. Initially, their concentration may be absorbed in isolating the movement of an individual finger to develop a level of motoric control that allows them to play one key at a time. They may then concentrate on mastering movements that allow them to play particular combinations of keys simultaneously, jump from one key to another at requisite speed, coordinate both hands playing together, or to lean on a key with just the right amount of weight or type of touch necessary to elicit the dynamic or produce the articulation indicated by a composer.

After these movements have been encoded, the musician's attention may then come to be absorbed in pairing together particular combinations of smaller movements or movement patterns that he or she has learned to allow for smoother transitions between different phrases or sections of a piece. Patterns that have been broken down into smaller components and learned at a slower speed to master their intricacies may be sped up to reach the appropriate tempo. As the musician's attention is freed to rest at higher levels of abstraction, pedaling movements may be incorporated as well as particular types of demonstrative gestures and posturing that communicate expressive intent. Once the musician has acquired a level of individual mastery of the instrument, he or she may then feel ready to begin playing this instrument in concert with other musicians.

Moving Together

Four rock musicians play together on stage at a crowded venue. As the final note of her guitar solo rings out, the lead singer and guitarist catches the eye of the rhythm guitarist. Maintaining this eye contact, she raises her right hand in front of her chest, palm facing out and fingers spread wide, before turning her palm to face the floor and lowering her hand from the level of her chest to the level of her hip. "Stop" and "decrescendo" appear to be the imperatives here. Receiving this communication, the rhythm guitarist lets the notes of the last chord he played ring out and quickly lowers the volume of his instrument. Out of the corner of her eye, the bassist notices the movements effected by the rhythm guitarist to adjust the volume of his instrument. She refrains from playing her next note and shifts her gaze to focus on the drummer, whose glance is fixated on the floor. She immediately shoots her left arm out, extending it down and away from her body. As her left hand falls in line with the drummer's glance, the bassist clicks her fingers rapidly. This flickering disrupts the drummer's trance, and he glances toward all three band members, who return his gaze expectantly. Accepting their invitation, he begins his drum solo. As the drummer's solo continues, the other band members begin to nod their heads to the beat, their three heads coming to rise and fall in unison. Over the course of his solo, the drummer works to double the tempo of the song. His band members continue to nod with increasing rapidity. As the solo draws to its end, the drummer looks at each of his fellow band members and grins. The lead guitarist also grins and, looking at the rhythm guitarist and the bassist, raises the index and middle fingers of her right hand in what looks like a peace sign. The rhythm guitarist and bassist return the lead guitarist's grin, and as the drum solo ends, the band launches into a special double-time rendition of the chorus of their song.

The above vignette, based on research data gathered during live performances, provides powerful examples of ancillary and communicative movements executed by musicians together during a performance. Eye contact, gesture, and posture play crucial roles in allowing musicians to effectively engage in moving together during performance. The process of entrainment, in which "independent rhythmical systems interact with each other" (Clayton 2012, p. 49), in some cases such that "they adjust toward and eventually 'lock in' to a common phase and/or periodicity" (Clayton, Sager, & Will 2005, p. 2), underpins this coordination. Entrainment exists both at an individual level (e.g., responding to self-generated rhythmic output as the drummer did during his solo) and at collective levels (e.g., responding to rhythmic output generated by another person, as the band members did when they nodded their heads together with the beat marked by the drummer).

Communicating Expressive Intent

Musicians' ancillary movement also communicates vital information about expressive ideas during a performance. Thought to originate from protomusical exchanges that consolidate emotional bonds between a mother and her infant, expressive gesture in music performance involves the music performer moving in a way that is above and beyond that which is required for technical mastery of an instrument alone. Crucially, movement during performance communicates expressive intent to an audience.

Movement is the most effective indicator of the emotional manner in which a musician intends to play, with visual information alone being found to communicate a musician's expressive intent to an audience more clearly during performance than sound alone and, curiously, more clearly than when visual information and sound are paired together. This speaks to the centrality of movement in a musician communicating expressive intent during a performance. The quantity of musician movement has also been found to be related to the perceived expressive intent of the musician during a performance, with larger movements corresponding to greater perceived expressive intent. Movements of the head, hips, and torso in particular have been found to communicate specific expressive intent to an audience more clearly than movements of other parts of the body.

Music gestures take several forms, with distinct functions: (1) *emblems* can be translated into a word, such as giving a thumbs-up for "OK," using two fingers to form a peace sign, waving a hand to say hello, or using a flat hand to indicate stop; (2) *illustrators* highlight some aspect of music structure, such as waving a hand up and down to mirror the shape of a melodic phrase or snapping fingers in time with the beat; (3) *affect displays* are movements that reflect an emotional state, such as smiling, frowning, or opening one's arms with joy; (4) *adaptors* are self-oriented gestures, such as brushing your hair out of your eyes or scratching your nose; and (5) *regulators* are movements intended to maintain the flow of information with audience members or fellow performers, such as nodding your head, making direct eye contact, raising your eyebrows, or winking. Regulators are important for audience members and musicians alike, and the forging of a strong connection to the audience has been found to be of central importance to musicians' experience of their performance. It is difficult to imagine how this connection could be established were it not for movement in music performance. More generally, movements that communicate expressive intent help a musician to establish, regulate, shift, and maintain a strong connection to an audience during a performance.

CONCLUSION

Movement is an integral and essential element of music performance. This chapter acknowledged the variety of movements present in music performance and then narrowed its focus to the relationship between human musician movement and music performance. It then established that musician movement is important in music performance because it initiates the process that results in the production of sound and because the actions are closely linked to the way in which this sound is perceived by listeners. Three different but interrelated types of musician movement in music performance were then explored: the movement required for playing an instrument, the movement demonstrated when playing an instrument with other musicians, and, lastly, the movement involved in the communication of expressive intent during a performance. During a performance, musician movement must serve to execute technical mastery, facilitate cooperation and coordination with other musicians onstage, and communicate expressive intent to the audience. How musicians build a capacity to move in ways that fulfill these criteria, the extent to which such movement occupies musicians' conscious awareness during a performance, and how musicians manage when movement in one domain may obstruct movement in another are examples of potential areas of interest that future study could address.

References and Further Reading

Clayton, M. (2012). What is entrainment? Definition and applications in musical research. *Empirical Musicology Review, 7,* 49–56.

Clayton, M., Sager, R., & Will, U. (2005). In time with the music: The concept of entrainment and its significance for ethnomusicology. *European Meetings in Ethnomusicology, 11,* 1–82.

Davidson, J. W., & Broughton, M. C. (2016). Bodily mediated coordination, collaboration, and communication in music and performance. In S. Hallam, I. Cross, & M. Thaut (Eds.), *The Oxford Handbook of Music Psychology* (2nd ed., pp. 615–631). Oxford, UK: Oxford University Press.

Geeves, A., McIlwain, D. J., & Sutton, J. (2014). The performative pleasure of imprecision: A diachronic study of entrainment in music performance. *Frontiers in Human Neuroscience, 8,* 863. https://doi.org/10.3389/fnhum.2014.00863

Geeves, A., & Sutton, J. (2014). Embodied cognition, perception, and performance in music. *Empirical Musicology Review, 9*(3–4), 247–253.

Repp, B. H., & Knoblich, G. (2004). Perceiving action identity: How pianists recognise their own performances. *Psychological Science, 15*(9), 604–609.

50. The Case of Ensemble Performance

Renee Timmers

Playing in a group with fellow musicians is an exciting experience. The jointly produced sound can be vast, and the interactions mind-bogglingly fast. In contrast to conversations, where it is one speaker at a time, musical interactions happen in parallel: multiple people perform, listen, respond, and adapt at the same time. Psychologists investigating ensemble performance are interested in discovering the processes that enable performers to play in time with each other and to adapt to one another while playing. These processes are often social as well as cognitive (skill-based): They concern the ways performers relate to each. Relevant research questions include the following examples: Do performers attend to a leader or divide their attention evenly? Are all musicians equally good in synchronizing or does this depend on their personality and skills? How do musicians communicate during a performance? What keeps them together? How is this practiced during rehearsals?

Many of the processes relevant in music performance are not unique to musicians. For example, nonmusicians may clap or sing together in time. However, musicians have taken these processes to a different level, accomplishing levels of precision and speed that are extraordinary and comparable to what top-level athletes achieve within their sports. Studying these processes within the context of music performance, therefore, not only gives insight into "the musician" but also tells us more generally what people's abilities are and how they communicate and align their activities and behaviors.

In this chapter, we will first consider some of the processes that allow musicians to play together in time. And, second, we will consider in what ways musicians communicate and respond to each other while performing in an ensemble. The aims of the chapter are to start thinking about ensemble performance from a psychological perspective and to get acquainted with some of the ways psychologists make sense of or explain the skills that enable performing in a group.

WHAT KEEPS MUSICIANS TOGETHER IN TIME?

Having a basic pulse or beat is a very common characteristic of music, and it was most likely already a characteristic of music making in early human civilizations. Interestingly, the ability to synchronize and sustain an audible beat is a typical human ability that our closest ape relatives do not show. It is not unique to humans, as some other species can synchronize to each other and to a beat, such as parrots. Synchronization of movement in a group creates a sense of coherence, or belonging, between people: It allows people to literally and figuratively join forces.

As the term *measure* indicates, it is the bar (measure) and the beats in the bar that form the units that segment time. Counting the beat to play musical rhythms is one of the first skills music students learn, and it is still a crucial skill for professional musicians. When playing in an ensemble, playing the right notes may matter less than keeping the beat and playing in time. As soon as the beats of different voices drift apart, the performance surely becomes a mess.

Having the beat as a timing reference gives musicians a powerful tool to be together in time. It allows large groups of musicians to play together, such as in the large orchestras of over one hundred musicians required for Mahler's Eighth Symphony or Wagner's *Ring des Nibelungen* opera cycle (with a total playing time of about fifteen hours!). Interestingly, it also allows musicians to play together even if they are not physically present at the same time. This has become common practice since the availability of multitrack recording. Parts are recorded separately and overlaid as part of the sound editing process. Such overlaying is facilitated by having performers play along with the same click track when recording or with earlier recorded tracks, in particular the drum and bass.

Having a reference beat is not just a matter of convenience; it is also a creative source. The beat itself may take various forms, from a slow ballad to an upbeat techno or a relaxed reggae to a thrilling high-speed metal song. Both slow and fast tempi are more difficult to synchronize with than the average tempo of around 120 BPM (beats per minute), and it is one of the key skills that musicians need to be able to entrain with a broad range of tempi. In some genres, the beat is very clearly present. In electronic dance music, for example, the beat is generally continuously audible, with sections where the beat is suspended (interrupted) having special status and emotional effect. In other genres, however, only some beats of the bar receive a drum stroke, or heavy beats receive light strokes while light beats receive heavy strokes. What instrument plays when is an important aspect of the musical ensemble.

A nice example is Stevie Wonder's "Superstition," which illustrates how different instruments combine together in establishing and playing with the beat. The song starts with a basic drum pattern where the beats of a measure are emphasized by the bass drum on the heavier beats (1 and 3) and the snare drum on the lighter ones (2 and 4). The high-hat plays eighth notes with "funky" variations, adding some dotted rhythms and sixteenth notes. Then, the guitars and keyboard come in, providing their own overlaid rhythms that fit the beat but simultaneously play with it: offbeats are emphasized, and the timings of tones slightly anticipate the beat. Next, the voice comes in, followed by the brass instruments. The timing of the brass is very tight and precise but hardly coincides with the strong downbeats. The timing of the vocals is more floating and fluid with respect to the underlying beat, partly due to the vocal ornaments and the adherence to the rhythm of the lyrics.

Psychological studies have demonstrated the consistency with which performers often deviate from mechanical, or strictly on-the-beat, timing, illustrating the temporal control and precision that performers have. It has also shown some of the expressive functions that playing with the beat may have. For example, adding offbeat notes to a rhythmic sequence may enhance listeners' urge to want to move to the music, which also increases the sense of "groove" in the music. In "Superstition," this is smartly done; the musical layers are added gradually, enabling listeners to hook onto and predict the rhythms while being challenged by added layers that ask for additional movement, possibly of different body parts, to accommodate the different patterns and forces in the music.

HOW DO MUSICIANS COMMUNICATE AND RESPOND TO EACH OTHER?

It should be clear then that a beat or metrical framework is central to successful ensemble performance, even though there are musical pieces that do not have a periodic beat (recurring at equal intervals) that can still be performed in an ensemble (such as free jazz). However, the role of the beat does not yet explain how variations in timing or speed (tempo) are communicated or how musicians ensure that they are in sync with the beat and with each other. The example given above of music that is constructed from separately recorded tracks of musical parts highlights that it is not necessary for musicians to see each other (or even to be present) for a coherent musical performance to be generated. Indeed, research has shown that audible cues are the most relevant for musicians to synchronize and play together—seeing each other does not always improve the ability to synchronize. At least, this is the case when two musicians play music together that offers sufficient auditory information to rely on. To start playing in a particular tempo or to continue performance after a pause, visible cues such as head nodding, breathing cues, or arm raising are necessary.

As with any group of people working on a shared task, there are many aspects that influence how people communicate with each other, including what words they use, who does most of the talking, what gestures are used, and how frequently and long people look at each other. In music, different genres have different rules of behavior in the form of etiquette, and conformity to these norms shapes participation. Social affiliations, familiarity with coperformers, and different levels of experience may also play a part. Hierarchies are a common feature of ensembles and may include formal roles, such as the leader in a string quartet, or arise from social relationships, such as when a more experienced member joins a novice group. Whatever the context, there is generally a need for a "tuning in" to a common approach. To achieve this during performance, communication happens through nonverbal and often mostly subconscious means that are implicitly rather than explicitly communicational.

Research has shown that performers respond to subtle differences in timing between their tone onsets and those of their coperformers and adjust the timing of subsequent tones accordingly. If these differences are small, players may not be consciously aware of the differences. Nevertheless, they will automatically adjust subsequent timing to ensure synchronization. If timing differences are larger and suggestive of a change in tempo, a more conscious effort will need to be made to adjust one's own tempo. You can imagine that making "automatic" timing adjustments to align with other performers' parts is not always desired, if deviations in timing are part of the expressive goal, as explained earlier. Indeed, musicians need to learn and practice to keep time amid other forces that may pull them in different directions. In a band setting, the bass and drum may coordinate strongly in time while the lead singer times notes more freely.

Psychological research has shown that musicians may add more body movement and body sway during a concert performance and in final rehearsals leading up to a performance. This suggests that these movements are intended for expressive and theatrical purposes. They may serve as communication with the audience and expression of the music rather than explicit communicational cuing to coperformers (although there may be some of that too). In expressive performances, both body movements and sound may show high levels of synchronization between performers. In other words, both the timing of auditory events and body movements are being coordinated. Nevertheless, the degree of phase locking (the degree to which something is synchronized in time) tends to be less strong for body movements than for auditory events. For example, if the members of a brass section raise their instruments for their entry, they may do this in a coordinated and synchronized manner, but this synchronization is unlikely to match their millisecond precision in musical timing.

One of the puzzles for research investigating gestures and body movements in performers is to distinguish between different types of movements: are movements necessary for tone production, are they the result of self-expression, or are they part of a communicative intention? We do know that gestures and movements strongly influence how the music is perceived. Appropriate movements may make the performances "sound" more expressive as well as of better quality!

Investigation of the synchronization patterns between musicians has generated some interesting insights into the interactional dynamics between players. It has been found that when two players play together and one is asked to lead, the players still tend to mutually adapt to each other. Unless the leader cannot hear the follower, the leader will keep adjusting to the follower as well as the follower to the leader. This is indeed the most effective way to assure synchronization. In a larger ensemble, such as a quartet, adjusting to all other parts is more difficult and puts a demand on attentional resources. Nevertheless, it has been found that performers in a quartet do adjust to all others but to varying degrees. It was not the case that all attention went to a single performer who was conceived to be the leader. At the start of a piece, however, more attention may go to the leader, who visually signals the start of the music.

Adjusting to the timing of others is not purely a matter of responding. In contrast, predicting the timing variations of a coperformer is particularly important. It has been shown using simple finger tapping tasks that two players who are both good predictors of timing variations show strong tapping synchronization. In subsequent studies, it was found that performers who score high in self-reported interpersonal empathy tend to simulate the actions of others more strongly, and this simulation is relevant for accurate synchronization. In other words, these studies indicate that people's ability to synchronize with a coperformer is partly related to their personal traits, such as their ability to predict and empathize with the actions of others. Interestingly, it also works the other way around: after playing in synchrony with fellow players for a while, feelings of empathy and agreeableness toward coplayers are stronger. This seems present even at a young age: toddlers are more willing to help an experimenter after the toddler and experimenter have moved in synchrony than when they have moved out of sync.

CONCLUSION

Timing, rhythm, and movement are central to ensemble performance, and psychological research has uncovered several processes that performers employ without explicit awareness to coordinate in time and play in synchrony with each other. Synchronizing with a beat and predicting when the next beat will come based on previous beats is something all of us can do, unless we have a particular type of amusia. However, these abilities are developed through musical experience and training, allowing musicians to synchronize with a wide range of tempi, coordinate in time even when playing different rhythms from each other, and play with the beat, playing laid-back or ahead. Many of these skills are learned on the job and are characteristic of particular genres. Finding novel ways of timing and moving is part of the continuous innovation that musical ensembles engage in.

Of course, ensemble performance is not only about timing and rhythm. Generating harmonious sounds and interweaving melodic patterns are also crucial elements of successful ensemble performance. Research is starting to address questions related to ways in which musicians improvise in ensemble contexts; how ornaments, including vibrato and glissando are used; how intonation may work; and so on. Additionally, ensemble performance is not only about highly skilled musicians performing together. In contrast, much music making happens in the context of amateur choirs, bands, and ensembles involving people of various ages and abilities. Participating in musical ensembles is musically enjoyable, and it also often has broader meaning and benefits for participants. Systematic research helps to demonstrate potential benefits in addition to uncovering processes that contribute to it.

References and Further Reading
Fabian, D., Timmers, R., & Schubert, E. (2014). *Expressiveness in Music Performance: Empirical Approaches across Styles and Cultures*. New York, NY: Oxford University Press.

51. Music and Dance

Mary Broughton

Imagine these scenes. In a city nightclub, a group of friends join a mass of others. The dance floor is packed with bodies all moving to the beat of the music. The music is being crafted and performed by a DJ. The dancers seem to be "worshipping" at the "altar" from which the DJ performs. On the other side of the world, a ritual is taking place to acknowledge and celebrate a significant cultural event. Singing voices, percussive music, and dancing bodies unite the community in the ritualistic practice. Elsewhere, a ballet performance takes place on a stage that has seen many performances over its one hundred years. Highly trained classical ballet dancers carry out sequences of well-rehearsed steps, movements, and postures accompanied by an orchestra performing music from a bygone era. Audience members attentively watch and listen from the theater stalls.

Across all cultures, we see diverse ways in which music and dance combine. In this chapter, you will discover why we make music and dance, what some of the psychological processes involved in dancing and making music are, and how these cultural practices contribute positively to our life experiences.

WHAT ARE THE ORIGINS OF MUSIC AND DANCE?

Many recent theoretical propositions revolve around the idea that music and dance evolved because they served some benefit to the survival of our ancestors. For example, social benefits may have stemmed from the capacity to cooperate and coordinate behaviors. Cognitive benefits could have followed from the development of skills in attention and pattern recognition across auditory, visual, and kinesthetic domains. Or they may have developed from the human capacity for affective, or emotional, engagement, as a special abstract system for us to share, understand, and change others' emotional states.

Alternatively, some theorists argue that art forms such as music and dance did not evolve because they have some benefit to our survival. Instead, they argue that art forms, rather than being encoded in our genes, are invented behaviors that capitalize on a range of skills and capacities that we developed for other biologically important purposes. For example, we may have developed skills in attention and pattern recognition to hunt successfully, and music and dance built on these skills. While a single comprehensive explanation for the origins of music and dance is not yet available, the idea that music and dance coexist as an outward expression of important socially relevant processes appears plausible.

MUSIC AND DANCE BEHAVIORS FROM INFANCY ONWARD

The connection between music and dance appears to be innate. Young children's early movements in response to music involve arm waving, or "conducting" movements, and head bobbing to the beat. As the child physically develops and can stand, the repertoire expands to include bobbing up and down, bending the knees, swaying from side to side, and stamping the feet in time to the music. As children exit the toddler period of life, their improvised dance movements to music become more complex, demonstrating increased physical coordination. Toward the end of the early childhood period, children begin to demonstrate the ability to dance cooperatively with others to music, and they begin to learn how musical styles and genres match with particular dance steps and styles. These early experiences are a foundation for learning and becoming fluent in the music and dance styles of their culture.

SOCIAL PROCESSES AND PURPOSES OF MUSIC AND DANCE

Music and dance feature in many social gatherings around the world. For example, people in Colombia might gather in a nightclub to dance the salsa or merengue. A block party in the United States might draw together members of a particular social group who enjoy hip-hop music and dance. Despite differences in musical and dance styles, culture, or geographical location, the act of people coming together to make music and dance reveals a range of social processes. These include bonding with other group members, presenting a social identity, playing out courtship behaviors, and engaging in community-based, and sometimes ritualistic, practices.

While music and dance go hand in hand in many social contexts, it is possible to differentiate the music and dance components. For example, salsa band musicians play the music while the dancers perform the dance movements. In other cultures, music and dance are inseparable. For example, the East African term *ngoma* refers to a cultural phenomenon combining music and dance—where the two concepts are inseparable. In both these contexts, music and dance are primarily participatory experiences. However, in many other cultural contexts, people come together to experience music and dance as audience members or observers.

OBSERVING MUSIC AND DANCE PERFORMANCE

Attending a dance performance, such as a ballet concert, as an observer exposes us to a wealth of sensory information. Our attention is primarily focused on what we see and hear. We receive visual information through our eyes about the dancers, their movements in time and space, and perhaps the costuming and sets. Our ears enable us to receive auditory information about the music connected with the dancers' movements.

The audio and visual information available to us shapes the way that we respond to the dance experience. If you were to close your eyes and just listen to the music, the experience would be very different from one where you are able to see and hear the performance. Likewise, if you were to place your hands over your ears, block out the sound, and just watch the dancers' movements, the performance experience would probably seem quite strange. The aesthetic experience for the observer, or audience member, of dance performance is often heightened through multimodal perception–seeing and hearing the performance simultaneously.

Some types of information about the dance performance can be quite effectively communicated through either visual or auditory channels. For example, emotional information, such as patterns of tension and release, can be communicated similarly through watching or listening only. Patterns of tension and release, experienced simultaneously through auditory and visual senses, creates redundancies, as the information is duplicated. Redundancies lead to faster and more effective communication of content.

However, while observers' perceptions of the dance performance may be influenced in a similar fashion by the combined audio and visual information available to them, individuals bring to the task of observing a dance performance their own mix of experiences in the world. These individual experiences shape the way that they perceive and respond to music and dance, even down to the basic level of brain activations. For example, when classical dance experts watch a classical dance performance, their brains show a similar pattern of activation. That is, their brains respond as if they were producing the movements themselves. The same situation exists for a musician watching someone play their instrument, such as a pianist watching the piano being played. The hypothesized human mirror neuron system is proposed to account for this similar pattern of firing for actions that are produced and perceived or observed. Mirror neurons were first discovered in research with monkeys (macques), where the same neurons fired when monkeys observed or performed a grasping movement.

Some researchers propose that the mirror neuron system helps us to understand the actions of others and to share emotional, or affective, experiences. The capacity to understand the thoughts, intentions, and emotions of others as we observe their actions and interactions is referred to as *theory of mind*. In lay terms, this is the capacity to "put yourself in another's shoes" and understand their thoughts and feelings. These cognitive and emotional (affective) elements as well as prosocial behaviors are cornerstones of empathy. The idea that we have capacity to share thoughts and feelings with others, which might be facilitated by a human mirror neuron system, is potentially highly important to understanding how and why we engage in sociocultural practices such as music and dance.

EXPERTISE IN MUSIC AND DANCE

To produce an artistic performance at a professional level takes years of training and experience. To achieve an expert level in a particular domain, such as music or dance, takes approximately ten thousand hours, or ten years, of deliberate practice. This practice changes the structure and function of the brain. For example, the size of areas of the brain involved in the specialist task increase, and the speed of processing task-relevant information is enhanced. Training also develops schemata, or mental representations for sound and body movements and positions in long-term memory. These shape our expectations for, and recognition of, music and dance material.

To dance or produce music performance also involves an array of senses and processes: auditory, visual, touch, kinesthetic, proprioceptive (related to knowing where the body is in space), vestibular (to help with balance and spatial orientation), motor (movement), and affective. The dancer or musician must use the sensory information arising from the body and its interactions with the environment in conjunction with knowledge in long-term memory for postures, movements, and sound to refine and enact motor plans in a continual loop of perception and action. The consequence of this intense training is that we see differences between experts and novices in how they produce, perceive, and respond to the type of artistic performance in which they are trained.

Music and dance, as artistic performance, show how thinking can be embodied in sound and action. The artistic performance demonstrates the operations of a highly attuned perceptual system to attend and respond to sensory information as well as specialist forms of knowledge in long-term memory. Knowing how to do something, such as dance, play an instrument, or ride a bike, is referred to as *procedural knowledge*. Knowing about something, such as what an *arabesque* means in the dance world, reflects declarative knowledge. Deliberate practice develops domain-specific long-term memory, such as how to play an instrument or what arabesque means and how to execute an arabesque dance movement.

When music is combined with dance in an artistic performance, the musical information can assist dancers in recalling movements from memory and maintaining the timing of their performance. Music can also be important for recalling dance sequences, and not just because it provides a referent framework for timing; it can also provide emotional information to help cue recall. Musical structure can assist in memory recall, as it exists as a hierarchy of elements that are *chunked* together. For example, musical notes are chunked into phrases (musical sentences), which are then chunked together to form sections of the piece. A chunk of musical material can cue dancers to recall a chunk of movement material.

Music is not just highly structured; sections of music often repeat. Repeated musical and dance material are likely to have a stronger presence in memory simply because of the repeated exposure. That is, when we frequently experience information, and information in association, such as music with dance, it becomes embedded in long-term memory. Composers and choreographers capitalize on these fundamental ways that we process and recall information for artistic and communicative purposes.

HOW DO WE SYNCHRONIZE DANCE MOVEMENTS TO MUSIC?

The capacity to detect rhythmic signals in external stimuli, such as the beat in music, and synchronize rhythmic behaviors with that signal facilitates complex human behaviors such as music and dance. We refer to this capacity to synchronize behaviors with the rhythmic signals detected in the environment as *entrainment*. Entrainment involves a range of sensory and motor systems to perceive rhythmic signals and produce synchronized rhythmic behavior. Synchrony is maintained by monitoring the sensory information available in an ongoing manner and adjusting behavior as necessary. An example of entrainment of movement to the rhythmic signals provided by music might be how workers, during the period of slavery in the United States, or prisoners would sing to coordinate rhythmic movements when working in the fields or on chain gangs. Aside from the rhythmic movement of the body to the beat of music that we can observe with our eyes, the electrical activity of the brain also entrains to the rhythmic signals, or regular periodicities, of the music, such as the beat. Entrainment is not simply a physical process; it also has social and emotional aspects.

Social entrainment is apparent when a person coordinates their movements in space and time with the rhythmic signals coming from another. A parent and infant entraining to each other's musical and movement signals can facilitate bonding. Or the physical and gestural mirroring of another's movement in interpersonal spoken communication or dance can facilitate a sense of mutual understanding, and shared meaning and emotion. This is often referred to as *empathy*. The implications of entrainment, which we see exemplified in music and dance, is that it is believed to be a key element of social coordination, cooperation, and bonding. This capacity for entrainment may well underpin our success as a social species by enabling us to coordinate large groups of people around a common goal, sharing intentions and emotions, and create change in the environment.

HEALTH AND WELL-BEING BENEFITS OF MUSIC AND DANCE

In healthy individuals, music and dance provide opportunities for maintaining physical, cognitive, and socio-emotional health and well-being. For example, taking part in dancing with others to music can be seen as a type of physical exercise. Learning new dance steps presents some cognitive challenges and capitalizes on the potential for *neuroplasticity*, which refers to the brain's ability to change in response to new experiences. Dancing provides the opportunity to develop social connections and a social identity, which is an affiliation and sense of belonging to a social group. Dancing with music also enhances emotional experiences and provides an outlet for self-expression.

Music and dance together can be used therapeutically with those facing psychological and neurological disorders and trauma. For example, dance movement therapy is a professional practice that uses movement and dance for the purposes of improving an individual's functioning in different areas of life. It can assist an individual with physical movement, such as balance and coordination; processing of emotional or traumatic experiences; developing social connections; cultural understanding; and improvement of cognitive (thinking) processes.

Music and dance may also be used in the treatment of neurological disorders, such as Parkinson's disease. Parkinson's disease is a progressive neurological degenerative movement disorder characterized by loss of movement control and diminished quality of life. Therapeutic interventions for Parkinson's patients that include music and partnered dance are proving effective and complementary to traditional physical therapies. Tango is one form of partnered dance used in such interventions. The basic movement is the long, slow step (forward and backward), upon which is built sequences of increasingly challenging steps and turns. Music and partnered dance appear to improve the control of certain types of movement and are enjoyable and motivating. Ongoing research is examining how the available cues, whether they are auditory from the music (such as rhythmic cues), visual, kinesthetic, or coming from the dance partner, might bypass the diseased neural area (the basal ganglia) and improve movement control.

CONCLUSION

Music and dance are fundamental human practices, and they offer benefits to spectators and participants practicing these art forms, whether they do so for pleasure, work, cultural or community reasons, or therapeutic purposes. For observers, they offer opportunities to experience aesthetic beauty, a range of emotions, and perhaps some cognitive challenges that are shared with others in a social context. Those engaged in practicing music or dance may experience health benefits from physical exercise in a social context while also developing perceptual and motor skills. Music and dance, for varied purposes, are a part of everyday life across cultures, although they may be enacted in different ways. Underpinning the variety of cultural practices we see is the idea that music and dance are important facets of the human experience for our optimal functioning as a social species.

References and Further Reading

Bläsing, B., Puttke, M., & Schack, T. (2010). *The Neurocognition of Dance: Mind, Movement and Motor Skills*. London, UK: Psychology Press.

Krumhansl, C. L., & Schenck, D. L. (1997). Can dance reflect the structural and expressive qualities of music? A perceptual experiment on Balanchine's choreography of Mozart's Divertimento no. 15. *Musicae Scientiae, 1*(1), 63–85.

Thompson, W. F. (2014). *Music, Thought, and Feeling: Understanding the Psychology of Music* (2nd ed.). New York, NY: Oxford University Press.

52. Why Do People Exercise to Music?

Thomas Hans Fritz

It is at mile seventeen that she puts in the earphones while running. She has been training hard for this marathon and has managed to work herself into a good position in the field, but the contest is tough and is taking a toll on her body. Synchronizing her steps to the beat of the pumping music always helps her to overcome the perception of exhaustion, which is crucial in the final third of the race. What she does not take into account is that the use of music during the race is illegal. So, when she crosses the finish line in first place, with her arms raised in triumph, celebrating her astounding performance, she is unaware that she is facing disqualification, and the organizers will justify their decision with photographs of her with earphones plugged in during the race.

Why is this happening to her? What could be wrong with listening to music while running a professional race? It is obvious that when people are listening to music, they may not be able to hear instructions from the announcers, which is relevant in athletic contests in which athletes must know when they are being addressed. But is listening to music a form of cheating, like doping?

Research into the effects of music during sports suggests it may indeed provide an advantage to athletes. Over the past twenty years, a wealth of evidence from sports science has revealed astounding effects of music on sports performance. It seems that music and sports go together naturally, and the majority of athletes who engage in sports exercise benefit from the use of music. How can this be so? Psychologists and physiologists have uncovered several mechanisms underlying the nature of this benefit.

SUBJECTIVE REASONS WHY PEOPLE EXERCISE TO MUSIC

People use music during sports differently depending on what they are trying to achieve. If they are an athlete trying to reduce their anxiety before a professional sports game, they might listen to calming music. If they want to motivate themselves, they might listen to upbeat music. At the gym, at least two groups can be differentiated: those who use music as a distraction (similar to watching TV while exercising) and those who use music to improve their workout success. When people are asked about their motivation for listening to music, they will typically give one of the following reasons: (a) music helps pass the time; (b) music is a source of energy; (c) music distracts people from the intense effort involved in a workout; (d) people like to synchronize their movements in time with music; (e) music makes exercise an aesthetically pleasing activity; or (f) using headphones helps people disengage from their surroundings and other people. These informal explanations explain why people listen to music while they exercise, but researchers are more interested in objective ways of measuring the benefits of music during exercise.

PSYCHOLOGICAL EFFECTS OF MUSIC DURING EXERCISE

One of the psychological benefits of music during exercise is that it reduces sensations of fatigue. Music listening seems to lower the perceived effort of exercise. According to one explanation, music listening leads to a "narrowing of the performer's attention," thereby diverting attention away from sensations of fatigue during exercise. This theory is based on the idea that only so much information can be processed in any single moment, so focusing on music means there is less attention available to focus on the effort of exercise. If people have a limited attentional capacity, it is advantageous to allocate some of their attention to music so that less attention is available to think about the effort of the exercise.

Interestingly, however, this benefit seems to work best for low-intensity exercise. For high-intensity exercise, music is not very good at decreasing the perceived effort. One reason is that with low-intensity exercise, people can more easily synchronize their movements to the beat of the music. That is, people benefit the most from music when they can align body movements to the rhythmical elements of music, and this is not very easy for high-intensity exercise.

Listening to music during physical exercise can also increase stamina and endurance, especially when participants listen to music that they find highly motivating and enjoyable. If people like the music they are listening to, they may continue the activity for a longer period of time.

Listening to music during or before a sports performance can also improve mood, and positive mood is known to benefit sports performance. In one study, 100 percent of weightlifters claimed that they use music to improve their mood, and 89.2 percent of them felt that the quality of their training improved with music. The benefit of music-induced positive mood on exercise occurs regardless of the perceived effort of the exercise and may be especially powerful for increasing exercise adherence, such as exercising regularly.

Aside from its effects on mood, music can also influence energy levels, also called *arousal*. The effect of music on arousal is so strong that many sport psychologists recommend music as a stimulant or a sedative. It can be used prior to a physical activity to prepare for a performance by increasing excitement (getting psyched-up) or for decreasing stress (calming down). It can also be used during physical activity so that the athlete's arousal level matches the type of sports activity. Music affects arousal because of acoustical properties such as loudness and tempo (louder and faster music tends to lead to greater arousal). Arousal can also be affected by extramusical associations, whereby certain types of music can promote thoughts that inspire physical activity or promote relaxation.

PHYSIOLOGICAL EFFECTS OF MUSIC DURING EXERCISE

Listening to music also has a number of physiological consequences, and some of these changes are beneficial for physical exercise. For example, it has been shown that listening to music can lead to greater muscle relaxation during performance, so the target muscle is activated more effectively. This effect can lead to improved motor performance and increased aerobic endurance. Music listening can also lead to changes in physiological measures, such as blood lactate, heart rate, and respiration rate. All these physiological changes influence our ability to exercise.

WHAT TYPE OF MUSIC IS OPTIMAL TO ACCOMPANY EXERCISE?

The types of music that people choose to listen to during physical exercise is often quite different from the music that they like to listen to at home. In general, people who are exercising choose music that is far more arousing, with a tempo between 125 and 140 BPM (beats per minute). Such fast-paced music is similar to dance music that you hear in a club and mirrors the heightened cardiovascular activity required in exercise, such as increased heart rate and breathing rate. Indeed, people in nightclubs often engage in intense physical activity in the form of dance.

HOW IS MUSIC SELECTED IN EXERCISE PLAYLISTS FOR GROUP EXERCISE CLASSES?

When exercise is choreographed for group classes, music playlists must be carefully selected so that participants can synchronize their movements to the music. Furthermore, class instructors find it helpful when the musical style reflects the musical tastes of the participants. In an ideal world, participants would be able to select their own preferred music during a class. Selecting their own music has the additional benefit that people enjoy it more and feel a greater sense of control, but individual music selection is not possible in group classes where everyone must listen to the same pieces of music to coordinate their movements.

JYMMIN: MAXIMIZING THE EFFECTS OF MUSIC ON SPORTS WITH INNOVATIVE TECHNOLOGY

Research conducted by the author of this chapter and colleagues in Leipzig, Germany, suggests that the intense effects of music on sports might relate to how we control our muscles. There are three types of systems that control movements: (1) deliberate movements, for example, when we pick up a glass of water and then put it back down; (2) automatic movements of muscles that occur without our conscious control, for example, reflexes and the movement of muscles in your intestines; and (3) emotional movements over which we only *sometimes* have control. For example, speaking emotionally comes naturally if we are in an emotional situation, but most people need acting training to speak emotionally in an artificial or theatrical situation. Without such training, people are surprisingly poor at accessing this type of emotional motor control. The movements needed to express emotionality, for example, in one's voice or body language, are controlled by a neuronal system called *emotional motor control*. Most people can only access this type of motor control in an authentic emotional situation, but finding ways to access this type of motor control may hold the key to athletic performance.

In recent years, a new music-sports technology has emerged that allows people to generate their own music during high-arousal physical workouts. This is an important development because the act of generating music may stimulate emotional motor control, which in turn may assist with athletic performance. The exercise system is called Jymmin, and involves using different types of movement to trigger changes in accompanying music. The system is a bit like singing while you work and changing the type of singing depending on the nature of the work. For example, making faster movements during exercise may increase the intensity of the accompanying music, and it may also affect the instruments that you hear. The result is a system in which the person's own movements determine the music, and that gives the person a strong sense of control that seems to help people exercise.

Should we be surprised? Not really. There are many examples of work songs throughout history, whereby music is used to increase endurance. In fact, most agrarian societies have work songs to accompany herding or harvesting. "Yankee Doodle" is thought to have originated as a harvest song. Jymmin was developed in recognition of the power of work songs, and it aims to rediscover the forgotten benefits of music for endurance. The exercise system can be performed individually or in groups such that each exercise movement or machine can be "played" just like a musical instrument (which might be the baseline and the electronic beats in a techno song or the string section in an orchestra). Moreover, several exercise movements or machines can be combined so that a more elaborate song with various instruments can be played by several people. The result can be a euphoric experience that is highly beneficial for endurance, and it may be a powerful tool for sports training.

Our research suggests that the benefits of passive music listening for endurance are strongest when participants imagine that they are *creating* the music themselves and are *in contr*ol of the music. This sensation is referred to as a *self-efficacy experience*, and it can be induced by coordinating the timing of one's movements with the beat of the music. Furthermore, Jymmin has been shown to result in beneficial cognitive effects, such as increased capacities for creative thinking and attention, which have been argued to be beneficial for sports performance.

Combining music with exercise can sometimes lead to altered states, such as euphoria or even trancelike states. Trance states are an ultimate distraction from the exhaustion of exercising, for they are characterized by a loss of a sense of self and have been argued to allow access to specific experiences that are not accessible outside of the trance state. It is now possible to systematically test such psychological effects of music in a laboratory setting by combining music making with an exercise sport workout.

Although it is tempting to suggest that the benefits of music on perceived exhaustion or exertion can be boiled down to distraction, there are problems with this simple explanation. For one thing, when people use Jymmin to exercise with music, they coordinate their movements to the music, and so they concentrate on their own body movements to control the music when combining coordination and strength training. One would in this scenario therefore rather speak of guided attention than distraction. That people feel less exhausted when they control music in this way would furthermore imply that something else besides distraction from physiological monitoring is going on. Exercise movements that seem to control music are less exhausting than exercise movements done for their own sake, possibly because people are engaging a different system for movement: the emotional motor system.

Using Jymmin also seems to release endorphins more efficiently than sports activities that do not involve music (e.g., running a marathon). Within only ten minutes, an increase in mood is observed in comparison to a conventional machine exercise workout, an effect often labeled a *runner's high*. This "high" was reported to last between ninety minutes and two and half hours, suggesting that it indeed was caused hormonally. Furthermore muscles during the Jymmin workout were observed to physiologically become more effective. Specifically, antagonist muscles were more relaxed during the workout, and so less oxygen was required to perform at the same level.

Not surprisingly, participants experienced a greater sense of internal locus of control and self-efficacy during Jymmin than during passive music listening, and this perception extended to their self-efficacy perception generally, that is, in their lives.

CONCLUSION

A variety of psychological and physiological effects of music on physical exercise have been reported, most notably a decrease in perceived effort, greater muscle relaxation, increased mood, and changes in arousal (energetic or relaxed). One of the most important concepts related to these effects is the idea of self-efficacy, or feeling in control. Feelings of self-efficacy seem to increase when music is performed actively as an integrated part of exercise. It is often said that the optimal workout movement should be executed with maximal control and deliberation to ensure the very best execution of movement. Although there is truth in this idea, it is necessary to reconsider exercise movements in light of modern concepts about motor control and to consider the importance of self-efficacy and emotionally motivated actions, which during physical exercise probably occur most naturally when exercise is accompanied by music.

References and Further Reading

Fritz, T. (2017). Jymmin—The medical potential of musical euphoria. In M. Lesaffre, P. J. Maes, & M. Leman (Eds.), *The Routledge Companion to Embodied Music Interaction* (pp. 278–283). New York, NY: Taylor & Francis.

Karageorghis, C. I., & Terry, P. C. (2009). The psychological, psychophysical, and ergogenic effects of music in sport: A review and synthesis. In A. J. Bateman & J. R. Bale (Eds.), *Sporting Sounds: Relationships between Sport and Music* (pp. 13–36). London, UK: Routledge.

Terry, P. C., & Karageorghis, C. I. (2011). Music in sport and exercise. In T. Morris & P. C. Terry (Eds.), *The New Sport and Exercise Psychology Companion* (pp. 359–380). Morgantown, USA: Fitness Information Technology.

Music and Health

53. Defining Music, Health, and Well-Being

Teresa Grimm and Gunter Kreutz

Most people listen to music, and some people play a musical instrument such as piano or guitar. However, when it comes to the many ways that music can be used to promote health and well-being, we should think of *music* as an umbrella term that embraces a wide range of activities. These activities include, but are not restricted to, listening to music, singing, dancing, playing an instrument, learning about music, and practicing on musical instruments. All of these activities can be carried out individually or with other people. Additionally, creating music by improvising, songwriting, composing music, and even designing and manufacturing new musical instruments are musical activities. Finally, in our digital online age, in which music is one of the most important contents on the Internet, people often create individualized music playlists and share their favorite music with other people. New software and hardware tools allow individuals with little or no specific musical training to find and select preferred pieces for listening and even to compose new music or perform music online. All these forms of musical behavior can help people to express their feelings, thoughts, and emotions in meaningful ways.

Both receptive (listening) and productive (performing) musical activities can promote health and well-being. However, not all uses of music are healthy. Playing music at very high loudness levels for leisure purposes or exposing individuals to music that they do not like can be a nuisance and even physically harmful in some cases. In rare cases, some uses of music have been described as a form of torture. In 1993, in Waco, Texas, investigators from the FBI blasted extremely loud and distorted music every night toward members of the Branch Davidian religion in the hope that they would leave the compound without the need to use other means of force.

WHY DOES MUSIC ENHANCE WELL-BEING?

Most people listen to music because they enjoy it, but we also initiate musical activities for pragmatic purposes that are linked to (primarily) positive emotions, well-being, and quality of life. For this reason, the psychological (or behavioral), physiological, and social consequences of music are of enormous interest to public health. Why should music have such powerful effects on us?

First, human musicality is deeply ingrained in our lives. There are both genetic and environmental influences on our responses to music that affect our musical development even before birth. The development of human musicality continues across the life span. Therefore, music can be a resource for health and well-being at any point in life regardless of our circumstances or health. People can develop expertise in music even if they have reduced hearing capacities, for example, or other disabilities that are acquired as a fetus, in early

Photo 53.1 Alberta Hunter Music Can Be a Resource for Health and Well-Being at Any Point in Life. (Photofest)

infancy, or later in life. When people play music together, feelings of happiness and well-being can be contagious, as exemplified in photo 53.1.

Second, we are all born into rich musical cultures that are characterized by a range of music genres. Different musical cultures have their own song repertoires that most or all members of that culture are exposed to during their development, and this exposure is part of their musical enculturation. For example, virtually everyone in Western industrialized societies has been exposed to the song "Happy Birthday," and most people have been exposed to music by popular bands such as the Beatles and Coldplay. However, people from other cultures might not have been exposed to this music. Thus, people from different cultures are familiar with different kinds of music, and this familiarity helps to shape their musical preferences. Such differences must be taken into account when using music interventions to improve well-being and health.

CAN MUSIC HAVE NEGATIVE EFFECTS ON US?

Although music usually contributes to health and well-being, it can sometimes have negative health implications. As an obvious example, prolonged exposure to very high sound pressure levels from sound sources, including music, can cause hearing problems such as tinnitus or hearing loss. Interestingly, playing music professionally can also have negative consequences. Performing music on a regular basis can be physically demanding, and it has also been associated with systemic health problems, including long-term psychosomatic and musculoskeletal disorders. The extent and complexity of health issues in professional musicianship has given rise to a specific medical field called *musicians medicine*, which underscores the view that playing music can have specific health implications not unlike playing sports.

Becoming a popular musician, such as a rap or heavy metal musician, also carries health risks related to the lifestyles that many such musicians lead. Popular musicians have a much higher risk than the general population in the United States of dying from an accident, suicide, or murder. Consequently, prevention and rehabilitation programs have been developed to counteract health risks and provide support for musicians who dedicate their lives and careers as highly trained artists.

SALUTOGENIC AND PATHOGENIC APPROACHES

The World Health Organization (WHO) defines *health* as "a state of complete physical, mental and social well-being and not merely the absence of disease or infirmity." In other words, being healthy is not just the absence of disease but is partly subjective. A healthy person is not only free of disease but also experiences well-being.

What factors influence such feelings of well-being? Aaron Antonovsky was a physician who tried to find the answer to this question by conducting extensive interviews with survivors of the Holocaust after World War II. Partly from these interviews, he developed a theory about how specific personal dispositions can make some individuals more resilient to the stresses of daily life. An important concept in his theory was *salutogenesis*. Salutogenesis is a medical strategy that tries to identify all the factors that support health and well-being rather than focusing on factors that cause disease. In other words, salutogenesis was proposed as an alternative to the more common *pathogenic* approach of focusing on illness, injury, and disease. Today, illness and health are considered to be endpoints of a continuum, and the resources that help us to maintain well-being are just as important as the treatment and rehabilitation that are needed to overcome illness. Music is one of many factors that can significantly promote health and well-being.

The strengths of the salutogenic approach are primarily seen in prevention and rehabilitation. This means that salutogenic strategies can work alongside medical treatment strategies as adjunct therapies. When it comes to music for health and well-being, musical activities in everyday life offer salutogenic potential, especially if they contribute to what Antonovsky has called a *sense of coherence* (SOC), meaning that musical activities are most beneficial when they are experienced as *meaningful, manageable,* and *comprehensive.*

THE PROFESSION OF MUSIC THERAPY

Music therapy is a clinical strategy in the treatment of a wide range of patient groups, and it is normally practiced by registered music therapists who have been trained at an accredited program of study. Professional music therapy is predominantly defined as a form of psychotherapy. Perhaps the most important defining criterion is the relationship between a client, usually a patient, and a registered music therapist. It is assumed that the effects of music therapy are dependent on both the musical activities and the social interactions within the client-therapist relationship. The format of music therapy may be extended to groups of patients through singing, drumming, and music and movement or dance as strategies.

MUSIC FOR HEALTH AND WELL-BEING

Music for health and well-being, by contrast, is a more general strategy of using music in everyday life and educational settings. Music-induced health benefits occur in a range of contexts beyond the client-therapist relationship. They are not restricted to particular forms of musical interactions or experiences, and it is also not always easy to pinpoint the specific musical components that lead to health benefits. One complication is that musical activities often occur in a social context and in presence of a wide range of environmental influences. These social and environmental factors can have health benefits on their own, so it may be difficult to separate the benefits of music from the benefits that arise from the many non-musical factors and environmental conditions that accompany the musical activity. Nonetheless, these musical activities can have significant health benefits without introducing risks or negative side effects. Whether music therapy is being practiced by a registered therapist or by other professionals, music is a highly effective tool for promoting well-being and for the prevention, intervention, and rehabilitation of mental and physical disease.

HOW ARE THE HEALTH BENEFITS OF MUSIC MEASURED?

It can be difficult to measure the positive or negative health and well-being consequences of music. Musical activities are complex, and there is no easy way to measure the relative importance of all the various features of a musical activity. If a musical intervention leads to health benefits, we do not know whether those benefits were caused by the social nature of the activity, the personal aspect of the music, the emotional qualities of the music, or the physical effects of moving to music. One way to ascertain the importance of these various aspects of music is to observe changes over time in comparison to other nonmusical activities, which may have similar features except for one or more of the components of the musical activity. For example, playing bingo has a social element, but it lacks other features of musical activities. Although comparing the benefits of musical and nonmusical activities (such as bingo) is a valuable scientific strategy, it cannot tell researchers everything they need to know. All human activities are highly complex and multifaceted, so any two such activities will differ in many ways.

The benefits that arise from musical activities reflect the fact that myriad variables can influence our health and well-being. Research designs can only consider a limited number of variables at any one time. Therefore, studying the benefits of musical activities is just as hard as, for example, trying to understand the benefits of yoga, meditation, or massage. Nonetheless, all of these experiences and activities can be studied at subjective levels to evaluate how they make people feel and at biological levels to address some of the physiological consequences of these activities. In recent years, there is a new trend to study endocrine responses by measuring the concentrations of specific molecules, including proteins and hormones, via salivary or blood samples. These substances can indicate activity in four bodily systems: (1) reward, motivation, and pleasure; (2) stress and arousal; (3) immunity; and (4) social affiliation.

WHAT DOES SCIENCE SAY?

A number of systematic reviews of research have confirmed that there are many benefits of musical activities for health and well-being. One review conducted in 2015 considered seventy-three randomized controlled trials (RCTs) on the effects of music listening on anxiety and pain in adult patients undergoing surgical procedures. A meta-analysis of these studies showed that music reduced postoperative pain, anxiety, and the use of analgesia. In addition, music patients were also more satisfied and made fewer complaints than controls. Another review was conducted in the same year on studies of children undergoing surgery. In comparison to standard care, children receiving music suffered significantly less pain, anxiety, and distress after surgery.

These two examples illustrate that scientific research on the health benefits of music are not merely anecdotal but meet the highest methodological standards of medical research. Despite this promising progress, however, more research is needed to achieve a complete understanding of the health benefits of music.

CONCLUSION

The study of music for health and well-being has emerged as a new interdisciplinary domain of empirical research in music psychology. Over the last decade, traditional music therapeutic approaches have been increasingly informed by scientific evidence. This evidence confirms that music is a powerful resource for enhancing health and well-being and that music-based interventions are effective in a wide range of clinical and nonclinical settings for prevention, intervention, and rehabilitation across the life span.

References and Further Reading
Hole, J., Hirsch, M., Ball, E., & Meads, C. (2015). Music as an aid for postoperative recovery in adults: A systematic review and meta-analysis. *Lancet, 386*(10004), 1659–1671. https://doi.org/10.1016/S0140-6736(15)60169-6
Lewis, A., Cave, P., Stern, M., Welch, L., Taylor, K., Russell, J., . . . Hopkinson, N. S. (2016). Singing for lung health—A systematic review of the literature and consensus statement. *NPJ Primary Care Respiratory Medicine, 26*(16080), 1–8. https://doi.org/10.1038/npjpcrm.2016.80

MacDonald, R. A. R., Kreutz, G., & Mitchell, L. (2012). *Music, Health, and Wellbeing.* Oxford, UK: Oxford University Press.

van der Heijden, M. J. E., Araghi, S. O., van Dijk, M., Jeekel, J., & Hunik, M. M. G. (2015). The effects of perioperative music interventions in pediatric surgery: A systematic review and meta-analysis of randomized controlled trials. *PLoS One, 10*(8), 1–11. https://doi.org/10.1371/journal.pone.0133608

54. Five Healthy Ingredients of Music

William Forde Thompson

Music can powerfully affect our moods and energy levels and can be used as a therapeutic tool for conditions such as anxiety, depression, post-traumatic stress disorder (PTSD), and social phobia. It can also be used to treat or alleviate symptoms of neurological disorders, such as memory loss from dementia, mobility problems from Parkinson's disease, and the inability to speak following a stroke (nonfluent aphasia). How is this possible? What are the ingredients of music that give it the capacity to affect people from all around the world and all walks of life and that make music a valuable tool for treating neurological disorders? Understanding these ingredients has been a long-standing ambition for scientists and music therapists who want to know why music engages us so powerfully and how it can trigger processes of recovery from brain injury and neurological disease.

MUSIC IS PHYSICAL

The first beneficial ingredient of music is that it is physical. Playing and dancing to music are by definition physical activities, but even passively listening to music has physiological consequences that affect heart rate, blood pressure, and respiration. It is well known that physical exercise can benefit a wide range of conditions by improving mood, promoting better sleep, increasing flexibility of movement, and boosting oxygenation throughout the body, including the brain. Physical exercise is good for one's immediate health, and it can also reduce the likelihood of developing neurological conditions later in life, such as dementia and stroke.

Music and movement are intimately connected. Music often encourages people to move in time with the music, whether tapping one's foot, clapping, or even dancing. In many places around the world, music is always accompanied by some form of dance, and musical rhythm can trigger activity in the motor areas of the brain, even when we are not actually moving. Many researchers believe that moving to music is more beneficial than physical exercise alone, both for cognitive (thinking) and physical health. In one study, 469 participants over the age of seventy-five were tracked for many years, and it was found that the risk of developing dementia was lower in those individuals who regularly engaged in dance than those who rarely or never danced.

Dancing to music can also be used therapeutically to improve the symptoms of Parkinson's disease. This disease typically leads to severe problems of movement (walking) and balance. When people with Parkinson's disease listen to music, their movements become easier and more fluid. At advanced stages of the disease, people may have considerable difficulty simply walking across a room, but in the presence of music, they can not only walk more easily but can often dance to the music. Such dramatic improvements in symptoms occur because music provides an external stimulus for timing their movements, replacing the internal timing mechanisms that are damaged by the disease.

By stimulating physical movement, music can reduce the risk of developing neurological disorders, alleviate symptoms of existing neurological disorders, and provide direct health benefits through increased oxygenation to the body and brain. Older adults may not always enjoy exercising for its own sake, but combining exercise with music can be a highly enjoyable activity that invites high participation levels.

MUSIC IS EMOTIONAL

One of the hallmark features of music is that it can trigger powerful emotional states, and these states act as a catalyst for a flood of associations and memories. These effects on emotion and memory are especially important for people with dementia, who can often recapture lost memories while listening to music and become emotionally energized and more "present." It may also be important for children with autism spectrum disorder, who may find music to be a valuable and accessible outlet for emotional communication.

For all people, emotional experiences to music are associated with the release of neurochemicals in the brain, including dopamine and noradrenaline. Some of these neurochemical changes may be important for brain plasticity, that is, the capacity of the brain to adapt to new circumstances. Music-evoked emotions are also linked to reward systems in the brain, so they tend to be pleasant experiences, even, paradoxically, if the music sounds sad. Because music is rewarding, people are usually happy to participate in music-based treatments.

One of the ways that music can induce emotional states is by reminding us of significant times in our lives. Music has the capacity to trigger autobiographical memories, even for people with dementia (such as Alzheimer's disease) who have impaired memory function. Such memories tend to induce positive emotions and are valuable in reminding people of their most personal memories. In the absence of music, people with dementia can be emotionally flat, and their difficulty with memory means they have only a faint sense of their personal identity. If you have forgotten who your spouse is, your children, where you lived, and other details of your personal life, it is hard to feel a strong sense of personal identity. Music, by stimulating autobiographical memories and generating positive emotional feelings, can help remind people with dementia of their personal identity and induce a positive emotional state.

MUSIC IS ENGAGING

A third feature of music is that it is highly engaging. Music captures our attention, both because it is interesting and because it triggers activation across many regions of the entire brain. Our tendency to pay close attention to music means that music experiences are richer and more engrossing than other daily activities, such as doing a crossword puzzle, washing the dishes, or talking on the telephone. This depth of experience is important because it can distract people from discomforts such as pain or anxiety.

In the field of neurorehabilitation, introducing highly engaging stimulation to patients is a treatment strategy called *environmental enrichment therapy*, and the benefits of this enrichment are well established. For example, people who have suffered a brain injury following an accident or a stroke can recover more quickly if they have a lot of environmental stimulation, including music. In one study, groups of patients who had suffered a stroke were given one of three types of therapeutic intervention: daily music listening, daily audiobooks, and standard care. People who engaged in daily music listening had better memory and attention than people who listened to audiobooks or received standard care.

Why should music have benefits for attention and memory? Attention may improve because music is a highly engaging source of environmental stimulation, so people willingly allocate their full attention to music. Focusing one's attention on music exercises our attentional capacities. It gradually improves our ability to attend to other aspects of our environment, leading to a general benefit to attention. Memory may improve because music is a powerful trigger of autobiographical memories. Many of our favorite songs bring to mind a particular time of our lives, for example, a time of life when we heard the song for the first time. By repeatedly triggering memories of special times, music may gradually refine the ability of people to retrieve memories, leading to a general improvement in memory function. The importance of engagement is underscored by the saying "use it or lose it." Because music is so engaging, it encourages us to use our mental capacities.

MUSIC IS SOCIAL

Most often, we engage in musical activities together with other people, and there is evidence that we feel strong connections with people who share in our music experiences, even if we do not know them. There is no better way to get a party going than putting on some good music, and music is used to support some of the most significant life events, such as graduations, marriages, birthdays, and anniversaries. Researchers have discovered that when people move together in a musical context, the neurohormone oxytocin is released into the body. Oxytocin functions, in part, to enhance feelings of social connection and empathy for others. Social connections are surprisingly important for neurological conditions, which can often lead to social isolation. Neurological impairment may physically reduce a person's ability to participate in social activities, and many patients avoid social situations simply because they are not feeling well. But social isolation can be dangerous. It not only slows recovery but can also lead to additional impairment to cognitive function, a kind of snowball effect.

One reason social support is important is that many cognitive functions—such as language fluency, memory, attention, and motor function—are subtly supported by our social environment. Have you ever reminded a friend of something that they had forgotten? Have you pointed out something interesting to a friend during a walk in the park? Have you ever said "watch your step" to help someone avoid tripping? In the absence of any social support, we are on our own in the world. We may not realize it, but social connections provide us with a continuous source of support and can be likened to a personal scaffold of psychological and physical support. Without our social scaffold, cognitive functions are likely to decline.

Another reason that social engagement is important is because social situations encourage us to draw upon a large number of cognitive processes, such as attention, working memory, verbal memory, and imagination. Our imagination helps us to anticipate what is going to happen next in social situations, either immediately or in the future. For most of us, these capacities come naturally, and we are not aware of them. But for people who have a neurological problem such as dementia, traumatic brain injury, or stroke, these capacities need to be exercised and rehabilitated.

That is where music comes in. Music therapists frequently use music to nurture feelings of social support and connection. For infants, music is one of the earliest forms of social communication. From adolescence to older age, familiar music nurtures social bonds with friends and family. Listening to unfamiliar music can even help us to understand and empathize with people from other cultures, thereby reducing prejudice. For people with neurological disorders, musical activities such as group singing are known to reduce agitation and isolation, increase positive mood, and improve communication. For children with autism spectrum disorder, music is often used to encourage greater social participation and engagement. These social benefits demonstrate that music is a powerful glue that holds friends and communities together, and it has the potential to create greater unity in the world.

MUSIC IS PERSONAL

The music from our past is deeply connected to our sense of identity. This is especially true when we are first finding ourselves as adolescents, but the connection between music and identity continues throughout our lives. When people develop a neurological disorder, it often disrupts their sense of self. Imagine an individual with dementia who starts to lose her memory of family members as well as her own past history. As her memory fades, so too does her sense of identity.

The loss of core physical functions can also disrupt our sense of self. Imagine an individual who has suffered a stroke that results in impaired motor functioning and the loss of speech. Whether he was formerly an athlete, or regularly enjoyed hiking and rock climbing, or is accustomed to having long conversations with family members, his physical and social identity will be severely disrupted.

But research has shown that both passive (listening) and active (performing) forms of music engagement are extremely powerful sources of personal identity. Music can remind us of our essential personality, and it can transport us back in time to significant moments in our lives. Reconnecting to our past experiences and identity through music has significant benefits, assisting in memory function and well-being.

When music is used as therapy, it is most effective in the form of a personalized playlist. Music that is personally meaningful is almost always more beneficial than music that is chosen by a care professional. As an example, some couples have a special song that is uniquely associated with their identity as a couple. These shared songs can remind a couple of a significant event or time in their relationship, such as when they first met, their wedding, or a time when they were separated and missed each other. As the saying goes, "Darling, they're playing our song."

A case that illustrates the power of "our song" was brought to the attention of myself and Amee Baird. At the time we were contacted, Barbara had been diagnosed with Alzheimer's dementia five years ago, and she often became confused and agitated. Increasingly, she stopped recognizing her husband, David, even though they had been together for almost sixty years. When she accused him of being an intruder and chased him out of their family home, David had no idea how he could make her understand that he was her partner of six decades. Barbara's dementia had rendered her with a form of Capgras delusion—the false belief that your spouse is an intruder.

But it was the power of song that brought Barbara back to David. On the night they first met, sixty years ago, they had danced to the last song of the evening, "Unchained Melody," by the Righteous Brothers. Now, on the advice of his insightful family doctor, David began singing their special song to Barbara every day. Eventually, in David's words, "She came back," and the episodes of her failing to recognize him stopped—almost as though Barbara was heeding the lyrics of the song itself, "I'll be coming home, wait for me."

CONCLUSION

Just like pharmaceutical treatments, music treatments work because they contain a number of "active ingredients." Music is a powerful treatment for a range of psychological and neurological conditions because it combines several powerful ingredients into a single package that is highly enjoyable and universally accessible to all. Music is at once physical, emotional, engaging, social, and personal, and combining these five ingredients means that it is among the most effective and readily available nonpharmaceutical interventions available. Although music that is played too loudly may damage our ears, for the most part, there are few negative side effects of music, especially when it is employed in treatment by a qualified practitioner. As evidence accumulates about the benefits of musical interventions, practitioners can refine music treatments to emphasize the active ingredients that best meet the special needs of individual patients, whether those needs concern mobility, emotional connection, cognitive function, social engagement, or a sense of identity.

References and Further Reading
Baird, A., & Thompson, W. F. (2018). The impact of music on the self in dementia. *Journal of Alzheimer's Disease, 61*, 827–841.
Baird, A., & Thompson, W. F. (2019). When music compensates language: A case study of severe aphasia in dementia and the use of music by a spousal caregiver. *Aphasiology, 33*, 449–465.

MacDonald, R. A. R., Kreutz, G., & Mitchell, L. (Eds.). (2012). *Music, Health, and Well-being*. Oxford, UK: Oxford University Press.

Thompson, W. F., & Schlaug, G. (2015). The healing power of music. *Scientific American Mind, 16*(5), 32–41.

55. Music Therapy

Felicity A. Baker

We have all experienced how music can affect our mood, causing us to smile, cry, or feel less stressed. It also energizes us to move—dancing at a rave or jogging in our neighborhood. Music can also assist our learning of nonmusical information; keep us focused when we study; help us meet people in social situations, such as a party; or distract us when we are in pain, for example while at the dentist. These potentials for music to effect change are drawn upon when music is used as a therapeutic tool. Music therapy is a discipline whereby a trained therapist draws on the potential of music and the relationships that can develop in and through music to address a range of clinical needs across the life span. In this chapter, you will learn about some of the populations that benefit from music therapy, the types of health and well-being outcomes music therapy can lead to, and the different applications of music that music therapists use when working with their clients.

WHAT IS MUSIC THERAPY?

Music therapy is practiced throughout the world over, and its definition is different in almost every country, determined by the clinicians who practice there and shaped by each country's perspectives on health care. Despite their subtle differences in definition and practice, several core concepts are shared. The World Federation of Music Therapy (WFMT), an organization composed of music therapists and music therapy associations from around the globe, has defined music therapy as follows:

> The professional use of music and its elements as an intervention in medical, educational, and everyday environments with individuals, groups, families, or communities who seek to optimize their quality of life and improve their physical, social, communicative, emotional, intellectual, and spiritual health and well-being. Research, practice, education, and clinical training in music therapy are based on professional standards according to cultural, social, and political contexts. (WFMT 2011)

In this definition, the important concepts articulated are delivered by a trained "professional." This means that although music can be therapeutic in and of itself, it is only considered music therapy when a trained professional delivers an intervention in a planned and systematic way. Take the example of a nurse who comes into the hospital room of a child being treated for cancer. She sings a song for the child that she knows he likes. The child may talk to the nurse and may visibly look happier, even if just for a brief moment. Clearly, there has been some benefit in this musical interaction; however, this is not music therapy. The nurse has no music therapy training and therefore no knowledge of how to assess and plan an appropriate and targeted program for the child.

In the WFMT definition, the phrase "music and its elements as an intervention" is articulated. Music is intentionally used as an intervention to address a health need, not as entertainment or for music education. These interventions may be delivered in hospitals and other medical settings, rehabilitation centers, aged care facilities, or within the community. They are also delivered in educational settings, such as mainstream schools or schools for children with special needs, and in home environments.

Presently, there is much debate about the word "intervention," as it implies that the therapy has the intention to act upon the person rather than acknowledging that the person is an active collaborator in achieving their own well-being. Many clinicians and researchers are striving to address the power relationship set up by the term "intervention" and indeed the term "therapist."

WHO IS MUSIC THERAPY USED WITH AND WHAT NEEDS DOES IT ADDRESS?

Research and outcomes from clinical practice have shown that music therapy can address a range of physical, social, psychological, emotional, intellectual, communicative, and spiritual needs for premature babies right through to elderly people who are preparing for imminent death. It is not possible to outline all the areas of clinical practice in detail, but they can be categorized into child, adolescent, and adult mental health; autism spectrum disorder and developmental disabilities; neurorehabilitation and neurodegenerative diseases; and terminal illnesses, grief, and loss. Each will be briefly described below.

Child, Adolescent, and Adult Mental Health

Music therapy has a long tradition of application in the mental health sector with acute hospitalized clients as well as those whose symptoms are well managed and living in the community. Some clinicians use musical encounters with clients to change their distorted thinking and help them to view themselves in a more positive way. In psychology, this model, termed *cognitive behavioral therapy* (CBT), involves the therapist drawing to the clients' attention how their faculty and negative thoughts and beliefs contribute to their everyday problems. Music therapists use musical experiences to draw clients' attention to their faulty thinking. For example, one music therapy method, songwriting, is used with clients who may be depressed. They may offer lyrical ideas for songs, such as "I have done nothing of value with my life," that are generally false statements. The music therapist will challenge this and help the clients to reframe how they see themselves and to recognize that this thinking is faulty and self-defeating.

Some clinicians will use music therapy approaches that are derived from what is known as *psychodynamic theory*. Here, it is understood that people's mental health issues stem from past experiences, particularly childhood traumatic experiences that have been repressed and hidden from conscious thought. To move to a better state of mental health, music therapists facilitate musical experiences that help their clients to connect with inner emotions and past experiences, stimulate memories, or simulate prior relationships through improvising on musical instruments. As music evokes emotions, associations, and memories, when clients improvise on musical instruments, they have the opportunity to explore the complexity and pain of their past experiences and address unresolved feelings toward others' past actions toward them. While the clients improvise with the therapist, they are communicating and interacting musically using the same interactional styles used in everyday life. Clients can sense how these may mirror interactions in real life when listening back to their improvisations and discussing what was heard with the therapist. Through repeated musical experiences, the clients work through these issues and internally resolve past traumas, feelings and experiences of destructive relationships.

Autism Spectrum Disorder and Developmental Disabilities

Music therapy has had a long history of contributing to the well-being of people on the autism spectrum and those who have complex developmental disabilities. For children with these developmental disabilities, music therapy may be practiced within a special education setting or a mainstream school. The clinician will work collaboratively with the children, teachers, and parents to facilitate a program that is meaningful, enables creative engagement in learning, and facilitates skill development. For example, music activities that involve instrument playing can be motivating and provide opportunities for children to develop gross and fine motor control. Playing a xylophone with a mallet requires eye-hand coordination and handgrip to play; these skills are integral to carrying out many of life's daily activities. For those people living with developmental disabilities that impact their ability to verbally communicate with others, singing and composing songs offer opportunities to acquire new language and practice articulating sounds that they may have difficulty producing. It is a common practice in education more generally to teach language through songs. For those children who have great difficulty in acquiring language, pairing music with words and sounds can be an effective approach to acquiring language.

Social skills are developmental skills that may be challenging for people with "developmental disabilities. They may not recognize social cues, understand turn taking in conversations or activities, tolerate conflict, or assert themselves when in uncomfortable situations. These are all skills that can be enacted during improvisational activities or other music-based games. The musical experiences provide a safe space to "try out" these social skills. Some group members may experience anxiety in unfamiliar places and circumstances, so the music therapy program is carefully designed to be predictable and safe, especially through the use of repetition of session structure and songs used. New material is introduced in staged approaches to avoid overwhelming the students. Here, music provides the container for group experiences.

Neurorehabilitation and Neurodegenerative Diseases

There has been a growing interest in the role of music therapy in the care of people with neurodisabilities (e.g., stroke, spinal cord injury, brain injury) and neurodegenerative diseases (e.g., motor neuron disease, Parkinson's disease, Huntington's disease, and Alzheimer's disease and other forms of dementia). When neurotrauma occurs, people can lose their ability to walk, talk, use their upper limbs, and access short-term memory and the ability to plan and execute activities of daily life. They may become dependent on nursing staff or family for their full care and may experience difficulty adjusting to the sudden change in their circumstances.

For those patients who have difficulty walking, there is one music therapy method, *rhythmic auditory stimulation*, that may assist patients to walk again. The principle of this method is that as rhythm is integral to movement (each muscle contraction or extension must be coordinated in time with other muscles to form a fluid movement), rhythm becomes an auditory cue to organize movement. The music therapist can create a musical frame for the patient to practice walking and gradually adjust the rhythm and tempo of the music as the patient becomes more able to move in time, at a faster pace, and for longer distances. Prerecorded music is not able to adapt in the moment as the patient becomes more able or begins to fatigue. Therefore, the expertise of a trained therapist who can create the musical frame in the moment is important here.

A common impairment seen in people with brain injury, stroke, and Parkinson's disease is paralysis or weakness of the facial muscles (dysarthria), or an inability to coordinate the movements of these muscles (dyspraxia). This means that patients have difficulty verbally communicating with others. Their speech may sound slurred, explosive in volume, or in contrast, breathy and soft, too fast or too slow, arrhythmic, or monotonal. They may not be able to sequence sounds together to form words. Carefully tailored singing programs can be used to assist clients to speak with clearer articulation. The music therapist creates a program in which the targeted sounds are identified and practiced within the context of a song. As clients practice and improve, the therapist modifies the program so that more difficult tasks are embedded within the singing activities to push the clients to further improve.

Acquiring a neurological injury or receiving the diagnosis of a degenerative disease may be received as a crisis. Clients are at risk of becoming depressed, angry, or frustrated, which impacts their own well-being as well as their relationships with the important people in their lives. Music is a tool within which people can express complex emotions and come to terms with the inevitable changes in their lives that are beyond their control. Listening to or singing songs that tell stories of similar experiences gives these clients "permission" to grieve their losses and to have insight and better understanding of the long-term implications of their condition. For example, R.E.M.'s song "Losing My Religion" can be used to explore themes of confusion, feeling trapped, self-imposed punishment, and identity. As the clients listen to the song, it evokes emotions. They can relate to the experiences of the songwriter and use this as a starting point to explore issues of grief, loss, acceptance, and change.

Another common approach to addressing psychoemotional adjustment is songwriting. Here, the music therapist facilitates a songwriting experience that enables clients to tell their stories or journeys of loss, recovery, and the like. Their songs become a powerful vehicle for self-expression, with the music adding emotional intensity to the lyrics created. Repetition of lyrics can be powerful in conveying the key messages or feelings being expressed in the songs and help to highlight the core issues being experienced by the person.

The use of music therapy programs in aged care settings is rapidly increasing as the world experiences an aging population crisis. Incidence of dementia is on the rise, and music therapy has been shown to assist in enhancing the quality of life for those living with the disease. Confusion, memory loss, and agitation are visibly reduced when a meaningful music therapy program is used for people living with dementia. As music has the capacity to evoke long-term emotions, popular music from the eras when these people were in their twenties and thirties can be used to access memories of the past. After listening to these "old timers' songs," people living with dementia are more talkative and coherent, recounting happy or painful memories. This evocation of memories (whether happy or painful) illuminates core aspects of the person. Family members experience joy when their loved ones appear lucid, coherent, and connected to reality.

Terminal Illness, Grief, and Loss

Reviewing one's life, resolving intrapersonal and interpersonal (family) conflicts, and dying at peace are often what people with a terminal illness strive to achieve before dying. Musical life review through the creation of a personal playlist of music is one approach music therapists use in the journey toward a peaceful death. As patients select and then listen to meaningful music, they may then discuss its meaning with the therapist within the context of their own lives. This helps patients to create a picture of their lives that captures key moments, incorporates key people, and highlights personal and professional achievements. Similarly, any unresolved intrapersonal issues can be explored through a similar process of listening to music and talking about issues that are the root of patients' anxiety and tension. Through listening, the underlying conflicting issues may become clear or better understood, thereby giving patients an opportunity to explore and resolve them.

Leaving a legacy is also important for some patients with a terminal illness. Songwriting is regularly used to send messages of love and appreciation to significant family and friends. The music therapist is key here, as the terminally ill patients may often become easily fatigued. The music therapist must act as scribe and help the patients create lyrics that adequately express the intended messages. Again, the music is used to create emotional impact and highlight the important messages being communicated. These legacies can play an important role in assisting the family and friends of the deceased to come to terms with their death.

CONCLUSION

Music therapy is a unique allied health profession that draws on the emotional, communicative, cognitive, and physical potentials of music to address a range of health needs. Through the carefully planned and tailored music-based programs, and with the special therapy skills of a music therapist, many people around the world can experience improved health and well-being as a direct consequence of their engagement in music therapy. The acceptance of music therapy as an integral part of health care is growing and with increasing research in the area, it is likely to be more widely used in the future.

References and Further Reading
Baker, F. A. (2015). *Therapeutic Songwriting: Developments in Theory, Methods, and Practice.* London, UK: Palgrave Macmillan.

Baker, F., & Tamplin, J. (2006). *Music Therapy in Neurorehabilitation: A Clinician's Manual.* London, UK: Jessica Kingsley.

DeBacker, J. (2014). *The Music in Music Therapy: Psychodynamic Music Therapy in Europe: Clinical, Theoretical and Research Approaches.* London, UK: Jessica Kingsley.

Humpal, M. (2012). *Early Childhood Music Therapy and Autism Spectrum Disorders: Developing Potential in Young Children and Their Families.* London, UK: Jessica Kingsley.

Silverman, M. (2015). *Music Therapy in Mental Health for Illness Management and Recovery.* Oxford, UK: Oxford University Press.

Wheeler, B. (Ed.). *Music Therapy Handbook.* New York, NY: Guilford.

World Federation of Music Therapy. (2011). *What Is Music Therapy?* http://www.wfmt.info/wfmt-new-home/about-wfmt.

56. Music and Healthy Aging

Jennifer MacRitchie

Healthy aging is a high priority for today's society, considering the rising number of people that can expect to live well beyond their sixties, seventies, and eighties. The World Health Organization (WHO), in its 2015 report on aging and health, stated that "healthy ageing is more than the absence of disease. For most older people, the maintenance of functional ability has the highest importance" (World Health Organization 2015). This does not just refer to physical function ability, that is, being able to move around independently, but notes that older adults also require the ability to be able to build and maintain relationships, grow, learn, make decisions, and, more broadly, contribute to society.

Music is consistently rated by older adults as a highly valued cultural activity. Music is extremely powerful in eliciting memories and emotions. Therein lies a lot of the appeal in its use as an activity that will both promote healthy aging behaviors in later life and stave off various mental and physical declines. When discussing music in a healthy aging context, it is important to acknowledge what type of activity is taking place, and this can often be determined by the amount of participation involved, from listening to background music, to playing a favorite song on an instrument, to improvising completely new musical material. Music encompasses a wide variety of activities and styles. So, what types of benefits can older adults gain from being involved in music, and what are the underlying mechanisms that make this happen?

THE BENEFITS OF A LIFETIME OF MUSIC

We build up a wealth of experience of music over our lifetimes, whether we play a musical instrument or not: nowadays, it is hard not to be exposed to music on a day-to-day basis. However, the benefits of musical experience over a lifetime are often described solely in terms of the benefits of continuing practice on a musical instrument. This is because those who have undertaken intense training on a musical instrument over a number of years show the most striking changes in brain structure and function when compared to nonmusicians.

Playing a musical instrument is an activity that requires the coordination of many different brain processes, from fine motor planning and function (when the player has to plan and execute the movements to press the piano key or bow the violin string) to auditory perception (processing the sound produced from the instrument through the ears). It is hypothesized that it is the involvement of all these areas, the strong links between auditory and motor processes and the fine control required over the timing of these actions over a long period of time, that makes playing a musical instrument such a unique brain-training activity.

When considering whether an activity promotes healthy aging, researchers are often interested in the transfer effects to general domains. That is, they want to understand whether training in this one activity will help with brain processes required in different tasks, that is, not the one that is already being trained.

Music itself is primarily aural; we are mainly focused on the sounds produced and perceived during a music performance. If music training leads to transferable skills in other domains, it is expected that these would arise in other activities that involve listening, such as general speech perception. A major issue for older adults is being able to accurately hear speech, particularly in noisy situations, as hearing losses and declines in brain processing speed in this age group make it an increasingly difficult task. Older adults generally experience a slower brain response when perceiving a speech sound than younger adults. However, older adults who have undergone a period of training in a musical instrument in earlier life now show less of these delays. Changes in brain function that are started in childhood with the help of playing a musical instrument are often retained into adulthood, and this is where these older adults are demonstrating advantages in processing sound.

But why do musicians see benefits in encoding speech? Aniruddh Patel's OPERA hypothesis suggests five conditions that promote brain plasticity in this instance—essentially the ability to learn

1. Overlap—The same brain networks are required to process auditory features that are common across all types of sounds, so some aspects of speech and music are processed in the same way.

2. Precision—The precision of processing required for music is much higher than for speech due to the often detailed nature of music at very short timescales.

3. Emotion—Listeners feel strong and positive emotions while listening to music.

4. Repetition—Music listening tasks are likely to be repeated, particularly due to the positive feelings we experience when we do them.

5. Attention—When listening to music, we are often paying very close attention to the task; this may be because of the level of detail at very small timescales.

These conditions all mention listening to music, not necessarily playing music, and of course someone who spends a lot of time listening to music may show similar benefits. Currently, it is thought that the extra time and attention given to music listening tasks when learning an instrument may be why we see this effect, particularly for those we class as musicians.

Music's effects are not just examined in closely related aural activities; they are also studied on a more general scale, for instance, in the assessment of general cognitive functions such as memory, attention, and brain processing speed. Although music mainly deals with the auditory domain, the combination of skills required in playing an instrument means that there is a large overlap with many other tasks that may not be closely related to listening. This is known as *far transfer*.

In 2011, Hanna-Plady and MacKay asked seventy older adults between the ages of sixty and eighty-three to take part in numerous standardized cognitive tests. At the same time, they registered details of the musical experiences they had accumulated over their lifetimes, such as age of onset and number of years of training. What they found was that adults who had at least ten years of musical experience showed advantages over nonmusicians in the performance of tests measuring word retrieval, executive processing, and nonverbal memory. Interestingly there were no differences in performance considering whether the older adult was still musically active or had ceased training years ago. This suggests that the transfer effects of at least ten years of music training for general cognitive processes last well into adulthood.

The majority of these studies mentioned the use of what is known as a *correlation paradigm*; it is an analysis of older adults at one point in their lifetime that takes into account the years of experience they report (and often the age they started) on a musical instrument. This is a great way of seeing the effects of music training over decades (which is difficult to do for any one research project), but it can be tricky to narrow down the exact relationship between the music training and the outcomes being tested.

What it does do is give researchers an idea of what the effects of music might be in terms of short-term interventions that can be subsequently tested. Short-term interventions involve participants being involved in a music program for a number of weeks (or months). These programs are often either evaluated for benefits on their own or comparatively against other types of intervention or groups of participants. The difference between short-term interventions and evaluations over a lifetime is that, for short-term programs, data can easily be collected before and after, making it easier to try and truly understand what the effects of the music program have been.

MUSIC PROGRAMS AND INTERVENTIONS

So, what about the older adult novice? For those who have not trained on a musical instrument before, all is not lost. The brain is still able to change as a function of experience across the whole of the life span. Research suggests that music may be able to promote healthy aging, even when it is experienced for only a short time, whether it is part of a community music program or a specific musical intervention.

There are many types of music programs on offer for older adults, and musical interventions can involve different levels of professional practice. Although all music can have therapeutic effects, not all music activity is therapy. We can begin to separate out these types of intervention by the level of professional therapeutic input required. For example, a low level of professional therapeutic input could be a community-led choir. Here, there are a lot of good potential side effects of doing the music activity, but the main focus is on creating art and a sense of community in general. An example of a high level of professional input is one-to-one music therapy. Music therapists are registered professionals who draw up a plan of treatment related to the individual's health goals, which may be physical, cognitive, emotional, or social. Musical activities are then chosen to elicit a specific outcome, and progress is checked throughout the program. Of course, there are many types of programs that fall in between these examples, and the wide variety of uses of music and other arts in health and health care practices can be difficult to define.

For healthy older adults, concerns are often focused toward staving off any cognitive or motor declines and to maintain independent living for as long as possible. In these cases, short-term programs of music training, from scat singing and improvisation to traditional piano lessons, have shown some success in terms of increasing aspects of cognitive function, such as verbal fluency and attention. Again, the mechanism behind these far transfer effects is thought to be linked to training executive function. However, it is not just cognitive and physical ability that is of concern. Unfortunately, loneliness, isolation, and depression can also be key features of aging. Here, music classes conducted in groups such as choirs and keyboard classes often aid older adults to build social connections as well as help them to form their own identities through music by being able to express themselves.

In older adulthood, many are already experiencing declines associated with different impairments. In Australia alone, as of 2014, musculoskeletal conditions (including arthritis) affect nearly 1.4 million people over age sixty-five. As of 2017, it is reported that approximately 400,000 Australians are living with cognitive impairments such as dementia. In these cases, music interventions have been examined as an optimal environment for aiding recovery and rehabilitation (where possible) or reducing behavioral symptoms (such as agitation and depression). Currently, the majority of evidence for benefits of music interventions are found for those affected by stroke, or people living with Parkinson's or dementia.

Playing along to a piece of music requires that we play sequences of notes in a particular temporal framework. It is this property of music that improves the motor function of adults as they try to learn a new (or relearn an old) action. For instance, moving along to a simple beat can help stroke patients with reaching actions. Piano playing interventions help stroke patients to retrain their affected hands. In this case, the external rhythm of the beat or the notes being produced may be acting as an external timekeeper for the brain. This is useful in conditions such as Parkinson's, where the internal timekeeping mechanisms in the brain have broken down. Compliance with rehabilitation programs is also aided by the enjoyment and reward experienced when playing a musical instrument. It helps that playing a song is more enjoyable than doing some other repetitive type of exercise.

That memory of music can be somewhat retained in the advancing stages of dementia (in particular in people living with Alzheimer's), and that it elicits strong emotions and memories in participants makes it a useful intervention. Benefits are particularly found in the reduction of anxiety, depression, and agitation that can accompany daily life for a person living with Alzheimer's. Various types of activities have been examined in this case, and participant-selected music listening, music with movement, singing, and music therapy all show these improvements. At this stage, it is difficult to determine whether music has a specific aspect that makes it the optimal activity in this case or whether it listening and singing are just pleasant activities to do. However, there are some effects of musical activities for cognitive functioning in people living with Alzheimer's suggest otherwise, although more randomized control trials are needed to fully explore these effects for those already suffering from severe cognitive impairments.

CONCLUSION

Music has been shown to be a pursuit that can offer a large number of cognitive, motor, social, and emotional benefits for healthy aging. Enjoyment in music is something we can share with others, whether we are talking about our favorite songs, having a singalong with other people, or performing for a family member or friend. Learning to play or to appreciate music is developing a skill, so this also provides an opportunity for intellectual growth and a sense of achievement.

There is evidence to show that the changes in the structure and function of the brain as a result of music training can provide some lifelong benefits that aid with increasingly difficult tasks in older age. However, those just starting to get involved as music novices can also experience benefits. Whether the benefits from music programs and interventions are mainly due to the effect of their involving an incredibly enjoyable activity that encourages attention to the task as well as motivating participants to repeat physical performances and frequently practice or whether there is something more special about music is still to be determined. However, we already see that aspects such as having an external rhythmic structure help in cases where participants are having problems controlling their movements. Some effects of cognitive transfer have been shown in both healthy older adults and those with cognitive impairments, but by no means is this effect robust in the literature.

As the aging population keeps growing and the use of music in health and community for this age group becomes more popular, there are many more questions to be answered and evidence to be gathered. Do music interventions truly work for everyone in the same way regardless of previous music experience? Will there be a difference for future generations now that younger people have had arguably more access to instrumental education and music listening experiences through increasingly accessible technologies? Time will tell how this will change our outlook on music and healthy aging.

References and Further Reading

Altenmüller, E., & Schlaug, G. (2012). Music, brain and health: Exploring biological foundations of music's health effects. In R. MacDonald, G. Kreutz, & L. Mitchell (Eds.), *Music, Health and Wellbeing* (pp. 12–24). Oxford, UK: Oxford University Press.

Baird, A., & Samson, S. (2015). Music and dementia. *Progress in Brain Research, 217*, 207–235.

Creech, A., Hallam, S., McQueen, H., & Varvarigou, M. (2014). *Active Ageing with Music: Supporting Wellbeing in the Third and Fourth Ages*. London, UK: Institute of Education Press.

Fancourt, D. (2017). *Arts in Health: Designing and Researching Interventions*. Oxford, UK: Oxford University Press.

Hanna-Pladdy, B., & MacKay, A. (2011). The relation between instrumental musical activity and cognitive aging. *Neuropsychology, 25*(3), 378–386. https://doi.org/10.1037/a0021895

Patel, A. D. (2011). Why would musical training benefit the neural encoding of speech? The OPERA hypothesis. *Frontiers in Psychology, 2*(142), 1–14. https://doi.org/10.3389/fpsyg.2011.00142

World Health Organization. (2015). *World Report on Ageing and Health*. Geneva: WHO.

Music Education

57. Music in Schools

Susan Hallam

Most young people experience some form of music education while they are at school. This may include a wide range of different activities, including moving to music, singing, playing an instrument, listening, discussing and evaluating music, improvising, composing, acquiring musical knowledge, and understanding national culture. These activities can take place in or out of school, in formal or informal contexts, or through exposure to music in everyday life. The nature of these activities typically differs depending on the age or existing musical experience of the learners.

Music education has a long history. There is evidence of its existence as early as the fifth and sixth centuries BCE, when schools of music were established in Athens, Greece. Young people were taught to play the lyre and kithara and to sing, accompanied by their teacher on the aulos. In the second century, in Italy, Guido Arezzo developed staff notation. This made it easier to learn new music and provided the basis for the sol-fa system. The introduction of printing technology in the nineteenth century further increased access to music making. When education became compulsory in much of the world in the eighteenth and nineteenth centuries, music was included in the curriculum. Typically, the focus was singing. The songs taught were influenced by political ideology, colonialism, and imperialism. As music education became more established, a range of different educational methods were developed. Many of these continue to influence the curriculum today, for instance, the works of Emile Jaques-Dalcroze (1865–1950), Carl Orff (1895–1982), Zoltan Kodaly (1892–1967), and Shin'ichi Suzuki (1898–1998).

Internationally, there are many approaches to music education. Even within countries, different states and other local bodies may define and provide different kinds of music education. The provision of music education is not universal, despite the United Nations Education, Scientific and Cultural Organisation (UNESCO) identifying that an education in the arts is a basic human right.

Much music education takes place outside the normal school curriculum as an extracurricular provision. This can include the withdrawal of pupils from normal school lessons to have instrumental or vocal lessons. More often, it involves participation in a range of activities outside school time. Extracurricular activities can include attendance at a music school, center, conservatory, or the premises of a private provider, where tuition and ensemble opportunities are available in the evenings, on weekends, or during the school holidays. Private studio teachers also provide instrumental and vocal lessons, usually individually, although sometimes in small groups. Technological advances have also opened up opportunities to learn musical skills and participate in a range of musical activities through the media. The family can also be an important provider of music education.

Overall, music education is multifaceted and complex. Learners can develop their musical skills in myriad ways in a range of environments. These may or may not complement each other. The challenge is to ensure that everyone who wishes to develop their musical knowledge and skills has the opportunity to do so.

FORMAL MUSIC EDUCATION IN THE EARLY YEARS

Music making in the early years often depends on parents and what they can provide at home. Recently, however, there has been an increase in the development of formal music education for very young children, including activities for mothers and babies, and provision in nurseries and preschools. Typically, activities include singing, often with movement, and exploration of simple percussion instruments. These support young children's musical and language development.

The human auditory system is functional three to four months before birth, and infants are sensitive to pitch and rhythmic grouping of sounds in similar ways to adults; however, the complex skills required for understanding the tonality of music take time to develop. It is not until about the age of five, depending on previous musical experiences, that children have a stable sense of tonality. Movement to music, particularly when coordinated with a beat, is important because it assists in the development of coordination and the neurological connections that assist in the development of literacy skills.

ELEMENTARY SCHOOL

There is huge variability in the elementary school music curriculum internationally. In some countries, there is a national curriculum that teachers are expected to follow; in others, guidelines are provided nationally, locally, or by professional organizations, and in some places, the onus is on the teacher to develop a suitable curriculum. Usually, there are no national assessment systems to determine what is taught and learned.

Historically, the elementary music curriculum was based on singing. This continues to be the most favored activity, in part because generalist class teachers, who typically teach music, tend to be more comfortable with singing than other activities. Commercially available sources of songs, which often include backing tracks, further support the teacher. The problem with these is that they do not support the teacher in improving the quality of the singing.

Nowadays, there are many similarities in the kinds of activities considered appropriate for the music curriculum in elementary and secondary music education: improvisation, composition, listening, discussing and evaluating music, performing, and knowledge of the historical and cultural roots of music education and its relationship to other arts. Guidance for teachers may also prioritize links with other areas of the curriculum. Types of world music and classical, folk, jazz, and popular music may be included. Offering opportunities to engage with a wide variety of music can support ongoing, lifelong engagement with a range of different musical styles. Being introduced to these early on is particularly important because young children are open-eared and do not have prejudices for or against different types of music.

Listening skills tend to be developed through active music making, although there are sometimes opportunities for attending live concerts and engaging with professional musicians in short-term projects (e.g., a visiting composer). At elementary schools, recorded music is sometimes played when children move around the school and prepare for school assemblies. Developing critical and appraising skills is central to all musical activity and is supported by teachers providing constructive criticism and asking pertinent and challenging questions about what might be improved in relation to improvisation, composition, or performance.

At the elementary level, generalist class teachers tend to lack confidence in introducing improvisation and composition. One possible starting point is through storytelling, with musical sounds illustrating elements of the story. Later, the focus may be a poem or a specific topic, for example, machines or advertising. Typically, the whole class works together. Professional animateurs can visit schools to undertake specific creative projects that last several weeks and involve one or more classes. For such projects to be successful, high levels of partnership are required and the commitment of school staff who maintain interest in the weeks when the animateur is not present.

Knowledge about music, its history, and its relationship to culture and the other arts; identifying instruments and different genres; and world music tend to be taught as specific pieces of music are learned. Where cross-curricula links are made, music usually complements other subjects; for instance, an overarching topic about the environment may be supported by a song about animals. There are materials that introduce elementary school pupils to key classical works, such as the BBC's Ten Pieces. These provide teachers with materials that support filmed performances and provide information about the composer, the historical context, and details of the structure of the music, instrumentation, and so on.

Instrumental tuition as part of the school curriculum is frequently on relatively simple instruments, for instance, tuned and untuned percussion, ukulele, recorder, or ocarina. However, in some places, whole class tuition is provided on a range of band, orchestral, and keyboard instruments. Some of these initiatives have been influenced by El Sistema, a musical social program developed in Venezuela. This program has spread internationally, although there is variation in its implementation. Such programs not only contribute to the development of the children's musical skills but can also enhance their personal and social development.

Music in elementary schools is usually taught by generalist class teachers. This raises issues about the quality of the tuition. There is ongoing debate about whether class music should be taught by generalists or visiting specialist music teachers. One view is that class teachers know the children better, can make links with other areas of the curriculum, and can use success in music to enhance self-esteem. But unless they have adequate musical skills or are supported by a strong music coordinator in the school, the quality of teaching tends to be limited. Music specialists are more consistent in delivering high-quality lessons. Opportunities for generalists to develop their musical skills through attending courses are few, as resources tend to be allocated to what are considered to be more important subjects, such as mathematics, even though short training opportunities can raise skill levels and confidence.

MUSIC IN SECONDARY SCHOOL

What is on offer in secondary school music education varies between schools as well as at local, national, and international levels, although there has recently tended to be a greater emphasis on music making, including improvisation and composition. There are wide differences in the ages at which music is no longer compulsory and becomes optional. Pressures on school budgets and raising performance in other subjects have led to music disappearing from the curriculum in some schools and only being available in a reduced form in others.

During the teenage years, a great deal of time is spent listening to popular music outside school. The movement toward making music education more meaningful and relevant to the everyday lives of young people and giving them greater control over the kinds of music they learn in school has led to moves that include popular music in the curriculum. In Scandinavia, jazz, rock, folk music, and pop were introduced into the curriculum in the 1970s. However, the speed with which new genres of popular music developed made it difficult for teachers to learn and be able to teach them; therefore, the curriculum became outdated very quickly.

Also attempting to bridge the gap between school music and that in everyday life, the Musical Futures approach was developed in the United Kingdom. This advocates the informal learning of music in small groups in the classroom. Popular recordings are copied through learning by ear. As learners become more experienced, they create their own compositions. The adoption of this approach has a positive impact on motivation and enables those who have no prior instrumental skills to develop them and enhance their musical skills. However, it presents considerable challenges for teachers, as they have to manage the activities of multiple small groups at the same time, some of whom may find working productively in this way challenging.

Maintaining a music curriculum that is broad and balanced is frequently problematic for teachers, as they cannot have expertise across all musical genres. Project work delivered by outside arts organizations can motivate young people and address this issue by introducing them to different genres. Such projects require strong partnerships working to ensure that there are ongoing opportunities for those participating to continue developing the skills learned. Cooperation with the other arts in schools can support the development of conceptual understanding and creativity, but there are challenges in ensuring that there is time for basic skills to be acquired in each subject.

At secondary school, there tends to be an increase in musical activity out of school. This may involve instrument or vocal lessons, formal ensemble activities, or informal music making with friends. Participation in ensembles plays a crucial role in the development of musical and social skills, including team working. The Internet also offers myriad musical resources, including performances to emulate, demonstration lessons, opportunities for interactive lessons, and making music with others. There is also an increasing number of electronic sources for learning to read notation, composing music, and supporting musical practice and performance. Whatever the nature of extracurricular activity, parents play a major role in supporting it, ensuring attendance, attending concerts, and supervising individual practice or ensuring that it is undertaken.

In secondary schools, there is a greater focus on the assessment of classroom work, including entry for national examinations, which may contribute to access to ongoing educational opportunities. Alongside this, there are independently organized graded music examinations for those learning to play instruments or having vocal tuition. These examinations provide a means for children, teachers, and parents to establish the extent of progress, ranging from those for beginners to levels required for entry to music programs in conservatories and universities. They have a powerful impact on the instrumental curriculum and determine much of what is taught.

THE CHALLENGES FACING FORMAL MUSIC EDUCATION

The overall quality of music in schools depends on a range of factors, not the least being the quality of the teaching and the extent to which music making is at the core of lessons. High-quality teaching requires senior management in the school to be committed to music and prepared to allocate resources for professional development, networking with colleagues in other schools and internationally, facilitating input from professional artists, and building relationships with others providing music education in the area, particularly those providing instrumental tuition and ensemble opportunities for pupils. Schools also need to provide opportunities for performance to engage parents in supporting their children's musical progress and success.

Although music should be included in the school curriculum as a subject that is appreciated and valued for itself, it has frequently been necessary to justify its place recently. This is not a new phenomenon. Music was initially justified in terms of religion and later as being a humanizing and civilizing force. More recently, its role has been justified in terms of its impact on the intellectual, personal, and social development of children, the way that it can promote creativity and artistic development, and its impact on well-being and happiness, which in turn supports motivation for learning more generally.

CONCLUSION

Internationally, the provision of music education varies enormously, as does the nature of the curriculum offered. While there is much evidence of the wider benefits of making music, not only in the school years but throughout the life course, it continues to be challenging for music to maintain its place in the school curriculum and for adequate resources to be made available to train teachers and support them in ensuring ongoing high-quality tuition.

References and Further Reading

Hallam, S. (2014). *The Power of Music: A Research Synthesis of the Impact of Actively Making Music on the Intellectual, Social and Personal Development of Children and Young People*. London, UK: iMERC.

Hallam, S., & Creech, A. (Eds.). (2010). *Music Education in the 21st Century in the United Kingdom: Achievements, Analysis and Aspirations*. London, UK: Institute of Education, University of London.

Lamont, A. (2016). Musical development from the early years onwards. In S. Hallam, I. Cross, & M. Thaut (Eds.), *Oxford Handbook of Music Psychology* (2nd ed., pp. 399–414). Oxford, UK: Oxford University Press.

McPherson, G., & Welch, G. (Eds.). (2012). *Oxford Handbook of Music Education*. Oxford, UK: Oxford University Press.

58. Music Learning across the Life Span

David E. Myers

A familiar saying in some folklore traditions states, "You can't teach an old dog new tricks." This can be taken to mean that it is difficult to change long-standing ways of doing things; or, it can be interpreted to mean that the older someone is, the harder it is for that person to learn something new. Realistically speaking, some aspects of learning, or acquiring new knowledge and skill, may become more challenging for some people as they get older. But this does not mean that they cannot successfully learn, regardless of their age. It only means that people may learn differently at different times of their lives. In fact, most people of any age who want to learn something new have to accommodate personal traits or characteristics that may make it difficult for them to learn. Perhaps they have a physical impediment, or numbers are hard for them to grasp, or they lack certain background knowledge, or they may have a learning disability. Everyone, at any age, experiences some learning that is more difficult and some that comes more easily.

Because music learning is complex, involving the senses, the mind, and the body, adults sometimes think they cannot be successful with music if they did not begin study at a young age. That may be true if one has a desire to become a professional musician. However, for most people who primarily want to make and understand music for pleasure or as a hobby, even at strong levels of proficiency, music learning can begin or continue at any age. Developing music knowledge and skill can be a source of joy and fulfillment from infancy through older adulthood.

AGING AND LEARNING

From the moment of birth, everyone is getting older; that is, they are *aging*. Chronological age is marked both by one's date of birth and the number of years one has been alive. Life cycle refers to the patterns that humans follow as they age, moving through infancy, childhood, adolescence, young adulthood, middle adulthood, and older adulthood. During childhood through young adulthood, the primary task people face is to learn as much as they can to lead fulfilling and successful lives. As their brains develop, they take in enormous amounts of knowledge—from learning to walk and talk, to learning to solve problems, to learning specific knowledge and skills for jobs and careers. Prior to about the last thirty years, scientists believed that after young adulthood, the brain did not continue to develop, and people primarily built on what they had learned earlier, even if they studied something new or acquired some new skills. In fact, it was commonly believed that learning something new was primarily a way of holding off the inevitable decline of mental abilities with increasing age.

More recently, however, it has become clear that learning at any age can positively affect the structure of the brain and that the act of learning new information or skills may be an important part of remaining vital throughout one's entire life span. In other words, learning throughout life is not just about avoiding declines in mental abilities (sometimes called "use it or lose it") but continuing to grow and develop, to learn completely new things, and even to increase mental functioning in adulthood. Scientists who study the brain and learning now refer to "changes" that may be associated with chronological age rather than "declines" assumed to inevitably accompany increasing age.

Music has always been a part of educating children and adolescents, whether formally in schools, in teacher-apprentice contexts (individual music lessons with a teacher), or in less formal ways, such as community gatherings, family activities, religious activities, and recreational experiences. As with all fields of study, some students become professionals in the field of music. However, for the vast majority of people, music learning is something that enriches their lives, serves as a means of transmitting and sharing important rituals and cultural traditions, and provides understanding of how life's deepest feelings can sometimes be expressed better through music than through language.

Although many adults continue to *participate* in music, this participation has often been attributed to their having learned to sing or play an instrument at an earlier age. Many other adults who for some reason did not gain music knowledge and skill as young people have thought that they are "too old" to take up music. What is known from research today is that music *learning* can begin at any age and that people can be successful music learners as middle-aged and older adults.

A big difference between youth and adult learners is that adults may need more time to acquire new knowledge, and older adults may need more time than younger adults. Scientists used to believe this was partly because mental ability was decreasing as people grew older. Now, however, there is evidence that as people age, they are dealing with more and more information, and there are complex relationships among different types of information that are organized in the brain. Thus, new learning has to be integrated into the large vault of accumulated knowledge adults have acquired, and thus it takes more time to fully incorporate new learning into previous knowledge. The longer one lives, the more knowledge is stored, and the longer it may take to process new knowledge. It is also true, however, that older adults' mental and physical capacities may slow down, which only means that they take more time to learn something new, not that they are unable to learn new things. Adults use *accommodations* to compensate for these changes, such as eyeglasses, hearing aids, better lighting, larger print, exercise, and other strategies.

MUSIC LEARNING AND THE LIFE COURSE

In infancy, all learning is imitative. Parents smile, coo, and sing to their babies, and the babies respond in kind. Singing games provide a way for children to practice using vocal pitches, clapping in time with music, and creating movements. In early childhood, simple instruments are introduced—such as rhythm sticks, xylophones, and recorders—and children may create instruments or use household items such as pots and pans to accompany singing and movement. Learning to "feel" music is very important, and depending on the society and culture, recordings or other live music experiences invite children to learn names of instruments and actively participate.

By age five, or even earlier, music notation may be introduced, and children will be encouraged to connect the sounds they make with the signs and symbols on the printed page. They will begin learning names of notes and note values. Ultimately, the process will be reversed, and children will interpret the signs and symbols as an avenue for making music. Some children will take private music lessons with a teacher, where they begin to excel in individual ways. They may join orchestras, choirs, bands, folk groups, rock groups, or other ensembles in which they make music with others. Ultimately, some will choose to become professional musicians, performing, composing, or teaching based on extensive learning they have acquired in universities or conservatories.

Music learning, like all learning, can be pictured as a spiral in which experiences lead to understanding that leads to further experiences and greater understanding. Sometimes, when considered from the teacher's perspective, this may be called *scaffolding*, which means that the teacher provides experiences to promote understanding that leads to the next level of experience and understanding. Over and over, the cycle repeats as the learner develops more and more capacity in the subject matter.

The spiral of music learning is similar no matter how young or old the learner may be. This is based on the fact that music begins as organized sound. The learner hears and responds to the music, participates in making music, and then seeks to understand why the music sounds the way it does. The teacher, who nurtures skill development and understanding, guides experiences and responds to the learner's desire (or need) to know, that is, to understand how the music works. As the learner is ready for new concepts, terms, and performance tasks, the teacher introduces them in ways that challenge the learner but are also within the student's abilities to be successful.

Whether an infant or elder, an amateur or a professional, a college student or a midcareer accountant, learning music essentially follows the same spiral from musical sound, to active music engagement, to understanding. In reality, all are occurring simultaneously rather than separately, but the sound and engagement may initially be mere actions that are later enlightened by understanding.

As an example, the familiar childhood song "Twinkle, Twinkle, Little Star" is often learned at home or in preschool. At first, the child simply imitates the teacher (or whomever is singing), echoing the tune and the words. Soon, the child can sing the entire song alone or with others, at which time movements may be added.

These movements may relate to the text (the words) or to the higher and lower succession of the pitches in the melody. Movements might be added to show the phrases of the song. The teacher may introduce the notation of the song, pointing out that some pitches are vertically far apart on the music staff and others are closer together. The child begins to apply the terms *step* and *leap* to the pitch differences. As children develop more understanding of the pitches, the phrases, and the rhythms, their singing of the song improves, and they are then able to apply this knowledge to new songs.

If the new music learner is sixty instead of preschool age, the spiral is the same, but the material is designed to suit the maturity and life experience of the student. Even if such a learner has no prior formal music education, it is virtually certain that he or she has been exposed to far more music than a preschool child. The teacher might ask the student to name a familiar song or choose a commonly known folk or popular song. After listening, the student would be engaged in singing the song. The teacher would call attention to the same basic concepts explored with preschool children but would use activities more appropriate to adults. Ultimately, the sound-participation-understanding cycle would be repeated, and both the student's understanding and performance would improve.

A LIFE SPAN VIEW OF MUSIC LEARNING

For many years, the field of music education, which deals with issues of learning and teaching music, focused almost all of its attention on the education of children and youth. Those who became professional teachers of music by studying at advanced levels in colleges and universities believed that if children were given systematic music instruction early in life, they would become lifelong participants in music. The basic idea was that teaching children and youth would lead them to appreciate and value music, attend concerts, and support professional musicians and music organizations in their communities.

In recent decades, music educators have developed a broader perspective that views learning music as something that can occur over an entire lifetime or that may begin at any time during life. For a variety of reasons, some children may not have music learning opportunities in schools and communities and may only as adults discover that they want to know more about music. Some adults may have had music instruction as children but were not interested at the time and have now become interested in understanding and performing music. Some parents may have discovered their own desires to learn music through the classes and lessons their children are taking. Some people who learned to perform music when they were younger may decide as an adult that they would like to compose music and need to know more about it. Some professional musicians may feel they need to reach a higher level of performance proficiency.

In other words, there are many reasons why adults may wish to begin or continue music learning, which means there need to be teachers who know how to teach adult learners. Even though the spiral of music learning is the same, adults of differing ages still need specific kinds of teaching that match their needs and interests. If a group of elders want to learn to compose music, they cannot be treated the same as a group of ten-year-olds who are learning to compose music.

Perhaps the most important aspect of adults' wanting to learn music is that they have many years of life experience that children do not have. They may have college degrees, a lot of experience in a profession, knowledge of how to raise children, and a strong ability to solve challenging problems. They may also be highly motivated and are choosing to study music rather than being required to do so by their schools or parents. However, they may also worry that because they did not study music when they were young they will not be successful. They may be fearful of not doing well. The teacher who works with adults must understand all of these things to be effective and help students meet their goals.

CONCLUSION

As older adults retire and seek interesting ways to spend their time, many choose to study music for the first time or to renew music study that they began when they were younger. Some research has shown important health benefits for older adults when they study music. Older adults also report that they enjoy the social aspects of making music together. One organization, the New Horizons International Music Association, has several thousand members from across the globe who play music in their communities and gather for festivals around the world. Unlike many organizations that largely focus on participation, New Horizons is an educational organization for both beginners and experienced performers.

There are also many community music schools around the world that provide opportunities to begin or continue music studies from infancy through adulthood. There are orchestras made up of doctors and nurses, choirs made up of the employees of various companies, and music ensembles for individuals who have Alzheimer's or other debilitating illnesses. All of these experiences involve learning music, and some of them include creating and composing music as well.

In some communities, organizations made up of different generations of students come together to make music. For example, a high school choir and a group of singers from an elder care center may present a joint concert. Or a school band and members of the community who play band instruments may join together to practice and perform. Although there are many good reasons to begin music studies in childhood, music study can begin at any time during one's life and bring great joy and fulfillment at any age.

References and Further Reading
Green, L. (2016). *How Popular Musicians Learn: A Way Ahead for Music Education.* Farnham, UK: Ashgate.

Judy, S. (1990). *Making Music for the Joy of It.* New York, NY: Penguin Putnam.

Myers, D. E. (2012). Including adulthood in music education perspectives and policy: A lifespan view. In P. K. Schmidt & C. Benedict (Eds.), *The Place of Music in the 21st Century: A Global View* (pp. 74–92). New York, NY: Teachers College of Columbia University and National Society for the Study of Education.

Myers, D. E., Bowles, C. L., & Dabback, W. (2012). Music learning as a lifespan endeavor. In K. Veblen (Ed.), *Community Music Today* (pp. 133–150). Lanham, MD: Rowman & Littlefield.

59. Music in the Community

Dylan van der Schyff and Marissa Silverman

Modern society offers a range of possibilities for people to engage in musical practice. These include music education programs in primary and secondary schools; specialized training in performance, theory, musicology, and composition at universities and conservatoires; and professional ensembles such as symphony orchestras. But people also create opportunities for music making outside of these formal institutional environments. In such contexts, musical activities are guided less by predetermined curricular requirements—or the demands of professional training and repertoire—and more by the interests of the participants and the characteristics of the local communities they share. This chapter introduces a variety of forms such community-based music making can take. In the process, you will learn about some areas of research in community music, what community music means for the people who participate in it, and what it offers for broader issues related to cultural identity, social justice, and sustainability.

COMMUNITY MUSIC: WHAT IS IT?

There is a sense in which all music can be thought of as community music. Music is, after all, a highly social activity requiring cooperation and a range of shared social and cultural understandings. And indeed, music making of all kinds, in configurations large and small—such as orchestra, rock bands, taiko drumming groups, and formal music education programs—all involve people working together. Those people all live in neighborhoods, towns, and cities that support and benefit from such activities. Researchers who study community music want to know more about the various forms it takes and what it means for the lives of the people who participate in it. Because of this, they have developed various ways of looking at the subject that can help us obtain a more detailed sense of what is involved.

For example, Lee Higgins (2012) suggests three main areas for research in community music. These involve (1) exploring the types of musical activity that characterize a particular community more generally, (2) examining how music is created communally between specific members of a given group, and (3) studying the ways community music programs are designed to foster positive forms of social engagement. The first of these areas is referred to by Higgins as the "music of a community." Here, one might think of the different musical environments created at an electronic dance music (EDM) event in Montreal, an outdoor performance of traditional folk music in Prague, or a church service in Alabama and the kinds of shared experiences and collective meanings such events have for the people who participate in them as performers and listeners. In line with this, the music of a community explores the significance of collective music making for a given culture or group of people. It involves the roles of both formal and informal types of learning and practice, and it examines the various functions music serves for the community as a whole. Put simply, the music of a community refers to the kinds of musical practices, styles, and genres that are associated with a given group and how the tapestry of musical activity contributes to the broader social and cultural identity.

Consider, for instance, the many ways in which drumming groups in Kopeyia, Ghana, contribute to a shared understanding of the peoples, places, beliefs, and histories of the society in which that music making happens. Consider, too, how this music of a community helps to strengthen social and cultural belonging among the people who participate in it, both as performers and listeners. To take some other examples, one might think of the musical communities associated with rap, metal, country, blues, punk, house, and jazz. In each case, the music making is deeply connected with a shared sense of identity, which can also be reflected in the ways people speak and dress and how they see themselves in relation to other social groups.

The second area of community music research mentioned above involves studying the activity of *communal music making*. Here, the level of inquiry shifts from the broader cultural concerns associated with music of a community to the more intimate level of musicians interacting in specific contexts. Consider again the example of Ghanaian drumming. The relationships between master drummer, supporting drummers, dancers, and various others involve bodily, sonic, emotional, spiritual, and other forms of social and musical communication. The ways these aspects play out may differ in performances, from group to group, and from person to person.

The unique character of specific groups and events within broader musical communities can also be examined in other contexts. Think, for example, about the variety of approaches to rap that emerged in Los Angeles in the 1980s and 1990s, or the house music of Chicago that emerged in the same period, or the many current instantiations of metal music around the world. Each of these communities are established by individuals and groups that share common experiences and ideals but who also express many differences in how they create and think about their music. Moreover, it is these differences within musical communities that keep them creatively vital. Accordingly, the theme of communal music making asks the researcher to examine the various ways specific members of a community go about making the music they do, how they interact with each other and collaborate, and what this means for their lives.

The third area of research involves exploring the ways communal music making programs are designed to serve as forms of active social intervention. It is these types of musical environments that many researchers refer to when they use the term *community music*. One of the main features that distinguishes this kind of community music is that it involves forms of musical learning and community building that are intentionally situated outside of music schools and conservatories. This is because it is thought that the kinds of musical practice and learning that occur in these institutional environments often reflect too strongly the musical ideals and practices of the dominant culture. As such, they tend to ignore cultural diversity and the needs of marginalized groups. In response to these concerns, community music organizations, programs, and facilitators offer opportunities for collective music making built on principles of hospitality, inclusivity, and respect for difference, where people of various backgrounds and abilities can come together and participate in the creation of a musical community.

Community music programs are guided by highly skilled facilitators who aim to foster creativity and collaboration among participants, where personal and social growth is as important as musical development. Ideally, the musical activities of these groups are not meant to adhere to some pregiven model but, rather, reflect the goals and backgrounds of the people who constitute them. As such, community music remains open to a range of musical and cultural perspectives— the music of a community and forms of communal music making mentioned above. However, as these programs often comprise people of various ages and cultural backgrounds, participants are encouraged to collectively develop their own approaches to music making. As a result, improvisation, exploration, experimentation, collaboration, and shared self-assessments play important roles in community music programs.

HISTORY AND USES OF COMMUNITY MUSIC PROGRAMS

Precursors to the kinds of community music programs just mentioned can be traced back to the early twentieth century. However, community music as a critical form of social intervention really only began in the 1960s and early 1970s in the United Kingdom, North America, and Australia as part of the broader *community arts movement*. This movement reflected the growing counterculture environment of the time, which developed alternatives to polarizing distinctions between "high/serious" and "low/vernacular" art. In doing so, it encouraged creative learning and social engagement through the arts that took the experiences, needs, and goals of participants seriously as guiding elements of practice. Today, community music programs can be found across the globe, with organizations such as the International Society for Music Education (ISME) offering important international forums (journals and conferences) where facilitators and participants can share experiences, ideas, and research. This has revealed a range of important applications for community music.

For example, programs have emerged that support intergenerational activities, where participants of various ages collaborate and learn from each other. This upsets the traditional adult-as-teacher/child-as-learner dynamic, affording environments where participants can act as both teachers and learners who engage in reciprocal acts of giving and receiving. Good examples of this can be found in the work of Canadian researchers and facilitators Carol Benyon and Chris Alfano. Benyon and Alfano have developed programs in which youth and senior citizens come together to sing and learn to play instruments. Documentation of these programs has shown that, in addition to musical learning, a deeper appreciation and understanding emerged across generational groups who participated. This helped to break down stereotypes and foster mutual forms of respect and support between participants. Similarly, across Canada and the United States, the New Horizons Bands—whose motto is "Music for life!"—offer similar types of intergenerational music-making opportunities.

Community music also serves an important role for socially marginalized groups and individuals. For instance, the Meet4Music program (M4M) in Graz, Austria, provides a safe environment where participants engage in weekly sessions involving musical and dance improvisation. The sessions are open to everyone in the community. However, a special effort is made to include recent immigrants and refugees. Research has shown that the open-ended and improvisational nature of this program provides a way for established participants and newcomers to interact, develop physical forms of communicating, and thereby build trust and friendships even when spoken language is difficult or impossible. These observations demonstrate the important role community music can play in fostering an openness to difference and for initiating new shared cultural understandings.

Similarly, community music programs have emerged in the context of music therapy (sometimes called *community music therapy*), where the healing effects of music are being developed in conjunction with the social benefits offered by communal music making. As with M4M, these programs encourage participants to express their own cultural experience and to make music creatively and collaboratively. This fosters a greater sense of identity, personal agency, and belonging whereby people can think of themselves as more than just patients. Promising outcomes for physical, mental, and social well-being are being shown in a range of clinical contexts.

Important projects have also been initiated to serve at-risk children and youth offenders, such as Youth Music in the United Kingdom and Musical Connections in New York City. These projects offer opportunities for participants to engage in activities that provide healthy diversions from harmful activities and promote self-worth and social integration. Related projects involve work with prison inmates, such as Mary Cohen's work with the Oakdale Prison Community Choir in Iowa. Likewise, the Dallas Street Choir (Dallas, Texas), facilitated by Jonathan Palant, invites homeless people to participate. These programs aim to promote personal transformations and positive social exchanges.

Additionally, because community music often involves the activities of specific groups of people in specific locations, it can also play a role in preserving indigenous forms of music making. Accordingly, a range of programs now exist that aim to both protect and extend traditional practices by sharing them with the broader community. For example, students at Queensland Conservatorium at Griffith University in Australia partner with indigenous musicians to develop collaborative performance opportunities. Such events are intended to foster positive forms of discussion and cross-cultural understanding. Similarly, an international research project called Sustainable Futures for Music Cultures investigated and compared conditions in nine musical cultures. In doing so, it explored the relationship between music and other aspects of these communities with the aim of developing strategies for ensuring the long-term preservation of cultural heritage.

CONCLUSION

This chapter has introduced some important aspects of what community music can entail. We have touched on its implications for positive social and personal transformation, social justice and sustainability, and human well-being more generally. There is, of course, much more to explore, and many new possibilities for community music are appearing on the horizon. The emergence of digital technology and the Internet means that musical communities can now be located online, with participants collaborating across the globe.

Additionally, community music is emerging as a field of study in academia, where a range of research projects have been initiated. Likewise, courses of study are becoming available, where aspiring researchers and practitioners can gain valuable practical experience and theoretical knowledge. For example, the Master of Arts in Community Music at the Irish World Academy at the University of Limerick (Limerick, Ireland) is both a theoretical and practical degree program. Here, students learn about various kinds of community music. They also participate in projects that engage members of the surrounding communities. These projects involve leading orchestras as well as initiating musical activities in hospitals, community centers, and more.

Lastly, it is possible that the introduction of community music into the academic sphere may help open a wider range of possibilities for formal music education programs, leading to a greater appreciation of the meaning of improvisation, creativity, collaboration, and other cultural perspectives for musical learning.

References and Further Reading

Bartlett, B. L., & Higgins, L. (2018). *The Oxford Handbook of Community Music*. New York, NY: Oxford University Press.

Higgins, L. (2012). *Community Music in Theory and Practice*. New York, NY: Oxford University Press.

Higgins, L., & Willingham, L. (2017). *Engaging in Community Music: An Introduction*. London, UK: Routledge.

Veblen, K. K., Messenger, S. J., Silverman, M., & Elliott, D. J. (2013). *Community Music Today*. Lanham, MD: Rowman & Littlefield.

60. Media and Technology in Music Education

Evangelos Himonides and William Forde Thompson

Listening to live "unplugged" music is enjoyable, but most of the time, the music that we listen to involves a lot of modern technology. Technology is used for amplifying instruments, for recording the musicians in a studio, for mixing tracks at the music production stage, for laying down the final polished "audio-master" track, and for delivering the music to our ears, whether through radio, television, or a digital audio device such as a smartphone. In contemporary society, a full understanding of music requires knowledge of the entire process by which music is produced, which includes all the technologies required to produce and deliver that music.

What counts as technology? Is technology limited to computer technology and studio gear? Not at all. In fact, anything that is created by humans and supports musical behaviors can be considered a technology. Every musical instrument is an example of technology. A piano is a type of technology for producing musical sounds, as is a flute or an acoustic guitar. The car that we use to drive to a concert is a technology that supports our music experience. Even the clothes that musicians wear while performing music and the rooms that they perform in can be considered technologies that support musical behavior. Technology is everywhere, and we need to adopt a much broader understanding of technology than what we usually learn in school. An appreciation of all forms of technologies that support musical behaviors can not only help us to understand our experiences of music but also to anticipate educational challenges, including the challenge of preparing young people for jobs or careers in music that have yet to become defined.

TECHNOLOGY IS UBIQUITOUS

Aside from singing in the nude in the woods, every musical activity that we engage in involves some form of technology. Even at the very early times of human evolution, our ancestors used technological "solutions" for our music making. For example, the oldest flute that archaeologists have found dates back approximately forty thousand years (the Aurignacian period flute). It is fair to assume that simpler technologies, such as sticks and other improvised percussion instruments, were used by ancestral musicians much earlier, perhaps as early as the very beginnings of our (and parent or cousin) species.

Given the large number of skills needed to become a musician and the fact that there are many possible paths to succeed as a musician, music educators are faced with the challenge of how to maximize career opportunities for their students. Learning about advanced harmony and counterpoint is important, but to get a job as a musician, students need more. For almost every musical profession, learning about technology is crucial for developing the musical knowledge and skills that are needed to become a professional musician. Understanding technology is important at any age and point along our musical journeys, regardless of our abilities, disabilities, cultural backgrounds, or socioeconomic status.

Photo 60.1　Two Young Girls in the Studio Exploring a Digital Vocoder and Desktop Looping Machine Together. (Photo by Evangelos Himonides. Used by permission.)

INTEGRATING TECHNOLOGY INTO MUSIC EDUCATION

One does not need to spend too much time browsing through music education–related materials (e.g., course outlines, textbooks, policy, curricula) to see that technology is usually present in one form or another. Many young children have been brought up with technology and feel comfortable using it, like the children shown in photo 60.1. Technology is also incorporated into classroom teaching of music, as shown in photo 60.2. Unfortunately, technology is often taught in disappointingly noncreative, superficial, and sterile ways. It is often presented as though it were detached from musical experience (listening, developing, learning, practicing, communicating) and as a technical addition to the curriculum in which students might learn about particular pieces of music software or hardware. This approach tends to discourage students from appreciating the fundamental role of technology in experiencing music and explains why many talented students prefer to identify as "nontechy, traditional musicians" who avoid areas that they perceive as "too technological."

But is this possible? Technology is everywhere, so it would be naive to believe that we are ever detached from technology. There are many tools that any musician or music student might use on a daily basis, such as a mirror, a piece of paper, a metronome, a tuning fork, and a piano. We take such "technologies" for granted, but if we consider that we have been making music from the beginning of our journey as a species, they are almost as modern as any software or hardware available. From the perspective of our evolutionary history, the wristwatch is a very modern invention, and one that is already being superseded by other technologies for keeping time. In other words, we are almost always engaging with technology in one form or another, and technologies are continuously being invented, refined, and replaced with something better.

Photo 60.2 A Group Keyboard Pedagogy Class at the University College London Institute of Education. (Photo by Evangelos Himonides. Used by permission.)

Why is it important to acknowledge the fundamental role of technology in our lives? Because our attitude toward technology will determine the level of our success in using technology effectively and whether we experience it meaningfully or not. It also defines our engagement (or disengagement) and our affection (or disaffection) about it. The good news is that young generations of students and learners are gradually becoming more acquainted with the role of science and technology in musical practice. It is important to take advantage of this momentum so that technology becomes accessible to all and less foreign to those who have not been introduced to its rich potential.

What are some ways that technology can be integrated into music learning? As one example, research has been done to evaluate the usefulness of real-time (moment-to-moment) visual feedback technology within a singing studio. The participants in the study were based in different singing studios in England and consisted of participants whose expertise in singing ranged from skilled amateur to advanced professional. The singers had access to visual representations of their singing, including a display of the frequency (pitch) contour of their voice, which reflects the sequence of notes being sung, and a display of spectral energy, which gives an idea of the timbre (overall sound) of the voice. The presence of this additional technology was found to positively affect the learning process. The feedback was valuable for both the singers and for their teachers, enriching the meaningful feedback that could be given.

TEN CORE USES OF MUSIC TECHNOLOGIES

How should educators and students understand the role of technology in music education? In what contexts are technologies most useful to us? Below, we identify ten different ways that technologies can be used in music education.

1. *Anything that helps us become a better musician:* Any tools that can be used for the development of specific musical skills must be considered technologies. Such tools may include aural training methods, books, and websites as well as encyclopedic materials and multimedia resources.

2. *Anything that helps us understand music and/or the wider impact that music has on our lives and ongoing development:* Within social networking platforms and online content sharing platforms, people often focus on the power of music. There are countless emotional accounts of the impact of music in everyday life, and such accounts may differ depending on social context, age group, and religious or political background. Such technology-supported accounts educate us about the power of music and develop our awareness of musical contexts that are outside of our own personal experiences.

3. *Anything that allows us to record, capture, experience, study, create, compose, document, analyse, and archive sound and music:* In contemplating these outcomes, most of us think of technologies such as notation software, sequencing software, and digital audio workstations (DAWs). However, we need to adopt an even broader definition of technology that includes any type of tool that people can use for these pragmatic purposes. Individual musicians

should be free to exploit whichever aspect of technology is suitable to their personal needs.

4. *Anything that enhances the teaching and learning experience in the music classroom:* Can an interactive whiteboard or a USB pen drive be "music technology"? Absolutely! When used effectively, they become crucial parts of a meaningful learning experience. Music technology is not necessarily something that requires a MIDI keyboard or a loop player.

5. *Anything that provides wider access to other people's music:* A fundamental characteristic of any meaningful educational and learning experience is *polyphony*, but in this context not *musical polyphony* but rather a varied, colorful, rich, and pluralistic sound (i.e., *polyphonic*) input. Any good musician will consider multiple sources of sound input, just as theologians study multiple religions, artists learn to appreciate many different art movements, and literary critics and writers consider the contributions of authors from different countries and eras. Media technology allows us to experience other people's music easily and effectively, and these experiences directly contribute to our musical understanding.

6. *Anything that allows us to experience music in new ways:* Before the invention of the gramophone and phonograph around the turn of the 1900s, there was no way to record music, so it was always experienced as a live performance. Technology now allows us to experience music in a plethora of ways, from a personal intimate experience while wearing headphones to a widely shared experience on a social media platform, and even as part of a virtual reality (VR) game. Technology continuously expands and enriches our experiences of music.

7. *Anything the allows people with special needs or disabilities to access music:* One of the most important uses of technology is to bring music to all people, regardless of ability. Not everyone has the fine and gross motor skills to play a violin or piano, but everyone can use technology to access, experience, and create music. Music technologies can be used for pleasure, rehabilitation, health, and well-being. New music programs (which are technologies) are dramatically changing and enhancing the lives of people with disabilities and supporting the development of children and young adults with learning difficulties.

8. *Anything that helps us monitor and assess teaching practice in the music classroom:* Education is most effective and meaningful when it has a meaningful and tangible impact on people's development. Educational assessments help us to understand the impact of education, whether through e-portfolios, digital assessment methods, classroom observation technologies, or analysis engines. Access to big data allows us to test different assessment strategies effectively across vast populations.

9. *Anything that allows us to monitor and assess students' learning experiences:* Over the last century, educational research has provided strong evidence that not all students learn in the same way; some students learn effectively and efficiently, but others do not. Technology offers immense potential in allowing

customized, student-specific educational experiences so that each student can receive an education that is optimally suited to their specific needs, aspirations, and passions.

10. *Anything that allows us to research, scrutinize, assess, and evaluate educational theories (and their application to practice) and allows us to develop new theory, practice, and policy for music education:* This last use of technology incorporates all previous uses together such that researchers and educators can continue to refine the applications of technology in music education. Educators can develop theories that suggest the development of new tools for learning, new methods to evaluate learning, and new ways to celebrate music. Examples of such technologies include online forums that advocate the importance of music education, archives that preserve the musical heritage and culture of indigenous populations, collaborative platforms, showcasing skills and new forms of performance, compositional tools, and novel musical instruments.

CONCLUSION

Technology and music are richly intertwined, and their interaction is fundamental to musical experiences. As new technologies become available, creative new musical practices come to life and are applied in creative ways. It is important to be open-minded about the nature of technology and what we can do with it. After all, technology is a fundamental part of being human as much as music is a fundamental part of humanity. We are not trapped or limited by technology. Instead, we should celebrate the freedom that technology can offer us and the creative and exciting opportunities that it affords. Anyone who aspires to develop as a musician should be given the opportunity to do so, whether they are prodigies, typical adolescents, or have a mental or physical disability. Technology can provide opportunities for all people to become the musicians that they want to be, so we should all embrace and celebrate the many technologies in our lives and develop them further.

References and Further Reading

Himonides, E. (2012). The misunderstanding of music-technology-education: A meta-perspective. In G. McPherson & G. F. Welch (Eds.), *The Oxford Handbook of Music Education* (Vol. 2, pp. 433–456). New York, NY: Oxford University Press.

Himonides, E. (2017). Narcissism, romanticism, and technology. In S. A. Ruthmann & R. Mantie (Eds.), *The Oxford Handbook of Technology and Music Education* (Vol. 1, pp. 489–494). New York, NY: Oxford University Press. https://doi.org/10.1093/oxfordhb/9780199372133.013.46

Himonides, E., & Purves, R. (2010). The role of technology. In S. Hallam & A. Creech (Eds.), *Music Education in the 21st Century in the United Kingdom: Achievements, Analysis and Aspirations* (pp. 123–140). London, UK: Institute of Education.

King, A., & Himonides, E. S. (2017). *Music, Technology, and Education: Critical Perspectives*. New York, NY: Routledge.

King, A., Himonides, E., & Ruthmann, A. (Eds.). (2017). *The Routledge Companion to Music, Technology, and Education*. New York, NY: Routledge.

About the Editors and Contributors

EDITORS

WILLIAM FORDE THOMPSON, PhD, is a distinguished professor in the Department of Psychology at Macquarie University in Sydney, Australia, and director of the Music, Sound, and Performance Research Group. He is author of *Music, Thought, and Feeling: Understanding the Psychology of Music* (2nd edition, 2014), and general editor of *Music in the Social and Behavioral Sciences: An Encyclopedia* (2014).

KIRK N. OLSEN, PhD, is a postdoctoral researcher and lecturer in the Department of Psychology at Macquarie University, Sydney, Australia, where he is also the research manager of the Centre for Elite Performance, Expertise, and Training and the Music, Sound, and Performance Research Group. His research interests include auditory perception and cognition, musical expertise, and the psychosocial impact of violence in music.

CONTRIBUTORS

FREYA BAILES, PhD, is an associate professor in music psychology at the School of Music, University of Leeds, United Kingdom. In addition to her research interests in musical imagery, music and memory, and cognitive and social processes in performance, Freya is a codirector of the Music for Healthy Lives Research & Practice Network. She is also the program leader of the masters, postgraduate diploma, and postgraduate certificate in music and well-being.

AMEE BAIRD, PhD, is a clinical neuropsychologist who has worked in clinical and research positions in London, Paris, and currently in Australia. She was awarded an Australian government Dementia Research Development Fellowship to investigate the relationship between music, memory, and the self in people with dementia, and is coeditor of the book *Music and Dementia: From Cognition to Therapy* (2019).

FELICITY A. BAKER, PhD, is a professor of music therapy at the Melbourne Conservatorium of Music, University of Melbourne. She is a former ARC future fellow and president of the Australian Music Therapy Association. Her main interests are in the area of songwriting as a therapeutic tool across the life span.

TONYA R. BERGESON, PhD, is an associate professor and chair of the Communication Sciences and Disorders program at Butler University in Indianapolis, Indiana, and a volunteer associate professor in the Department of Otolaryngology at the Indiana University School of Medicine. She is also cofounder of the Urban Chalkboard play cafe and learning studios in Carmel, Indiana. Her research interests involve focus on the effects of early auditory experience on speech, language, and music development in infants and children with hearing impairment.

JEANETTE BICKNELL, PhD, is an independent scholar based in Toronto, Canada. Her main areas of research are the philosophy of music and the philosophy of art. She is the author of *Why Music Moves Us* (2009); *Philosophy of Song and Singing: An Introduction* (2015); and numerous articles in philosophical journals.

MARY BROUGHTON, PhD, is a psychology of music lecturer in the School of Music at the University of Queensland. Her research focuses on embodied cognition, investigating the role of the body in music performance production, perception, and communication. She is a reviewer for many peer-reviewed journals in the fields of music and psychology, such as *Music Perception* and *Frontiers in Psychology*.

KAREN BURLAND, PhD, is a professor of applied music psychology and the head of the School of Music at the University of Leeds, in the United Kingdom. She has research interests in musical identities and their role in musical participation in a variety of contexts. Her book *Coughing and Clapping: Investigating Audience Experience*, edited with Stephanie Pitts, was published in December 2014.

ANNE CACLIN, PhD, is a researcher in the Lyon Neuroscience Research Center in Lyon, France. Her research focuses on auditory cognition and its disorders at the behavioral and cerebral levels.

ALEX CHILVERS, PhD, is an Australian music composer, researcher, and educator based at the Sydney Conservatorium of Music, where he completed his PhD. His music and research explore the relationship between centuries-old musical traditions and contemporary approaches to composition. He is the editor of the *Sydney Undergraduate Journal of Musicology* and is an associate of the Australian Music Centre.

AMY CLEMENTS-CORTÉS, PhD, is an assistant professor at the Faculty of Music at the University of Toronto, an instructor and supervisor at Wilfrid Laurier University, an academic coordinator and instructor of interdisciplinary studies at

Ryerson Chang School, a music therapist, and a registered psychotherapist. She is the author of *Voices of the Dying and Bereaved*, the past president of the World Federation of Music Therapy (WFMT), and the managing editor of the *Music and Medicine* journal.

MEAGAN CURTIS, PhD, is an associate professor of psychology at Purchase College, State University of New York. She is a singer and cognitive psychologist. Her research explores the use of music as a tool for mood and pain management, motivation during boring or challenging tasks, and its numerous interpersonal functions.

JANE W. DAVIDSON, PhD, is the chair of the Creativity and Wellbeing Research Initiative and the associate dean of research for the Faculty of Fine Arts and Music at the University of Melbourne, Australia. She is coauthor of *Music in Our Lives* (2012), *My Life as a Playlist* (2014), and *Music, Nostalgia & Memory* (2019).

STEPHEN DAVIES, PhD, teaches philosophy at the University of Auckland. His books include *The Artful Species* (2012), *The Philosophy of Art* (2nd edition, 2016), and *Adornment: What Self-Decoration Tells Us about Who We Are* (2020). He is a former president of the American Society for Aesthetics.

TIA DENORA, PhD, is a professor of sociology of music in the Department of Sociology, Philosophy and Anthropology at the University of Exeter, United Kingdom. She is Professor II in GAMUT, the University of Bergen. She has published widely in the areas of music and daily life and music and well-being and currently collaborates with music therapists on a project examining music in late and end of life.

SAMANTHA DIECKMANN, PhD, is an associate professor of music at the University of Oxford, where she teaches music education and community music. Her program of research examines how intercultural relations play out in a range of music education settings, with a focus on the musical lives of migrant and former refugee communities in resettlement contexts.

CHRIS DROMEY, PhD, is an associate professor of music at Middlesex University, the coeditor of *The Classical Music Industry* (2018), and author of *The Pierrot Ensembles: Chronicle and Catalogue, 1912–2012* (2013). His research has also appeared in *Stravinsky in Context* (forthcoming), *Music in the Social and Behavioral Sciences* (2014), and *Zemlinsky Studies* (2007). He writes program notes for Kings Place, London, and is a trustee of the Society for Music Analysis.

TUOMAS EEROLA, PhD, is a professor of music cognition at Durham University, in the United Kingdom, and the codirector of the Music and Science Lab. He obtained his PhD in musicology in 2003 from the University of Jyväskylä, Finland. He has published widely on perception of rhythm and timbre and induction and perception of emotions in music.

THOMAS HANS FRITZ, PhD, is the leader of the Music Evoked Brain Plasticity research group at the Max Planck Institute for Human Cognitive and Brain Sciences in Leipzig. He is also a visiting professor for empirical music research at the Institute for Psychoacoustics and Electronic Music (IPEM) at Ghent University.

SANDRA GARRIDO, PhD, is a research fellow at the MARCS Institute for Brain, Behaviour & Development and a senior lecturer in psychology at Western Sydney University. Her research focuses on music and mental health. She is the author of *Why Are We Attracted to Sad Music?* (2017) and coauthor of *Music, Nostalgia & Memory* (2019).

ANDREW GEEVES, PhD, is a sessional academic and clinical psychologist. He currently works between hospital and private practice settings in Queensand, Australia and will begin the Postdoctoral Program in Psychoanalysis and Psychotherapy at New York University in 2021. His clinical and research interests include relational psychodynamic psychotherapy and the experience of music performance for professional musicians.

JESSICA A. GRAHN, PhD, is an associate professor at the Brain and Mind Institute and Department of Psychology at the University of Western Ontario in London, Canada, where she directs the Music and Neuroscience Lab. She has degrees in neuroscience and piano performance from Northwestern University as well as a PhD from Cambridge, England, in the neuroscience of music. Her research interests include how music makes us move, how musical training changes brain structure, and whether music can benefit patients with neurological disorders, such as Parkinson's disease.

DAVID M. GREENBERG, PhD, is a Zuckerman Postdoctoral Scholar at Bar-Ilan University and an Honorary Research Associate at Cambridge University. His research investigates how music impacts the brain and society through big data, social neuroscience, and clinical trials.

TERESA GRIMM, MA, is a doctoral candidate at the Department of Music at the Carl von Ossietzky University of Oldenburg, Germany. In her dissertation project, she investigates the psychophysiological effects of music on people with disorders of consciousness (DOC).

SUSAN HALLAM, PhD, is an emerita professor of education and music psychology at the Institute of Education, University of London. Her extensive publications in music psychology and music education include *The Power of Music* (2001, 2014) and *Music Psychology in Education* (2005). She is coeditor of *The Oxford Handbook of Psychology of Music* (2009, 2016) and *Music Education in the 21st Century in the United Kingdom*. She was awarded an MBE for services to music education in 2015 and has been recognized by the International Society for Music Education, the British Psychology Society, and SEMPRE through honorary lifelong membership.

ERIN E. HANNON, PhD, is an associate professor of psychology at the University of Nevada, Las Vegas. Her research examines music, dance and language, with a focus on child development. She is interested in how our cultural environments shape our perceptions and experiences of music. She also investigates similarities between music, language, and other skills and behaviors as they develop during infancy and how individuals learn to move with music.

EVANGELOS HIMONIDES, PhD, FRSA, FBCS CITP, is reader in technology, education, and music at University College London (UCL), United Kingdom. His research and public output span various fields, including technology, psychoacoustics, education, research design, information engineering, special needs, big data, singing, health and wellbeing. Evangelos has developed all Sounds of Intent–related technologies and a number of open-access technologies, such as inspiremusic, the online Afghan Rubab Tutor (OART), and the Continuous Response Measurement Apparatus (CReMA).

MARTIN W. B. JARVIS, OAM, PhD, FRSA, FIMT, is based at Charles Darwin University; however, he is also a visiting professor at the Anhui Normal and Hainan Universities in China. He was the artistic director of the Darwin Symphony Orchestra for twenty years, and besides authoring many journal articles, he is the author of *Written by My Mrs Bach* and *The String Players' Pocket Dictionary*.

FRINI KARAYANIDIS, PhD, is a professor at the School of Psychology at the University of Newcastle, Australia, and the director of the Functional Neuroimaging Laboratory. Her research focuses on understanding how cognitive control processes are supported by the brain across the life span and impact decision-making in everyday life.

MICHELLE KELLY, PhD, is a senior lecturer in clinical psychology in the School of Psychology at the University of Newcastle, Australia. She is a founding member of the Australasian Society for Social and Affective Neuroscience, and her research focuses on the measurement and treatment of social cognitive impairments in those with neurological conditions. She is also an art and science devotee and has recently curated a public exhibition called *Brain*.

GUNTER KREUTZ, PhD, is a professor of systematic musicology at the Carl von Ossietzky University Oldenburg, Germany. He is interested in the psychophysiological and social effects of music and helped to establish wellbeing and health as a field in music psychology research.

JACQUES LAUNAY, PhD, has conducted research related to music and social bonding at Western Sydney University; Oxford University, United Kingdom; the University of London, Goldsmiths, United Kingdom; and Brunel University. He is currently a senior policy advisor in the Department for Environment, Farming, and Rural Affairs.

STEVEN R. LIVINGSTONE, PhD, is a senior lecturer in computer science at the University of Otago, New Zealand. His research is in affective data science, where he applies programming, statistics, and machine learning to understand emotion and its related disorders. His research focuses on developing techniques and technologies that can recognize, predict, and express emotion.

JENNIFER MACRITCHIE, PhD, is a senior research fellow in health and wellbeing at Western Sydney University, working across the School of Humanities and Communication Arts and the MARCS Institute for Brain, Behaviour and Development. With a background in both electrical engineering and music, her research focuses on the acquisition and development of motor skills in instrumental performance and how these can be used to promote health and well-being. Her studies range from looking at movements of novices to experts and from those who have studied music from a young age to those who are rediscovering music in retirement.

ELIZABETH HELLMUTH MARGULIS, PhD, is a professor at Princeton University, where she directs the Music Cognition Lab. She has a PhD from Columbia University and is the author of *On Repeat: How Music Plays the Mind* (2014) and *The Psychology of Music: A Very Short Introduction* (2019).

KATRINA SKEWES MCFERRAN, PhD, is a professor and the director of graduate studies in the Creative Arts and Music Therapy Research Units (CAMTRU) at the University of Melbourne. Her research has been focused on the ways that young people use music to promote health and well-being in therapy and everyday life. She has written a number of books, including *Adolescents, Music and Music Therapy* (2010) and *Building Music Cultures in Schools* (2014), and she is also creator of the MOOC How Music Can Change Your Life (Coursera).

GARY E. MCPHERSON, PhD, is the Ormond Professor of Music at the Melbourne Conservatorium of Music, University of Melbourne, Australia. His research examines the acquisition and development of musical competence and motivation to engage and participate in music from novice to expert levels.

ANDREW J. MILNE, PhD, is a musician and a senior research fellow in music cognition and computation at the MARCS Institute for Brain, Behaviour & Development, Western Sydney University. Funded by a prestigious Australian Research Council Discovery Early Career Researcher Award, he develops computational models of music perception and uses these models to shed light on human cognition, to drive creative musical outputs, and to inform the development of educational tools for mathematics and music.

MIRIAM A. MOSING, PhD, is a senior research fellow at the Melbourne School of Psychological Science in Melbourne, Australia, and an associate professor at the Neuroscience Department and the Department of Medical Epidemiology and Biostatistics at the Karolinska Institutet in Stockholm, Sweden. Her research investigates (1) expertise development and (2) quality of life throughout the lifetime and in the aged, using interdisciplinary approaches to quantify the inter-play between genes and the environment.

DAVID E. MYERS, PhD, is a professor emeritus and former school director at the University of Minnesota and is currently head of music studies at Augsburg University. His work in life span music learning includes research, writing, and lecturing, and he serves in community arts leadership roles for the St. Paul Chamber Orchestra, the MacPhail Center for Music, and Vocalessence—all of which serve cross-age audiences. For ten years, he was an evaluation consultant for the League of American Orchestras. He is coauthor of the 2017 book *Redefining Music Studies in an Age of Change: Creativity, Diversity, Integration.*

KARLI M. NAVE, PhD, is a doctoral student at the University of Nevada, Las Vegas, where she is pursuing her PhD in experimental psychology under the men-torship of Dr. Erin Hannon and Dr. Joel Snyder. Her research interests include auditory neuroscience, rhythm perception and production, musical beat and meter, and children's development of auditory rhythm processing.

MICHAEL NILSSON, MD, PhD, is the director of the Centre for Rehab Innova-tions (CRI) and the Global Innovation Chair of Rehabilitation Medicine at the University of Newcastle. He is a fellow of the Australasian Faculty of Rehabilita-tion Medicine and the Royal Australasian College of Physicians.

ADAM OCKELFORD, PhD, is a professor of music and the director of the Applied Music Research Centre at the University of Roehampton, London, United Kingdom. His research interests include exploring how all humans make sense of music without the need for education and training and the factors that contribute to special musical abilities and needs. He is author of *Comparing Notes: How We Make Sense of Music* (2018).

GEMMA PERRY is a PhD candidate in the Department of Psychology at Macquarie University in Sydney, Australia. She investigates the effects of chanting meditations on emotional and cognitive processes. Her interests are primarily in how the chanting of specific sounds can decrease psychological and physiological stress, increase social connection, and ultimately expand states of awareness.

VINCE POLITO, PhD, is a research fellow in the Department of Cognitive Sci-ence at Macquarie University. His research investigates altered states of con-sciousness, beliefs, and self-representation.

MATTEO RAVASIO, PhD, is a postdoctoral fellow at Peking University's School of Arts, where he works under the supervision of Professor Peng Feng. He obtained his PhD from the University of Auckland under the supervision of Professor Ste-phen Davies. Most of his work concerns problems in musical expressiveness.

STEPHANIE ROCKE, PhD, is a research associate of the ARC Centre of Excellence for the History of Emotions at the University of Melbourne. Her current interests include music as ritual in a secularizing world and the interrelationships between emotion and music reception.

EMERY SCHUBERT, PhD, is a professor of music at UNSW Australia. He is leader of the Empirical Musicology Group and Music-Science at UNSW. His primary research area is in music psychology, with particular interest in emotional responses to music. He serves on the editorial board of key journals in the field of music psychology and is a founding member of the Australian Music and Psychology Society (AMPS), which he has served in various positions over the years.

MATTHEW SCHULKIND, PhD, is a professor in the Psychology Department at Amherst College. His work on music cognition has examined how people identify and distinguish familiar melodies. In addition to his music cognition research, he also investigates questions surrounding individual differences in autobiographical memory.

WILLIAM A. SETHARES, PhD, is a professor in the Department of Electrical and Computer Engineering at the University of Wisconsin–Madison and is a scientific researcher at the Rijksmuseum in Amsterdam. His research interests include adaptation and learning in audio and image processing, and he is the author of five books, including *Tuning, Timbre, Spectrum, Scale* (2nd edition, 2006) and *Counting Vermeer* (2018).

MARISSA SILVERMAN, PhD, is an associate professor and undergraduate coordinator at the John J. Cali School of Music, Montclair State University, New Jersey. A Fulbright scholar, her research agenda focuses on dimensions of music philosophy, artistic interpretation, community music, and interdisciplinary curriculum development. She is author of *Gregory Haimovsky: A Pianist's Odyssey to Freedom* (2018) and coauthor of the second edition of *Music Matters: A Philosophy of Music Education* (2015).

DEAN KEITH SIMONTON, PhD, is a distinguished professor emeritus in the Department of Psychology at the University of California, Davis. He is the author of *Origins of Genius* (1999), *Creativity in Science* (2004), and many other influential books. He has received numerous prestigious awards, including the Robert S. Daniel Award for Four Year College/University Teaching (APA 2006); the Theoretical Innovation Prize (APA 2004), the Award for Excellence in Research (Mensa Education and Research Foundation 1986, 2009, 2011), and the Lifetime Achievement Award (Mensa Foundation 2019).

GRAEME SMITH, PhD, is an adjunct senior research fellow at the Sir Zelman Cowan School of Music, Monash University. He has written extensively on the sociology of popular music in his books and academic articles and has a particular interest in folk, ethnic, and country music scenes in Australia and throughout the world.

ERIC S. STROTHER, PhD, is a part-time faculty member at Anderson University in Anderson, Indiana, where he has taught courses in American popular music and film music. His research interests include the intersections of music and religion, race, gender, and social movements.

MARCO SUSINO, PhD, is lecturer in creative arts in the College of Humanities, Arts and Social Sciences at Flinders University, Australia, and recipient of an Endeavour Research Fellow at the Juilliard School, New York. His research focus is emotion in music, with particular interest in culture effects on music cognition, and interest of musical emotions across the performing and visual arts.

JOHN SUTTON, PhD, is a professor of cognitive science at Macquarie University in Sydney, Australia, and the director of the Centre for Elite Performance, Expertise, and Training. He is coeditor of *Collaborative Remembering: Theories, Research, and Applications* (2018) and *Embodied Cognition and Shakespeare's Theatre: The Early Modern Body-Mind* (2014). His current research addresses skill, autobiographical and social memory, and embodied cognition.

ERIC TAYLOR, PhD, studies artificial cognition—the science of decision-making in artificial intelligence systems—at the Vector Institute for Artificial Intelligence in Toronto, Canada. Previously, he worked as a management consultant in behavioral economics designing experiments for major corporations and nonprofit institutions. Eric has completed research fellowships and lectured extensively at the University of Toronto and the Brain and Mind Institute at Western University. He earned his PhD in cognitive psychology from Purdue University, studying perceptual decision-making and attention. In his spare time, Eric plays board games and guitars, and enjoys climbing and hiking.

BARBARA TILLMANN, PhD, is a CRNS researcher and the leader of the Auditory Cognition and Psychoacoustics team at the Lyon Neuroscience Research Center, France. Her research in the domain of auditory cognition uses behavioral, neurophysiological, and computational methods to investigate healthy and pathological brain functions. For example, she is investigating how the brain acquires knowledge about complex sound structures, such as music and language, and how this knowledge shapes perception and memory.

RENEE TIMMERS, PhD, is a professor in the psychology of music at the University of Sheffield, United Kingdom, and the director of the Music Mind Machine research center. She is coeditor of *The Routledge Companion to Music Cognition* and *Expressiveness in Music Performance: Empirical Approaches across Styles and Cultures*. Her publications address emotion in music, psychology of performance, and multimodal experiences of music.

SANDRA E. TREHUB, PhD, is professor emeritus in the Department of Psychology at the University of Toronto Mississauga. Her research primarily focuses on the perception of musical patterns by infants and young children and on the nature and consequences of maternal singing. Among her many honors is a Lifetime Achievement Award from the Society of Music Perception and Cognition.

FREDRIK ULLÉN, PhD, is a professor of cognitive neuroscience at the Karolinska Institutet. His research focuses on the neuropsychology of expertise and creativity, using music as a model. He is also active as a professional pianist and is represented on more than twenty albums, many of which have received outstanding reviews and awards from the international press. He is a fellow of the Swedish Royal Academy of Music (2007) and Academia Europaea (2017).

DYLAN VAN DER SCHYFF, PhD, is a senior lecturer in jazz and improvisation at the Melbourne Conservatorium of Music, University of Melbourne. He completed his PhD at Simon Fraser University in British Columbia, Canada. His research interests include music cognition, improvisation, and music education.

CHRISTINA M. VANDEN BOSCH DER NEDERLANDEN, PhD, is a postdoctoral fellow in the Music and Neuroscience lab at the University of Western Ontario. She received her PhD in 2016 from the University of Nevada, Las Vegas. Her research involves examining how music and language are processed throughout the life span, including how children with and without dyslexia neurally entrain to speech and song.

NARESH VEMPALA, PhD, is a data scientist at Nuralogix, a Toronto-based affective intelligence company, where he leads the research team in developing machine learning models for predicting health vitals. He is the cofounder and chief organizer of CogMIR, a community of academic and industry researchers that meets annually to present topics that explore cognitively based music informatics. His research interests include music cognition, music emotion, melodic similarity, and understanding cognitive processes using computational models.

JONNA K. VUOSKOSKI, PhD, is an associate professor in the Departments of Psychology and Musicology at the University of Oslo, Norway, and a core member of the RITMO Centre for Interdisciplinary Studies in Rhythm, Time and Motion. Her main areas of research are music and emotion, music and individual differences, and the social and embodied cognition of music.

Index

Note: Page numbers in *italics* indicate photos; page numbers followed by *t* indicate tables and *f* indicate figures.

Absolute pitch
  formal musical training and, 55
  general intelligence and, 60
  genetics and, 65
  musical aptitude and, 44
  musical savants and, 90, 91, 92, 94
  natural ability and, 81
Acculturation, 214, 216–217, 219
  Berry, John W., on, 214
  Nettl, Bruno, on, 216, 217
  strategies of ethnocultural groups
    (Berry), 215*t*
  strategies of larger society (Berry), 215*t*
  syncretism and, 216
  typology of processes (Nettl), 217*t*
Advertising, music and, 192–197
  music as lure into consumer environ-
    ments, 193–194
  product choice and consumer satisfac-
    tion, 195
  psychological explanations, 196
  spending and, 194–195
  use of music in advertising, 193
Aerophones, 3
Aging
  aging brain, 104
  brain changes and, 101–103
  brain development and, 104
  health benefits of music, 306–308
  learning and, 316–317
  music and healthy aging, 305–310
  music programs and interventions,
    308–310
Alexander, Joey, 86–87
Amplitude, 10
Amusia. *See* Tone deafness

Armstrong, Louis, 77
Asymmetries, 19–20

Bach, Anna Magdalena, 130, 131–132
Bach, Johann Sebastian
  musical genius and, 60, 64
  spirituality and, 170–171
Balakirev, Mily, 125
Beethoven, Ludwig van
  musical genius and, 58, *59,* 60, 62
  research on, 36
Beethoven's Nightmare (all-deaf
    contemporary rock band), 4–5
Belief, music and
  advertising and, 192–197
  healing rituals and, 197–204
  lyrics and, 188–192
  religion and, 183–187
  See also Religion, music and
Beyoncé, 53, 129, 134
Blacking, John (ethnomusicologist), 7
Bowie, David, 53
Brain research. *See* Neuroscience and
    music

Cello, 9, 17
Chopin, Frédéric, 71, 79, 92, 126, *126,*
  129, 179
Chromatic scale, *24,* 24–25, 27
Circular breathing, 3
Class. *See* Social class
Coltrane, John, 62, 86, 170–171
Community, music in the, 321–325
  definition of community music,
    321–323
  history and uses of, 323–324

Competitions, music, 69–74
  American Idol (television program), 72
  America's Got Talent (television program), 72
  classical music, 70–71
  Eurovision Song Contest, 72
  history of, 70
  judging expertise, 73–74
  Music Performance Assessment (MPA) and, 70
  Opportunity Knocks (television program), 72
  Pop Idol (television program), 71
  Popstars (television program), 71–72
  popular music, 71–72
  psychology of expectation and, 72–73
  recency effect and, 72
  The Voice (television program), 70, 72, 119
  World Federation of International Music Competitions, 74
  The X Factor (television program), 70
Consonance, 13, 45
Creativity, musical
  Alexander, Joey, 86–87
  definition and assessment of creativity, 85–86
  prodigies and, 84–89
  Sullivan, Quinn, 88
  Zakir, Hussain, 87–88
Cross-cultural research
  acculturation, 216–217
  fieldwork, 38
  in music psychology, 36–41
  musical similarities and differences, 39–41
  research challenges, 37–38
  See also Culture
Cultural identity, 124–129
  folklore studies and ethnomusicology, 124–125
  Herder, Johann Gottfried, on, 124, 128
  human universality and, 125
  music without borders, 128
  musical nationalism, 125–127
  socialist realism, 127
Cultural markers, 185–187
Culture
  Bourdieu, Pierre, on, 35, 136–137
  challenges of cross-cultural research, 37–38

cross-cultural research in music psychology, 36–41
cross-cultural similarities and differences, 39–40
cultural events, 32–33
cultural scene, 32
defining, 31–36
Douglas, Mary, on, 34
Durkheim, Emile, on, 31, 33–34, 35
enculturation, 42, 46, 54, 291
expectancy, 40–41
fieldwork, 38
functions of, 33–34
high culture, 35, 136, 137
music across, 37
musical subcultures, 32
nature versus nurture, 41–47
negative effects of, 34–35
as object and activity, 31
physical and psychological constraints, 39
playlists and, 32
power, segmentation, and conflict, 34–35
psychological basis of cross-cultural similarities and differences, 40–41
purposes and roles of, 33–34
similarities and differences in musical behaviors across cultures, 42
taste publics, 32, 35

Dance, music and, 278–284
  expertise in, 281–282
  health and well-being benefits of, 283
  observing performances, 280–281
  origins of, 279
  social processes and, 279–280
  synchronizing dance movements to music, 282
  young children and, 279
Deafness
  music listening and appreciation and, 4–5
  sign language interpretation, 4
  See also Tone deafness
Death, music and, 177–182
  in ancient cultures, 178
  in fifteenth to nineteenth centuries, 179
  in medieval times, 178–179
  music history and, 178–180
  music to facilitate lamenting and mourning, 180–181

rites of passage, 175–176
in twentieth and twenty-first centuries,
 179–180
use of music in dying and grieving,
 181–182
Defining music, 1–7
 American Heritage Dictionary
 definition, 3–4
 dictionary definitions, 3–4
 emotion, 6
 entrainment, 6
 floating intentionality, 5
 as organized sound, 7–8
 Oxford Universal Dictionary definition,
 3–4
 purpose-built instruments, 6
 qualities of good definitions, 5
 Random House College Dictionary
 definition, 3
 scale, 6
 social activity, 6
 song, 6
 sound, 4–5
 thick description, 7
 universals and family resemblances,
 6–7
Deliberate practice, 55, 58, 83, 281
Dissonance, 13, 43, 45, 179, 232
Durkheim, Emile, 31, 33–34, 35

Earworms, 258–263
 blocking, 262
 individual differences in experiencing,
 261–262
 music we imagine, 260
 possible causes of, 261–262
 science of, 259–260
Ecstatic states, music and, 167–171
 case study (John Coltrane),
 170–171
 definition of ecstatic state, 167
 in Hinduism, 169
 in Judaism, 168
 process of achieving spiritual
 transcendence through music, 168*f*
 in Shamanism, 169–170
 in Sufism, 168–169
Education. *See* Music education
Emotion, music and
 across cultures, 243–248
 aesthetic judgment and, 232
 brain stem reflexes and, 232

BRECVEMA model of, 236–237
cognition and, 227–228
contemporary research, 233–238
contour and convention of musical
 emotion, 230
cross-cultural communication and,
 244–246
cultural cues, 247
Darwin, Charles, and, 228
Descartes, René, and, 228
dimensions of emotions and rating
 scales, 234
emotion management, 238–243
emotional contagion and, 232
episodic memory and, 232
evaluative conditioning and, 232
expectations and, 230–231
Huron, David, on, 40, 246
mental health and well-being,
 240–242
music as language of emotions, 230
music sounds as emotions feel, 230
physiological and neuroscientific
 research on, 235
psychological models of emotion,
 227–229
rhythmic entrainment and, 232
sources of experience of musical
 emotionality, 231–232
theories of, 227–233
two-dimensional representation of
 emotion, 229*f*
universal and multimodal cues, 246
valence-arousal theory, 228–229,
 234–235
visual imagery and, 232
Enculturation, 42, 46, 54, 291
Ensemble performance, 274–278
Ethnomusicology, 7, 48, 51,
 124–125, 216
Exercise, music and, 284–289
 Jymmin exercise system, 286–288
 physiological effects of music during
 exercise, 286
 playlists for group exercise classes, 286
 psychological effects of music during
 exercise, 285–286
 subjective reasons people exercise to
 music, 284–285
 types of music and, 286
Expectancy, musical, 40–41, 231–232,
 236, 237

Expertise, musical, 53–58
　assessment of, 54–55, 57–58
　competitions, 69–74
　defining expertise by ability, 56–57
　definition of, 53
　enculturation and, 54
　Ericsson, K. Anders, on, 55, 56, 83
　experiments in, 57
　formal musical training, 55
　genetic syndromes and, 66
　genetics and, 64–69
　music practice and, 65–66
　musical families, 65
　musical knowledge in general
　　population, 53–55

Frequency
　amplitude and, 10
　fundamental frequency, 8–12, 16
　harmonics, 11–12
　hearing range of dogs, 9
　intervals and, 22–23, 49
　overtones, 11–13, 16, 29
　partials, 11
　pitch and, 8–10, 14–16
　ratios, 49
　sound waves and, 8–10
　timbre and, 10–12, 18

Gamelans, 27, 29, *29,* 47, 54
Gender bias, 129–135
　Bach, Anna Magdalena, 131–132
　case studies, 131–133
　handwriting and, 133–134
　Hildegard von Bingen, 130
　history of, 130
　masculine versus feminine, 130–131
　Mozart, Marie Anne, 132–133
Genetics
　chromosomes, 68–69
　gene finding methods, 67–68
　genes of potential interest, 68–69
　genetic syndromes, 66
　measuring genetic influences on
　　musicality, 66–68
　musical expertise and, 64–69
　twin studies, 68
　See also Nature versus nurture
Genius, musical, 58–64
　achieved eminence and, 61–63
　Bach, Johann Sebastian, 60, 64
　Beethoven, Ludwig van, 58, *59,* 60, 62

creative productivity and, 63–64
　definitions of genius, 59–63
　general intelligence and, 59–60
　Karas, Anton, 63
　Mozart, Wolfgang Amadeus, 60
　Shakira, 60–61
　talent or giftedness and, 60–61
Giftedness, 60–61, 75
Globalization, 36, 128, 173, 215, 222
Grieg, Edvard, 125
Guitar
　acoustic, 156, 325
　classical, 258
　"Edelweiss" *(The Sound of Music)* and,
　　8
　electric, 80, 145, 156
　first seven pitches of harmonic series,
　　13*f*
　harmonics and, 12–13
　lead, 271
　as "masculine" instrument, 122
　movement and, 271
　musical prodigies and, 80, 88
　musician personality and, 145
　rhythm, 271
　rock musicians, 271
　"Superstition" (Stevie Wonder) and, 290
　timbre and, 11–12, 113
　tuning and, 27
　violent music and, 155, 156

Harmonics, 11–12
Harp, 9, 71, 182
Harpsichord, 132, 145
Healing rituals, music and, 197–204
　altered states of consciousness, 202
　breathing and, 201
　Buddhism, 199
　expectations and, 202–203
　focused attention and, 201
　Hinduism, 199–200
　indigenous Australians, 198
　Islam, 199
　Native Americans, 198
　science of, 200–203
　secular Western culture, 200
　synchrony and, 201–202
Health, music and
　definition of health, 292
　five healthy ingredients of music,
　　295–300
　healthy aging, 305–310

measurement of health benefits of music, 293–294

music as emotional, 296

music as engaging, 296–297

music as personal, 298–299

music as physical, 295–296

music as social, 297–298

music therapy, 292–293, 300–305

negative effects of music, 291–292

salutogenic and pathogenic approaches to, 292

science of, 294

well-being, 290–295

Heavy metal, 35, 50, 138, 142, 158, 180, 186, 196, 239, 292

Hildegard von Bingen, 58, 62, 77, 130

Hip-hop, 32, 35, 45, 128, 186–187, 191, 241, 247, 279

Identity, music and

in adolescence, 120

cultural identity, 124–129

defining ourselves through music, 119–124

gender bias in music history, 129–135

listening and connecting with others, 120–121

live music events and, 120–121

making music as adults, 122–123

music in school, 121–122

social class, 135–139

Immigration and migration, 34, 55, 128, 214, *215*, 323–324

Indigenous populations

acculturation and, 216

community music programs and, 324

Confederated Salish and Kootenai Tribes (North America), 216

didgeridoo (indigenous Australians), 3, 20

drum circles, 169–170

indigenous Australians, 3, 127, 198, 324

music rituals, 198

music technologies, 330

musical nationalism, 127

musical preferences, 45

Native Americans, 169–170, 198, 216

Tsimané (Bolivia), 45

Infancy

pitch and, 161–162, 205, 208, 312, 318

rites of passage, 172–173

See also Lullabies; Maternal singing

Intercultural psychology, 214–220

acculturation, 214, 216–217, 219

Berry, John W., on, 214

Nettl, Bruno, on, 216, 217

strategies of ethnocultural groups (Berry), 215*t*

strategies of larger society (Berry), 215*t*

syncretism and, 216

transformative power of music, 217–219

typology of processes (Nettl), 217*t*

Intervals, 22–24

chroma, 23, *24*

combining, 23

expressed in cents, 23–24

frequency and, 22–23, 49

just (pure) intervals, 23, *24, 25*

musical fifth, 23

octave, 22–24

pitch and, 22–23, 27

ratios and fractions, 23–24

sound waves and, 12–13

tone and, 22–23, 48–49

tone height, 23

Isochronous beats, 19

Jay-Z, 128, 187

Kolberg, Oskar, 125

Korngold, Erich, 76, 77, 79

Language, music and

the brain and, 113

Broca's area and, 113–115

communication of ideas, 114

expectations, 113–114

grammar of music, 111, 114

neural overlap, 114–115

shared elements, 112–113

Life span, 100–105

aging brain and, 104

brain changes and, 101–103

brain development and, 104

music learning across, 316–320

See also Aging

Liszt, Franz, 53, 62, 70, 74, 79

Love, music and, 210–214

biology of, 210–211

role of music in, 211–213

songs of heartbreak, 213

ritual and, 174

Love songs, power of, 265–266

Lullabies
    communication and, 188
    cross-cultural similarities of, 40
    effects on infants of, 208
    importance of, 209
    infants' musical preferences and, 162
    maternal singing and, 162–163, 165
    play songs compared with, 172–173
    social bonding and, 205–209
    universality of, 50–51
Lyrics, 188–192
    song meaning, 189–190
    songs as communication, 188–189
    truth in songs, 190–191

Maternal singing
    bonding rituals and, 161–167
    consequences of, 165–166
    descriptive features of, 163–165
    factors that compromise, 165
    Motherese, 50–51, 205, 206
    See also Lullabies
Media and technology, 325–330
    integrating technology into music
        education, 327–328
    ten core uses of music technologies,
        328–330
Mehta, Bejun, 76–77, 78–79
Memory, music and
    ability to think and, 254–255
    earworms, 258–263
    intellectual tasks, 255–257
    melody identification, 249–251
    memory for music, 249–253
    mnemonic capacity of music, 251–253
    music as distraction, 257–258
    music-evoked autobiographical
        memories (MEAMs), 263–268
    science of earworms, 259–260
    studying and, 253–258
Metric hierarchies, 19
Migration and immigration, 34, 55, 128,
    214, 215, 323–324
Monk, Thelonious, 53, 86
Monks, religious, 62, 168, 181, 185
Motherese, 50–51, 205, 206
Movement, music and
    communicating expressive intent,
        272–273
    dance, 278–284
    ensemble performance, 274–278
    exercising to music, 284–289

    importance of movement in music
        performance, 269–270
    music performance, 269–273
    musicians moving together, 271–272
    playing an instrument and, 270–271
Mozart, Marie Anne ("Nannerl"), 82, 130,
    131, 132–134
Mozart, Wolfgang Amadeus
    musical expertise and, 53
    musical genius and, 60
    musical prodigies and, 76, 79,
        81, 82–83
    requiem masses, 179
    Rondo alla Turca, 93
Mozart effect, 255
Music education
    across the life span, 316–320
    in the community, 321–325
    integrating technology into music
        education, 327–328
    media and technology, 325–330
    in schools, 311–316
    ten core uses of music technologies,
        328–330
Music therapy, 292–293, 300–305
    for autism spectrum disorder, 302
    for child, adolescent, and adult mental
        health, 301–302
    definition of, 300–301
    for developmental disabilities, 302
    for neurorehabilitation and
        neurodegenerative diseases, 303–304
    for terminal illness, grief, and loss, 304
Musical ability, 43
Musical aptitude, 43–44
Musical preferences, 45–46
Music-evoked autobiographical memories
    (MEAMs), 263–268
    Alzheimer's dementia and, 264–265
    brain storage of, 266–267
    definition of autobiographical memories,
        263–264
    love songs and, 265–266
Musicians, personality and, 145–150
    characteristics of musicians,
        145–147
    kinds of musicians, 147–148
    performance anxiety and,
        148–149

Naming notes, 22
Naming scales, 24–27

Nas, 187
Nationalism, musical, 125–127
Nature versus nurture, 41–47
  absolute pitch and, 44
  cross-cultural research on, 43
  cultural similarities and differences in
    musical behaviors, 42
  musical ability, 43
  musical aptitude, 43–44
  musical preferences, 45–46
  singing, 44–45
Neuroscience and music
  across the life span, 100–105
  aging brain and, 104
  blood-oxygen-level-dependent (BOLD)
    responses, 97–98
  brain development and, 104
  brain lesion studies, 96–97
  Broca's area and, 113–115
  contemporary approaches, 95–99
  electroencephalography (EEG), 98–99
  functional magnetic resonance imaging
    (fMRI), 97–98
  language, 111–116
  magnetoencephalography (MEG), 99
  music processing distributed throughout
    brain areas, 101f
  neuroplasticity, 100, 102, 104
  prosody, 104, 109, 112
  tone deafness, 105–110

Octave
  equivalence, 22–23, 46, 48
  interval of, 22–24
  melody and, 48
  musical universals and, 48–49

Parker, Barbie (sign language interpreter),
  4
Partch, Harry, 25, 25, 26, 27
Perfect pitch. See Absolute pitch
Personality, music and
  Big Five theory, 140–141, 143,
    145–146, 151–152
  definition of personality,
    140–141
  listeners, 140–145
  music listening and, 142–143
  music preferences, 141–142
  musicians, 145–150
  sad music, 150–154
  violence, 154–160

Piccolo, 9
Pitch, 14–16
  ambiguous pitch, 16
  complex tone and, 15
  contour and, 230
  cross-cultural research and, 40
  definition of, 8, 14
  emotion and, 230, 232, 234, 244
  E-natural, 10, 12
  enculturation and, 54
  frequency and, 8–10, 14
  harmonic complex tone and, 15
  harmonic scale and, 13f
  infancy and, 161–162, 205, 208, 312,
    318
  intervals and, 22–23, 27
  language and, 112–115
  mating and, 211
  melody and, 14
  melody identification and, 250–251
  mourning rituals and, 181
  music education and, 318, 319
  musical expertise and, 54–55, 56, 57, 60,
    65
  musical universals and, 49–50
  neuroscience and, 95, 97, 98, 103
  pure tone, 8–11
  relative pitch, 60, 68, 253
  ride cymbal and, 15f
  sad music and, 150
  scales and, 21, 27, 48–49
  sound and, 14
  sound waves and, 8–10, 14
  timbre and, 10–12, 16, 18
  tone and, 8–10
  tone deafness and, 107–110
  train sound and, 15f
  unpitched sounds, 8, 9, 10, 260
  violin note and, 15f
  See also Absolute pitch
Pitch perception, 57, 68, 112, 115
Playlists
  cultural identity and, 129
  culture and, 32
  emotion and, 227, 239–241
  exercise, 286
  musical knowledge and, 54
  musical life review and, 304
  personal well-being and, 290, 299
  personality and, 140
  rites of passage and, 172
Polyrhythms, 20

Prodigies, musical
  Armstrong, Louis, 77
  Curtis Institute of Music and, 84
  definition of gifted, 75
  definition of prodigy, 75
  definition of talent, 75
  deliberate practice and, 83
  distinguishing characteristics of, 80–81
  environmental influences on, 82–84
  Garland, Judy, 79
  gifts and talent development, 76–78
  Korngold, Erich, 76, 77, 79
  Mehta, Bejun, 76–77, 78–79
  modern education and, 79
  Mozart, Wolfgang Amadeus, 76, 79, 81, 82–83
  musical creativity and, 84–89
  natural abilities and, 81–82
  in performance, 80–84
  personality and, 76
  potential, chance, and personal change, 78–79
  self-generated learning and, 77
  stereotypes of, 83–84
  See also Savants, musical
Prosody, 104, 109, 112

Rachmaninoff, Sergei, 53, 61
Rap and rappers, 36, 128, 135, 138, 155, 158, 186, 187, 191, 322
Religion, music and, 183–187
  Buddhism, 168, 181, 183, 184, 185, 199, 200, 201, 203
  Christianity, 38, 130, 176, 181, 183–187, 200
  Hinduism, 136, 167, 169, 171, 172, 175, 183–185, 199–200, 202
  Islam, 168, 175–176, 183–185, 199
  Judaism, 167, 168, 169, 171, 173, 176, 183–185
  religion as cultural marker in music, 185–187
  ritual use of music, 183–185
  Shamanism, 167, 169–170, 171
  Sufism, 167, 168–169, 171, 185
Rhythm, 18
Rites of passage, music and, 172–177
  in birth and infancy, 172–173
  "Bridal Chorus" from Wagner's *Lohengrin,* 175
  coming of age, 173
  death and funeral traditions, 175–176

marriage, 174–175
  romantic love and heartbreak, 174
Ritual, music and
  consequences of maternal singing, 165–166
  death, 177–182
  descriptive features of maternal singing, 163–165
  ecstatic states, 167–171
  factors that compromise maternal singing, 165
  maternal songs as bonding rituals, 161–167
  rites of passage, 172–177

Sad music, 150–154
  capacity for absorption and, 151
  culture and, 150
  emotional expression of, 152
  empathy and, 152–153
  mood management and, 151
  openness to experience and, 151–152
  rumination and, 153–154
Saint-Saëns, Camille, 60
Savants, musical, 89–94
  absolute pitch and, 90, 91, 92, 94
  Down, J. Landgon, on, 89
  examples of, 90–93
  Paravicini, Derek, *93*
  prodigious savants, 89
  savant syndrome, 89
  as self-taught, 89–90, 91
  teaching savants, 94
  Treffert, Darold, 89, 89
Scales, 21–22
  chromatic scale, *24,* 24–25, 27
  historical and cultural differences, 25, 27
  instruments for 43-tone just scale, *25, 26, 27*
  just intonation scales, 25
  naming, 24–27
  purpose of, 21–22
  Western tradition and, 24–25
Schools, music education in, 311–316
  challenges of formal music education, 315
  early years, 312
  elementary school, 312–314
  secondary school, 314–315
Shakur, Tupac, 58, 186
Singing, 44–45. *See also* Maternal singing
Smetana, Bedřich, 125

Social bonding, music and
  intercultural relations, 214–220
  love, 210–214
  lullabies, 205–209
  social grooming, 220–224
Social class, 135–139
  Bourdieu, Pierre, on, 136–137
  cultural capital, 136–137
  cultural homology theory, 137–138
  Fabbri, Franco, on, 135
  omnivores and univores, 137–139
  preferred music genre by gender and
    social class, 136*t*
  social influences on musical preference,
    135–136
Social grooming, music and, 220–224
  human evolution and social behavior,
    221–222
  music as social grooming, 222–224
  primate social bonding and, 221
The Sound of Music (musical), 8
Sound waves, 7–13
  amplitude, 10
  frequency, 10
  intervals, 12–13
  loudness, 10
  origins of sounds, 8
  pitch, 8–9
  timbre, 10–12
  vibrating pattern of sine wave, 10*f*
Sullivan, Quinn, 88

Talent, 60–61, 75
Talent development, 76–78
Taste publics, 32, 35
Technology. *See* Media and technology
Thalberg, Sigismond, 70
Timbre, 16–18
  sound waves and, 10–12
  sympathetic resonance and, 12
  tone and, 10–12
  vibration patterns of a string, 11*f*
Time scales, perceptual, 18–19
Tone
  complex tone, 15
  emotional tone, 97, 174, 212
  harmonic complex tone, 16
  intervals and, 22–23, 48–49
  loudness and, 8–11
  movement and, 275, 276, 277
  naming notes and, 22
  naming scales and, 24–27

overtones, 11–13, 16, 29
pitch and, 8–10, 97
pure tone, 8–11
semitone, 12, 49, 107
sound waves and, 9–16
timbre and, 10–12
vibrating pattern of sine wave, 10*f*
vocal tone, 104, 153, 161, 163, 206
Tone deafness, 105–110
  acquired amusia, 105–106
  congenital amusia, 65, 106, 107, 108, 110
  deficits in distinguishing and
    memorizing tones, 107–108
  impaired access to consciousness and, 109
  language processing and, 108–109
  musical handicap, 107
  neuroimaging and, 108
Tuning instruments, 27–28
  early eighteenth-century, *28*
  gamelans, 27, 29, *29*
  guitar, 27
  piano, 27
  tanbur, *28, 29*

Universals, musical, 47–52
  emotion and, 246
  entrainment and social uses of music, 50
  grouping and regularity, 49–50
  lullabies, 50–51
  musical family resemblances and, 6–7
  Nettl, Bruno, on, 48
  pitches and scales, 48–49
  search for, 48

Varèse, Edgard, 7–8
Violent music, 154–160
  AC/DC and, 156
  benefits from listening to, 159
  Cannibal Corpse and, 155–156
  definition of violence, 155
  fans of, 157
  negative outcomes from listening to,
    157–158
  personality and, 157
  sound of, 156
  violent lyrics, 155–156

Wagner, Richard, 58, 129, 175, 275
West, Kanye, 187
Wu-Tang Clan, 187

Zakir, Hussain, 87–88

www.ingramcontent.com/pod-product-compliance
Lightning Source LLC
Chambersburg PA
CBHW080411270326
41929CB00018B/2983